TROPOLOGIES

ReFormations

MEDIEVAL AND EARLY MODERN

Series Editors:
David Aers, Sarah Beckwith, and James Simpson

RECENT TITLES IN THE SERIES

Against All England: Regional Identity and Cheshire Writing, 1195–1656 (2009)
Robert W. Barrett, Jr.

The Maudlin Impression: English Literary Images of Mary Magdalene, 1550–1700 (2009)
Patricia Badir

*The Embodied Word: Female Spiritualities, Contested Orthodoxies, and
English Religious Cultures, 1350–1700* (2010)
Nancy Bradley Warren

The Island Garden: England's Language of Nation from Gildas to Marvell (2012)
Lynn Staley

Miserere Mei: The Penitential Psalms in Late Medieval and Early Modern England (2012)
Clare Costley King'oo

The English Martyr from Reformation to Revolution (2012)
Alice Dailey

Transforming Work: Early Modern Pastoral and Late Medieval Poetry (2013)
Katherine C. Little

*Writing Faith and Telling Tales: Literature, Politics, and Religion in
the Work of Thomas More* (2013)
Thomas Betteridge

*Unwritten Verities: The Making of England's Vernacular
Legal Culture, 1463–1549* (2015)
Sebastian Sobecki

Mysticism and Reform, 1400–1750 (2015)
Sara S. Poor and Nigel Smith, eds.

The Civic Cycles: Artisan Drama and Identity in Premodern England (2015)
Nicole R. Rice and Margaret Aziza Pappano

RYAN McDERMOTT

TROPOLOGIES

ETHICS AND INVENTION
IN ENGLAND,
C. 1350–1600

UNIVERSITY OF NOTRE DAME PRESS

NOTRE DAME, INDIANA

University of Notre Dame Press
Notre Dame, Indiana 46556
www.undpress.nd.edu

Library of Congress Cataloging-in-Publication Data

Names: McDermott, Ryan, 1978– author.
Title: Tropologies : ethics and invention in England, c. 1350–1600 / Ryan McDermott.
Other titles: Ethics and invention in England, c. 1350–1600
Description: Notre Dame, Indiana : University of Notre Dame Press, 2016. |
   Series: ReFormations : medieval and early modern | Includes
   bibliographical references and index.
Identifiers: LCCN 2016004189| ISBN 9780268035402 (paperback) | ISBN
   0268035407 (paper)
Subjects: LCSH: English literature—Middle English, 1100–1500—History and
   criticism. | English literature—Early modern, 1500-1700—History and
   criticism. | Bible—Criticism, interpretation, etc.—History. |
   Bible—Influence. | Bible—In literature. | Bible and literature. | Ethics
   in literature. | Religion and literature. | BISAC: LITERARY CRITICISM /
   Medieval. | LITERARY CRITICISM / Renaissance.
Classification: LCC PR275.B5 M33 2016 | DDC 820.9/3823—dc23
LC record available at http://lccn.loc.gov/2016004189

∞ *This paper meets the requirements of ANSI/NISO Z39.48-1992*
(Permanence of Paper).

Contents

List of Illustrations   ix
Acknowledgments   xi

Introduction   1

1 Tropological Theory   11

2 How to Invent History: *Patience,* the *Glossa ordinaria,*
and the Ethics of the Literal Sense   87

3 "Beatus qui verba vertit in opera": Langland's Ethical
Invention   144

4 Practices of Satisfaction and *Piers Plowman*'s
Dynamic Middle   189

5 Tropology Reformed: Scripture, Salvation, Drama   238

6 Mirror of Scripture: Ethics and Anagogy in the York
Doomsday Pageant   291

Conclusion   371

Bibliography   383
Index   420

Illustrations

Fig. 1.1.   Detail of "October," *Les très riches heures du duc de Berry*. Chantilly, Musée Condé MS 65, fol. 10v. Reprinted by kind permission of RMN-Grand Palais/Art Resource, NY.   54

Fig. 1.2.   Oxford, Bodleian Library, MS Digby 171, title page. Reprinted by kind permission of The Bodleian Libraries, The University of Oxford.   82

Fig. 2.1.   *Biblia pauperum*, London, British Library, Kings MS 5 (Netherlands, c. 1405), fol. 20, detail. Reprinted under a Creative Commons license by the kind permission of The British Library. http://www.bl.uk/catalogues/illuminated manuscripts/.   100

Fig. 2.2.   Translation of the first page of the *Glossa ordinaria* on Jonah set in modern typeface, emulating the Rusch 1480/81 *editio princeps*. Originally published in McDermott, "The Ordinary Gloss on Jonah."   104

Fig. 6.1.   Christ displays his wounds at the Last Judgment. York
Minster, MS XVI.K.19, fol. 31r. © Chapter of York:
Reproduced by kind permission.   303

Fig. 6.2.   Christ judges the good and the evil souls on Doomsday.
York Minster, MS Add. 2, fol. 208r. © Chapter of York:
Reproduced by kind permission.   305

Fig. 6.3.   New York, Pierpont Morgan Library, MS Morgan 1089,
fol. 118v. Northern Italy, possibly the Veneto, c. 1425–1450.
Reprinted by kind permission. Photo: The Pierpont
Morgan Library, New York.   306

Fig. 6.4.   John Foxe, *Actes and Monuments* (London: John
Day, 1563). Oxford, Magdalen College, Old Library,
Arch.B.I.4.13. Title page of the first edition. Reprinted by
kind permission of the President and Fellows of Magdalen
College Oxford.   350

Acknowledgments

This book is the result of a natural tropology. The words and deeds of many people are here converted into a work that would be impossible without their prior acts of invention, and it is a delight to be able to express my gratitude.

I have been fortunate to write this book in intellectual communities that are at once peaceful and critical, nurturing and emboldening. At the University of Pittsburgh, Hannah Johnson and Jennifer Waldron have thought through every phase of this project with me. Pitt has a strong culture of collegial mentoring. I am particularly grateful for the friendship, advice, and example of Jonathan Arac, Don Bialostosky, Renate Blumenfeld-Kosinski, Nancy Glazener, Jim Knapp, Dennis Looney, Marianne Novy, Chris Nygren, Gayle Rogers, Johnny Twyning, and Bruce Venarde at Pitt, and to Peggy Knapp across the bridge at Carnegie Mellon. At the University of Virginia, I enjoyed the inspiring dissertation guidance of A. C. Spearing, Kevin Hart, and Peter Ochs. As director of the thesis that eventually grew into this book, Bruce Holsinger taught me how to work across disciplines and has always been there for savvy professional advice. Many of the initial ideas for this book emerged in the last seminar taught by the late Barbara Nolan, on the ethical Chaucer. I am sorry that she could not have been involved in the project that grew out of expansive discussions in class and her generously leisurely office hours. I wrote my dissertation in the invigorating interdisciplinary community of the Institute for Advanced Studies in Culture. At Duke Divinity School, Boyd Taylor Coolman introduced me to the wonders of medieval exegesis, and Reinhard Hütter opened my eyes to the timeliness of premodern philosophy and theology.

This book has benefited from the countless attentions, large and small, of many colleagues beyond those institutions. Cristina Maria Cervone has read every part of the book, at nearly every stage (even the many stages that did not make it into the book); her large- and small-scale contributions have improved every page. Andrew Cole, Rachael Deagman, Michelle De Groot, Ashley Faulkner, Chris Hackett, Eleanor Johnson, Billy Junker, Steven Justice, David Lavinsky, Allan Mitchell, Mary Raschko, Jennifer Rust, and Macklin Smith read substantial parts of the manuscript at critical junctures. Ann Astell, John Bugbee, Theresa Coletti, Ed Craun, Kantik Ghosh, Gabriel Haley, Ralph Hanna, Jeanne Krochalis, Alastair Minnis, Peter Ramey, Will Revere, Jennifer Rust, Kurt Schreyer, Vance Smith, Fiona Somerset, Beth Sutherland, Nicholas Watson, Nicolette Zeeman, and the participants in the seminar on Drama, Phenomenology, and Periodization at the 49th International Congress on Medieval Studies all responded to parts of the book and made it much better. Nina Appasamy and Zachary Herbster, rare multilingual undergraduate research assistants, contributed to the bibliography and checking of foreign-language quotations. Many other colleagues and students, too many to name here, contributed in countless other ways; without the intellectual community they created, a book like this would not be possible. All errors and infelicities are surely my own.

Along the way I have been fortunate to receive the support of the James B. Skinner Scholarship of St. Paul's Episcopal Church (Charlottesville, VA), the Dolores Zohrab Liebmann Foundation, and the Harvey Fellows Program. At the University of Pittsburgh my research has been supported by grants from the Dietrich School of Arts and Sciences Central Research Development Fund, the University Center for International Studies, and the Department of English. The Richard D. and Mary Jane Edwards Endowed Publication Fund made it possible to reprint images and to produce the book with footnotes. The Hillman Library's area specialists for English and medieval and early modern studies, Robin Kear and Clare Withers, have been unfailingly solicitous and inventive during a period of difficult financial constraints; I have not wanted for any resource.

The University of Notre Dame Press has been a delight to work with. Stephen Little and Rebecca DeBoer deserve particular thanks for their cheerful collaboration and sound advice. By inventing this ReFormations series, David Aers, Sarah Beckwith, and James Simpson inspired the present volume, which should be a testament to the intellectual power of the often tedious task of editing a book series.

Introduction

Tropological discourse has a long, distinct tradition that writers in the late Middle Ages traced to Gregory the Great. Gregory's *Moralia in Job* is perhaps the most concentrated, sustained project of tropological exegesis in Western Christianity: half a million words, occupying three volumes of the Corpus Christianorum. In the preface, Gregory explains that the "brothers" who asked him to write a commentary were not satisfied that he should "only explicate the words of the history according to the allegorical senses," but wanted him to "go on to turn [*inclinarem*] the allegorical senses into writing about the moral sense."[1] In asking Gregory to turn or incline himself to the *moralitas*, the brothers recapitulate the etymology of the exegetical term *tropologia*. In classical Greek, the root, *tropos*, means a turn or a way of life. The first sense—"turn"— is poetic or rhetorical, in a manner familiar to modern literary critics: a trope was a turn of phrase, and "tropology" treated any use of figurative language. Early Christians capitalized on the term's double meaning of

Unless otherwise noted, all English biblical quotations are cited from the Challoner revision of the Douay-Rheims, and Latin from the Stuttgart Vulgate; both are available in parallel online at www.latinvulgate.com.

1. Gregory the Great, *S. Gregorii Magni Moralia in Job*, ed. M. Adriaen, CCSL 143 (Turnhout: Brepols, 1979), Epist. 1.

"turn" and "way of life" to name the sense of scripture that involves the conversion or turning around of life, the moral sense. According to tropological theory, interpretation is never complete without action, and that action can take the form of writing. Tropology, in other words, is never simply an analysis of one text. It is also an invention of another—a fruitful activity, acted out in the production of life and literature, even profane literature.

Medieval exegetes typically identified three spiritual senses of scripture: the allegorical, the tropological, and the anagogical. According to the allegorical sense, key people, things, and events in the Old Testament correspond metaphysically to Christ's life, death, and resurrection in the New Testament. (Modern exegesis tends to speak of these correspondences in terms of "typology," and Erich Auerbach identified them influentially for medieval studies as *figura*.)[2] The allegorical sense thus teaches the doctrines of the Christian faith. The tropological sense involves the conversion of those Christian doctrines into one's own actions on the way to the kingdom of heaven. The anagogical sense concerns the final fulfillment of those doctrines in the contemplative union of the soul with God and the historical consummation of the church in the kingdom of heaven. Because tropological reading and action convert allegorized history back into lived history, they perform a vital circulatory function. According to Paul's sophisticated exegetical theory, the literal-historical sense of scripture "killeth" unless the spirit of allegorical and anagogical interpretation "quickeneth" (2 Cor. 3:6). On the other hand, as the Epistle of James insists, "so also faith without works is dead" (James 2:26). Without tropological interpretation and action, the Bible would be not only a dead letter but dead spirit as well. Letter and spirit require each other in order for the word of God to have life. Through the habits of tropology, living people keep the literal and spiritual meanings of scripture in circulation through practices of contemplation and action.

As they developed into the Middle Ages, the theory and practice of the moral sense of scripture functioned in several interrelated registers.

---

2. Erich Auerbach, "Figura," in *Scenes from the Drama of European Literature*, trans. Ralph Manheim (Minneapolis: University of Minnesota Press, 1984), 11–76.

In terms of history, tropological theory enabled theologians and exegetes to articulate how readers in the present could re-present and collaborate with the distant persons, things, and events to which the text of scripture granted access. In terms of the present, tropological reading of scripture asks what a passage means for us, today. Tropological reading overlays the text with the reader's array of ethical options; it transposes the text's *Sitz im Leben* from its original lifeworld to the present life. Consequently, tropological reading and invention involve much more than moral concepts and images—in fact, a literally moral text such as the Ten Commandments is least amenable to tropological interpretation, for tropology is not discourse *about* ethical concepts or images. Rather, it is a practice by which readers are led by the hand (*manuductio*) from history through doctrine (the allegorical sense) to action, converting the perverted will in the process, and lighting the path to the future consummation of the good (the anagogical sense). This "hermeneutic committed to human progress," as Gilbert Dahan calls it, assumes that scripture dynamically corresponds to the pilgrim movements of readers and communities.[3] These readers *invent* goodness in both senses of the rhetorical term: they discover moral sources in the Bible, and they create new works that participate in the goodness for which the God of the Bible created the world.

This book makes four related arguments. First, for many medieval and early modern exegetes, poets, and dramatists, the tropological sense of scripture was the key to any successful literal, allegorical, or anagogical reading because it circulates the hermeneutical endeavor out into the reader's life, where the reader's actions can render him or her a fit interpreter. Writers capitalized on this circulatory dynamic to turn words, especially the words of sacred scripture, into works—books as well as deeds. Second, this kind of tropological making entails a literary ethics distinct from rhetoric and moral philosophy and theology, though also overlapping in important ways.[4] Tropology situates ethics within biblical

---

3. Gilbert Dahan, *L'exégèse chrétienne de la Bible en Occident médiéval, XIIe–XIVe siècle* (Paris: Cerf, 1999), 51.

4. "Literary ethics" names the ideas and practices involved in communities' efforts to make and use texts to form individuals and institutions and to foster human flourishing and due care for the world.

history, both as a linear progression of events and as a narrative in which readers can participate sacramentally—the story of salvation, oriented toward the union of the soul with God and of Christ with his bride, the church. The tropological inventions that occupy this book place literary ethics within a sacramental economy that links literature to liturgy, performativity to penance, and poetic making to habituation in virtue. Third, this habit of tropological invention inspired a shadow tradition of English poetry and drama that has been obscured by Chaucerian, laureate narratives of the invention of English literature.[5] For all its ethical commitments and rootedness in biblical traditions, this literature is no less inventive and productive of new literary formations than its laureate counterpart. Finally, tropological invention was hardly a proprietary practice of medieval Catholics, spurned by literal-minded Reformers. In fact, it survived as the most important principle of continuity between "medieval" and Reformation biblical cultures, inspiring exegesis, poetry, and drama even in the court of the radical reformist King Edward VI. *Tropologies* demonstrates that the Bible, long seen as a major fulcrum of Reformation ruptures, could foster ethical and hermeneutical practices that united Protestants and Catholics spiritually, if not ecclesially, across confessional and temporal divides.

In the works studied here, ethics according to the tropological sense works dynamically and flexibly, irreducible to a single moral. So it is wrong to read the history of exegesis as a set of codes with which to decrypt the meanings, ethical or otherwise, encoded in late medieval literature. This was the putative, and at times actual, sin of D. W. Robertson, perhaps the most controversial figure in Anglo-American medieval literary studies well beyond his death in 1992. But sustained critical attention to the supple dynamics of medieval ethical literature demonstrates why Robertson's research into the history of exegesis was a great stride in the right direction, opening a way to think about medieval literary ethics beyond the rhetorical tradition. Looking back across the decades, it seems that the answer to all that ailed "Robertsonianism" (to the extent that such a school ever existed) was not to abandon research on the Christian exegetical sources of medieval literary invention, but

---

5. On the fifteenth-century construction of Chaucer as the father of English literature, see Seth Lerer, *Chaucer and His Readers: Imagining the Author in Late Medieval England* (Princeton: Princeton University Press, 1993).

to probe those traditions with greater dexterity, especially in an effort to understand how classical-rhetorical forms of literary ethics and the forms that emerged from spiritual exegesis relate to each other.

The shibboleth of "Robertsonianism" has not been so intimidating as to ward off all comers. Alastair Minnis, Mary Dove, Lesley Smith, and E. Ann Matter, to name just a few, have reinvigorated the historical study of exegesis by and for literary scholars. Yet it does seem as though the embargo laid on Robertsonianism has forestalled inquiry into the area where spiritual exegesis and ethics overlap, precisely because Robertson's most memorable "totalizing" claim was that exegetical research allowed modern readers to decode every medieval text for an ethical lesson about the love of God and neighbor. The research on theological exegesis of the past few decades has enabled us now to specify *how*—when medieval literatures did indeed seek to lead to love of God and neighbor—they invented their diverse ways and manifold proximate ends.

William Langland's long alliterative dream vision *Piers Plowman* occupies a central place in this book because it gathers and redeploys multiple earlier tropological traditions, Latinate and vernacular. Its diversity of tropological forms, topoi, and methods furnishes a critical apparatus by which to recognize tropological inventions in other works. As extensive research on manuscript production, use, and transmission has demonstrated, *Piers Plowman* functions as "a visible, and far from unique, connective between diverse versions of local community" in late medieval England.[6] And because it exerted direct and indirect influence on a wide ideological range of reformist thought and literature through the seventeenth century, *Piers Plowman* opens up comparative perspectives across a *longue durée*.

Chapter 1, "Tropological Theory," distinguishes the unique role of tropology from the overlapping discourses of rhetoric and moral philosophy and theology. Scholars of medieval literature are accustomed to thinking of poetry as a branch of ethics, which in turn is a part of philosophy. Poetry then employs the tools of rhetoric to move readers and listeners to the good. But in a large segment of medieval intellectual life,

---

6. Ralph Hanna, *London Literature, 1300–1380* (New York: Cambridge University Press, 2005), xvii.

ethics was considered more a part of biblical study than of philosophy. And although biblical literature also invested in rhetoric, its ultimate goal was not to move people to good action but to draw them into participation in the story of salvation narrated in scripture and fulfilled tropologically in the present. This chapter surveys this distinctive understanding of tropological exegesis from Augustine to Erasmus, with special attention to Gregory the Great, Bernard of Clairvaux (*Sermons on the Song of Songs*), and the high Middle Ages' most ambitious theorist of tropology, Bonaventure (*On the Reduction of the Arts to Theology*). Like these exegetes, the poets and dramatists studied here practice a tropological ethics that merges the eternal and mystical calling of the soul with the historical specificity of practical action. A final section of the chapter explores how *Piers Plowman* theorizes tropology in a vision of Piers sowing the seeds of the virtues in scripture and cultivating them by exegesis. *Piers Plowman* also furnishes examples of five varieties of tropology that will be encountered throughout the book, including the work of Stephen Batman, an important Protestant reader of *Piers Plowman* who employs tropology to bridge the intellectual and ecclesial gap opened by the Reformation.

Chapters 2 and 3 are concerned with how exegetical habits—literal and tropological, respectively—contribute to literary invention. In chapter 2, "How to Invent History: *Patience*, the *Glossa ordinaria*, and the Ethics of the Literal Sense," I argue that the author of *Pearl, Cleanness, Patience*, and *Sir Gawain and the Green Knight* develops his distinctive "realizing imagination" in order to open the literal history of scripture to affective and ethical participation. Focusing on the Jonah story in *Patience*, I compare the poet's interest in literal narrative detail and psychology to that of academic commentaries on Jonah, particularly the *Glossa ordinaria*. If the *Patience*-Poet has a literal imagination, then it is one that opens up the brute facts of linear history to the providential ordering of salvation history, with its meaningful intervals between corresponding people, things, and events. He can do this not because he can expect his readers to have an experience of the seamless ordering of history to salvation, but because the theology that underwrites the *Glossa ordinaria*'s inventive exegetical habits provides him with tools to reimagine story and history. The poet portrays Jonah's dilemma as a conflict between God's transcendent interests and Jonah's own immanent, historical exigencies. *Patience* adapts the theology of allegory to set up non-Christological correspondences that stage the argument not only between Jonah and God, but between the literal sense and the spiritual senses in order to reconcile them. This kind of historical imagination allows the spiritual sense of tropology to flourish within the literal sense of scripture, reconciling the potential conflicts of literal and allegorical reading. The *Patience*-Poet's project, then, can be read as cognate to the fourteenth-century scholastic project to integrate literal and spiritual senses. The poem models a practice of biblical paraphrase with tropological purpose that flourished across the Reformation, especially in the English reception of Erasmus's *Paraphrases on the New Testament.*

Patience assumes a metaphysics of history according to which readers of scripture can actually participate in its history by inventing new works. However, this metaphysics can seem to risk either absorbing the past into the present's exigencies or rendering the present a mere reiteration of the past. Tropological invention therefore raises the literary and ethical problematic of originality and repetition, understood in the rhetorical tradition according to the figure of model and copy. Chapter 3, "'Beatus qui verba vertit in opera': Langland's Ethical Invention," investigates the phenomenology of literary and ethical invention in *Piers Plowman* in order to inquire how writers and ethical agents can participate in the world of scripture without being absorbed into it—how they can both copy an all-encompassing model and create entirely unique, unforeseeable phenomena. In the Pentecost episode in *Piers Plowman*, Will and Conscience find themselves on the scene in first-century Jerusalem, inventing with the gathered crowd one of the most famous hymns of the liturgy, the sequence *Veni, Creator Spiritus.* Like the apostles who are speaking in tongues, the crowd invents a completely new song— indeed, invents the Christian liturgy—but it is already a copy of the Holy Spirit's gift. Such a "copy" defies classical rhetorical models, according to which an invention must vie with and displace its model. Unlike Rita Copeland's Chaucer, who translates classical antiquity in order to supersede it, *Piers Plowman* eschews competition, seeking to conserve its biblical and liturgical models, yet nevertheless inventing previously unforeseeable phenomena. Some of the most original and powerful literature of the period displays a similarly harmonious, irenic relationship with its sources, seeking to embody them rather than to overturn them in an agonistic struggle for literary supremacy. Such works strive to incarnate their source texts *as literature*, while also moving readers to enact their ethical directives.

Chapter 4, "Practices of Satisfaction and *Piers Plowman*'s Dynamic Middle," addresses the crucial passage from a literary mode of participation in the history of salvation to the sacramental mode that has often been considered more central to the Catholic Church's understanding of salvation. This chapter probes the overlap between word and sacrament in the climactic passūs of *Piers Plowman* that are structured by the Holy Week liturgy, where Will's participation in the Mass frames his writing of the poem. These scenes of writing as sacramental participation shed light on Reformation-era debates about penance and the role of good works in the Christian life. *Piers Plowman* ends with the corruption of the church and the undoing of the penitential self as the pitiful Contrition abandons his own allegorical essence and "clene forȝete to crye and to wepe."[7] No wonder some of the poem's best readers have identified failure as its chief engine of invention and closure. Nevertheless, Langland designs the work to subordinate the poem's failures to the productive work of satisfaction, the third "part" of the sacrament of penance. Langland conceives of sacramental and literary satisfaction not as the termination of a discrete penitential sequence (contrition, confession, satisfaction), but as an ongoing, open-ended habit of beginning again and making good ends. If we can understand Langland's tropological invention as satisfactory, we can better appreciate the failures and successes of penance in the late Middle Ages, and better recognize practices of satisfaction across the Reformation that narratives of decline and loss tend to overlook. Langland's vision also helps us understand the penitential thought that animates early Reformation literature of conversion, especially Sir Thomas Wyatt's *A Paraphrase of the Penitential Psalms* and

---

7. William Langland, *Piers Plowman*, C.22.369. Unless otherwise noted, I quote from *Piers Plowman: The C Version*, ed. George Russell and George Kane (Berkeley and Los Angeles: University of California Press, 1997); *Piers Plowman: The B Version*, ed. George Kane and E. Talbot Donaldson (London: Athlone Press, 1988); and *Piers Plowman: The A Version*, ed. George Kane (London: Athlone Press, 1960). I have also consulted *Piers Plowman: A Parallel-Text Edition of the A, B, C and Z Versions*, ed. A. V. C. Schmidt, 2 vols. (Kalamazoo: Medieval Institute Publications, 2011).

the glosses of *Piers Plowman*'s first editor, the radical Protestant Robert Crowley. Uniting all three beyond their deep differences of practice and theology was the scriptural belief that the phenomenon of sacramental penance appears fully only when seen in eschatological perspective.

What becomes of tropological participation in the history of salvation when the sacramental economy goes into eclipse? Chapter 5, "Tropology Reformed: Scripture, Salvation, Drama," argues both that tropology became an important channel of exegetical and ethical continuity between late medieval and early Reformation English religious culture, and also that tropology enabled various Protestant writers to bypass the sacramental economy on which Langland's practice of tropology depended. The first part of the chapter tracks permutations of tropological theory and practice in the theological and exegetical works of Erasmus, John Calvin, Martin Luther, William Tyndale, Thomas More, and Martin Bucer. These discourses frame the dramatic culture of the court of the Reformed boy-king Edward VI, who himself likely acted in apocalyptic, anti-Catholic plays and revels scripted by scholars steeped in Erasmian (Nicholas Udall) and Bucerian (Bernardino Ochino) tropological theory. Figures from that culture of court drama reappear during the reign of Mary in Coventry, where one John Careless, imprisoned for radical Protestant street drama, is released temporarily to perform in the city's traditional mystery plays. Careless's letters from prison to fellow radicals, recorded in John Foxe's Book of Martyrs, movingly capture him reinventing practices of consolation and tropological participation in biblical history that he learned from Coventry's medieval dramatic culture. As he scripts his own martyrdom from the tropes of biblical drama, Careless bears testimony to radical Protestantism's ability to sustain a participatory understanding of ethics and salvation despite its rejection of the sacramental economy.

Chapter 6, "Mirror of Scripture: Ethics and Anagogy in the York Doomsday Pageant," imagines the tropological possibilities of the "medieval" York Play during the last decade of its performance in a Protestant age. Entertaining critiques of "works righteousness," this speculative reformist performance of the play stages a confrontation between the tropological and anagogical senses to challenge the efficacy of good works and maintain the gratuitous judgment of Christ the King. At the same time, the thought experiment reveals how the play's original

Catholic theology contains resources for thinking beyond merit when considering the relationship between virtue ethics and salvation. Specifically, the chapter considers how medieval biblical drama enlisted optical theory to address obstacles to ethical participation in the story of salvation. In several episodes, the York Play deploys the image of a mirror to articulate the complex moral and soteriological functions of a performed Bible. Combining two pervasive mirror topoi—the mirror of scripture and the mirror as moral exemplar—the play displaces the topoi from their conventional medium, the book, onto drama, thus exploring what would become another pervasive mirror topos, the drama-as-mirror. The Doomsday pageant presents God as a judging spectator and the audience as the object of scrutiny. The pageant fosters an eschatological conversion of the gaze. Truly to see means to be seen truly. So while the York Play certainly endeavors to train its audience to be good spectator-participants, the Doomsday pageant seeks to render them the spectated-participated, thereby throwing their "goodness" into eschatological question. Other pageants in the play critique ecclesial pretensions to control the body of Christ in the transubstantiated Eucharistic host, but the Doomsday pageant defies the pretensions of a virtuous laity to possess the body of Christ through ethical works of mercy. As it rebuffs claims to Eucharistic hegemony, the pageant also invites a redefinition of "sacramental theater" that affirms the function of both the social body and the Eucharistic body in making Christ present.

By attending to tropology, this study illuminates changes and continuities in ethical thought and literature during a period of energetic reform in English religious culture from roughly 1350 to 1600. In debates about the revelatory and ethical functions of scripture, poetry, and drama, reformist writers acknowledged the tropological imperative that Christians embody the text of scripture in their actions. By studying tropology as an engine of literary invention in the poetry, religious literature, and drama of this long age of reform, *Tropologies* shows how the possibilities of poetry and drama changed as theology reconceived scripture's salvific power and institutions reformed laypeople's access to it. This approach demands that we treat works of narrative poetry and drama as powerful theological thought machines in their own right, thereby integrating vernacular literary texts more richly into the history of exegesis and religious reform.

1

Tropological Theory

This is a book about exegesis that treats relatively little biblical commentary, as traditionally understood. That is because tropology is the one mode of interpretation that cannot be successfully practiced by commentary alone. To write the history of literal, allegorical, and anagogical exegesis, we can remain within the glossed margins of innumerable biblical manuscripts, in sermon collections, catenas, lectures, *postillae*, and the theoretical apparatus that taught people how to produce them. But the moral exegesis we find in those places is always only a trace of the tropological endeavor, a husk of an act of invention—or the seed of another—because tropological interpretation is never complete without a corresponding movement of the will that issues in new action. Tropological invention can take many forms, and most of them vanish in the small and unremarkable actions that compose a life. But it can also take the form of literary invention, a responsive re-creation of the biblical material in surprisingly original yet recognizable renderings. Those inventions of biblical poetry and drama are the subject of this book, and this chapter explains why literature is an especially apt product of tropological invention.

The first part of this chapter develops a theory of tropology from the commonly acknowledged history of exegesis. My argument is cumulative, and it begins with a reorientation of the field of medieval literary ethics to appreciate how tropological exegesis and invention are distinguished from rhetorical and moral-philosophical discourses by their object of interpretation, the Christian Bible. Medieval theorists are prepared to extend tropological theory to all manner of interpretable objects, cultural and natural, but the Bible remains the conceptual center of gravity because it presents the story of salvation. For medieval exegetes, biblical reading ideally involves participation in the spiritual and historical realities to which the Bible bears witness. More than a hermeneutical fusion of horizons, "spiritual exegesis" entails a participatory metaphysics according to which created beings come to participate in the uncreated divine life. Allegorical and anagogical exegesis speaks *about* this participation, but tropological interpretation is different: it draws the ideas of allegory and anagogy into the lived present, interlacing readers' concrete actions with the biblical history to which the literal sense of scripture bears witness. While allegory traditionally calls for the exercise of faith and anagogy for that of hope, tropology is enacted in love, the greatest of these. Tropology therefore performs a vital circulatory function, channeling the meanings of scripture into readers' lives, where they can effect the proper disposition for right interpretation: love. Tropology might be thought of as the church's circulatory system: it pushes the blood of the literal sense into action and circulates it through the lungs of the allegorical sense in order to animate and inhabit the body with an anagogical completeness.

The Bible presents its readers with the tropological imperative to turn its words into works. These works, these tropological inventions, take innumerable forms, and one of the most durable, and so most available to study, is the invention of literature. Narrative poetry and drama engage in tropological interpretation and invention on a scale we do not encounter in line-by-line biblical commentary. Just as in the history of exegesis, where it has become apparent that the practice of exegesis is as important a source of exegetical theory as explicitly theoretical texts, our best source for understanding literary tropology is the works of literature themselves. The second part of this chapter makes good on the foregoing argument by studying biblical poetry—in this case, *Piers Plowman*—as a source of tropological theory and as an anatomy of tropological modes that show up in the other texts treated in this book. Although this chapter dwells on the medieval exegetical tradition, it turns at the end to a Protestant elaboration of Langlandian tropology that gestures toward Reformation-era transformations of tropological theory, the subject of chapter 5.

The History of Exegesis and Tropological Theory

Disciplinary Reorientation: Beyond the *Accessus ad Auctores* Tradition

Tropological ethics overlaps with much that we already know about rhetorical ethics and moral philosophy and theology, but not all ethical discourse is tropological. Tropology is *for us*, while other ethical discourses can be impersonal. Tropology is ordered toward participation in salvation history, while other ethical discourses can adopt more narrowly circumscribed horizons. Tropology situates the good within the horizon of salvation, while rhetoric can adopt cynically utilitarian specifications of the good. Tropology demands application of the moral, while one can discuss moral philosophy or theology ad nauseam without applying the moral. Tropology tends to draw a moral from something that is not explicitly ethical, to enact a *translatio* by shifting the frame of reference around the object of interpretation. Moral philosophy and theology, by contrast, deal explicitly with ethical matters within ethical conceptual frames. Most importantly, tropology necessarily draws moral interpretation and invention into the world of Christian scripture. These contrasts require a disciplinary reorientation, a reevaluation of the limits of the rhetorical traditions and of the medieval fields of moral philosophy and theology.

In order to appreciate tropological theory's significance for Middle English poetry and drama, we have to take a step back from the intricate theories of authorship refined by university-based scholastics in the twelfth and thirteenth centuries. Literary historians know a great deal about these theories, thanks to the late-twentieth-century rediscovery of "medieval literary theory and criticism."[1] According to medieval

---

1. The indispensable anthology of this body of work is A. J. Minnis and A. B. Scott, eds., *Medieval Literary Theory and Criticism, c. 1100–c. 1375: The Commentary Tradition*, rev. ed. (Oxford: Clarendon Press, 1988).

introductions to classical and patristic writing, the *accessus ad auctores*, ethics is the part of philosophy to which poetry belongs. Poetry is therefore considered a part of philosophy, and what modern scholars call literary ethics becomes a subfield of moral philosophy or moral theology. This classification of poetry as ethics, taken over from Greek commentators on Plato and Aristotle, shaped the disciplinary approach by which high medieval and late medieval scholars encountered classical literature and, eventually, the way they interacted with the Bible, early Christian authorities, and contemporary poetry.[2] Poetry's affiliation with philosophy, the most prestigious discipline in the Aristotelian hierarchy of the sciences, elevated its status. Meanwhile, by the early fourteenth century academic theologians had come to understand the language of scripture, rather than the history to which it referred, as the primary site of revelation, with the result that "the Bible became more like poetry."[3] These affinities could then be turned, in the hands of a subtle humanist such as Boccaccio, to the theological defense of poetry on the grounds that scripture and poetry "share a common mode of treatment."[4] The classification of poetry as moral philosophy has also guided two generations of modern inquiry into medieval literary theory, particularly the theory of what Judson Boyce Allen called "the medieval ethical poetic."[5]

---

2. On the classical origins of the tradition, see Edwin A. Quain, "The Medieval Accessus ad Auctores," *Traditio* 3 (January 1, 1945): 215–64; on the application of this tradition to scripture and patristic authorities, see Alastair Minnis, *Medieval Theory of Authorship: Scholastic Literary Attitudes in the Later Middle Ages*, 2nd ed. (Philadelphia: University of Pennsylvania Press, 2011), 40–72.

3. Christopher Ocker, *Biblical Poetics before Humanism and Reformation* (New York: Cambridge University Press, 2002), 78.

4. Giovanni Boccaccio, "Short Treatise in Praise of Dante," in *Medieval Literary Theory and Criticism, c. 1100–c. 1375: The Commentary Tradition*, rev. ed., ed. A. J. Minnis and A. B. Scott, trans. David Wallace (Oxford: Clarendon Press, 1988), 495. This narrative is engagingly limned, with updated bibliography, in the preface to the reissued second edition of Minnis, *Medieval Theory of Authorship*, ix–xxvi.

5. "There is no better method of tapping into the deep sources, the fundamental assumptions, of poetic theory in medieval Latin than to consider

However, most of the poetry and drama treated in this book, while saturated with scripture and ethical intentions, was produced and used neither as biblical scholarship nor as poetry in the humanist sense. The biblical literature studied here belongs more fittingly to what we might call lived theology than it does to the academic world of philosophy, theology, and biblical scholarship. This literature shares more with the discourses of exegesis, homiletics, pastoralia, and mysticism than it does with the increasingly scientific milieu of the theology faculties of the thirteenth and fourteenth centuries.[6] As Alastair Minnis has argued, medieval intellectuals treated poetry differently depending on whether they were considering it in terms of the Aristotelian *Organon*, as they did in the *accessus* tradition, or in terms of biblical interpretation.[7] Ethics likewise receives an alternative treatment. Unlike the *accessus* tradition, medieval introductory guides to exegesis and the intellectual

---

what the *accessus ad auctores* have to say." Alastair Minnis, "The Trouble with Theology: Ethical Poetics and the Ends of Scripture," in *Author, Reader, Book: Medieval Authorship in Theory and Practice*, ed. Stephen Bradford Partridge and Erik Kwakkel (Toronto: University of Toronto Press, 2012), 21. For prominent treatments of the *accessus* tradition as literary theory and specifically a key to literary ethics, see Judson Boyce Allen, *The Ethical Poetic of the Later Middle Ages: A Decorum of Convenient Distinction* (Toronto: University of Toronto Press, 1982), 3–66; Minnis, *Medieval Theory of Authorship*, 23–27, 177–90; Vincent Gillespie, "The Study of Classical Authors from the Twelfth Century to *c*. 1450," in *The Cambridge History of Literary Criticism*, vol. 2, *The Middle Ages*, ed. Alastair Minnis and Ian Johnson (New York: Cambridge University Press, 2005), 160–78.

6. For an approachable conspectus of the process by which theology became a specialized science, see Philipp W. Rosemann, *The Story of a Great Medieval Book: Peter Lombard's "Sentences"* (Toronto: University of Toronto Press, 2007), especially 184–91.

7. "Poetry continued to be demoted within the *Organon*, even as it was promoted within theologians' accounts of the *multiplex modus* of scripture." Minnis, "The Trouble with Theology," 28. Two other versions of this important revision of Minnis's early work on the *accessus* tradition appear as the preface to Minnis, *Medieval Theory of Authorship*, ix–xxvi; and as "Ethical Poetry, Poetic Theology: A Crisis of Medieval Authority?," in *Medieval and Early Modern Authorship*, ed. Guillemette Bolens and Lukas Erne, SPELL: Swiss Papers in English Language and Literature 25 (Tübingen: Narr, 2011), 293–308.

practices of the Christian life introduce an alternative disciplinary heading for ethics under scriptural exegesis, which is ordered to contemplative participation in divine wisdom. According to guides such as Hugh of St. Victor's *Didascalicon* and Bonaventure's *De reductione artium ad theologiam*, which permeated literate culture far beyond their monastic origins, ethics belongs to the tropological or moral sense of scripture, which teaches what you ought to do—*quid agas docet*, according to the widely cited distich of Augustine of Denmark.[8] At the same time, a great deal of poetry and drama made the Bible available beyond the bounds of the Vulgate proper, functioning like liturgy and preaching to disseminate scriptural knowledge and experience.[9] In this large body of vernacular biblical literature, literary ethics enters the purview of *sacra scriptura*. The exegetical theory of tropology illuminates literary phenomena at the boundaries of poetry and scripture that medieval theories of authorship do not, on their own, comprehend.

---

8. "Littera gesta docet, quid credas allegoria, / Moralis quid agas, quid speres anagogia" (The letter teaches what happened, allegory what you should believe, / tropology what you should do, anagogy what you hope for). Augustine of Denmark, *Rotulus pugillaris*, in "Augustini de Dacia, O. P.: 'Rotulus pugillaris,'" ed. A. Walz, *Angelicum* 6 (1929): 253–78, at 256. For Nicholas of Lyra's citation of the distich, see Minnis and Scott, *Medieval Literary Theory*, 267. On the distich's popularity and adaptation, see Edward Synan, "The Four 'Senses' and Four Exegetes," in *With Reverence for the Word: Medieval Scriptural Exegesis in Judaism, Christianity, and Islam*, eds. Jane Damman McAuliffe, Barry D. Walfish, and Joseph W. Goering (New York: Oxford University Press, 2003), 226–36; François Châtillon, "Vocabulaire et prosodie du distique attribué à Augustin de Dacie sur les quatre sens de l'écriture," *L'Homme devant Dieu: Mélanges offerts au Père Henri de Lubac*, 3 vols. (Lyons: Aubier, 1964), 2:17–28; Henri de Lubac, *Medieval Exegesis: The Four Senses of Scripture*, trans. Mark Sebanc and E. M. Macierowski, 3 vols. (Grand Rapids, MI: William B. Eerdmans, 1998–), 2:33–39.

9. The outlines of this vast field of English literature are sketched in James H. Morey, *Book and Verse: A Guide to Middle English Biblical Literature* (Urbana-Champaign: University of Illinois Press, 2000). On the diffuse modalities of scriptural knowledge and experience beyond strictly defined Vulgate literacy, see Eyal Poleg, *Approaching the Bible in Medieval England* (Manchester: Manchester University Press, 2013).

These discourses all draw, to varying degrees, on Gregory the Great, whose tropological imagination profoundly shaped the high and late medieval projects of scholasticism and pastoral care. In the *De reductione artium ad theologiam*, Bonaventure divides the arts by analogy to the four senses of scripture. All knowledge concerned with practical action falls under the tropological sense. Extending the analogy according to causal analysis, Bonaventure classifies everything relating to efficient causation under the tropological sense. If you want to know all about this tropological phase or mode of knowledge, he says—that is, if you want to know about the order of living and the activities (*effectus*) of practical reason, including rhetorical invention, the exercise of the senses, the making of armor, or the producing of plays (*ludendi continens*)—you should turn to Gregory the Great, who is the master of tropology.[10] Bonaventure shares his esteem for Gregory's moral exegesis with many other medieval theologians, early and late. Gregory is the dominant post-Aristotelian authority in Thomas Aquinas's treatise on the vices.[11] Gregory's *Moralia in Job* was the most prominent source for the *materia* of Peraldus's mid-thirteenth-century *Summa de vitiis et virtutibus*, a work that almost single-handedly supplied the moral discourse for penitential practice and theology after the Fourth Lateran Council, and inspired many academic and vernacular adaptations.[12] Scholarship on late medieval literary ethics has been dominated by the discourses of moral philosophy, moral theology, rhetoric, and exemplarity. However, as the example of Gregory suggests, the late medieval figures who shaped those discourses were keenly aware of tropology as an ethical discourse more intimately in touch with *sacra scriptura* and

---

10. Bonaventure, *Saint Bonaventure's "De reductione artium ad theologiam,"* trans. Emma Thérèse Healy, 2nd ed. (Saint Bonaventure, NY: The Franciscan Institute, 1955), 5.

11. Matthew Baasten, *Pride according to Gregory the Great: A Study of the "Moralia"* (Lewiston, NY: E. Mellen Press, 1986), 119–38.

12. F. N. M. Diekstra, ed., *Book for a Simple and Devout Woman: A Late Middle English Adaptation of Peraldus's "Summa de Vitiis et Virtutibus" and Friar Laurent's "Somme Le Roi": Edited from British Library Mss Harley 6571 and Additional 30944* (Groningen: Egbert Forsten, 1998), 317, 327.

therefore more fundamental than the *scientia divina* and *pastoralia* that developed later.[13]

Tropological theory helps us to understand the distinctive ways in which literary ethics functions in the traditions of biblical literature, in contradistinction to, but also in productive conversation with, academic theology. Although the exegetical terminology and theory on which I draw originated in monastic and scholastic contexts, along with the *accessus* tradition and its theories of authorship, I use them throughout this book to discover and articulate the often underarticulated theoretical work being performed in vernacular religious writing and biblical poetry and drama. This theoretical work is distinctive and in many cases supplements or diverges from the medieval academic theories with which modern scholars are most familiar.

Disciplinary Reorientation: Beyond Rhetoric and Moral Philosophy

Like tropology, rhetoric concerns the movement from interpretation to action, the turning of idea into affect, and the fulfilling of an affective potency in executive action. And like the theory of tropology, the rhetorical tradition supplied medieval writers with a robust theory of invention. Yet the rhetorical tradition's literary affordances, as modern scholars have come to know them, are only obliquely related to biblical literature. To be sure, Mary Carruthers's work in *The Craft of Thought* on the rhetorical "machines" of medieval invention emerges from a study of Cistercian and Carthusian reading communities. Yet in that work, Carruthers does not take up the ethics of reading scripture, instead referring the reader to her suggestive but unfocused chapter on "the ethics of reading" in *The Book of Memory*.[14] Carruthers's practical separation of the disciplines of rhetoric and *sacra scriptura* reflects a

---

13. For an even-handed account of analogous developments in scholastic theology, see Rosemann, *The Story of a Great Medieval Book*, 185–91.

14. Mary Carruthers, *The Craft of Thought: Meditation, Rhetoric, and the Making of Images, 400–1200* (New York: Cambridge University Press, 2000), 22–23; *The Book of Memory: A Study of Memory in Medieval Culture*, rev. ed. (New York: Cambridge University Press, 2008), 195–233.

similar bifurcation in medieval studies at large.[15] Tropology happens where the practices of rhetoric and *sacra scriptura* meet. My investigations of tropological theory take up the rhetorically inclined scholarship on didascalic literature and ethical reading and extend it into the theology of scripture and the practice of biblical exegesis.[16]

Moral philosophy, what Aristotle called ethics, has its own account of the movement from interpretation to action in the doctrine of prudence and related analyses of the will and action (action theory).[17] Tropology shares characteristics with the Thomistic-Aristotelian ethical synthesis, but it specifies different poles of movement from interpretation to action and different contexts in which the movement takes place. The context is not just any array of exemplars, any idea or image of a good that attracts and moves the affection. The idea or image that tropology turns into affect is not just any norm or precept, but rather

---

15. A natural point of convergence for rhetoric and *sacra scriptura* is homiletics. *Piers Plowman* studies have yielded some productive work along these lines, even if this work draws the poem further into the territory of rhetoric. See, notably, Carruthers, *The Craft of Thought*, 36n72. Copeland's article "*Pathos* and Pastoralism: Aristotle's *Rhetoric* in Medieval England," *Speculum* 89, no. 1 (2014): 96–127, demonstrates that at least one fifteenth-century reader of *Piers Plowman* applied to it an idea he appreciated in Aristotle's *Rhetoric*. In the margins of Cambridge University, MS Peterhouse 57, William of Moerbeke's translation of the *Rhetoric*, alongside Aristotle's discussion of the emotion of *amicitia* (friendliness), this reader has written, "O pers plwman. iust is thy life / thw livist of thi labor with owt ani strife" (114–15). This could be a case of mistaking Aristotle's *Rhetoric* for a homiletical aid of a nonrhetorical sort, namely, as a kind of maxim collection. The *Piers Plowman* gloss, itself in verse, draws the *Rhetoric* into the world of vernacular biblical literature, here especially the wisdom-literature thread of *Piers Plowman*. This annotator, as Copeland notes, seems not to grasp how the *Rhetoric* really functions and is only interested in maxims, which he has copied out at the end of the volume (108).

16. This book's contributions to *Piers Plowman* studies could be read as a reinvention of Mary Carruthers's first book, *The Search for St. Truth: A Study of Meaning in "Piers Plowman"* (Evanston, IL: Northwestern University Press, 1973), by way of her two, much later studies of reading, ethics, and invention in *The Book of Memory* (1990) and *The Craft of Thought* (1998).

17. See Daniel Westberg, *Right Practical Reason: Aristotle, Action, and Prudence in Aquinas* (Oxford: Clarendon Press, 1994).

Christian doctrine actualized in the history of salvation.[18] Nor is the action that tropology entails simply "good" action, defined as virtue in contrast to vice, but rather good action on the way to the kingdom of heaven in the company of other pilgrims (the church). Aristotelian (and modern) virtue ethics can be criticized for overlooking interpersonal relationships, but late medieval tropological ethics tends to resist individualism and to insist on normative particularities—determinatively, the norm of the Christian scriptures as the unique textual "face" or site of moral encounter with the Other.[19] These distinctive features of tropological theory and practice argue for a redrawing of the disciplinary lines that presently guide the study of late medieval literary ethics. Although "biblical ethics" is a subfield of modern theological ethics, scholars of medieval moral philosophy have not recognized a similar discourse, nor has medieval scholarship in general appreciated the prominence of biblical ethics in clerical as well as lay intellectual life.[20]

The modern term "biblical ethics" is a good starting point for a definition of tropology. The term "tropology" is widely used in me-

---

18. "The history of salvation is . . . an overarching reality or world which encompasses a self's present relation to God or Christ, together with the history of such relations and the factual occurrences in which it was embodied, as witnessed by the Bible." Hans W. Frei, *The Eclipse of Biblical Narrative: A Study in Eighteenth and Nineteenth Century Hermeneutics* (New Haven: Yale University Press, 1974), 181.

19. Moral philosophy and theology can tend, when read as discrete discourses, to emphasize individuals over communities. For a critique of liberal-individualist readings of medieval theology and ethics, see David Aers, *Faith, Ethics, Church: Writing in England, 1360–1409* (Cambridge: D. S. Brewer, 2000), 13–20.

20. For example, the *Cambridge History of Later Medieval Philosophy*, which has long sections on ethics, includes no reference to the properly ethical component of exegesis and exegetical theory. See especially Alan Donagan, "Thomas Aquinas on Human Action," in *The Cambridge History of Later Medieval Philosophy: From the Rediscovery of Aristotle to the Disintegration of Scholasticism, 1100–1600*, ed. Norman Kretzmann, Anthony Kenny, and Jan Pinborg (New York: Cambridge University Press, 1982), 642–54; and in the same collection, George Wieland, "Happiness: The Perfection of Man," 673–86.

dieval exegetical theory and biblical commentary, but it is less frequently encountered in biblical literature more broadly conceived, and the term drops out of use among Protestant reformers. I adopt the term throughout this book to speak about a range of interpretive and inventive practices that concern the conversion of words into works, within the context of the history of salvation as witnessed in and beyond the Christian scriptures. The medieval and early modern authors discussed in this book are primarily interested in the words of scripture and the works that grow out of scripture. But scripture, as we shall see, can be understood very capaciously—even, as Chaucer puts it, as "[a]l that is writen . . . for oure doctrine."[21] In the milieu of medieval biblical literature, the Bible is best imagined not as a single book but as a diffuse network of manuscript transmission complicated and enriched by all manner of contamination, interpolation, and performative variation, and then further extended in its liturgical and homiletical modalities. Because this diffuse Bible permeated so many forms of textual and performance culture, medieval writers and readers frequently thought about the conversion of even profane words into works by adapting the theory and practice of tropological interpretation and invention—which I will hereafter simply call tropology. As I conceive of it in this book, then, tropology extends far beyond the discourses in which it is named "tropology." At the same time, as pervasive as tropology may be, it functions differently from the more familiar practices of moral philosophy, moral theology, and rhetoric. By studying what is distinctive about tropology, we will be able to make finer distinctions about the kinds of ethical work performed by medieval and early modern literature. Before proceeding to those distinctions, I pause to anticipate the objection that the diversity of medieval scriptural discourses defies the traditional, ostensibly simplistic schematic of the four senses of scripture, and so attenuates the critical purchase of the language of tropology.

---

21. Geoffrey Chaucer, *The Canterbury Tales*, in *The Riverside Chaucer*, 3rd ed., ed. Larry D. Benson (Boston: Houghton Mifflin, 1987), *Retr.* 10a.1083. Hereafter cited by fragment and line number.

Tropology and the History of Exegesis: An Objection

Any consideration of tropology must begin from an understanding of the spiritual senses of scripture and their relationship to the literal sense and to each other. Medieval theology of scripture depends on an analysis of letter and spirit, derived from the writings of the Apostle Paul. According to this understanding, the letter of the text was unlocked and opened by Christ. Thomas Aquinas, for example, locates the opening precisely in Christ's passion: "[scripture] was closed before the Passion, but it was opened after the Passion because those who since then have understood it consider and discern how the prophecies are to be explained."[22] The New Testament recapitulates the Old, fulfilling its persons, things, and events in repetitions rendered different and spiritually fulfilled by Christ's life, passion, and resurrection. The Holy Spirit fills the literal sense of the text with other, higher, deeper spiritual meanings. These spiritual senses are commonly identified as allegorical, tropological, and anagogical. Spiritual exegesis, then, is exegesis of these senses, which are sometimes collectively called allegorical. Spiritual exegesis necessarily happens beyond or at a deeper level of the literal sense. Because these senses are animated by the Holy Spirit, they are related to each other and depend on each other. As the circulatory system of scripture, tropology brings the doctrinal ideas of allegory into lived application, where they can in turn be embodied in new history, a history directed toward the fulfillment of anagogy's eschatological visions.[23]

---

22. Thomas Aquinas, *In Psalmos Davidis expositio*, 21.11, www.corpus thomisticum.org.

23. As Lewis Ayres glosses de Lubac, "the Christian reader moves from one sense to another, not by leaving behind the previous sense but by seeing with more intensity and complexity the mystery of God's action in Christ. Thus, tropology discloses not simply the moral implications of Christian belief, but the shape of the life of one who lives within Christ, within the ecclesia. This disclosure is only possible when one has discovered the doctrinal matrix disclosed by allegorical reading. The two reading practices are thus part of one whole: the deeper one penetrates the mystery of God's action in Christ the more one comes to see how the action of Christ as and on the church is an action which

However, these theoretical schematics, as helpful as they can be in an introductory context, risk obscuring the diversity of exegetical theory and practice at any given time and their diachronic variation. The history of late medieval exegesis has grown in the past fifteen years into a cottage industry, and as we have learned more about the sheer volume of exegetical writing and the diversity of opinion and practice, the schematics that didascalic writers used to talk about exegesis have come to seem less adequate. Henri de Lubac's theoretically breathtaking *Exégèse médiévale: Les quatre sens de l'écriture*, which took those very medieval schematics as its *forma tractatus*, no longer seems to map onto the landscape that has been explored by three generations of followers of Beryl Smalley.[24] Smalley began the monumental task of sketching the institutional settings, academic and pastoral applications, and intellectual genealogies of late medieval exegesis—work that has only recently begun to crystallize into some kind of a clear picture.[25] The clearer the picture becomes, the more urgent seem studies of local centers of exegetical activity and networks of transmission—in short, those types of

---

shapes each Christian." Lewis Ayres, "The Soul and the Reading of Scripture: A Note on Henri de Lubac," *Scottish Journal of Theology* 61, no. 2 (2008): 175.

24. Henri de Lubac, *Exégèse médiévale: les quatre sens de l'écriture*, 4 vols. (Paris: Aubier, 1959–64).

25. Smalley's foundational book is *The Study of the Bible in the Middle Ages* (Oxford: Blackwell, 1952). The most significant recent developments that owe their course of research directly to Smalley's proposals center around the origins and authorship of the *Glossa ordinaria*. See especially Alexander Andrée's work on the earliest major glossators: Alexander Andrée, ed., *Anselmi Laudunensis Glosae super Iohannem*, CCSL 267 (Turnhout: Brepols, 2014); Alexander Andrée, "Anselm of Laon Unveiled: The *Glosae super Iohanem* and the Origins of the *Glossa ordinaria* on the Bible," *Mediaeval Studies* 73 (2011): 217–40; the introduction to Alexander Andrée, ed., *Gilbertus Universalis: "Glossa ordinaria in Lamentationes Ieremie prophete," Prothemata et Liber I: A Critical Edition with an Introduction and a Translation* (Stockholm: Almqvist and Wiksell, 2005); and Alexander Andrée, "The Rhetorical Hermeneutics of Gilbert the Universal in His Gloss on Lamentations," *Journal of Medieval Latin* 17 (2007): 143–58. Most of what we know about the development of the *Glossa* is presented in the landmark study by Lesley Smith, *The "Glossa ordinaria": The Making of a Medieval Bible Commentary* (Leiden: Brill, 2009).

institutional, sociological, codicological, and material-cultural inquiry for which the new philology has prepared medieval studies. This is why John Contreni, in an otherwise appreciative review of the English translation of de Lubac's magnum opus, can complain: "Built on *a priori* assumptions about the Bible and how learning and scholarship are transmitted across cultures and centuries (seamlessly and atemporally it would appear) and devoid of a sense of Christianity as a historical religion, *Medieval Exegesis* strikes me as terribly dated and largely irrelevant to current scholarship on biblical exegesis."[26] The consistency of medieval exegetical categories belies the diversity of actual practice and the wide variation in how theoretical terminology is used.

Historicist perspectives such as Contreni's, however, can obscure how and why medieval exegetes themselves so comfortably rehearsed the theory of fourfold (or threefold) exegesis and why they thought they were practicing exegesis accordingly. The theology of scripture has a long history of thinking about the unity of scripture alongside its multiplicity of senses. Such a plenitude can only arise, Augustine taught, through love. By the later Middle Ages, the Augustinian doctrine of scripture as a text full of love that invites loving interpretation from its readers informed discussions of unity and multiplicity. Henry of Ghent, for example, considers the various numbers assigned to the senses of scripture by the pseudo-Dionysius (two), Hugh of St. Victor (three), Bede (four), Augustine (five), and theorists working in the rhetorical tradition (as many as there are figures of speech). Henry goes on to argue for the appropriateness of four as the number of senses, but the important point is that all agree on the multiplicity of senses, which comes about, as Augustine says, because of the opening of scripture to the law of love that Christ inaugurated. Ever since Christ, the meaning

---

26. John Contreni, "Review of *Medieval Exegesis, Vol. 1: The Four Senses of Scripture* by Henri de Lubac," *The Medieval Review*, August 13, 1999, http:// hdl.handle.net/2022/4700. For an alternative view of de Lubac's intentions and the limitations and affordances of *Medieval Exegesis*, see Ryan McDermott, "Henri de Lubac's Genealogy of Modern Exegesis and Nicholas of Lyra's Literal Sense of Scripture," *Modern Theology* 29, no. 1 (2013): 124–56.

of scripture cannot remain closed in itself, but must be opened out, or must set out pilgrim-like, toward the goal of love:

> "Wherefore, when anyone has come to understand that the goal of God's commandment is love that proceeds 'from a heart that is pure, a clear conscience and faith that is sincere,' and if he determines to relate the entire process of understanding the divine Scriptures to those three things, then he may approach the task of treating of the Scriptures with confidence." . . . So every exposition of Holy Scripture must be aimed towards these three, in accordance with the rule of faith, namely that things worthy of belief be believed, things worthy of love be loved, and things worthy of hope be hoped for.[27]

Henry rhetorically doubles the most important terms—belief/believed, love/loved, hope/hoped for—because Christian scripture comes similarly doubled, or folded, by love, which functions both as efficient cause and final cause, the source of invention and the goal toward which further invention must tend. As we shall see in the second half of this chapter, this doubling of the same, this eschatological extension and deferral of what is already here, animates Langland's allegory of scripture.

Henry of Ghent and Langland find diversity, variation, and complexity in the theory and practice of exegesis to be not just tolerable but stimulating and productive. More recently, these characteristics are sometimes invoked as reasons to reject any but purely historical engagement with theories of manifold exegesis. Frances Young, for example, contends "that neither the self-conscious practice of detailed exegesis, nor its broader hermeneutical principles, are properly attended to by the standard analysis into senses."[28] But diversity and variation can be exaggerated. One wonders whether Young's own analysis of five types of

---

27. Henry of Ghent, *Summa quaestionum ordinariarum* 16.3; in Minnis and Scott, *Medieval Literary Theory*, 257–58. Citing Augustine, *De doctrina christiana* 1.11, citing 1 Tim. 1:5.

28. Frances Young, *Biblical Exegesis and the Formation of Christian Culture* (New York: Cambridge University Press, 1997), 201.

literal sense, eight types of allegory, four types of type, and six types of reading strategy constitutes "proper attention" to "detailed exegesis" or just a more cumbersome version of the fourfold mnemonic rehearsed by so many exegetes.[29] Such an approach can obscure commonalities, the habits of religious reading shared by exegetes across time and place. Ideally, the history of exegesis would be able to recognize variation in the enumeration, relations, and boundaries of the senses across eras, schools, and individual theorists, at the same time developing supple and agile general categories for thinking about what is happening trans-historically.

This field dominated by historicist methodologies stands to gain from comparative religious studies a more nuanced understanding of exegetical theory and its change over time. In a study of "religious reading" practices in first-millennium Indian Buddhism and third- to fifth-century Roman African Christianity, Paul Griffiths compares these disparate communities' attitudes about sacred texts and shared practices of reading from a social-anthropological standpoint. The method necessarily generalizes and analogizes, but the results—revelatory of likeness, difference, and nuance—are hardly totalizing. Griffiths describes "religious reading" as a "practice" that

> has to do primarily with the establishment of certain relations between readers and the things they read, relations at once attitudinal, cognitive, and moral, and that therefore imply an ontology, an epistemology, and an ethic. . . . The first and most basic element in these relations is that the work read is understood as a . . . vastly rich resource, one that yields meaning, suggestions (or imperatives) for action, matter for aesthetic wonder, and much else. . . . The second . . . is that readers are seen as intrinsically capable of reading and as morally required to read. . . . The work's . . . fecundity as a resource is thus matched by the reader's . . . ingenuity as a discoverer or uncoverer.[30]

---

29. Ibid., 186–213.

30. Paul J. Griffiths, *Religious Reading: The Place of Reading in the Practice of Religion* (New York: Oxford University Press, 1999), 41–42. Three of the

Medieval exegetes sketched a manifold model of spiritual exegesis because they were involved in something like religious reading as Griffiths expresses it here. The ontology of the text as infinite resource entails spiritual, or allegorical, meaning: if it always means something more, it must always mean something *else*. Readers' fitness for reading and their corresponding moral responsibility require something like a tropological sense. In religious communities with an eschatology, religious reading also requires something like an anagogical sense. The infinity of a text opens out toward an end that consummates the reading practices (in the Christian West, an infinitely satisfying repetitive stasis, and in the Christian East, an infinite, epectatic progress further into the divine life).[31]

Of course, despite these features shared among religious reading communities, differences in theology and practice will produce different forms of religious reading. In the Christian reading communities treated in this book, the nature of religious reading depends on a metaphysics of participation, a concept I will develop in the next section. Although other religious communities might develop an ethics of reading ordered to the consummation of the good, this reading will not be tropological in the sense of addressing the specific ways that medieval theorists understood tropology as participation in the divine life—a view that entails particular metaphysical and ontological positions. A social-anthropological inquiry into religious reading, then, reveals the importance of theological questions, for only particular kinds of theological metaphysics and ontology will even begin to entertain the kind of textuality that a community of religious reading presupposes.

Tropological theory provides a way to talk about the ethical component of religious reading that is historically contemporary with Middle English literature while also linking the late Middle Ages to earlier and later ethical interpreters of the Bible. Theologians always contested

---

ellipses elide expressions of textual and subjective "stability"—a term Griffiths qualifies elsewhere, but which I find unhelpful in the present context.

31. For a conspectus of these options, see Paul J. Griffiths, *Decreation: The Last Things of All Creatures* (Waco, TX: Baylor University Press, 2014), 21–28.

the meanings and boundaries of the manifold senses of scripture, but they contested them in a surprisingly consistent range of terms, habits, and theological *loci*. We can take advantage of this consistency by adopting the terms of their debates for our theoretical discourse. Far from imposing a universal notion of tropology on Middle English literature, then, this type of study contributes to our understanding of the diversity of the practice of tropology in the late Middle Ages.

Tropology as Spiritual Exegesis

Tropological ethics is distinct from other forms of ethical discourse because it opens human action to participation in God's action in human history. As one of the "spiritual senses" of scripture, the tropological sense requires an approach by readers that accesses the mystical depths of the scripture, its divine inspiration, and its origin and consummation in divine love. "There *are* constants in Christian exegesis," de Lubac avers,[32] and in one of the more recent systematic studies of late medieval exegesis, Gilbert Dahan seconds this premise of de Lubac's project, stressing "the importance of this binary conception [letter and spirit], since it is the passage from the letter to the spiritual or mystical senses that sets in motion the mechanisms of *translatio* [transfer of meaning]."[33] The dynamic between spirit and letter that animates spiritual exegesis arises from the differences and similarities between a complex, variegated literal-historical sense and the spiritual senses, and it activates an interpretive and inventive process by which scripture opens up to readers in what Pier Cesare Bori calls "infinite interpretation."[34] The *translatio* that is the dynamic essence of spiritual or mystical exegesis takes the form not of schematic rules for interpretation, but of "a spiritual-contemplative way of life that is often called 'mystical,' even though the term is not really accurate," as Hennig Reventlow remarks

---

32. Henri de Lubac, *Scripture in the Tradition*, trans. Luke O'Neill (New York: Herder and Herder, 2000), viii.

33. Dahan, *L'exégèse chrétienne*, 55.

34. Pier Cesare Bori, *L'interpretazione infinita: L'ermeneutica cristiana antica e le sue trasformazioni* (Bologna: Il Mulino, 1987).

of Gregory the Great's *Moralia in Job*.[35] "Mystical" can be a misleading term if it is taken to denote merely a higher range of meanings achievable only through mystical contemplation. Rather, spiritual exegesis entails a metaphysics of the text and of history according to which individuals and communities can participate in the history of salvation revealed in scripture. This "hermeneutic committed to human progress," as Dahan calls it, assumes that scripture dynamically corresponds to the pilgrim movements of readers and communities.[36]

Scripture can correspond to human lives because the key to scripture is Christ's life. Just as the Old Testament is read in light of the New Testament's revelation of Christ,[37] so all literal scripture is read in terms of the theological virtues of faith, love, and hope that activate the allegorical, tropological, and anagogical phases of the literal sense. Indeed, the spiritual senses are "above" the literal senses, analogous to the way the theological virtues are "above" the natural, cardinal virtues, as Bonaventure suggests: "Because the way to God is through faith, hope, and love, every creature is a suggestion of what we should believe, expect, and do. And parallel to this, there is a threefold spiritual meaning: the allegorical concerning what we should believe, the anagogical concerning what we should expect, and the moral concerning what we

---

35. Hennig Graf Reventlow, *Epochen der Bibelauslegung: Von der Spätantike bis zum Ausgang des Mittelalters* (Munich: C. H. Beck, 1994), 2:111.

36. Dahan, *L'exégèse chrétienne*, 51.

37. Thomas Aquinas distills a long tradition of seeing Christ's life, passion, and resurrection as the key that opens the spiritual senses of the Old Testament when he writes, "Now this spiritual sense has a threefold division. For as the Apostle says (Heb. 10:1) the Old Law is a figure of the New Law, and Dionysius says (*Coel. Hier.* i) 'the New Law itself is a figure of future glory.' Again, in the New Law, whatever our Head has done is a type (*signa*) of what we ought to do. Therefore, so far as the things of the Old Law signify the things of the New Law, there is the allegorical sense; so far as the things done in Christ, or so far as the things which signify Christ, are types (*signa*) of what we ought to do, there is the moral sense. But so far as they signify what relates to eternal glory, there is the anagogical sense." Thomas Aquinas, *Summa theologica*, trans. Fathers of the English Dominican Province, 5 vols. (New York: Benziger Bros., 1948; repr. Notre Dame, IN: Ave Maria Press, 1991), I.1.10.

should do, for love leads to action."[38] For Bonaventure, any text can be read for a moral, to inculcate natural virtue. But when the virtue in question is the theological virtue of love (*caritas*), and this virtue is conceived as "the way to God," then this ethical reading is properly tropological and situated in productive tension between allegorical and anagogical senses.[39] Faith reveals the presence of Christ in scripture; hope elicits a vision of the promised end; and love must extend the life of Christ and his promises into the reader's own life.

This involvement of the reader in the biblical narrative entails what Matthew Levering has called a "participatory metaphysics of history."[40] Most late medieval exegetes assumed that history involves more than a diachronic parade of events. As John Wyclif rightly observed, if you are going to begin to make claims that put a text into some kind of causal relationship with salvation and God, you must perforce rethink your notions of eternity and creation's participation in its creator.[41] Medieval exegetes assumed that

> [s]ince reality includes the triune God, creatures cannot be fully understood by attending solely to their linear historicity. Rather, creatures, in their historicity, bear a participatory relation to God metaphysically and Christologically-pneumatologically.

---

38. Bonaventure, *Collations on the Six Days*, in *The Works of St. Bonaventure*, vol. 5, trans. José de Vinck (Paterson, NJ: St. Anthony Guild Press, 1970), 13.11.

39. On Bonaventure's understanding of tropology's circulatory function, mediating between allegory and anagogy, see the section "*Ordo Interpretandi, Ordo Agendi*" below in this chapter.

40. Matthew Levering, *Participatory Biblical Exegesis: A Theology of Biblical Interpretation* (Notre Dame, IN: University of Notre Dame Press, 2008), 32.

41. John Wyclif, *On the Truth of Holy Scripture*, trans. Ian Christopher Levy (Kalamazoo, MI: Medieval Institute Publications, 2001), 97–117. See Beryl Smalley, "The Bible and Eternity: John Wyclif's Dilemma," *Journal of the Warburg and Courtauld Institutes* 27 (1964): 73–89; and Ian Christopher Levy, *John Wyclif: Scriptural Logic, Real Presence, and the Parameters of Orthodoxy* (Milwaukee: Marquette University Press, 2003), 47–62, 81–122.

In bearing participatory reference to divine and created realities, the words of the Gospel [the context here is Thomas's exegesis of John 3:27–36] refer to both the linear and participatory historical dimensions of these realities—to the creative and redemptive
work of the Son and Holy Spirit that make creatures' metaphysical
participation and their deeper participation of grace possible.[42]

Readers of scripture consequently participate in the history of salvation
when they turn the words about salvation history into works in their
own lives. This participation is possible because the metaphysics of history allows for contingent persons, things, and events to take part in an
eternally significant story. The way to eternity is through contingency,
and the way to the spiritual is through the literal.

Levering's formulation speaks deftly for a long tradition that found
the metaphysical basis of spiritual exegesis in the eternal Word's syn-
chronic presence to all time and simple unity in all diversity. Augustine's
meditations on eternity in Book 10 of the *Confessions* animate his later
doctrine of scripture, where God's eternity undergirds the unity of the
Christian canon and its historical disposition: "You remember that one
word [*sermo*] of God is extended throughout all of the scriptures, and
through the many mouths of the saints one Word [*Verbum*] sounds, because in the beginning he was God with God, and there he did not have
syllables, because he did not have time."[43] Wyclif takes a fairly typical
fourteenth-century line when he calls scripture "a mirror in which the
truths of eternity are reflected, the way by which the pilgrim [*viator*] is
led to the goal of salvation, and the place of comfort [*consolatorium*]
where the mind of the languishing is strengthened."[44] The "way" of the

---

42. Levering, *Participatory Biblical Exegesis*, 32.

43. Augustine, *Enarrationes in Psalmos*, 103.4.1; PL 37:1348.

44. John Wyclif, "Principium," ed. Gustav Adolf Benrath, in Gustav Adolf
Benrath, *Wyclifs Bibelkommentar* (Berlin: Walter de Gruyter, 1966), 345. Wyclif
may have pushed his doctrine of the eternity of the Word further than his contemporaries, however. On "the fourth weapon" of scriptural logic, "the lofty
metaphysic declaring that all things which once had been, or will be in the
future, exist now in the presence of God," see Wyclif, *On the Truth of Holy*

scriptures reflects the true way of eternity so that by traveling along the way of the scriptures, the pilgrim also travels along the way of eternity "to the end of salvation." In this pilgrim ethic, practical movement through life corresponds to and participates already in eternity because it is ordered toward either eternal salvation or damnation. This *ordo*-in-action generates the diversity of interpretive modes and ethical practices that medieval theorists called tropology.

Natural Tropology and Mystical Tropology

Although this book focuses on the dimension of tropology that involves participation in the history of salvation, medieval exegetes recognized that all texts, including those having nothing to do with Christianity, have tropological potential. Even within traditions of biblical interpretation, because the order of reading and the relations between the senses never stay the same, it is more accurate to speak of a variety of tropologies. De Lubac discerned two relatively distinct types of tropological interpretation running through medieval exegesis: natural and mystical. Natural tropology concerns practical morality: virtues and vices, *quid agas*, what you should do. Nearly all texts have such a tropological sense or can be read tropologically. Natural tropology animated medieval philosophical and theological meditations on the *proprietates rerum*, such as Alexander Neckam's encyclopedia *De naturis rerum*, the ideal reader of which "internalizes the moral message until all the world becomes a book, a guide for a traveler whose ultimate destination is beyond the confines of matter."[45] Such encyclopedias were mined for exegetical and homiletic purposes, such as Wyclif's extended consideration of the moral properties of hyssop, which must have taken up at least ten minutes of his fifty-minute inaugural lecture as doctor of theology.[46]

Scripture, 124–26. See also Levy, *John Wyclif*, 81–122, and Smalley, "The Bible and Eternity."

45. Tomas Zahora, *Nature, Virtue, and the Boundaries of Encyclopaedic Knowledge: The Tropological Universe of Alexander Neckam (1157–1217)* (Turnhout: Brepols, 2014), 8.

46. Wyclif, "Principium."

And it was natural tropology that could survive the Enlightenment and find eloquent expression in Ralph Waldo Emerson's meditations on nature:

> All things are moral; and in their boundless changes have an unceasing reference to spiritual nature. Therefore is nature glorious with form, color, and motion, that every globe in the remotest heaven; every chemical change from the rudest crystal up to the laws of life; every change of vegetation from the first principle of growth in the eye of a leaf, to the tropical forest and antediluvian coal-mine; every animal function from the sponge up to Hercules, shall hint or thunder to man the laws of right and wrong, and echo the Ten Commandments.[47]

In Emerson's project, just as in medieval discourses, natural tropological interpretation is meant to motivate action by uniting intellectual apprehensions of the good to movements of the affections and the will.

Natural tropology concerns the moral sense of all things and texts; mystical tropology, in contrast, concerns only sacred scripture and the history of salvation. Mystical tropology is best understood as an aspect of the theological metaphysics of the text. The Christ event radically determined the Christian metaphysics of history and of the texts that bear witness to that history. Consequently, the whole Bible, including the Hebrew scriptures, teaches the saving doctrine of Christ, and it is this doctrine to which the allegorical sense of scripture grants access. The tropological aspect of this metaphysics concerns the participation of the reading community, that is, Israel and the Church, in the salvation history to which the allegorical senses bear witness. De Lubac adopts the common figure of head and body to express the relationship. "If allegory, starting from the facts of history, envisions the mystical body in its head or in its totality, tropology envisions it in each of its members: 'From history we have heard what we may marvel at; from the head we know what we may believe; now, from the body, we consider what we

---

47. Ralph Waldo Emerson, *Essays and Lectures*, ed. Joel Porte (New York: Viking Press, 1983), 28.

may hold in living life. For we ought to transform what we read within ourselves.'"[48]

Some medieval accounts draw sharp distinctions between natural and mystical tropology. For Honorius of Autun, natural tropology unites the faculties of the person, aligning will and intellect to produce good work, while mystical tropology unites the soul to God by charity.[49] Some demarcate the boundaries between natural and mystical tropology strictly along the lines separating the active and contemplative modes of life. In his preface to his commentary on the Song of Songs, Giles of Rome is eager to dissociate the mystical tropology of charitable contemplation from the natural tropology of mere good works. The science of sacred scripture, Giles remarks,

> is described as promoting the love of and affection for God . . . [B]ecause spiritual goodness is not dependent upon exterior actions but rather upon the condition and works of charity, Holy Writ, which is directed towards this sort of goodness, should not be called practical. . . . Likewise, theology, which is directed towards the affection or love of charity (because works of this sort are not exterior), must derive a special name from these qualities [i.e., affection and love] and must be described as affective and concerned with love, and not as practical.[50]

Giles's strict distinctions may reflect a monastic preference for contemplation over action, or perhaps his subject, the Song of Songs, skews his distinctions away from practical morality because it was widely held not to have a literal sense. But as we will see, the distinction between natural and mystical tropology is often blurred, since the same act of interpretation can issue in good works and in union with Christ. And as

---

48. De Lubac, *Medieval Exegesis*, 2:132. De Lubac is citing Gregory the Great, *Moralia in Job*, 1.24.33.

49. De Lubac, *Medieval Exegesis*, 2:132.

50. Giles of Rome, *Commentary on the Song of Songs*, Prol. 1; in Minnis and Scott, *Medieval Literary Theory*, 247.

Suzanne Lavere has demonstrated, even the *Glossa ordinaria* on the Song of Songs erodes any putative active/contemplative binary, turning exhortations to contemplation into calls for pastoral action.[51]

Signs Are Things; Things Are Signs

Action is vital to mystical tropology because of the value the Christian exegetical tradition placed on things as signs. From very early in the practice of Christian exegesis, its hallmark was the special signifying function it assigned to certain historical events and persons.[52] Augustine famously draws a distinction between signs in words and signs in things (*res*),[53] and understands the Pauline practice of allegory (reading Abraham's lineage as prefiguring the Church [Gal. 4:24]) to elevate signs in things over signs in words.[54] Augustine's theology of history—according to which God redeems the world through the movements of history—later suggests a hierarchy of signs, where signs in events (which are a kind of thing) accrue greater dignity than words, which are iterable in a way events are not. Thus Bede influentially distinguishes between *allegoria in factis* (allegory in deeds or events) and *allegoria in verbis tantummodo* (allegory in words alone), emphasizing that salvific events and people produce meaning through historical correspondence and development, potentially ramifying further than allegories in words alone, which function literarily or rhetorically.[55]

---

51. Suzanne Lavere, "From Contemplation to Action: The Role of the Active Life in the *Glossa ordinaria* on the Song of Songs," *Speculum* 82 (2007): 54–69.

52. The breakthrough study of this theory is Auerbach, "Figura."

53. Augustine, *On Christian Doctrine*, trans. D. W. Robertson (Upper Saddle River, NJ: Prentice-Hall, 1958), 2.10.15.

54. Augustine, *The Trinity*, trans. Edmund Hill (Brooklyn, NY: New City Press, 1991), 15.9.15.

55. Bede, *De schematibus et tropis*, 2.2.12; in Bede, *Opera didascalica*, ed. C. B. Kendall, CCSL 123A (Turnhout: Brepols, 1975). In saying this, Bede does not diminish the value of words and literary tropes; if a hierarchy is established, it is one of causes, not value (events functioning as first and final causes, words

Hugh of St. Victor goes further, positing a metaphysical hierarchy among words, things, and ideas that is reflected in scripture as in no other text: "The philosopher knows only the significance of words, but the significance of things is far more excellent than that of words, because the latter was established by usage, but Nature dictated the former.... From this is most surely gathered how profound is the understanding to be sought in the Sacred Writings, in which we come through the word to a concept, through the concept to a thing, through the thing to its idea, and through its idea arrive at Truth."[56] For Hugh, we need words, but only to get started. Interpretation "only succeeds when it goes beyond words to a kind of participation in the truth of things."[57]

---

and tropes as efficient and formal causes). Eleanor Cook has traced the tendency of modern translations of works on allegory to devalue words relative to events, when in fact relative value is not at issue. See especially Eleanor Cook, "The Figure of Enigma: Rhetoric, History, Poetry," *Rhetorica* 19, no. 4 (2001): 374–78. On Bede's significance in the development of the theory of allegory, see Rita Copeland, "Medieval Theory and Criticism," in *The Johns Hopkins Guide to Literary Theory and Criticism*, 2nd ed. (Baltimore: Johns Hopkins University Press, 2005), http://litguide.press.jhu.edu/.

56. Hugh of St. Victor, *The Didascalicon of Hugh of Saint Victor: A Medieval Guide to the Arts*, trans. Jerome Taylor (New York: Columbia University Press, 1991), 5.3.

57. Ocker, *Biblical Poetics*, 34–35. Ocker, following Yves Delègue, credits Thomas Aquinas with the insight that revised Victorine hermeneutics came to dominate the late Middle Ages: "The verbal signs of scripture, and not the 'things' indicated by them, are revelatory—as words. The mind acting upon words constitutes religious knowledge, not mental acts reaching beyond words. What is so important about Aquinas' use of verbal signification is this: it means that in addition to straightforwardly indicative or hortatory literal statements, there is a kind of figurative explanation that remains literal. . . . The effect of verbal signification as a foundation of Bible reading was to introduce a new definition of biblical discourse as a medium of religious knowledge; it was to open another avenue to the communion between the mind and God *within* biblical discourse, spiritual ecstasy regardless. If the words of scripture, as Aquinas taught, could signify in and of themselves, one must account for obscure language by means of rhetoric, that secular thing" (40–41).

This understanding informs Hugh's theory of natural tropology.

[I]t is more the meaning of things than the meaning of words which seems to pertain to [tropology]. For in the meaning of things lies natural justice, out of which the discipline of our own morals, that is, positive justice, arises. By contemplating what God has made we realize what we ourselves ought to do. Every nature tells of God; every nature teaches man; every nature reproduces its essential form, and nothing in the universe is infecund.[58]

Hugh's metaphysics of creation, in which the creator has placed things that signify naturally rather than conventionally, entails a corresponding metaphysics of history. Things are more significant than words, and some things—namely, people and events—are more significant than others. Not only has the creator provided things such as water, wine, and bread that lead by sacramental reinterpretation to the most mysterious truths, but God has also presided over history, bestowing on it certain patterns through the work of chosen individuals and communities. Their exemplary characters and actions in cooperation with divine grace have prepared the way for what from all time was intended to be the definitive event of human history: the Christ event.[59]

Hugh's analysis of the event-oriented nature of the allegorical sense became the touchstone for later exegetical theory. Alexander of Hales, in his influential *Summa* questions on exegesis, singles out the event as the hallmark of allegorical signification. If "understanding is through the signification of the events described, . . . it is allegorical, as Hugh says: 'allegory occurs when some other event either in the present or in the future or in the past is signified by that which is said to have happened.'"[60] The preeminent instance of allegorical interpretation happens when readers recognize the Christological consummation of an Old

---

58. Hugh of St. Victor, *Didascalicon*, 6.5.
59. Ibid., 6.3.
60. Alexander of Hales, *Summa theologica*, 1.4.4; in Minnis and Scott, *Medieval Literary Theory*, 221.

Testament person or event in a New Testament person or event. A concordant allegorical theory of history, then, implies a metaphysics of the event, of people acting with God to make history. It is necessary, then, that tropological interpretation should be consummated in deeds: little events of the conversion of words into actions.

Ordo Interpretandi, Ordo Agendi

This hierarchy of words and deeds is reflected in a widespread, though by no means unanimous, understanding of tropology as the consummation of an interpretive process that begins with the letter and proceeds to allegory. The levels of exegesis may be understood as stages of interpretive progress—not absolutely but mnemonically and heuristically, as Carruthers suggests when she speaks of them as

> *gradus* (stairs) of a continuous action, and the four-fold way (or three-fold, as the case may be) as a useful mnemonic for readers, reminding them of how to complete the entire reading process. *Littera* and *allegoria* (grammar and typological history) are the work of *lectio* and are essentially informative about a text; tropology and anagogy are the activities of digestive meditation and constitute the ethical activity of making one's reading one's own.[61]

Such an account does not adequately describe much exegesis as we find it in undigested commentaries and sermons, especially since we have no way of examining "the entire reading process" in real time, as it were. Instead we encounter, at best, only two stages of the process at a time, for example, in a glossed copy of Augustine's *Enarrationes in psalmos*, where we find ethically motivated annotations on Augustine's commentary in two hands separated by a century.[62]

---

61. Carruthers, *The Book of Memory*, 205.
62. See Michael P. Kuczynski's analysis of the layers of Augustine's commentary and readers' notational *meditatio* in Newberry Library MS 13 and MS Bodley 554, in Michael P. Kuczynski, *Prophetic Song: The Psalms as Moral Discourse in Late Medieval England* (Philadelphia: University of Pennsylvania

But at least in medieval theory, tropology is commonly, though not always, understood to be the necessary consequence of the allegorical sense. This may be in part simply a deep-seated convention established by the acknowledged master of the tropological sense, Gregory the Great.[63] In the "Epistle" preface to his *Moralia in Iob*, as I observed at the start of my introduction, Gregory tells how the "brothers" who asked him to write a commentary were not satisfied that he should "only explicate the words of the history according to the allegorical senses." They wanted him to "go on to turn the allegorical senses into writing about the moral sense [*exercitium moralitatis*], which is still more serious."[64] When he deems it appropriate, then, Gregory progresses from one sense to another in a definite order: "For first, we lay the foundations of history; next, using the craft of thought [*fabricam mentis*] we erect a citadel of faith out of the allegorical sense [*significationem typicam*]; and finally, with the loveliness of the moral sense we adorn the building, as it were, with painted colors."[65] Not only does Gregory express the ordered passage from letter to allegory to tropology, but he habitually follows the order in the first two books of the *Moralia*, however otherwise scattered and unsystematic it may seem.[66]

Press, 1995), 68–77. On the limitations to studying "the entire reading process," see John Dagenais, *The Ethics of Reading in Manuscript Culture: Glossing the Libro de Buen Amor* (Princeton: Princeton University Press, 1994), 26–29.

63. "Sensus moralis . . . maxime docet Gregorius." Bonaventure, *Saint Bonaventure's "De reductione artium ad theologiam,"* 5.

64. Gregory the Great, *S. Gregorii Magni Moralia in Job*, ed. Adriaen, Epist. 1.

65. Ibid., Epist. 3. Gregory does not assume that every passage bears interpretation according to all of the senses: "But it should be understood that there are some parts that we treat with historical exposition, while in some we treat types allegorically, and in others we handle only the moral sense of the allegory; then there are some that we investigate more carefully according to all three senses at once."

66. Other responsibilities kept Gregory from revising and filling out the third book (1.1.2). In the early portions of the commentary, Reventlow notes, "A distinctive feature is the strict division into the three methodological and content-based steps: the exposition of the plain sense = history, then of the typological sense = the meaning concerning Christ and the Church, and finally,

Alan of Lille adopts the agricultural imagery of the Song of Songs to express this movement:

> *Early in the morning let us rise to the vineyards*, i.e., rising from the letter to the spirit, from history to the mystical sense, let us approach the sacred scriptures; in which the leafy boughs of history grow green, the flower of allegory gives off its scent, the fruit of tropology suffices. . . . *If the flowers bring forth fruits*, through the moral understanding; since, just as the fruit follows after the flower, so the moral understanding comes to inform us after allegorical interpretation.[67]

In these figurative expressions of exegetical theory, it is appropriate to say that allegory is not complete without tropology, for all of the senses must be consummated in a reading subject who embodies the meaning and participates in the text by enacting it.[68]

---

as the culmination (*Krönung*), the exposition of the moral (tropological) sense. . . . Gregory holds the three steps clearly separate from each other by treating a specific passage first according to the first sense, and then according to the second sense, and then returns to the beginning of the previously discussed text to treat of the third sense." Reventlow, *Epochen der Bibelauslegung*, 111–12.

67. Alan of Lille, *Elucidatio in Cantica*, PL 210:102c–d; cited in de Lubac, *Medieval Exegesis*, 2:133.

68. For Hugh of St. Victor, who follows Gregory in his enumeration and figurative descriptions of the senses, the senses of scripture are epistemologically parallel to the disciplines of the *trivium*. "First of all, the student of Sacred Scripture ought to look among history, allegory, and tropology for that order sought in the disciplines—that is, he should ask which of these three precedes the others in the order of study." Hugh of St. Victor, *Didascalicon*, 6.2. Like Gregory in the early parts of the *Moralia*, Hugh deliberately proceeds from literal-historical commentary to allegory and tropology, as he remarks in *De sacramentis*: "Since I previously dictated a succinct book on the first discipline of sacred speech, which consists of historical reading, now I have prepared this [book] for those who are to be introduced to the second discipline, which consists of allegory. If they establish their minds on this foundation of interpretation according to faith, they will endure unshaken, and other things will be able

Modern readers might object that such a conception of graduated progress forecloses interpretation and ethical action because it too clearly identifies the end point of reading and understanding. Doubtless, medieval readers did at times settle for simplistic, self-serving reading, presumably the kind of reading that Chaucer's pilgrims deride as "glosing." Properly understood, the anagogical sense ensures that any tropological consummation remains provisional. In chapter 6 I show how the anagogical orientation of the York Doomsday pageant challenges complacent tropologies that would locate ethical perfection within the interpretive community. But the main reason the *ordo legendi* did not foster complacent, totalizing interpretation is that it could also be practiced as a way of life, a ritual that was iterative, peformative, and communal, and that served to keep members of textual communities in a continuous circulation between text and world, reading and writing, inner and outer person, letter and spirit.

Bonaventure's account of the "threefold intellect" captures this intermediate, circulatory function of tropology, which may be practical and exterior but is also open toward the contemplative and interior:

> [T]he intellect has . . . a threefold directive condition *(habitus)*. For if we consider intellect in itself, defined thus it is truly speculative and is brought to perfection by the condition which exists purely for the sake of contemplation and which is called "speculative knowledge." But if we consider it as being created in order to be extended to achieve some task, it is brought to perfection by the condition which exists so that we may become good; and this is practical or moral knowledge. But if in some middle way it is considered as being created to extend to moving the affections, considered thus it is brought to perfection by a condition which lies between the purely speculative and the practical, and which embraces both. This condition is called wisdom, and it expresses both cognition and affection. As Ecclus. 6[:23] says: "For the wisdom of

---

to be built upon it either by reading or by hearing." Hugh of St. Victor, *De sacramentis christiane fidei*, prol., 1; PL 176:183.

doctrine is according to her name." So, this condition exists for the purpose of contemplation, and also that we may become good, but principally that we may become good.[69]

"Wisdom" is what Bonaventure calls the "middle way" that joins practical moral knowledge and ethical action to the speculative intellect "for the purpose of contemplation," that union with Christ in charity through which "we may become good." Here we verge into mystical tropology, the operation by which the soul is united to Christ through a participation in salvation history that occurs in the little events of one's own life. This uniquely exegetical account of human action resolves the moral-philosophical disjunction between beatific (traditional Christian) and worldly (neo-Aristotelian) happiness in an ethical *habitus* fulfilled in the reading and acting out of scripture.[70] Tropological ethics is unique because it opens the properly superrational (and so nonphilosophical) realm of the beatific vision to practical reason by means of graced participation.[71]

But this participation is hardly otherworldly. Indeed, tropological interpretation consummates the entire history of redemption and the three other senses of scripture on a daily basis, as a *catena* of de Lubac attests:

> *Moraliter, intrinsecus* and *quotidie* are three adverbs that go together. "The present reading," says Hervaeus of Bourg Dieu in a homily, "has been completed historically once in fact, but with respect to the spiritual sense it is being fulfilled every day." Each day, deep within ourselves, Israel departs from Egypt; each day, it is nourished with manna; each day it fulfills the Law; each day it must

---

69. Bonaventure, *Commentary on Peter Lombard's* Sentences, preface, q. 3, resp.; in Minnis and Scott, *Medieval Literary Theory*, 227.

70. On this contrast as it relates to literary ethics, see Jessica Rosenfeld, *Ethics and Enjoyment in Late Medieval Poetry: Love after Aristotle* (New York: Cambridge University Press, 2010), 6–9.

71. Thomas Aquinas, *Ethicorum Aristotelis expositio*, I.9.13, www.corpus thomisticum.org.

engage in combat . . . ; each day the promises that had been made to this people under a bodily form are realized spiritually in us. Each day also the Gentiles give themselves over to the worship of their idols; each day the Israelites themselves are unfaithful; each day, in this interior region, the land devours the impious . . . Each day again, there is the Lord's visit; each day he approaches Jerusalem, coming from Bethphagê. Each day is his advent: "The Lord coming in the flesh has visited us: and, morally, we also discern this come about every day." "Within those who are devoted, he comes every day." Now everything that came about for the first time in history had no other end than that. All that is accomplished in the Church herself had no other end. Everything is consummated in the inner man.[72]

The quotidian rhythm of tropology creates a medieval and properly exegetical version of the hermeneutical circle: events signify other events, which inspire a scriptural record, which may then be interpreted by a reader, whose consequent action makes another event, which then extends, and so changes, the history in which the original event participates. The reader may respond, may act, by writing, which is in any case a doing, and so actions and words are placed in a mutually creative orbit.

Tropological Creativity

Thomas Aquinas describes a similar oscillation when he explains the phenomenon of multiple meanings in the literal sense: "The senses are not multiple because a single word can mean several things, but because the same things that the words signify can be signs of other things." This creates a potentially infinite spiral of signification, in which things can become signs and words become things.[73] The passage from such a hermeneutic to a theory of invention is intuitive, and it underwrites the

---

72. De Lubac, *Medieval Exegesis*, 2:138.
73. Quoted in de Lubac, *Exégèse médiévale*, 4:282. On the circular nature of this aspect of Thomas's thought, see 4:283–86.

"semantic memory model" of semiotic activity developed by Umberto Eco. He proposes that each semantic unit, or sememe, be thought of as an encyclopedia, with entries for all of its possible meanings. Each person, whether writer or reader, carries a unique and limited encyclopedic "competence" for each sememe. The "problem," as Eco calls it, "is that *every semantic unit used in order to analyze a sememe is in its turn a sememe to be analyzed.*"[74] Eco is therefore describing "a process of *unlimited semiosis.*" In theory, "from a sign which is taken as a type, it is possible to penetrate, from the center to the farthest periphery, the whole universe of cultural units, each of which can in turn become the center and create infinite peripheries."[75] In practice, the semantic memory model is not so much an infinitely recursive problem as it is the "model of linguistic creativity."[76]

Eco's semiotics may demonstrate the vitality of a Thomistic sign theory, but it does not quite appreciate how concrete the medieval theories of tropological invention could become, for tropology invites practical and even institutional—not just linguistic—creativity. The invention of theological and exegetical writing can be considered in terms of things and events, often using analogies to building. Hugh of St. Victor instructs the student of sacred scripture and theology how to construct an edifice of doctrine out of the many books he must interpret: "See now, you have come to your study, you are about to construct the spiritual building. Already the foundations of history have been laid in you: it remains now that you found the bases of the superstructure. You stretch out your cord, you line it up precisely, you place the square stones into the course, and, moving around the course, you lay the track, so to speak, of the future walls."[77] It is then but a short leap for Thomas of Ireland to consider the university institution (both thing and event at

---

74. Umberto Eco, *A Theory of Semiotics* (Bloomington: Indiana University Press, 1976), 121, original emphasis.

75. Ibid., 122.

76. Ibid., 124.

77. Hugh of St. Victor, *Didascalicon*, 6.3.4. On exegesis as building, see Hennig Brinkmann, *Mittelalterliche Hermeneutik* (Darmstadt: Wissenschaftliche Buchgesellschaft, 1980), 132–40.

once) as the result of tropological invention: "According to the moral sense one can say that the house which the Wisdom of God the Father has built is the University of Paris. The foundations of this house are the Faculty of Arts. The two walls, which sustain and protect both our health and our possessions, are the Faculties of Medicine and Law. The roof, which covers and completes the whole building, is Theology."[78] The interpretation of books turns into action that surpasses mere thought, even thought *about* interpretation, in order to proceed to the foundation of institutions, disciplines, and communities through which the house of God can continue to expand through history.

Martha G. Newman has argued that twelfth-century Cistercian reformers conceived the monastic ideal of contemplative *caritas* to be bound up with social, ecclesiastical, and political *caritas*, so that "the Cistercians' own distinction between an ideal contemplative state and the realities of the human condition led them to insist that the demands of a communal life and a concern for the salvation of others were essential to learning to love the divine."[79] Though Thomas of Ireland was not himself a Cistercian, his strong sense of the providential purpose of his home institution, the University of Paris, bears a resemblance to the Cistercian understanding of *caritas*. Thomas uses tropological theory to express how the practices of a "textual community" impact social and ecclesial communities at large.[80] In his exegesis, natural and mystical tropology complement each other, since even natural cultural institutions participate in the providential ordering of history for the salvation of humanity.

---

78. Paris, BNF, MS Lat. 16397, fol. 12v, quoted in Éduard Jeauneau, "Thomas of Ireland and His *De tribus sensibus sacrae scripturae*," in *With Reverence for the Word: Medieval Scriptural Exegesis in Judaism, Christianity, and Islam*, ed. Jane Dammen McAuliffe, Barry Walfish, and Joseph Ward Goering (New York: Oxford University Press, 2003), 287.

79. Martha G. Newman, *The Boundaries of Charity: Cistercian Culture and Ecclesiastical Reform, 1098–1180* (Stanford, CA: Stanford University Press, 1996), 10.

80. Brian Stock, *The Implications of Literacy: Written Language and Models of Interpretation in the Eleventh and Twelfth Centuries* (Princeton: Princeton University Press, 1987), 90; and on Bernard and Cistercians, 403–54.

The example of Thomas of Ireland suggests how tropology can keep individual holiness and communal justice in virtuous circulation when it is practiced as a mediating instrument between practical and speculative sciences, and between natural and mystical goods. Tropology's social and institutional momentum can draw ethics beyond individual character formation. In subsequent chapters we will see how *Piers Plowman* activates tropology's social potential, but also how an exclusively natural tropology can arrest the pilgrimage of the Christian life and turn it into a static, lifeless moralism.[81] For without the other senses of scripture drawing the moral sense beyond natural ethics, tropology can turn into complacent moralizing and self-centered character formation, narcissistically detached from the concrete history that occasioned scripture and insouciant about the final destination of the earthly sojourn, the judgment seat of Christ.[82] In chapter 6, we will see how the Doomsday pageant of the York Play exposes this risk of bad tropology.

---

81. My focus is more on Langland's productive, robust tropology than on his critique of reductive tropology. For a more thorough, trenchant analysis of what happens when virtue is removed from its native habitat in scripture and appropriated by cardinals, see David Aers, "Langland on the Church and the End of the Cardinal Virtues," *Journal of Medieval and Early Modern Studies* 42, no. 1 (2012): 59–81, especially 63. Although Aers does not use tropological theory, his Langland situates ethics within the history of salvation as witnessed and imaginatively made available in scripture. Aers's Augustinian Langland, negotiating the claims of nature and grace, is working on the same issues as exegetes who seek to reconcile natural and mystical tropology, just in a different framework. (If the present book approaches Langland by way of de Lubac's exegetical theory, then Aers approaches Langland by way of de Lubac's major contribution to modern theology, his rereading of the Thomist account of nature and grace through Augustine, which culminated in *Augustinisme et théologie moderne* [Paris: Aubier, 1965]. It may be that *Piers Plowman* presents an opportunity to pursue that hitherto elusive goal of demonstrating the homology and joint significance of de Lubac's two major projects.) The Langlandian theology of nature and grace appears most firmly embedded in scripture in the chapter on the Good Samaritan episode in David Aers, *Salvation and Sin: Augustine, Langland, and Fourteenth-Century Theology* (Notre Dame, IN: University of Notre Dame Press, 2009), 83–131.

82. For a powerful account of nonparticipatory virtue ethics developed by reading *Piers Plowman* and Thomas Aquinas's *Summa theologica* in produc-

Tropology and Scriptural Practices

The textual relics of Bible reading rarely afford a glimpse of the application phase of tropology, the stage of the *ordo legendi* when a reader
turns the words of scripture into works. And the mystical depths of tropology, the participation of individuals and communities in the history
of salvation, are even more elusive. Yet late medieval writers of poetry
and drama came to see the activity of writing as ethically significant in
itself. What we encounter on the page, then, *is* the work, the consummation of the *ordo legendi*. In this way tropology mediates between
scripture and the sacraments as the practice by which the biblical narrative is joined to the institutions of salvation in individual Christian
lives and the communion of the church. For William Langland, as I
argue in chapter 4, the work of writing *Piers Plowman* is a work of mercy
that constitutes penitential satisfaction for the author. In some cases
like this, tropological invention leads directly into sacramental participation. Alternatively, it can constitute a parasacramental form of imaginative participation that merges with sacramental liturgy in the shared
scriptural tissue of the liturgy (like the York Play, which adapts scripture
in the context of Eucharistic devotion). But in many other cases, tropological invention is a nonsacramental form of participation in salvation
history. In inventions of literary tropology, we witness words turned
into works and thereby gather some sense of how other forms of tropological invention—social, political, economic—might have functioned.

Much of this book focuses on texts studied primarily by scholars of
English literature. *Piers Plowman, Patience,* the York and Coventry cycle
plays—these are not prominent titles in the histories of exegesis. The
tropological explorations in these texts stretch the boundaries of what
the history of exegesis has been prepared to recognize as tropology and,
indeed, as exegesis. These "literary" works give us a better sense of the
mystical depth of tropology and extend the purview of exegetical studies

---

tive tension, see Sheryl Overmyer, "The Wayfarer's Way and Two Texts for the
Journey: The 'Summa Theologiae' and 'Piers Plowman,'" Ph.D. diss., Duke University, 2010, 160–208.

beyond prologues, sequential biblical commentary, and homilies. *Piers Plowman* is an exegetically capacious work that deftly employs nearly all of the tropological traditions and practices we will encounter in other texts. It provides an excellent example of how literary works can themselves theorize tropology and perform tropological interpretation and reinvention of the Bible.

Tropological Reading and the Ethical-Hermeneutical Circle

Piers Plowman's exegetical theory takes up broader concerns in late medieval academic theology about the relationship between ethical character and biblical interpretation. The theological consensus, expressed by Augustine, was that it was not enough to have knowledge of "unfamiliar signs"; the fit interpreter of scripture must also be "gentle and humble of heart, meekly subjected to Christ."[83] For Thomas Aquinas, interpretation requires wisdom, which is a gift of the Holy Spirit, made manifest in piety. Piety and right interpretation, then, are effects of conformity to Christ by grace.[84] But in order to be conformed to Christ, one must know Christ, whose life and character are revealed in scripture.[85] In John Wyclif's theology of scripture, to which I turn shortly, these two competing priorities—ethical disposition and understanding of scripture—created a catch-22. In order to understand scripture, one needs to be virtuous, but in order to become virtuous, one needs to understand scripture.

These concerns reflected at a practical level widespread theoretical disagreements in the late thirteenth and fourteenth centuries about the relative priority of grace and the human will. As D. Vance Smith has ar-

---

83. Augustine, *On Christian Doctrine*, 2.42.

84. Thomas Aquinas, *Summa theologica*, II-II.45.1. For a fuller discussion, see E. F. Rogers, "How the Virtues of an Interpreter Presuppose and Perfect Hermeneutics: The Case of Thomas Aquinas," *Journal of Religion* 76, no. 1 (1996): 64–81.

85. Ian Christopher Levy, *Reading the Scriptures: Holy Scripture and the Quest for Authority at the End of the Middle Ages* (Notre Dame, IN: University of Notre Dame Press, 2012), 7–8.

gued, these debates were ultimately about beginnings, about the invention of salvation. Who moves first—God or the human? Traditional Augustinians insisted on the priority of a prevenient grace, while so-called semi-Pelagians required an antecedent movement of the will in order to secure the freedom of its assent to grace. Situating *Piers Plowman*'s penitential theology in the context of these debates, Smith argues that "the poem separates out the different beginnings that are entailed in a theology of redemption, but makes no explicit attempts to resolve contradictory connotations or to assimilate them into an analytic framework."[86] Langland similarly refuses to identify the beginning of the ethical reading of scripture. Instead, through the extended agricultural metaphor of the cultivation of scripture, Langland redirects concerns about priority to emphasize the cyclical, habitual nature of scriptural practices—reading, meditation, spiritual exegesis, preaching, prayer, and so on. This intervention requires Langland to develop a supple tropological theory that envisions how loving reading can lead to individual and communal flourishing. The result is a theological version of the hermeneutical circle, according to which interpretive activity circulates out into the ethical life of the reader, whence it returns to the text as the condition of right interpretation, defined as ethical participation in the history of salvation. This view of Langland requires a further look at the allegory of the cultivation of scripture, Wyclif's catch-22, and *Piers Plowman*'s allegory as a solution for Wyclif's dilemma.

---

86. D. Vance Smith, *The Book of the Incipit: Beginnings in the Fourteenth Century* (Minneapolis: University of Minnesota Press, 2001), 171–211; 173. According to Smith, Langland refuses to put forward a conclusion on the priority of grace and free will, but because he is so concerned with Will's and the will's beginnings, the poem's narrative treatments of these issues reflect semi-Pelagian voluntarism. Smith's occasional statements such as "the poem's theology is voluntarist" (172) overstate what is otherwise a helpful distinction between Langland's theology and the poem's *forma tractatus* constituted by successive beginnings (81). David Aers distinguishes between this form and Langland's Augustinian theology of grace and will in Aers, *Salvation and Sin*, 83–97.

The Allegory of the Cultivation of Scripture

In *Piers Plowman* B.19/C.21, the personified Grace establishes the church of Christ and provides for its proper functioning.[87] Grace's ecclesiological establishment revolves around the figure of Piers Plowman, whom he has appointed to serve as procurator, reeve, and registrar under King Conscience (C.21.258–59) and as Grace's "plouhman . . . on erthe" (260). To help him cultivate truth ("for to tulye treuthe"), Grace will equip Piers with the Evangelists/Gospels and a team of patristic exegetes (261):

> Grace gaf Peres a teme, foure grete oxen.
> That oen was luc, a large beste and a lou chered,
> And Marc and Mathewe the thridde, myhty bestes bothe;
> And ioyned til hem oen iohann, most gentill of all,
> The pris neet of Peres plouh, passynge alle oþere.
> And grace gaef Peres of his goednesse foure stottes,
> All þat his oxes erede they to harwen aftur.
> Oen hihte Austyn and Ambrose anoþer,
> Gregory the grete Clerk and þe gode Ieroem;
> Thise foure, the fayth to teche, folewede Peres teme
> And harwed in an handwhile al holy scripture
> With two aythes þat they hadde, an oelde and a newe:
> *Id est vetus testamentum & nouum.*
>
> (21.262–73a)

The allegory of the four doctors of the Church plowing and harrowing scripture can seem straightforward, and the four oxen and four draft horses plowing and harrowing a field evoke all of the densely

---

87. It is worth noting that in this late and arguably programmatic episode, grace narratively prevenes the activity of the human will, challenging the "voluntarist" narrative patterns that Smith identifies in earlier parts of the poem. Cf. D. Smith, *The Book of the Incipit*, 172–73.

agricultural-religious imagery developed through the Western tradition from the Old Testament onward.[88]

Yet this passage is hardly straightforward. For starters, Langland activates the terms of the allegory so that they function as metaphor. The shifting relations of vehicle and tenor create a complex of moving parts that we associate more with theological argument than with allegory as an elementary mnemonic tool.[89] The image can remind us of the four great evangelists, but it is doing much more than that. Langland deploys traditional imagery to express a nuanced and supple theology of exegesis that is best understood as tropological.

The extended metaphor calls on the practices of medieval agriculture. In the fourteenth century, unbroken ground was first tilled, then plowed to open furrows for planting, then sown, and finally harrowed to chop up clumps of dirt, mix the seeds into the soil, and get rid of weeds:[90]

---

88. See Stephen A. Barney, "The Plowshare of the Tongue: The Progress of a Symbol from the Bible to *Piers Plowman*," *Mediaeval Studies* 35 (1973): 261–93.

89. As I employ the terms here, metaphor is a figure of speech in which one thing or state of affairs is spoken of using language normally used to speak of another thing or state of affairs. The tenor is the thing spoken of, while the vehicle is the other thing that lends its language. The metaphor is the interplay of vehicle and tenor, such that it is inaccurate to say that Y is a metaphor for X. Y may be a vehicle for X tenor, but the metaphor comprises the ensemble of X/Y. In the following analysis, I am indebted to Janet Martin Soskice, *Metaphor and Religious Language* (Oxford: Clarendon Press, 1985), and to the theory of metaphor developed in Cristina Maria Cervone, *Poetics of the Incarnation: Middle English Writing and the Leap of Love* (Philadelphia: University of Pennsylvania Press, 2013), 19–55.

90. Langland's use of the terminology is not consistent. He uses ME "tillen" to mean both to break ground and to cultivate crops. ME "plouen" and "eren" seem to be used interchangeably to signify both the breaking of ground and preparation of already broken ground for sowing. "Harwen" is more consistent and precise: it follows plowing and sowing. A harrow pulled by a single horse may be seen in action in fig. 1.1. The March illumination of the *Très riches heures* depicts plowing with a team of two oxen.

broadcast sowing (as opposed to dibbling or drilling) was the only common propagation technique in Europe, despite its high cost in seeds. There were, however, two different procedures. Sowing could be done *after* ploughing, with the seeds being covered afterwards with a harrow. Or it could be done *before* ploughing, where the ploughing itself would cover the seeds. In this case, the sower followed the ploughman and dropped the seeds into the open furrow that the plough-share would cover in its next passage; but this particular technique required much more care and time.[91]

In Langland's use of the imagery, the steps of this process serve as vehicles for a metaphorical discourse in which the tenors are constantly changing. Piers drives the team of the "foure grete oxen" (262), who figure both the Evangelists and the Gospels that go by their names. Grace also gives Piers four "heavy work horses" ("stottes")[92] to harrow the field plowed by the Gospels. Unlike the team of oxen, these horses do not seem to be ridden or driven by Piers, since they "folwede Peres teme" (271). Perhaps we should imagine them individually harrowing the field, like the lone horse pulling a harrow (and ridden, not driven) in the October calendar illumination in the *Très riches heures du duc de Berry* (fig. 1.1). Or perhaps they go in pairs, each pair pulling one of the "aythes," or harrows,[93] that represent the Old and New Testaments,

---

91. Georges Comet, "Technology and Agricultural Expansion in the Middle Ages: The Example of France North of the Loire," in *Medieval Farming and Technology: The Impact of Agricultural Change in Northwest Europe*, ed. Grenville Astill and John Langdon (New York: Brill, 1997), 26. An informative discussion of medieval harrowing may be found in Perrine Mane, *Le travail à la campagne au Moyen Age: Étude iconographique* (Paris: Picard, 2006), 141–51.

92. See the note in Langland, *Piers Plowman: A Parallel-Text Edition*, ed. Schmidt, 2:708.

93. Noted by both Schmidt (ibid., 2:709) and Skeat as an extremely rare derivation from OE *egþe*. William Langland, *The Vision of William Concerning Piers the Plowman*, Vol. 2, *Preface, Notes, and Glossary*, ed. Walter W. Skeat (Oxford: Oxford University Press, 1885; repr. 1961), 270.

respectively. But since none of these patristic commentators focused solely on the Old or New Testament, we perhaps should imagine that each horse is dragging two harrows, one behind the other—a practice envisioned and in fact encouraged as ideal for rough ground by the nineteenth-century farming manual *Household Cyclopedia*. The manual also reveals that harrowing after plowing to refine the tilth requires multiple passes of the harrows, which is why it would be helpful to have multiple harrows at work in order to harrow a plowed field "in an handwhile" (272).[94]

Up to this point the metaphor is fairly straightforward, until we ask what the field—the ground plowed and harrowed—signifies. Some commentators have assumed that the ground is the same "mannes soule" in which Piers sows the seeds of the cardinal virtues (275).[95] But the field has two, more proximate tenors within the passage quoted above that describe the gift of farm animals to prepare the ground: the horse-exegetes plow and harrow "treuthe" (261) and "holy scripture" (272). *Treuthe* just as likely takes the entire horticultural process—tilling to harvesting—as its vehicle, or could even be thought to eschew a vehicle and to shimmer with that delightfully oversignified, potent vagueness that so often accrues to Langland's favorite words and concepts.[96]

---

94. Henry Hartshorne, ed., *Household Cyclopedia* (New York: Thomas Kelly, 1881), 22–23.

95. Barney, "The Plowshare of the Tongue," 281; William Langland, *Piers Plowman: The C-Text*, ed. Derek Pearsall (Exeter: University of Exeter Press, 1994), 352n262; D. W. Robertson and Bernard F. Huppé, *"Piers Plowman" and Scriptural Tradition* (Princeton: Princeton University Press, 1951), 220–21.

96. "The central effort of [Langland's] poem, despite the use it makes of analytic methods, is directed against the making of intellectual distinctions and towards the building up of large, theologically undefined ideas which will have the power to stir men's emotions and move them to action. One means he uses to this end is the kind of verbal repetition that fuses intellectual concepts into what we might call significant vaguenesses." A. C. Spearing, "Verbal Repetition in *Piers Plowman* B and C," *Journal of English and Germanic Philology* 62 (1963): 737. While "treuthe" surely has a glow of vagueness by this point in the poem, Langland spends the next twelve lines in his equally potent mode of significant precision.

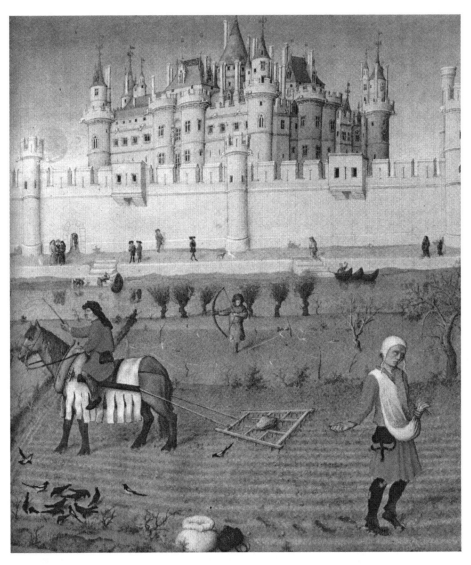

Fig. 1.1. Detail of "October," *Les très riches heures du duc de Berry.* Chantilly, Musée Condé MS 65, fol. 10v. Reprinted by kind permission of RMN-Grand Palais/Art Resource, NY.

"Holy scripture," however, unambiguously takes the vehicle of the ground being harrowed by the four horse-exegetes, and since they are harrowing the same ground that the oxen-Evangelists plowed, and since "Holy Scripture . . . is the very revelation of truth itself,"[97] the Evangelists must be thought to plow "al holy scripture" as well. The resultant poetic effect of this interplay of vehicle and tenors is both complex and dynamic. The vehicle of the field remains stable, while different tenors pass across it in succession, like the multiple passes of plow and harrow, creating a metaphor-in-motion. Taken together, the series of metaphors formed by new combinations of vehicle and tenor, as well as their ensemble motion, reflects the manifold and dynamic practice of spiritual exegesis. The historical exegetes interpret scripture; later readers use the exegetes to interpret scripture; the interpreters of scripture use the New Testament to interpret the Old and the Old to interpret the New; they use the Gospels to interpret the rest of the New Testament; and all of holy scripture interprets all of holy scripture as part interprets whole and as the whole gives meaning to the parts.

Langland's deployment of agricultural imagery in this particular section is remarkable because he does not attempt to make the developing metaphor express the most well-attested biblical and exegetical use of such imagery, namely, the preaching of the Gospel (the seed) to souls (the ground) for the sake of producing virtues (fruits) that are harvested at the Last Judgment.[98] Langland of course is aware of this evangelical-soteriological configuration of the agricultural imagery; it is the figural world in which Piers Plowman and the poem named after him spring to life, and the same world back into which the allegory passes in line

---

97. Wyclif, *On the Truth of Holy Scripture*, 97. The belief that scripture, the body of Christ, and truth are coterminous or isomorphic was widespread. For a catalogue of such teachings, see de Lubac, *Medieval Exegesis*, 2:107–8.

98. See Barney, "The Plowshare of the Tongue," 262–81, for the prominence of this theme. Barney assumes that this passage is "a pageant-like emblem of the operation of Grace in the world" (282), without attempting to explicate the shifting metaphorical relations or noting the conspicuous absence of the traditional tenors of human hearts, virtues, and the Day of Judgment.

274 with the introduction of the seeds of the virtues.[99] However, before that turn is made, the conceptual frame concerns the theology of exegesis and what Wyclif would call the metaphysics of holy scripture.

The metaphysical and theological effects are produced by a metaphor folded back on itself, with the Evangelists as the crease. When the Evangelists are considered as tenors, they take oxen as their vehicle. But when Matthew, Mark, Luke, John, and the oxen are considered as vehicles, they carry the Gospels as their tenor. Or when the Evangelists are considered to sum up and comprehend the entire New Testament, that is, when they are considered as truth/scripture, they become tenors once again, taking the field as their vehicle. The relations are further complicated by the distinction between "al holy scripture" in its totality, the duality of the Old and New Testaments, and the representative, summative priority of the Gospels.[100] Langland thus multiplies our vision of scripture by making the Gospels and Old and New Testaments (in their multiplicity) the instruments by which the Bible (in its unity) is prepared for planting. The Evangelists plow the New Testament, of which they are a part. The New Testament harrows "al holy scripture," of which it and the Gospels are parts. And the Old and New Testaments harrow "al holy scripture," of which they are all parts. If we are to consider the passage at C.21.262–73a as a discrete literary allegory, then, it is one that depends on the moving parts of an extended metaphor to figure forth a theology of scripture and its exegetical possibilities.

Langland doubles down on this complexity by recapitulating the allegory forty lines later (309–16), this time with the expected figures of seeds and virtues folded in. In doubling the allegory, Langland mimics the doubled structure of an Augustinian doctrine of scripture, discussed

---

99. Langland also deploys the imagery in discrete local contexts that are not related by plot to Piers and his half acre, such as when he provides the following etymological gloss for the heathen Britons converted by Augustine of Canterbury: "Heþen is to mene after heeþ and vntiled erþe" (B.15.459).

100. The widely held view that the Gospels effectively summarize the whole Bible is well expressed in Langland's oft-repeated phrase "lawe of loue," which he asserts as the full meaning of Old and New Testaments when he superimposes Christ's writing in the sand to forgive the woman caught in adultery over the inscription of the Ten Commandments (C.14.37–43).

above, whereby the meaning and unity of scripture emerge only in the multiplication of its senses by *caritas*. Langland doubles the allegory of scriptural farming in order to interrogate a classic theological dilemma of nature and grace. Which came first: the seed or the fruit? Writing the dilemma into his allegory of the seeds, Langland figures the virtues' fragility with metaphors that slip from one frame to another. We will return to the second frame later in the chapter, but for now, following on from the passage just discussed, the frame is planting and growing. The seeds are not the virtues themselves, but virtues *in potentia*. The addition of "spirit" may draw a distinction between the active virtue and the spirit that animates it. The seeds, then, would be powers that could be acted on or not, developed or not. (Accordingly, habitual action contrary to the spirit of virtue is a sin against the Holy Spirit, who is the spirit or principle of virtue and whose spirit intrinsically animates all virtuous action.) But then the frame slips to eating, collapsing the interval of growth from seed to fruit: "*Spiritus prudencie* the furste seed hihte / And hoso ete þat ymageny he sholde, / Ar he dede eny dede deuyse wel þe ende" (276–78). The other virtues are treated the same way. All are sown in "mannes soule" (275), but Grace describes each as if it were a fruit that a person (a soul) must eat in order to partake of its virtue, tangling the common biblical trope according to which the fruits of the Spirit are invariably the actions or dispositions *produced* by a person who works virtuously. The soul is thereby doubled; it is simultaneously the organic source of the fruit and the gustatory partaker of it. But it would be rash to insist on the simultaneity of planting and partaking, for the conjunction of these moments on either end of the food economy raises the question of ethical and interpretive priority: Does one first have to be innately good, with the natural virtues having been implanted by grace at birth (or baptism)? Or must one actively internalize the virtues so that, as Gregory the Great puts it, we might "transform what we read within our very selves, so that when our mind is stirred by what it hears, our life may concur by practicing what has been heard"?[101]

---

101. Gregory the Great, *Moralia in Job*, 1.33, cited in Carruthers, *The Book of Memory*, 205. On reading as spiritual digestion for the sake of moral metabolism and self-constitution, see 202–12.

Langland's language equivocates on the answers to these questions. Grace's descriptions rely heavily on the semantically ambiguous verb *shulen*. For example, "He þat eet of [*Spiritus temperancie*] hadde such a kynde: / Sholde neuere mete ne meschief maken hym to swelle / Ne sholde no scornare out of skille hym brynge / . . . / Sholde no curious cloth comen on his rugge" (282–84, 287). *Sholde* is a modal auxiliary, but does it express futurity or duty? It is unclear whether "hoso ete þat" virtue will in the future definitely behave accordingly, or whether eating the seed/fruit imparts ethical responsibility, a debt to be paid for the gift given (277).[102] Ever since the innovation of Guilelmus Peraldus's extremely influential *Summa virtutum et vitiorum* (c. 1236–48), discourses on the vices and virtues had gone beyond scholastic interest in the nature and distinctions of the habits to take on rhetorical, and therefore homiletic, utility. Peraldus's concern, and that of the long tradition he spawned and in which *Piers Plowman* participates, was "to help his readers overcome sin by making the vices [and virtues] known to them and furnishing reasons to [delight in good and to] detest evil as well as remedies against it. His final cause, therefore, is not theological clarification but rhetorical persuasion."[103] If we isolate the descriptions of the virtues, a homiletic mode makes good sense of the modal auxiliaries, which function both descriptively and prescriptively: describing for the sake of recognition and discernment, and prescribing for the sake of exhortation. But if the discourse on the virtues is a sermon, its position in the structure of the passus casts its adequacy, indeed its very purpose, into doubt.[104] For no sooner has Piers sown the seeds of the virtues than

---

102. Only *spiritus fortitudinis* is not modified by *shulen*. *Spiritus temperencie* relies heavily on *shulen*.

103. Siegfried Wenzel, "The Continuing Life of William Peraldus's *Summa vitiorum*," in *Ad litteram: Authoritative Texts and Their Medieval Readers*, ed. Mark D. Jordan and Kent Emery (Notre Dame, IN: University of Notre Dame Press, 1992), 152.

104. The latter half of the passus contains clear structural divisions. The agricultural imagery takes a roughly chiastic form: plowing and harrowing to prepare ground (261–73a); sowing of seeds (274–309); harrowing to remove weeds (309–16); preparing for harvest (317–34). This chiastic episode is dis-

they are attacked by vices. By the end of the passus we have witnessed the abrupt destruction and derangement of the previous section's elaborate agricultural-ecclesial complex. In a final parody of reform, the king uses the language of virtue to rebrand a platform of patently unjust policies. One imagines a medieval *accessus* on *Piers Plowman*: "Guilelmi forma tractandi calamitosa est." So while the descriptions of the virtues might help people recognize them, they also expose the gifts' contingency and vulnerability because they exhort the audience—if we read *shulen* as expressing duty—to practice the very virtues they are trying to learn. Langland's slippery allegory of the origins of the cardinal virtues befits their mystery and appreciates how difficult it can be to discern those virtues in others, especially when you do not possess them fully yourself.

Wyclif's Ethical-Hermeneutical Catch-22

This dilemma is pronounced in the work of John Wyclif, and his treatment of it proves an instructive contrast with Langland's approach by way of agrarian imagery. Consistent with a tropological understanding of scripture, Wyclif believed that readers could become good through their encounter with scripture, especially with the Christ of the Gospels. In his *Postilla* on Matthew, Wyclif takes the Sermon on the Mount as the tropological center of the Gospels. The beatitudes, he says, are designed to counter the vices and instill the virtues. The beatitudes detail the ethical form of the virtuous life, which is summed up in Christ, who teaches by his own example what the beatitudes formulate abstractly.[105] As Wyclif repeatedly intones, "Omnis Christi accio est nostra instruccio"

---

tinctly demarcated. It begins with Grace's gifts and instructions to "tulye treuthe" (261) and ends with the summary remark that Grace "wente / As wyde as the world is with Peres to tulye treuthe" (332–33). Although a great deal has happened in the intervening lines, it has happened for the purpose of etiology, providing a rather idealistic outline of the way truth and the virtues are meant to be cultivated in the church.

105. Gustav Adolf Benrath, *Wyclifs Bibelkommentar* (Berlin: Walter de Gruyter, 1966), 113–14.

(Every action of Christ is our instruction).[106] And what Christ teaches in his own example and in the Sermon on the Mount not only must be fulfilled but, more importantly, *can be fulfilled*. Jesus wraps up the Sermon on the Mount with the words, "every one therefore that heareth these my words and doth them, shall be likened to a wise man that built his house upon a rock" (Matt. 7:24). Commenting on this verse, Wyclif speaks directly to the problem of interpretation and action: "Nor is the fulfillment of the aforesaid law of Christ impossible or unprofitable, for everyone who hears the law in order to learn it and does works in order to fulfill it is like the wise man, intentionally and objectively building the whole sum of the works of his life upon Christ."[107]

But how can one who is not already holy hear the law of God in scripture? Wyclif repeatedly insisted that the interpreter of scripture must be conformed to Christ.[108] In the pursuit of "theological wisdom," the order of the affections precedes the order of the intellect. "Theological truths may not be acquired without the due ordering of the will. This is why, however much the infidel, the heretic, or the man entangled in any mortal sin thinks that he understands the wisdom of scripture sufficiently, he nevertheless errs in this because he does not taste with the due sense of taste on account of a disorder [*discrasiam*] in the power of the will, since theological truth may excellently be called wisdom, the prudent science, as it were."[109] Even to understand the basics of moral philosophy—which most theologians agree to be helpful in understanding scripture—one needs to understand scripture. "Sacred scripture is full of the theology of moral philosophy, without which, as it happens, the theologian does not learn any of the lessons [*sentencia*] set forth in philosophical books."[110] So Wyclif is left, as we have noted already, with a hermeneutical catch-22: in order to be good you have to understand

---

106. Cited in ibid., 33.

107. Cited in ibid., 113n99.

108. For a catalogue of these passages, see Levy, *Reading the Scriptures*, 80–81.

109. Wyclif, "Principium," 340.

110. Ibid., 344–45.

scripture, but in order to understand scripture you have to be good.[111] Wyclif and later Wycliffites lean on a neo-Augustinian doctrine of illumination for a theoretical way out of this bind, according to which, as Kantik Ghosh has argued, "the Bible is . . . no longer a verbal text demanding interpretation but the discourse of true belief originating in God and existing in the hearts of the faithful."[112] Even if this extreme position is not a necessary conclusion of Wyclif's principles,[113] it nevertheless points to a troubling impasse in exegetical theory and moral theology when the theoretical orders supplied by these discourses are applied to the order of practical interpretation and action.

Langland's Circulatory Tropological Theory

One facet of this hermeneutical-ethical dilemma appears at the end of *Piers Plowman* 21, with the calamity discussed above in which the vices attack the virtues and the king co-opts the language of virtue to disguise a platform of unjust policy. In that case, Grace's sermon on the virtues proved ineffective because it fell on the ears of people who, in Wyclif's terms, lacked the requisite ordering of the will to receive the truth. But as is often the case in *Piers Plowman*, a solution to this dilemma was proposed earlier in the allegory of the cultivation of scripture, where Langland turns Wyclif's catch-22 into a chicken-and-egg scenario. Which came first? The answer doesn't matter because the cultivation of

---

111. Cf. David Lyle Jeffrey, *People of the Book: Christian Identity and Literary Culture* (Grand Rapids, MI: William B. Eerdmans, 1996), 175–78.

112. Kantik Ghosh, *The Wycliffite Heresy: Authority and the Interpretation of Texts* (Cambridge: Cambridge University Press, 2002), 43; on Wycliffites, 117–18. Wyclif could be understood to bypass tropology altogether by insisting on a radically prevenient grace that would take over the natural intellect and appetites, with both understanding and virtue necessarily infused directly from above. Compare Ghosh's sharp commentary on "hermeneutics . . . displaced by 'right living'" (60–66).

113. Levy contends that Wyclif held no position that was not common among his contemporaries and forerunners, pointing out that the doctrine of illumination and the belief that the good interpreter must be conformed to Christ were deeply embedded in the tradition (*Reading the Scriptures*, 80–81).

crops is a natural, yearly routine such that we have no doubt about its possibility (though we do have doubts about the fortunes of climate and pests). The agricultural metaphors resist the orders of priority and of the faculties with which moral philosophy and theology deal. In Langland's agrarian imagination, neither right reading of scripture nor the virtue of the interpreter ever has absolute priority. The solution to the crisis of ethical interpretation cannot be derived from a better theory or method of exegesis, nor can it depend on a flash of illumination. According to the order of society and church that Grace has established and entrusted to Piers, the ethical crisis is not just a matter of ethics, judgment, or epistemology. The crisis requires a more targeted solution than an epistemological, hermeneutical, or ethical correction. It requires practices of scripture—reading, meditation, prayer, preaching, liturgy, and so on—cultivated with the cyclical regularity, discernment, and dogged reliability required by good farming.

While scriptural practices are the answer to the catch-22, they are not a purely technological answer, as the farming analogy might initially suggest. No methodology, no *ordo* of study, prayer, and proclamation, is going to solve this bypass. The allegory of scriptural cultivation insists that love must be involved, and that love has to be expressed communally, by all the estates. Holy Scripture and her interpreters drive out the vices and cultivate the growth of love. Piers's injunctions about interpretation, teaching, and action extend the responsibilities for cultivation of the virtues by scripture to all people endowed with natural reason: "'Harweth alle þat conneth kynde wit bi consail of this doctours / And tulieth to here techynge the cardinal vertues'" (315–16). Where the first iteration of the cultivation metaphor had an episcopal Piers as plowman and foreman, this recapitulation commands the entire *commune* to participate in the cultivation of virtue.

But how can those who do not yet possess the virtues cultivate virtue when the requirements of virtue are unclear, even in the light of scripture? Furthermore, how can those who recognize virtue handle hypocrisy—an urgent question, especially among Wycliffites?[114] Lang-

---

114. On the same concern in Wycliffite sermons, see Ghosh, *The Wycliffite Heresy*, 116–18.

land confronts these difficulties directly in his treatment of justice and then suggests the way toward a solution. Justice gets tripped up by guile because it is his virtue to do "equite to alle eueneforth his knowyng" (308), but he must judge within the bounds of the judicial system, which is vulnerable to the baldfaced lie and the dissembler of virtue. The crisis of interpretation causes Langland to recapitulate the scriptural part of the allegory:

> Thise foure sedes Peres sewe and sennes he dede hem harewe
> With olde lawe and newe lawe that loue myhte wexe
> Among the foure vertues and vices distruye.
> "For cominliche in Contrayes cammokes and wedes
> Fouleth the fruyt in the feld ther thei growe togyderes
> And so doth vices vertues; forthy," quod Peres,
> "Harweth alle þat conneth kynde wit bi consail of this doctours
> And tulieth to here techynge the cardinal vertues."
>
> (309–16)

Here Langland suggests two ways to cultivate the virtues and kill the vices. Reading scripture cultivates love in and among the natural virtues, elevating them to Christian virtues and destroying the vices. In the first iteration of this allegory, plowing and harrowing figured the opening up of the literal sense of scripture to the Spirit. Now scripture harrows the souls in which Piers sowed the seeds of the virtues, seeking openings in the souls like those opened by spiritual interpretation in scripture.

Scripture acts on the souls of its readers to increase love. Love—for Augustine, the vivifying and authorizing spirit of good interpretation— grows up in the spaces and intervals among the virtues. But although love grows (waxes) in this image, it is not figured as a plant, and Langland calls our attention to its herbicidal function. Love kills the "cammokes and wedes" of vice (312), and its selectivity is noteworthy. As a selective herbicide, love discerns which plants are good and which are bad. And "cammokes" may not just be redundant for the sake of alliteration: its modern English name is rest-harrow, for its ability to arrest the harrow, or as the medieval Latin name for the cammock would have it, to arrest the ox who pulled the plow.[115] These are weeds that not only kill desirable crops but hinder the work of weeding itself (for harrowing was and still is the most effective natural way to get rid of weeds).[116] They also hinder plowing, that figure for the whole of the evangelical enterprise in *Piers Plowman*. So when Piers urges all people possessed of natural intellect to harrow the weeds of vice out of the soil of the individual and communal heart, he appoints a difficult task indeed. The Old and New Testaments are the harrows with which they will do the weeding, according to the counsel and teaching of the four exegetes previously figured as four "stottes" (267). Not only does one need to discern the good plants from the bad, but the scripture used for harrowing needs strong oxen to pull it and, the image suggests, to steer it. The exegetes, then, work in accord with the love that waxes in the first image, discerning good from bad, and by their teaching and counsel guiding the reading of scripture to cultivate virtue and uproot vice.

Reading scripture is not enough for the fruits of virtue to grow and resist the weeds of vice. The interpretation and discernment the exegetes

---

115. "It has been called in Latin *remora aratri, resta bovis*; in French Arrête-boeuf; in English Rest-harrow, and by synonymous terms in other languages, in reference to its strong, creeping, tangled roots, which retard the operations of the ploughman." Benjamin Herbert Barton, Thomas Castle, and John Reader Jackson, eds., *The British Flora Medica: A History of the Medicinal Plants of Great Britain* (London: Chatto and Windus, 1877), 344. See *MED*, s.v. "cammok" (a), which cites John Mirfeld's *Sinonoma Bartholomei*, 36: "Resta bovis herba est retinens boves in aratro: cammoc" (The *resta bovis* is a plant that holds up the oxen when plowing: a cammock).

116. "The ploughshare is of such a size as to turn over the clods. People immediately sow seeds and drag the harrow over the land. Land that is thus seeded does not need weeding, but it is with ox teams of two or three pairs that they plough in this manner." Pliny the Elder, *Historia Naturalis*, 18.48; quoted in Georges Raepsaet, "The Development of Farming Implements between the Seine and the Rhine from the Second to the Twelfth Centuries," in *Medieval Farming and Technology: The Impact of Agricultural Change in Northwest Europe*, ed. Grenville Astill and John Langdon (New York: Brill, 1997), 43. Raepsaet observes, "The framed harrow is still used today in numerous countries, pulled by oxen" (60).

provide come, like the seeds of virtue themselves, *in potentia* as the first movement of tropological interpretation. In order to complete the interpretation, the Christian *commune* must cultivate holiness in itself. Immediately after Piers gives instructions for harrowing, Grace instructs him to build the barn of Unity—the church—to keep the fruit of his labors. No sooner has he built it (out of the wood of the cross and the crown of thorns) and commenced to "tulye treuthe" (333) than Pride attacks Conscience, all Christians, and the crop of virtues, blowing them down, breaking them, and biting the roots apart (335–38). In answer to this attack, the church must redouble its husbandry, with each individual member cultivating holiness:

> Ther ne was cristene creature that kynde wit hadde
> . . . .
> That he ne halpe a quantite holinesse to wexe,
> Somme thorw bedes biddynge and somme bi pilgrimage
> Or oþer priue penaunse and somme thorw pans delyng [giving
>   alms].
> And thenne walled [wept] watur for wikked werkes
> Egrelich ernynge [running] oute of menne yes.
> Clannesse of þe comune and clerkes clene lyuynge
> Made vnite holi churche in holinesse stande.
>
> (372, 374–80)

The growth of holiness has been transposed into another allegorical frame, but the images overlap. Formerly those in possession of "kynde wit" used it to harrow the weeds; now they turn to repentance, a kind of self-harrowing. Their practices of piety increase holiness, the Christian form of the natural virtues. In this allegorical frame, holiness is a moat of defense around the tower/barn of Unity. Penitents' tears fill the moat but also, according to the previous allegory, water the virtues. The allegory of the crops of holiness returns in passus 22, where the Antichrist parodies Piers's plowing, harrowing the roots of "the crop of treuthe"— holiness, the virtues, Christian souls—and planting guile in their place (22.53–57). This final iteration of the allegory emphasizes the problem of interpretation, demonstrating the intimate connection between growth in holiness and the ability to distinguish truth from falsehood. Recognizing the natural virtues is not enough, as Piers insists, for the Antichrist comes clothed in apparent virtue. Only Holy Scripture, opened as a vessel for the spiritual senses, can discern good from evil and root out guile. At the same time, scripture needs to be interpreted, which requires the exegetical tradition and the practices of interpretation it teaches. Those practices are the invention of love, which grows out of scripture interpreted in love and culminates in active love, works of holiness. Interpretation is irreducibly ethical, for it happens in and through active love, and ethical action is irreducibly interpretive, for it must constantly discern, by reference to scripture and the exegetical tradition, the fruit from the weeds. Langland's allegory of the cultivation of scripture solves the hermeneutical-ethical catch-22 that vexed many of his contemporaries by applying agrarian categories that resist, with their rhythms of cyclical growth and emphasis on praxis, the orders of priority and of the faculties that dominate philosophical and theological treatments of the dilemma.

Langland's cyclical approach to scriptural ethics reflects the circulatory function of tropology. It also challenges understandings of the Bible as a moral code, a repository of timeless, universally applicable laws. If the Bible were such a moral code, it would suffice to read it once, or even to read a summary of its edicts. By contrast, the allegory of the cultivation of scripture situates interpretation and invention in an iterative practice of religious reading, whereby the tropological imperative resounds not as a command to do this or that good deed, or to fulfill one's duty, but to apply one's reading today, however that might happen, and to become thereby the sort of person who habitually participates in the story of salvation and whose happiness will be fulfilled in that story's ending. Such a conception resists detaching ethics from scriptural practices and sacraments, or natural virtue from grace, and it creates a space for critique of ethical discourses and practices that would claim hegemony over love, whether by institutionalization, methodological correctness, or possession of the proper objects of love.[117]

---

117. See chapter 6 for an example of this critique in the York Play.

An Anatomy of Tropologies

In what follows, I anatomize some types of uses to which Langland puts tropology and adduce examples. This catalogue is not meant to be exhaustive, but rather to suggest directions for further thought about the diverse ways in which tropology functions in literary texts. Elizabeth Salter observed in her anatomy of *Piers Plowman's* allegorical modes that the poem deftly coordinates literary allegory with the allegory of spiritual exegesis (or figuralism, as she called it).[118] The same may be said of tropology. *Piers Plowman* contains natural tropologies, or set pieces of moral conversion when characters convert their behavior by interpreting the ethical sense of a situation, as well as exegetical tropologies, such as Reason's or Conscience's sermons on moral themes from the Bible or moral theology. It contains tropological interpretation of natural phenomena; of recent history; of salvation history; of fantastic visions; of liturgy; and countless examples of corrupt interpretation of scriptural and ecclesiastical authority in order to justify political, economic, and social abuses. It represents or models in its own making countless events of tropological invention, of the conversion of words into works. And preeminently, as I will argue in chapters 2 and 4, *Piers Plowman* invites readers to participate imaginatively in its paraliturgical, scriptural world as a way to foster metaphysical and sacramental participation in salvation history.

Ethical Discourse That Is Not Properly Tropological
Piers Plowman is full of ethical discourse that is not tropological, strictly speaking, because it treats explicitly of ethics and requires no *translatio*, no shifted frame of reference in order to derive a moral sense. Most of this nontropological ethical discourse occurs within a literary-allegorical frame.

---

118. Elizabeth Salter, "Introduction," in *Piers Plowman*, by William Langland, ed. Elizabeth Salter and Derek Pearsall (Evanston, IL: Northwestern University Press, 1967), 9–28.

The tradition of moral personification allegory provides one such frame. The parade of vices in C.6–7 couples named vices with confessional soliloquies and narrative that dramatize the vices' characteristics. There is little gap between the literary mode of allegory and the ethical interpretation of it. Of course, Langland's parade of vices is more interesting at times than, say, Prudentius's, and the passages of low mimetic realism, such as when Glutton "pissede a potel in a paternoster whyle" (C.6.399), invite readers' humorous participation. But on the whole, the literary personification allegory is coextensive with the moral, requiring no ethical *translatio*.

Other literary allegories frame debates that are explicitly ethical. Most of C.9 consists of direct, explicit discussion of labor ethics, couched in allegorized terms. Truth sends a letter to merchants "vnder his secrete seal," as if he is sending them a papal bull or a pardon (C.9.27). The contents of the letter exhort the merchants to

> . . . bugge [buy] boldly what hem best likede
> And sethe sullen [sell] hit aȝeyn and saue þe wynnynge,
> Amende mesondewes [hospitals] þerwith and myseyse men fynde
>   [support the poor]
> And wyckede wayes with here goed amende
> And brugges tobrokene by the heye wayes
> Amende in som manere wyse and maydones helpe.
> (C.9.28–33)

The list goes on, mirroring mainstream fourteenth-century ecclesiastical views of what the merchant class owes society at large.

There is nothing tropological about this discourse, but the merchants' response to Truth's letter is tropological, for they interpret the plain-sense ethical directives as a unified means of grace purchased by Piers Plowman for their salvation: "Tho were Marchauntes mury; many wopen for ioye / And preysede Peres the plouhman þat purchased þis bulle" (C.9.41–42). The merchants thus contribute to the allegoresis of economic law by identifying its ethical directives as a gift *for them* that moves them to affective response, which in turn allows them to identify the laws' involvement in the grand scheme of salvation.

Natural Tropological Exegesis

Especially in the central passūs that focus on *kynde* (nature), Langland likes to draw ethical and soteriological significance from the natural world. He associates natural tropology largely with classical antiquity and the natural intellect. "Kynde wittede men can a clergie [know a body of knowledge] by hemsulue; / Of cloudes [clothes] and of costumes they contreuede mony thynges / And markede hit in here manere and mused þeron to knowe" (C.14.72–74), such as the moral exemplarity of the peacock and parrot, which "with here proude fetheres / Bytokenen riht ryche men þat reygne here on erthe" because "men reuerenceth more þe ryche for his mebles [possessions] / then for eny kyn he come of or for his kynde wittes" (C.14.172–73, 181–82). The character Imaginatif respects such natural moral lore, but finds it potentially misleading if it is not supplemented by tropology ordered toward salvation:

> Ac thorw here science sothly was neuere soule ysaued
> Ne brouhte by here bokes to blisse ne to ioye,
> For al here kynde knowing cam bote of diuerse syhtes,
> Of brides and of bestes, of blisse and of sorwe.
> Patriarkes and prophetus repreuede here science
> And saide here wordes ne here wysdomes was but a folye;
> As to þe clergie of crist thei counted hit but a tryfle:
> *Sapiencia huius mundi stulticia est apud deum.*
>
> (C.14.77–83a, original emphasis)

But Imaginatif is not the final authority in these matters (nor in others), and Langland elsewhere approves of and pursues a natural tropology that harmonizes with revealed learning. In order to convert Will away from Rechelesnesse and toward Reason, Kynde comes to the aid of Clergie and shows him the order of the natural world in the "myrour of mydelerthe" (C.13.132). Kynde presents the mirror for the benefit of both Clergie and Will. Clergie needs to learn "To knowe by vch a creature kynde to louye" (133), and Will needs to learn the value of measure by comparing the procreative "resoun" of the beasts to humans who "out of resoun . . . ryde and rechelesliche taken on / As in derne dedes, bothe drynkyng and elles" (154–55). The vision of order, wonder, fullness, and beauty in the natural world causes Will to desire the same for humans.

Circulating Tropology

Of the historical figures mentioned in *Piers Plowman*, "Gregorie þe grete clerk and þe goode pope" (B.10.298) is perhaps the most prominent. Langland mentions the widely acknowledged master of tropology eight times, and Clergie cites his *Moralia in Iob* by title (B.10.299). Langland prizes Gregory in part because his *Moralia* does ethics as tropological commentary in reaction to the political, social, and spiritual crises of Gregory's day.[119] Gregory never wrote an ethical treatise, but in the high Middle Ages, academics digested the *Moralia* into their systems of moral philosophy and theology. Peraldus, author of the *Summa de vitiis et virtutibus*, and his successors broke up the *Moralia's* exegetical rhythms, rearranging Gregory's *materia* to fit their *schemata*.[120] In vernacular biblical literature, though, tropological ethics persisted. Langland keeps coming back to Gregory, I think, because he sees himself engaged in a similar project, one where Dowel, Dobet, and Dobest cannot simply be analyzed according to vices and virtues but entail a life-long participation in the history of salvation encountered in and recapitulated through scripture.

In *Piers Plowman*, Clergie (B.10.298–304) and Reason (C.5.146–51) cite the *Moralia* for an exemplum about the tensions between the active and contemplative lives. It turns out that the exemplum does not occur in the *Moralia*,[121] but Gregory does deploy the same image of a fish in

---

119. Catharina Greschat, *Die "Moralia in Job" Gregors des Grossen* (Tübingen: Mohr Siebeck, 2005), 3–9.

120. See Grover A. Zinn, "Exegesis and Spirituality in the Writings of Gregory the Great," in *Gregory the Great: A Symposium*, ed. John Cavadini (Notre Dame, IN: University of Notre Dame Press, 1995), 168–80.

121. A similar proverb is found in the *Legenda Aurea's* Life of St. Anthony. An abbot asks Anthony what he should do. Anthony replies, "Sicut pisces, si in sicco tardaverint, moriuntur, ita et monachi extra cellam tardantes aut cum viris saecularibus immorantes a quietis proposito resolvuntur." Jacobus de Voragine, *Legenda aurea: Vulgo historia lombardica dicta*, ed. Johann

and out of water to discuss the topic of action and contemplation. Leviticus prohibits eating fish without fins, Gregory remarks, because the fish that have fins tend to leap above the water. "Therefore the only people who enter the body of the elect, as if they were food, are those who devote themselves to serve in the humblest matters, and who know from time to time to ascend to the heavens by leaps of the mind, lest they always lie hidden in the depths of their busyness, lest no breeze of the heights of love as of the open sky brush across them."[122] Gregory wants the elect, like the fish they eat, to alternate between passionate engagement with the humblest tasks of the fleeting world and restful contemplation of eternal peace.

Clergie and Reason in *Piers Plowman* make the opposite point when they claim Gregory's authority for the assertion that

> Ryht as fysches in floed whan hem fayleth water
> Dyen for drouthe whenne they drye lygge,
> Ryht so religioun roteth and sterueth
> That out of couent and Cloystre coueyteth to dwelle.

(C.5.148–51)

The point of the exemplum is that religious should *not* alternate between contemplation and action, at least not out in the world. But Gregory himself, in the same *Moralia* passage mentioned above, does an about-face to affirm the basic point of Langland's exemplum: "Therefore those who are occupied with temporal things order their external affairs well only when they anxiously flee back to interior affairs; when they never delight in the hubbub of commotion outside, but take their rest within themselves in the bosom of tranquility."[123]

In apparently reversing himself, Gregory has pulled off a Langlandian trick by rotating the frame of reference around the constant

---

Georg Theodor Grässe (Dresden and Leipzig: Impensis Librariae Arnoldianae, 1846), 21.4.

122. Gregory the Great, *Moralia in Job*, 5.11.

123. Ibid.

terms of an image. First, the fish with fins could escape the turmoil of worldly affairs only by leaping out of them, ever so briefly, into the free air of contemplation. But now those to whom the fish are compared must submerge themselves, taking refuge within rather than without. As so often happens in *Piers Plowman*, the kinetic logic of the imagery mimics the thematic logic of the argument. The interior and exterior alternate as sites of rest precisely because Gregory advocates an alternating rule of life. He wants his readers to learn constantly to circulate between the humble turmoil of the world and contemplative rest in the divine peace of prayer. He wants to teach his readers an ethical habitus, and to do so he leads them through all of scripture in a wandering, circulatory manner, at times ascending to heights of mystical contemplation, but also descending to worldly affairs and the ethical dilemmas they entail.

This circulating itinerary defines Gregory's tropological method. Tropology in Gregory never merely reveals the good course of action; rather, tropology runs every ethical question through the texture of scripture (what we might call the literal sense), the history of salvation (what we might call allegory), the practicalities of worldly affairs (what we might call morals), and the heights of contemplation (what we might call anagogy). I have called this tropological and figural movement Langlandian, but of course Langland learned a great deal from Gregory. Langland's Gregorian tropological imagination, then, keeps him from letting a simplistic exemplum about stability get in the way of a complex political theology that can appreciate the social benefits of monastic activity. It keeps the senses of scripture in circulation and encourages a mixed life envisioned as a healthy alternation between active and contemplative states.

Literary Allegory That Requires Ethical Translatio
More often than he writes explicit moral allegories, Langland stages allegorical dramas that require their fictional participants, the dreamer, and the reader to figure out what the moral point of a vision is: what it means to do well in a given situation, or what an authoritative figure would have them do. We find each of these phases of tropological interpretation in the pardon scene in C.9. Piers gives an extended exegesis of the pardon he has received from Truth—119 lines of specific moral di-

rectives (C.9.159–277). But when a priest demands to read Piers's pardon, he is disappointed to find "no pardoun," just two lines that he translates as "'do wel and haue wel, and god shal haue thy soule / And do yuele and haue euele and hope thow non oþere / Bote he þat euele lyueth euele shal ende'" (C.9.289–92). The priest and Piers dispute over the pardon, but their discussion wakes Will, who is ambivalent about Piers's prolific capacity for tropological interpretation. How could Piers get 119 lines out of three lines?

Will's puzzlement prompts his own act of tropological interpretation upon waking from the dream. When Piers showed the pardon to the priest, Will stood behind them, looking over their shoulders. Now awake, he figuratively retains the same position, interpreting not only the text of the pardon but the drama of interpretation that he had dreamed. While Piers could quickly translate the pithy pardon into a capacious vision of social and economic ethics, Will's tropological disposition leads him to slow down and meditate on the strange interaction between Piers and the priest:

> Musyng on this meteles [with no food] A myle way y ȝede.
> Mony tyme this meteles [dream] hath maked me to studie
> Of that y seyh slepynge, if hit so be myhte,
> And of Peres the plouhman fol pencyf in herte
> And which a pardoun Peres hadde the peple to glade
> And how þe prest inpugnede hit thorw two propre wordes.
>
> (C.9.297–302)

Will is reluctant to accept Piers's exegesis at face value because he wants to translate the drama of interpretive conflict into ethical meaning that *he* can take away from it. He briefly wonders about the legitimacy of dream interpretation (303–4), but then quickly launches an extended defense of the practice from biblical precedent (305–17). All of this defers his interpretation even as it impresses the value of interpretation, meanwhile coaxing the reader, who virtually looks over Will's shoulder as Will looked over Piers's shoulder, to engage in ethical interpretation himself or herself. Will's waking delay, his languorous "studie," buys time for the reader to recognize how odd it was that the priest could find no pardon.

When Will finally comes out with his own tropological reading of the situation, fifteen lines later, it comes as some surprise that he makes no mention of Piers but assumes *the priest* to have performed a bold tropological exegesis in his rejection of the two lines as a pardon:

> Al this maketh me on meteles [dreams] to studie
> And how þe prest preuede no pardon to do wel
> And demede þat dowel indulgences passeth,
> Bionales and trionales and bisshopes lettres.
> For hoso doth wel here at þe day of dome
> Worth [will be] fayre vnderfonge [received] byfore god þat tyme
> So dowel passeth pardoun and pilgrimages to Rome.
>
> (318–24)

Will assumes that the priest, in finding no pardon, was not making a remark about the legal and soteriological status of the documentary evidence before him. Rather, he assumes that the priest's remark was tropological: the priest shifted the frame of reference from forensic or legal justification—the kind of thing you expect to find in a pardon or a papal bull—to what *he* should do for the salvation of his soul. The priest found no pardon, no free pass *a pena et a culpa*, because he took seriously the ongoing tropological imperative, translating the declarative, descriptive Latin—"qui bona egerunt" (those who do good deeds)—into an English imperative: "do wel and haue wel" (287, 290).

In his own appropriation of the priest's tropological reading, Will, like Piers, addresses the moral to the public: "Forthy y rede [advise] ʒow renkes [people] þat riche ben on this erthe" (333). But he quickly moves into the mode of collective tropology, emphasizing his solidarity with the people in their common need for grace to do well for the salvation of their souls. Note how quickly the prophetic first-person singular shifts into a collective, supplicating first-person *plural*:

> Forthy y consayle alle cristene to crye god mercy
> And marie his moder be *oure* mene to hym
> That god gyue *vs* grace here ar *we* go hennes
> Suche werkes to worche the while *we* ben here

> That aftur *oure* deth day dowel reherce
> At þe day of dome *we* dede as he tauhte.

(347–52, my emphasis)

Will would answer his own call if only he could find Dowel. But the beginning of the next passus has him roaming about "Alle a somur seson for to seke dowel" (C.10.2). The quest for salvation remains in a tropological mode, between allegory and anagogy, between salvation history and the hoped-for rest in God. Will can grasp the essential tropological meaning of Truth's pardon, but it does not end his quest for Dowel because the pardon signifies nothing other than the tropological imperative, a command to continue tropological interpretation and invention. Tropology and Dowel, then, name the same ethical condition of the Christian soul *in via*.

Tropological Reception of Piers Plowman
Annotations of *Piers Plowman* manuscripts can afford glimpses of how readers, in John Dagenais's apt phrase, "negotiate . . . between the letter of the text and their own lives."[124] The "prolific" mid-fifteenth-century

---

124. Dagenais, *The Ethics of Reading*, 14. Although I focus here on presumably spontaneous annotation by engaged readers, a large proportion of annotations in medieval manuscripts, especially of *Piers Plowman*, reflects professional contributions to the text's *ordinatio*. These were reading aids that were prepared in advance and often standardized, much like the sets of glosses that accompanied texts of the Bible and canon law. For example, even the frequently thoughtful and moral annotations in the Douce 104 manuscript of *Piers Plowman* were probably copied from an exemplar, "not the stuff of a quill-happy owner, but real scriptorium slog-work." Kathryn Kerby-Fulton and Denise L. Despres, *Iconography and the Professional Reader: The Politics of Book Production in the Douce "Piers Plowman"* (Minneapolis: University of Minnesota Press, 1999), 68–69. Yet only with an individualist vision of ethics and reading could one conclude that professional glossing does not translate the literal sense of the text into readers' lived experience. Professional glossing "depends ultimately upon a system of values that directs the flow of the letter's play and ultimately closes it off at the point at which the letter meets the life experience of" the community of readers for which, and often in which, the glossator

annotations of the B-text in London, British Library, MS Additional 35287 reveal a reader "at once viscerally engaged in the text and sensitive to the very same conflicts that trouble Will the dreamer."[125] As Christine Schott has demonstrated, "Hand 3" adopts different voices in his glosses, now echoing the text verbatim, now paraphrasing its imperatives, now "noting" something of interest. He is the source of tropological theory—echoing Reason's sermon, "That ye prechen þe peple, preue it yowselve" (5.42)—as well as its addressee. When Imaginatif exhorts Will to "[a]mende þee while þow myȝt" (12.10), Hand 3 takes the admonition personally and communally, as Will did in his exegesis of the pardon discussed above, glossing the line with "Emendemus dum temporum habemus" (Let us amend ourselves while we have time).[126] Amendment of life could take very practical forms, as the scribe's interest in quotidian, but nonetheless moral, matters suggests. An allegory depicting baptism in terms of landlord/tenant relations suggests to Hand 3 that peasants should not enter into contracts without their landlords' permission (11.127). Other moral annotations are less specific—"dowell superest Indulgencias" (Dowel is better than indulgences) (7.175)—or more political-theoretical, as when he paraphrases Trajan's opinion that people should serve their lords "magis propter amorem quam pecunie stipendium" (more for love than for monetary pay) (11.175). In Hand 3's habit of annotation, "the pursuit of salvation blends," as Schott remarks, "almost seamlessly into the pursuit of right action in the world."[127]

A similar pursuit, though with more literary ambition, motivates the anonymous author of a new ending to *Piers Plowman* A in the Duke of Westminster's MS (*olim* Eaton Hall). The ending is one of three con-

---

labored—though even in this quotation I have had to suppress "the individual reader." Dagenais, *The Ethics of Reading*, 15. Further, just because an annotator was professional does not mean he or she could not also be an "intimate reader." See Christine Schott, "The Intimate Reader at Work: Medieval Annotators of *Piers Plowman* B," *Yearbook of Langland Studies* 26 (2012): 163–85.

125. Schott, "The Intimate Reader," 164, 171.

126. Ibid., 178–79.

127. Ibid., 173–74.

tinuations that readers added to the end of *Piers Plowman*, and the manuscript is one of six that display "the capacity of *Piers Plowman* to elicit response, to generate active participation in the literary and social experience it evidently constituted for near-contemporary readers."[128] Like the other two continuations, the Westminster ending, written by a hand other than the main scribe and signed "R H," expresses ethical aspirations that are clearly inspired by the experience of reading the poem to that point. R. H. adopts Will's persona in order to ventriloquize and recapitulate the opening lines of *Piers Plowman*:

> And when I wos wytterly awakyd I wrote all thys dreame
> And theys mervellys þat I met [dreamed] on mawlverne hyllys
> In a seyson of sommer as I softe nappyd
> For þe peeple after ther power wold persen after Dowell
> That ys treysure moost tryed and tryacle [medicine] at neede
> Now god gravnt vs hys grace to make a good end
> And bryng vs all to þe blysse as he bowghte vs on þe Roode amen
>
> R H[129]

R. H.'s prayer for "grace to make a good ende" merges his own making of an end to the poem with the anagogical phase of Dowel as it is oriented toward the end of the pilgrimage of this life on Doomsday. The final line looks back to the biblical history of the crucifixion in order to aspire prayerfully to the bliss of heaven, at the same time making a

---

128. George Kane, "The Text," in *A Companion to Piers Plowman*, ed. John A. Alford (Berkeley and Los Angeles: University of California Press, 1988), 182. Besides the Westminster manuscript, the other continuations are John But's ending to the A-text in Oxford, Bodleian Library, MS Rawlinson Poetry 137, and Stephen Batman's brief couplet, discussed below, in Oxford, Bodleian Library, MS Digby 171. My understanding of tropological invention in and beyond *Piers Plowman* is shaped by Anne Middleton, "Making a Good End: John But as a Reader of *Piers Plowman*," in *Medieval English Studies Presented to George Kane*, ed. Edward Donald Kennedy, Ronald Waldron, and Joseph S. Wittig (Wolfeboro, NH: D. S. Brewer, 1988), 243–63.

129. *Piers Plowman: The C Version*, ed. Russell and Kane, 185.

literary good end in the present. The plea for grace in the penultimate line echoes Conscience's cries as he "grade aftur grace" in the final authorial line of the poem (C.22.386 [B.20.386]), thus inscribing the authorial ending's open-endedness into this additional ending and locating it temporally alongside Conscience's ongoing quest for *Piers Plowman*. Just as Hand 3 of Add. 35287 blended an interest in quotidian ethics with his pursuit of salvation, R. H. joins Will and William Langland in ethical literary invention for the sake of salvation. By recapitulating *Piers Plowman*'s biblical-historical and anagogical orientations, he or she participates in the poem's participation in salvation history. The Westminster manuscript's additional ending illustrates how tropological invention begets more tropological invention.

That desire for more tropological invention is in evidence in a much later instance of annotative participation, namely, Oxford, Bodleian Library, MS Digby 171, an incomplete C-text owned and annotated by Stephen Batman, a Protestant clergyman who acquired the manuscript in 1578.[130] The manuscript breaks off at line 15.65, adjacent to which Batman has crammed an invented line that *rhymes* with the last line of the authorial text and then occasions a further couplet. I transcribe here the final three lines of the authorial text (15.63–65), with Batman's additions in bold:

> Paciense was wel a paide : of þis proper seruyse
> And mad mirthe with þis mete : ac y mornede euere
> For a doctor at þe heie deys : drank wyn faste / **I wolde this vers**
> **were not ye laste**
> **Although this work be harde to finde**
> **Yet it is good for a christian minde**[131]

---

130. According to an inscription on the recto of the front flyleaf in what Simon Horobin has identified as Batman's hand. Horobin, "Stephen Batman and His Manuscripts of *Piers Plowman*," *Review of English Studies*, n.s., 62, no. 255 (2010): 368.

131. Oxford, Bodleian Library, MS Digby 171, fol. 64r.

The concern that "this work be harde to finde" probably bespeaks Batman's concerted efforts to collect and collate multiple versions and copies of *Piers Plowman*.[132] His continuation of this premature ending, then, follows the logic of Langland's authorial ending and R. H.'s invented ending in the Westminster manuscript insofar as the former imagines an open-ended quest for Piers Plowman the oversignified salvific figure, and the latter for *Piers Plowman* the book. But continuing the quest in the tropological present is now more complicated because a perceptible historical gap has opened up between R. H.'s present and Batman's present. And so Batman's verses accentuate the temporal distance even as they work to build a bridge back to Langland's present. As stilted as his rhyming verses may be, they translate Langland's lines into a prosody more familiar to the late sixteenth century. At the same time, by rhyming with Langland, Batman creates an aural continuity with this antique work.

Batman was particularly interested in continuity, for antiquarian, propagandistic, and pastoral purposes. Serving as Archbishop Matthew Parker's book collecting agent, by his own reckoning Batman procured some 6,700 books for Parker's project to recover "'monuments of antiquity' recuperable for Protestant national identity."[133] Parker's ambitious project of book collecting and library making thus invented historical and theological continuity, a continuity made possible by the violent disruption of the monasteries, the sources of most of the manuscripts that eventually crossed Batman's acquisitive path.

But this was not the kind of continuity that most interested Batman. His personal collection, extant in twenty-three manuscripts, closely mirrors the ensemble of biblical and pastoral "London literature" produced and consumed by the scribal, religious, and lay social circles

---

132. Horobin, "Stephen Batman."

133. Rivkah Zim, "Stephan Batman," in *The Oxford Dictionary of National Biography*, ed. H. C. G. Matthew and B. Harrison (Oxford: Oxford University Press, 2004), www.oxforddnb.com; Jennifer Summit, *Memory's Library: Medieval Books in Early Modern England* (Chicago: University of Chicago Press, 2008), 111.

among whom and for whom Langland probably composed *Piers Plow-man*.[134] In fact, Batman acquired for his own use a major network hub of the mid-fourteenth-century London book trade, Cambridge, Magda-lene College, MS Pepys 2498, a massive miscellany that Ralph Hanna describes as a "deliberate and major gathering of texts, virtually every-thing we know of early fourteenth-century prose"—all of which "pro-vide reasonably direct access to biblical texts" in English.[135] The center-piece of Pepys 2498 is the Middle English *Mirror*, a translation of Robert of Gretham's Anglo-Norman sermon cycle, itself an adaptation of Greg-ory the Great's forty Gospel homilies. Unremittingly tropological, the cycle is directed to lay readers and hearers (not, like so many other cy-cles, to pastors who need help thinking up a homily).[136]

The *Mirror* not only makes Gospel texts and exegesis available in English, but explicitly theorizes a tropological engagement with scrip-ture, using the same agrarian imagery that Langland employs. In the Gospel for the fifth Sunday after Epiphany, Jesus likens the kingdom of heaven to a field where a farmer sows wheat and his enemy sows tares; the two are allowed to grow up together, and then are separated at the harvest. In the *Mirror* this vision mirrors the church in its mixture of good and bad people—a community of individuals each of whom can change from good seed into bad seed, and vice versa. The way to remain or to become a good seed is to cultivate holiness by listening to scripture attentively and turning its words into works:

> Vnderstondeth now þis lessoun, ȝe þat louen God, & skile & resoun
> what þat it is to menen. Ffor wite ȝe wel, he þat vnderstondeþ it wel
> & doþ þerafter, it wole profyte hym gretliche. . . . Ffor wordes ben
> ordeyned þerfore, for þat man schal ȝeue vnderstondynge þerto; &
> vnderstondynge comeþ no good of but ȝif men don it in werk to

---

134. M. B. Parkes, "Stephen Batman's Manuscripts," in *Medieval Heri-tage: Essays in Honour of Tadahiro Ikegami*, ed. Masahiko Kanno et al. (Tokyo: Yushodo Press, 1997), 125–56; Hanna, *London Literature*, 1–43.

135. Hanna, *London Literature*, 156 and 7, respectively.

136. Ibid., 183–202.

Godes worschupe. Ne men may neuere more se þe kirnel of þe note but ȝif þe schelle be broken first. No more ne may Goddes word ben vnderstonden ariȝt but ȝif it be opened openlicher to mennes vnderstondyng. And þerfore Iesus Crist hymseluen wolde vndo þis & open þis ariȝt to oure vnderstondynge for to helpen us, & for to confounden his enemyes, & þat ne wole no þing ȝeue hem to but for to vnderstonde þe letter. Þe seed is Iesus Crist & his wordes & his werkes þat he spac & dide.[137]

The *Mirror* identifies the good seed sown in the parable as the scriptural record of Christ's words and works. While an intuitive reading of the parable suggests that the seeds are souls, perhaps even the souls of the elect, the *Mirror* translator layers another sense over this one, the Bernardian idea that Christ's life set down in scripture might be taken up and incarnated in one's own life. In the analogy of the kernel and nut, the *Mirror* aligns the breaking of the nut with the doing of the word. Hearers of scripture only truly understand it when they do it. How? Jesus Christ "undoes" and "opens" it. But if the only way it can be opened is in the doing, then this must mean that Christ cooperates with the hearer to perform the word. And so the seed that the farmer plants can signify both souls and Christ's words and works at the same time, for in tropological agriculture the only good seed is the one that participates in the life of Christ by hearing and doing his words and works.

This exegesis helpfully frames the frontispiece that Stephen Batman lovingly designed for his used, incomplete copy of *Piers Plowman C*, and now featured on the cover of this book. A large title heading declares, "This Booke is clepped: Sayewell, Doowell, Doo Better, & Doo Best," while a subtitle remarks, "Souche a book, az diserveth the Reeding" (fig. 1.2).[138] The good speech of *Piers Plowman*, its good words, its *gospel*—these are never explicit in the poem's most vivid figures and

---

137. Robert de Gretham, *The Middle English "Mirror": An Edition Based on Bodleian Library, MS Holkham Misc. 40*, ed. Kathleen Marie Blumreich (Tempe: Arizona Center for Medieval and Renaissance Studies, 2002), 88–89.

138. Oxford, Bodleian Library, MS Digby 171, title page.

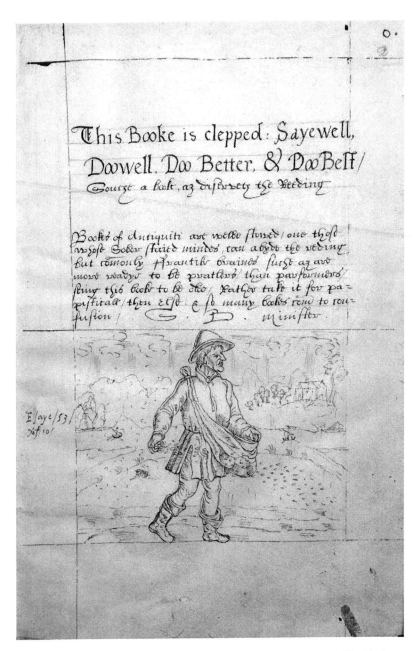

Fig. 1.2. Oxford, Bodleian Library, MS Digby 171, title page. Reprinted by kind permission of The Bodleian Libraries, The University of Oxford.

prominent ordering rubrics, Dowel, Dobet, and Dobest. But by drawing
Piers Plowman's gospel, its "Sayewell," into the title along with the familiar trifecta, Batman features the first part of the tropological imperative,
the words that must first be encountered, digested, and repeated (according to the monastic reading sequence: *lectio, meditatio, oratio*) before they can be turned into works.

Beneath a seven-line epigraph, Batman's drawing of a sower in a
field occupies the lower half of the page. The epigraph makes an apology
for medieval books and instructs readers how best to approach them:

> Bookes of Antiquiti are welbe stowed one / those whose Sober
> staied mindes can abyde the redyng but commonly Frantik braines
> suche az are more readye to be prattlers / than parformers / seing
> this book to be olde / Rather take it for papisticall / then else. & so
> many bookes com to confusion / S. B. Minister

Batman associates knee-jerk anti-papists with people who only "prattle"
but do not "perform." It is not enough to "Sayewell"; one must also
"Doowell." Old books like this require tropological readers "whose
Sober staied mindes" will seek to turn the words into good works. Batman's bridge across the Reformation is tropological reading. The continuities he values are scriptural continuities, and these make the reading
of Catholic literature worthwhile, "good for a christian minde," as his
couplet concludes *Piers Plowman*.

The portrait of Piers Plowman on the title page—sowing truth
(C.7.183–88) or virtues (C.21.275–311)—calls up the rich imagery of
scriptural cultivation. The rubric referencing Isaiah 53:10 sets up a
clever pun on the dreamer's name: "he shall see a longlived seed, and the
will of the Lord shall be prosperous in his hand." The allusion to Isaiah
activates related seed imagery of the word proceeding from God's
mouth to give seed to the sower and prosper all growth.[139] This suggests

---

139. "And as the rain and the snow come down from heaven, and return
no more thither, but soak the earth, and water it, and make it to spring, and give
seed to the sower, and bread to the eater: So shall my word be, which shall go

that *Piers Plowman* is a very good place to encounter the sowing and cultivation of God's word—even, perhaps, that the poem is scripture or contains scripture. The term is one Batman uses generously. Prefacing the *Stimulus amoris* in Cambridge, Trinity College, MS B.14.19, Batman remarks, "In mani placis of this Stimulus amoris (this pricke of Love) are veraye good & sounde documents of scripture, and what the rest are. consider the tyme."[140] That Batman saw no need to warn readers of *Piers Plowman* to "consider the tyme" in which it was written, coupled with the title-page iconography of scriptural sowing, strongly suggests that he accorded at least parts of the poem the status of "good & sounde documents of scripture."

If Batman's epigraph to *Piers Plowman* constitutes a blanket defense of medieval religious literature against knee-jerk destroyers of papist works, his other prefaces are more cautious, counseling shrewd discrimination of truth. The preface to *Stimulus amoris* chides those who would burn "ancient Recordes," and vaguely gestures toward "meanes and wayes. to preserve the good corne by gathering oute the wedes."[141] Jennifer Summit has characterized Batman's cautious selectivity as distinctively Protestant, the opposite of the medieval meditative reading promoted by the very texts he opportunistically appropriates.[142] But Batman's selectivity, in particular his orientation to usefulness, is actually consistent with medieval habits of tropological annotation, certainly those modeled by the professional readers of *Piers Plowman* manuscripts who, in John Dagenais's words, "read piecemeal, in patches, like scavengers combing our master text for whatever they can use. They are self-centered, greedy, disrespectful. They are reductive."[143] Compared to Dagenais's hyped-up portrait of such medieval readers, Batman is a veritable shepherd of the premodern tradition.

---

forth from my mouth: it shall not return to me void, but it shall do whatsoever I please, and shall prosper in the things for which I sent it" (Isa. 55:10–11).

140. Cited in Horobin, "Stephen Batman," 369.

141. Cited in ibid.

142. Summit, *Memory's Library*, 116–17.

143. Dagenais, *The Ethics of Reading*, 213.

Batman in fact does not extract the good parts from the rest, as Summit suggests. Taking the parable of the wheat and the tares seriously, he urges readers to leave complete texts intact. His verse preface to *Ancrene Wisse* in Pepys 2498 judges the first part "veri good" but the second half "not sound." Yet he pleads, "Teare not this book. but kepe it in store, / thow maiest else misse for knoweng of more." Protestant readers might want to know more in order "To answer the ennemy" with proof that "theire owen penns svch errowres have tolde." The "ennemy" recalls the sower of tares elsewhere in Pepys 2498, and Batman's insistence that "one with out the other thow cannot be / Else falsehood with trwthe mixed thow cannot see" perhaps echoes the *Mirror*'s exegesis of the parable, "Ffor ȝif þe wicked were casten out, how schulde þe goode ben proued?"[144] In order to access Christ's words and works, the *Mirror* imagines, one has to encounter and discriminate between both good and bad seeds. This of course makes sense of the visible church, a notoriously motley crew. But Batman's understanding of how scripture can persist in medieval texts suggests that the discrimination of good and bad seeds and fruit applies also to reading practices, medieval as well as early modern. While Batman is certainly on the side of Protestant modernity—"Here is to be senne the ignorance of tyme past / Praie that soche tyme be neuer a gayne"[145]—the continuities he seeks are tropological, and these trump the discontinuity of religious progress. Once the reader has recognized historical discontinuity and taken due precautions, he or she can get on to the far more important matter of continuity. That continuity is provided not so much by good moral material as it is by scripture made available for tropological interpretation and invention—practices that Batman himself models in his frontispiece and brief continuation of *Piers Plowman*.

The narratives studied in the rest of this book approach ethics and the Bible in ways that Batman could appreciate. In these poems and

---

144. The full preface is transcribed in Parkes, "Stephen Batman's Manuscripts," 140–41; Gretham, *The Middle English "Mirror,"* 92.

145. Batman is referring to the penitential work *Psalterium Sancti Hieronymi.* Cited in Summit, *Memory's Library,* 117.

plays that invite affective and ethical participation in the biblical history of redemption, we encounter tropology on a salvation-historical scale. The relative importance of situational ethics ("what should I do now?") diminishes. Ethics shifts from the narrow confines of local and immediate right action to the broad expanse of the Christian life, featuring habituation in virtue, the graces of the sacraments, the bonds of community, and the mediations of the institutional church: Dowel, Dobet, and Dobest under the condition of communal pilgrimage. For the users of this biblical literature, the lineage of commentarial traditions—the source-critical work that has dominated so much modern exegetical scholarship—recedes into practical irrelevance as affective and liturgical participation gains prominence. At the same time, the scope and rhythms of literary tropology can help historians of exegesis recognize the participatory and mystical dimensions of moral exegesis in traditional biblical commentary, as I argue in the next chapter, where *Patience* teaches us to read the *Glossa ordinaria* on Jonah.

2

How to Invent History

Patience, *the* Glossa ordinaria, *and the Ethics of the Literal Sense*

The Jonah of *Patience* likes to complain, and we like to listen to his *sotto voce* grumblings directed at no one and everyone, including his "Syre," God.

> "Oure Syre . . .
> . . . gloumbes [frowns] ful lyttel
> Þaȝ I be nummen in Nunniue and naked dispoyled,
> On rode rwly torent with rybaudes mony."[1]

We like to listen because Jonah is funny, and he is funny because he is realistic: we know his self-pitying mumblings and their accompanying psychological profile all too well from our neighbors, our children, even

---

1. *Patience*, in Malcolm Andrew and Ronald Waldron, eds., *The Poems of the "Pearl" Manuscript: "Pearl," "Cleanness," "Patience," "Sir Gawain and the Green Knight"* (Exeter: Exeter University Press, 2002), ll. 93–96. Hereafter cited in the text.

ourselves. But Jonah is also speaking allegorically when he timorously imagines the "rode" on which he might be "torent," for the *rode* might be either a road or Christ's cross. Such is the occupational hazard of the prophet: allegory happens.[2] And it can happen to implicate the prophet in a vocation of suffering he never, in his comic *grucchyng*, intended. Realism has consequences, especially if it develops within a history that is always already allegorical, where each realistic word implies an extra-linguistic person, thing, or event that anticipates a historical series of events that can transfigure the original referent, solemnizing a comic word and investing it with salvation-historical significance.[3] Such is Jonah's fate when Jesus cites him in Matthew 12:40 as a "sign" of his own resurrection. The Gospel's forceful interpolation of Jonah into its Christian allegorical imaginary runs the risk of totalizing Jonah's own history. In *Patience*, Jonah is keenly aware that God's plans threaten to drown his own initiatives in an abyss of transhistorical allegorical correspondence. The Jonah of *Patience* identifies one of the great challenges to tropology, the possibility that the imitation of Christ will efface all that is unique about his own concrete existence. *Patience* dramatizes this problem while opting for an alternative understanding of tropology, one that emphasizes participation over imitation. The *Patience*-Poet communicates this alternative understanding exegetically and stylistically, trafficking in allegory in conversation with Jerome and the *Glossa ordinaria* but also applying his famous "realizing imagination" to work closely with the literal senses of the biblical story.[4]

In *Patience*, then, allegory is not the opposite of realism, but rather the mode according to which the real appears. The literal sense is the

---

2. See chapter 1 for the sense in which I am using allegory here: the correspondence between people, things, events, and texts in history that is divinely ordered to the salvation of the world.

3. On this semiology of history as developed by the Victorines and modified by Thomas Aquinas, see chapter 1, section "Signs Are Things; Things Are Signs," and Ocker, *Biblical Poetics*, 31–43.

4. A. C. Spearing, *The "Gawain"-Poet: A Critical Study* (Cambridge: Cambridge University Press, 1970), 55–65. See also Malcolm Andrew, "The Realizing Imagination in Late Medieval English Literature," *English Studies* 76, no. 2 (1995): 113–28.

complement, not the alternative, to the allegorical sense. And because literal and allegorical modes interanimate each other, readers and writers have more of a chance to convert the words into salvific actions than if the *Patience*-Poet's literal description were to distance narrative from salvation history.[5] The last chapter presented the tropological sense as the circulatory mechanism of the four senses of scripture. The aim of this chapter is to further develop the mutual interiority of the literal and spiritual senses and to show one way in which narrative poetry creates a productive relationship between biblical history, ethical practice, and the participatory metaphysics by which readers write themselves into the history of salvation.

As Richard Newhauser has noted, "the poet adapts Biblical narratives in a way which frequently does not deny their allegorical or typological potential, but which also demonstrates his great interest in their literal level, as stories of understandable human psychology."[6] I want to take this attention to the literal level further, to bring it full circle, by considering the *Patience*-Poet's delight in historical detail when "history" is already typological or allegorical. That is, what constitutes "realistic" in the poet's "realizing imagination" if his sense of the literal emerges from the complex of scriptural senses that include also allegorical, tropological, and anagogical modes? What exactly does this story that "is not exactly allegory" still have "in common with allegory"?[7] These questions are particularly important if we are to understand how

---

5. On the meaning of "salvation history," see chapter 1, section "Tropology as Spiritual Exegesis." Here I adopt the term "salvation history" rather more loosely than it was meant by the nineteenth-century proponents of *Heilsgeschichte*, but I intend by this term to address a problematic similar to the one those theologians faced: how to relate the "history" of the Bible to the scientific-critical account of history vigorously on the rise in mid-nineteenth-century Germany. See Frei, *Eclipse*, 179–82.

6. Richard Newhauser, "Sources II: Scriptural and Devotional Sources," in *A Companion to the "Gawain"-Poet*, ed. Derek Brewer and Jonathan Gibson (Woodbridge, Suffolk: D. S. Brewer, 1997), 259.

7. Priscilla Martin, "Allegory and Symbolism," in *A Companion to the "Gawain"-Poet*, ed. Derek Brewer and Jonathan Gibson (Woodbridge, Suffolk: D. S. Brewer, 1997), 320.

imaginative literature that did not profess a disciplinary or official affiliation with *sacra scriptura*—a description that fits nearly all the vernacular works studied in this book—could appropriate the theoretical assumptions of biblical commentary and accomplish many of the same functions, while also forming virtue and granting access to salvation history—qualities often ascribed to the Bible itself.

Patience's form and plot dramatize the tensions between the literary (often associated with humanity and literal, realistic detail) and the theological (associated with God and allegory). The poet amplifies the Vulgate extensively, and all critics agree that most of the additions involve realistic description rather than theological commentary, though it is description not for the sake of "realism" but rather as "a powerful narrative tool for dramatizing the limitations of human experience" and for giving readers an experience of the stories narrated.[8] For Lynn Staley, narrative detail does not distract from figural signification, but literal description is not the focus. "Though the details themselves help to create a world that appears 'real,'" she argues, "ultimately these details, like the equally multitudinous details of late Gothic art, are at the service of a good beyond verisimilitude."[9] Although for Sandra Pierson Prior, the poem deploys allegory to link readers to the "good beyond" of providential history,[10] Jay Schleusener detects in its figural typology a grim competition between God and humanity. "Men frame their goals to their own purposes, but because they are caught up in a greater plan

---

8. Sarah Stanbury, *Seeing the "Gawain"-Poet: Description and the Act of Perception* (Philadelphia: University of Pennsylvania Press, 1991), 2.

9. Lynn Staley, *The Voice of the "Gawain"-Poet* (Madison: University of Wisconsin Press, 1984), 21.

10. Sandra Pierson Prior, for example, concludes that "The lesson for Jonah, and for the poem's audience, is to stop concentrating on the distant apocalypse and instead to bring God's Kingdom into the present—and thus paradoxically to go one step beyond apocalypse. Going beyond apocalypse involves moving away from the linearity of an eschatological perspective and replacing the linear *forme* of judgment with the circular and open-ended *forme* of conversion." Sandra Pierson Prior, *The Fayre Formez of the Pearl Poet* (East Lansing: Michigan State University Press, 1996), 146.

conceived not by them but by God, the success or failure of their effort depends on its conformity to his hidden will."[11] In Schleusener's reading, Jonah is trapped by his own typological relationship to Christ. He "has a role in one plot while he *figures* in another, but in that other he has no role, his deeds no sense, his life no goal intrinsic to itself. The function of his figure is not an inward and unique but an outward and universal order." Typology constrains freedom, and descriptive, narrative detail comes about *in spite of* the poet's "firmly believed and deeply felt conception of providential history."[12] Sarah Stanbury approaches the poem's figures of constraint and limitation from a different direction, arguing that apparently realistic description is always refracted through a limited perspective. The poem's most vivid passages of description all concern places in which Jonah is contained—the ship, the whale, the woodbine—and in which he is cut off from the knowledge and will of God. But unlike Schleusener, Stanbury finds this containment to open out to providential history, not to be constrained by it.[13] For Stanbury, mimetic, literal description grants readers access to symbolic salvation history. Through "surprising coalescences between physical and spiritual locations . . . we can move between the sea bottom (despair, the bound soul, the mystics' dark night) and God's court."[14]

This is surely right: the daily lives of common people are linked to providential history by the "coalescence" of two representational modes, mimetic and symbolic. But the dramatic conflict Schleusener identifies between Jonah and God shows how hard-won any coalescence

---

11. Jay Schleusener, "History and Action in *Patience*," *PMLA* 85, no. 5 (1971): 959.

12. Ibid., 960.

13. "Characteristic of the treatment of space in this poem is a coalescence of multiple viewpoints. . . . In the episode of the whale in *Patience*, God's providential sphere in effect encases the whale swimming with Jonah in its maw, but does not disempower it; even as we as readers are reminded by references to God that the whale and the prophet are vassals in God's court, we are simultaneously seduced through graphic sensory detail to participate in the unfolding drama." Stanbury, *Seeing the "Gawain"-Poet*, 84–85.

14. Ibid., 86.

would be, and Jonah's own speeches adopt the narrator's representational modes to contrary purposes. By pointing up these conflicts, the *Patience*-Poet is working through fourteenth-century conflicts in exegetical theory and practice. He finds in the *Glossa ordinaria* and in the Jonah exegesis it represents what many modern critics have been unable to find: a flexible, open-ended view of salvation history that can contemplate providence, teleology, and anagogy in order to engage in free invention of the literal sense.

The poet's moral purpose and his delight in literal narrative detail mutually inform each other. *Patience* springs from, and seeks to instill, a desire to participate in a signal event in salvation history by adding to the literal details of the story and thereby inventing more history. Critics have missed how the invention of the poem is itself a part of history—as understood by late medieval Christian theology—the same history over which providence presides and in which people, events, and things correspond in history-making ways to other people, events, and things. The realistic style of *Patience*—the *forma tractatus* resulting from the poet's predilection for realistic description and his tendency to amplify the literal sense—derives from a theological and ethical impulse similar to the one that drives *Piers Plowman's* allegorical imagination (as developed in the next chapter), but it is more consistently embedded in the literal-historical sense. In order to understand the realistic style and allegorical moments at the same time, we have to grasp the *Patience*-Poet's realism as a finely attuned method for developing an intensely allegorical view of history that attends with equal intensity to the contours of the real in history. *Patience* enlists exegetical techniques shared by the most influential biblical commentary of the age, the *Glossa ordinaria*, in order to invent poetry that writes readers into the history of salvation.

By the term "realizing imagination," I intend to index and reassess a particular genealogy of exegesis that associates the rise of critical historicism in biblical studies with the decline of figural realism. In the most influential version of this genealogy, Hans Frei argues that modern hermeneutics has lost the ability to encounter scripture as "realistic narration."[15] Modern criticism mistakes history for reality, and when the

---

15. Frei, *Eclipse*, 142–54.

biblical narrative's ability to refer to history comes into question, its status as truth declines. Premodern exegesis, by contrast, attended to a feature of narrative that Frei calls "figuralism," adopting the term from Erich Auerbach, whose understanding of *figura* and "realism" looms large in Frei's project. It is precisely this habit of figural reading that Frei sees going into eclipse "when the identity of literal sense and historical reference is severed."[16] In an influential essay on allegorical exegesis, Auerbach places the eclipse of figuralism much earlier; by the late Middle Ages, figuralism's irreducibly historical and sensual correspondences between persons, events, and things have been replaced by the mystical and ethical *meanings* to which fourfold exegesis points, so that "the text becomes, to a far higher degree, sensually enfeebled and historically evacuated."[17] Auerbach laments scripture's lost capacity to evoke sensual experience by giving forms that convey "part of the substance [of] the sensually real present or past."[18] As Niklaus Largier argues, Auerbach's concept of *figura* always retains its etymological link to the visual arts, but even more importantly, to the plastic arts. In the literature of figural realism, Auerbach finds this sensual, reality-saturated, concrete presence translated into "a rhetorical texture, a linguistic reality, that emphasizes forms of figural likeness and is primarily an aesthetic-sensual experience."[19] Extending this analysis beyond the historical terminus Auerbach assigns it, Largier observes that for Henry Suso, "affect adapts itself" to the "figural levels" by "the assimilating

---

16. Ibid., 37.

17. "[D]er Text wird in einem weit höheren Masse sinnlich entkräftet und geschichtlich entleert." Erich Auerbach, "Figura," in *Gesammelte Aufsätze zur Romanischen Philologie* (Bern: Francke, 1967), 79. The sensual aspect of this effect gets lost in the standard English translation: "the text loses far more of its concrete history than in the figural system" (Auerbach, "Figura," in *Scenes from the Drama of European Literature*, trans. Manheim, 55). In general, the Manheim translation reads the "Figura" essay back through *Mimesis*'s concerns with the origins of modern realism, and thereby obscures the separate genealogy of exegesis that Auerbach pursues in the essay.

18. Auerbach, "Figura" (1967), 67.

19. Niklaus Largier, "Allegorie und Figuration: Figuraler Realismus bei Heinrich Seuse und Erich Auerbach," *Paragrana* 21, no. 2 (2012): 42.

practice of *imitatio* in an overwhelmingly absorbing manner."[20] Largier's argument about Suso thus revises Auerbach's genealogy of *figura*, demonstrating the ongoing practice of figural reading in the fifteenth century.

In these terms, then, the realizing imagination is the inventive faculty by which the multidimensional, textured, sensual experience of concrete historical events is translated into poetic language that then makes those events available to readers for affective, cognitive, and ontological participation. Late medieval exegesis integrated the literal and spiritual senses, and the realizing imagination similarly integrates sensual details, ideas, and spiritual realities with the lives of the imagining writers and readers. By analogy to Michelle Karnes's argument concerning Will's use of imagination in *Piers Plowman*, the *Patience*-Poet and his readers can "unite the spiritual to the natural so firmly that the spiritual simply becomes natural, [and they] simply live biblical narrative."[21] As I argue at the end of the chapter, this stylistic analysis of theological exegesis also applies to humanist and Protestant theories of biblical paraphrase and retellings of the Jonah story. What medieval scholars have recognized as the *Patience*-Poet's realizing imagination persists into the Reformation, and it conserves a tropological understanding of how writers and readers can participate in biblical history. These comparisons allow us to reassess genealogies of exegesis that identify Reformation valorizations of the literal sense as fatal ruptures, and they suggest new ways to situate realistic biblical narrative in early modern literature. The Protestant tropological theory that informs this continuity will be taken up in further detail in chapter 5.

How to Invent History: Amplification and the Literal Sense

Like many fish stories, the biblical story of Jonah gets bigger in *Patience*, swelling from around a thousand words, in the Vulgate version, to well

---

20. Ibid., 43–45.

21. Michelle Karnes, *Imagination, Meditation, and Cognition in the Middle Ages* (Chicago: University of Chicago Press, 2011), 179–80.

over four thousand. Scholars have long inquired about the poet's methods and resources for this expansion. Where do the extra words come from? Early source criticism turned up a range of analogues in patristic and early medieval exegesis and in late Latin literature.[22] Several readers have pointed to the traditions of homiletic manuals and aids as reference points for the poem's structure and model of amplification.[23] But although no reader can miss the poem's few but strategic Christological markers, which invite a comparison between Christ and Jonah, no one has seen exegetical habits as the inventive impetus for the *Patience*-Poet's amplification.

In the Bible, the whole story of Jonah occupies four short chapters. *Patience* retains the chapter divisions, marking them out in the manuscript with decorated initials. But *Patience* magnifies or amplifies each element of the story roughly by a factor of four. The scale of amplification can be judged by comparing *Patience* to the biblical account of Jonah being swallowed by the whale: "Now the Lord prepared a great fish to swallow up Jonah: and Jonah was in the belly of a fish for three days and three nights" (Jon. 2:1). That's it: one verse. An additional eight verses report Jonah's prayer from within the fish's belly, upon which we are told, "And the Lord spoke to the fish: and it vomited out Jonah upon the dry land" (2:11). These two verses bookend chapter 2 of Jonah.

The *Patience*-Poet's version, in contrast, runs as follows:

A wylde walterande whal, as Wyrde þen schaped,
Þat watz beten fro þe abyme, bi þat bot flotte,
And watz war of þat wyȝe þat þe water soȝte,
And swyftely swenged hym to swepe, and his swolȝ opened;
Þe folk ȝet haldande his fete, þe fysch hym tyd hentes;

---

22. For surveys of sources and analogues scholarship, see Newhauser, "Sources II"; William Vantuono, "The Structure and Sources of *Patience*," *Medieval Studies* 34 (1972): 401–21; and Francis Cairns, "Latin Sources and Analogues of the Middle English *Patience*," *Studia Neophilologica* 59 (1987): 7–18.

23. See especially Charles Moorman, "The Role of the Narrator in *Patience*," *Modern Philology* 61 (1963): 90–95; and Vantuono, "The Structure and Sources of *Patience*."

Withouten towche of any tothe he tult in his þrote.
Thenne he swengez and swayues to þe se boþem,
Bi mony rokkez ful roȝe and rydelande strondes,
Wyth þe mon in his mawe malskred in drede.

(247–55)

The Bible gives us myth, while the *Patience*-Poet's mimetic detail
verges on realism.[24] The fish of the Bible is *dag gadol*, a great fish without species, but one associated in the ninth-century Rabbinic commentary *Pirke de-Rabbi Eliezer* with Leviathan, that creature of primal chaos
who in the Babylonian creation myth *Enuma Elish* merges with the god-
dess of the sea, Tiamat, representing prime matter and prime chaos.[25]
The biblical account is designed to convey existential truth without historical verisimilitude. One could say that the Bible, by portraying the
great fish in two brief, mythical sentences, gives us the truth *of* the story,
rather than the truth *about* the story.

Not so in *Patience*, where the fish has the species of whale—and a
whale with foresight and intention, who propels himself up from the
deep (note the reflexive "swenged hym" [250]) and floats beside the ship,
waiting for Jonah. And now time freezes, and we see Jonah in a threshold moment between ship and whale's belly, with the alliteration accentuating the three points of contact: folk, feet, and fish. With the folk still
holding his feet, the fish snatches him away. Then the pace speeds back
up and the next line replays the same scene in fast motion: "Withouten
towche of any tothe he tult in his þrote" (252). As the whale takes Jonah
away, we watch him wend his way to the bottom of the ocean. *Patience*
supplies ample truths *about* the story.

---

24. By "myth" I mean a mode of narrative that conveys not history as sci-
entifically verifiable data, but "a 'true story' . . . that is a most precious possession because it is sacred, exemplary, significant . . . [and] gives meaning and
value to life." Mircea Eliade, *Myth and Reality*, trans. Willard R. Trask (New
York: Harper and Row, 1963), 1.

25. Emil G. Hirsch, Karl Budde, and Solomon Schechter, eds., *Jewish Encyclopedia* (New York: Funk and Wagnalls, 1906), s.v. "Jonah."

Why this transformation from myth to realistic description? Critics have often answered similar questions with reference to the poem's generic frame. This is a poem that seems to begin as a sermon on the virtue of patience. But *Patience* actually has little in common with the homiletic tradition.[26] A frequent attendee at Mass in late-fourteenth-century England would think the poem an odd homily. For one thing, she might never have heard a homily on the most wondrous part of the story—the part about Jonah and the whale. Although a lesson from Jonah was appointed in the Sarum rite for Monday in Passion Week, it concerned the conversion of the Ninevites, and it was the only reading from Jonah in the church year.[27] Clergy or parishioners with good Latin might pick up on the reference to Jonah's figural resurrection from the whale in Adam of St. Victor's sequence hymn for Easter Monday,[28] and mothers might cherish the reference to Jonah in the collect for a woman with child,[29] but otherwise the book of Jonah was never encountered in the liturgy, much less preached on. Even these liturgical references probably owe more to Jesus' remarks about the "sign of Jonah" in Matthew 12:38–41 than they do to the Old Testament book of the minor prophet. But even the Matthean Jonah passage received relatively little attention in vernacular sermons. Of some fifteen hundred extant Middle English

---

26. For studies that emphasize the dissimilarities with homiletic literature, see Ordelle G. Hill, "The Audience of 'Patience,'" *Modern Philology* 66, no. 2 (1968): 103–9; and Ad Putter, *An Introduction to the "Gawain"-Poet* (New York: Longman, 1996), 103–16.

27. J. Wickham Legg, ed., *The Sarum Missal: Edited from Three Early Manuscripts* (Oxford: Clarendon Press, 1916), 87.

28. John B. Friedman, "Figural Typology in the Middle English *Patience*," in *The Alliterative Tradition in the Fourteenth Century*, ed. Bernard S. Levy and Paul E. Szarmach (Kent, OH: Kent State University Press, 1981), 103.

29. "O God, Who didst sanctify the blessed Virgin-Mother, Mary, both in her conception and delivery; and by Thy mighty power didst deliver Jonah from the whale's belly, protect Thy servant who is great with child, and visit her with Thy salvation that the child she beareth may be safely delivered, and may attain unto the grace of the laver of salvation." A. Harford Pearson, ed., *The Sarum Missal Done into English*, 2nd ed. (London: The Church Printing Company, 1884), 567.

sermons, only four cite the Matthew passage and none the comparable Luke 11:29–32, while of eleven sermons that mention Jonah, only two consider him in relation to Christ.[30] So even if *Patience* is considered a homily, it would be the only extant vernacular homily that considers both Jonah's relationship to Christ and the Ninevites' repentance; the only homily to take the Jonah story as an occasion to talk about poverty and patience; and the only homily to avoid direct reference to the liturgical seasons of Easter and Lent.

A reader surprised by the choice of text would be even more surprised by the style of the narrative that follows the sixty-line homiletic introduction. The narrator or preacher sets up the Jonah story as an *exemplum*, a little story inserted into a sermon to illustrate the theme. *Exempla* were the bread and butter of vernacular preaching. As Robert of Basevorn puts it in his vastly influential preaching manual of 1322, "The third way of reasoning is by example; this avails much with lay people who are pleased with examples."[31] But Robert advises preachers to use at least *three* examples in a sermon, each of which supports the threefold subdivision of the theme. "Amplification" as a technical rhetorical tactic, then, means the ordered division and subdivision of a threefold theme set out at the beginning of the sermon. For example, a preacher might divide the theme of patience into (1) our patience toward others, (2) our patience toward external adversities, and (3) God's patience toward us. Another way to amplify a theme is to divide it

---

30. For this analysis I have consulted the indices in Veronica O'Mara and Suzanne Paul, eds., *A Repertorium of Middle English Prose Sermons*, 4 vols. (Turnhout: Brepols, 2007). The two Christological sermons are a Wycliffite sermon for Feria 4 in Week 1 of Lent, in Anne Hudson and Pamela Gradon, eds., *English Wycliffite Sermons* (Oxford: Clarendon Press, 1983), 3:74–76; and an Easter Day sermon translated from the twelfth-century Latin *Filius matris* sermon cycle and found in London, British Library, MS Harley 2276 (see O'Mara and Paul, eds., *Repertorium*, 2:1268–70). The other nine sermons that mention Jonah all concern Lent, fasting, and how to avert judgment by repentance.

31. Robert of Basevorn, *Forma praedicandi*, trans. Leopold Krul, in *Three Medieval Rhetorical Arts*, ed. James J. Murphy (Tempe: Arizona Center for Medieval and Renaissance Studies, 2001), 114–215; quotation at 182.

according to its allegorical, tropological, and anagogical senses. But although the poem does function allegorically and tropologically, it never directly allegorizes Jonah as a Christ figure in the manner of the *Biblia pauperum* (see fig. 2.1) or countless historiated initials to the "Jonah Psalm," Psalm 68.[32] The marginal gloss to the *Biblia pauperum* illustration ends with the statement, "Jonah, who after three days emerged from the fish, figured Christ, who after three days emerged from the tomb and resurrected." The *Patience*-Poet, however, conspicuously avoids explicit Christological allegory such as this (although, as we shall see, he invests in more oblique, ironic correspondences). He is much more concerned with the literal-historical sense of Jonah. So instead of following any of the rhetorical and homiletic guidelines for amplification, the *Patience*-Poet simply launches into a lengthy exemplum. How, then, does he invent so much new material, if not by following a conventional sermon format and not by allegorical amplification? Where do the more than three thousand extra words come from?

I propose that the extra words come from a habit of literal and tropological invention native to the biblical commentary tradition, and that this habit is developed in *Patience* in order to allow the writer and readers to participate in the narrative. I will show in some detail how the *Patience*-Poet accomplishes this aim. But first, some examples from the biblical commentary tradition are pertinent.

Patience and the *Glossa ordinaria*

The *Glossa ordinaria* was the most widely used edition of the Bible in the later Middle Ages and well into the sixteenth century. This was the form in which the educated elite most commonly encountered the Bible, and the commentary element of it was the "Gloss" to which theologians as diverse as Thomas Aquinas, Bonaventure, John Wyclif,

---

32. On illuminations of Psalm 68, see Prior, *The Fayre Formez of the Pearl Poet*, 86–91. On other related iconography, see Friedman, "Figural Typology in the Middle English *Patience*."

Fig. 2.1. Biblia pauperum, London, British Library, Kings MS 5 (Netherlands, c. 1405), fol. 20, detail. Reprinted under a Creative Commons license by the kind permission of The British Library. http://www.bl.uk/catalogues/illuminatedmanu scripts/.

and Martin Luther habitually referred. A school of scholars gathered around Anselm of Laon compiled the Gloss around 1100 from patristic authorities, the text was fairly well-established by 1140, and by 1200, portions of the *Glossa* were in every European monastic and scholastic library.[33]

---

33. The best introduction to the *Glossa ordinaria* is Lesley Smith, *The "Glossa ordinaria."* This paragraph is adapted from the introduction to my translation of the *Glossa ordinaria* on Jonah, from which I take all quotations in this chapter: "The Ordinary Gloss on Jonah," *PMLA* 128, no. 2 (2013): 424–38.

There is substantial evidence that the *Patience*-Poet was deeply familiar with the *Glossa ordinaria* on Jonah. William Vantuono has argued that the poet knew Jerome's commentary on Jonah because he appears to be aware of Jerome's Latin translation of the Septuagint when he describes Jonah's response to the forgiveness of Nineveh.[34] Jonah 4:1 in the Vulgate reads, "Et afflictus est Ionas afflictione magna, et iratus est" (And Jonah was exceedingly troubled, and was angry), while Jerome's translation of the Septuagint reads, "Et contristatus est Ionas tristitia grandi et confusus est" (And Jonah was exceedingly grieved, and was confounded).[35] Verses 4 and 9 also present the *iratus*/*contristatus* option. The *Patience*-Poet manages to render both emotions in the poem's fourth division, which corresponds to the fourth chapter of Jonah. Immediately after he learns that God has forgiven Nineveh, we find a rough paraphrase of Jonah 4:1: "Muche sorȝe þenne satteled vpon segge Jonas; / He wex as wroth as þe wynde towarde oure Lorde" (409–10). Later, after his woodbine is destroyed, Jonah "weped for sorȝe; / With hatel anger and hot, heterly he callez" (480–81). The poet, Vantuono argues, "reveals his protagonist's great conflict by portraying the prophet's grief in union with his displeasure. It is a double emotion, with the stress on anguish rather than on anger alone."[36] The Vulgate's 4:1 also presents a double emotion, but Vantuono is right that God's subsequent admonitions in verses 4 and 9 choose to focus on Jonah's anger rather than his grief. *Patience* maintains the complexity of Jonah's emotional state throughout the poem's fourth division. This strongly suggests that the poet was aware of the Septuagint translation.

But it is more likely that the poet was aware of the Septuagint and Jerome's Latin rendering of it through the *Glossa ordinaria* than that he had access to Jerome's commentary on Jonah. The *Glossa* on Jonah and

---

34. Vantuono, "The Structure and Sources of *Patience*," 416–18.

35. Jerome, *Commentarium in Ionam*, in *Commentarii in prophetas minores*, ed. M. Adriaen, CCSL 76 (Turnhout: Brepols, 1969), 411. For my English translation of Jerome's Septuagint Latin, I adopt the Douay-Rheims translations of *contristatus* and *confusus* in other passages (e.g., 2 Sam. 13:21 and Isa. 33:9).

36. Vantuono, "The Structure and Sources of *Patience*," 417.

the other minor prophets derives almost exclusively from Jerome's commentary.[37] The *Glossa*, by selecting from and condensing Jerome, maintains Jonah's emotional complexity even more than Jerome, whose brief remarks about Jonah's interior disposition are scattered among a diverse range of other considerations, including a polemic about the proper Latin word for the "woodbine." The *Glossa*, by contrast, offers a sustained reading of Jonah's anger and suffering on its own terms and as an allegorical prefiguration of Christ's distress in the Garden of Gethsemane. The outer gloss on 4:1 reads,

> **And Jonah was tormented** [*Et afflictus est*]: He is not grieved [*contristatur*] that a great number of the Gentiles are being saved, but that he sees his own people perish, and he, chosen out of such a great number of prophets, who announced the ruin of his own people through the salvation of others, is now in a certain way despairing of the salvation of Israel. Thus the Lord wept over Jerusalem, and he did not want to cast the bread of the children [to the dogs] [Matt. 15:26, Mark 7:27].[38]

The gloss smoothly reads "contristatur" for "afflictus," tacitly accepting Jerome's pronouncement that the words are interchangeable.[39] And just as *Patience* extends Jonah's grief to other circumstances besides the Ninevites' forgiveness, so does the *Glossa* use *tristitia* to connect Jonah's request that God take his life to Jesus' ordeal in the Garden of Gethsemane. The interlinear gloss above 4:3 ("And now, O Lord, I beseech thee take my life from me") reads, "My soul is sorrowful [*tristis*] even unto death," and, again, "Into your hands, Lord, I commend my spirit."

---

37. I have found only two glosses on Jonah that I cannot trace back to Jerome's commentary as edited in Adriaen's CCSL edition.

38. McDermott, "The Ordinary Gloss on Jonah," 436.

39. "Verbum Hebraicum hadra lach, et iratus es tu, et contristatus es tu, transferri potest" (the Hebrew word *hadra lach*, [the Vulgate's] *you are angry*, and [the Septuagint's] *you are grieved*, are interchangeable). Jerome, *Commentarium in Ionam*, 412.

Two more glosses move easily back and forth between anger and grief, but this should suffice to show that the *Patience*-Poet probably encountered the complex sense of Jonah's emotions conveyed by the two alternative Latin translations in the *Glossa ordinaria*.

The *Ductus* of the *Glossa ordinaria*

In the *Glossa ordinaria* on Jonah, literal-historical exegesis and allegorical exegesis animate each other. Here we are light-years away from the mechanistic "levels" of scripture that many literary scholars once imagined as fourfold exegesis. Instead of a schematic semiosis where the literal sense = x and the allegorical sense = y, the *Glossa ordinaria* sets historical and figural reading in productive oscillation. A good example of this is the opening of Jonah, displayed here in my adaptation of Adolf Rusch's printed *editio princeps* of 1480/81 (fig. 2.2). It presents a typical arrangement of large-point biblical text and smaller-point commentary in a mutually informative tension. Outer glosses are keyed to the main text by large-point lemmas—quotations from the biblical text—and often concern large themes or narrative movements, while interlinear glosses hover above the line and tend to comment on individual words or phrases.

The large drop cap begins the first words of Jonah, "And the word of the Lord was made to Jonah." In the outer gloss area, there are two glosses (callouts 1 and 2) on the first word, "And," explaining both the source of the author's invention and the odd stylistic quirk of beginning with a conjunction. The first gloss reads, "**And**: To those things that were being revolved in the mind of the prophet by the Spirit is joined this conjunction—namely, *and*." The second gloss reads, "**And the word of the Lord was made**: Seeing many things in the Spirit, as is the custom of a prophet, concerning these many things, he bursts forth into these words." We should note that these are historical-critical comments. Like modern-day form critics in biblical studies, the glossator determines the context of composition, its *Sitz im Leben*—in this case, a prophetic ecstasy—in order to explicate the passage's form and style and find clues about its purpose.

¶Jonah the dove and the grieving son of Amathi who was from Gath which is in Ofir is sent to proclaim to the Gentiles. Having been sent, he scorns; scorning, he flees; fleeing, he sleeps. Because of him, the ship is imperiled. But the lot reveals him lying hidden. The whale devoured him after he had been cast out, and spewed him back as he was praying. Having been thrown back, he preached destruction. But he is saddened by the repentance of the city, and he begrudges the salvation of the Gentiles. He even enjoys a bower of green ivy, and he is pained by its sudden withering. He even is pointed out in one of the cities of Gath, in a hamlet that is at the second milestone on the road to Sepphoris, on the road by which he goes to Tiberias.

¶No one is a better interpreter of a type of himself than he who inspired the prophets and guided them along certain lines, as it were, of the truth that would

¶And: To those things that were being revolved in the mind of the prophet by the Spirit is joined this conjunction—namely, *and*.

1

that had been announced against Nineveh to be revoked. What happened to Jonah also had happened to Saint Elisha, who did not recognize the son of the Sunamite woman as dead [2 Kings 4]. So Jonah, having suffered something human, thought that he would flee from the sight of God, saying with David, *"Where shall I go away from your spirit, and where shall I flee from your face?"* [Ps. 138.7].

¶The argument begins

Jonah the beautiful dove, prefiguring the passion of the Lord by his shipwreck, calls the world back to repentance, and he announces salvation for the Gentiles under the name of "Nineveh."

Chapter 1

And the word of the Lord was

* Christ, over whom the Spirit in the appearance of a dove [appeared], who also is suffering on our behalf.
‡ Of truth; God is truth.
§ The Father to the Son.

3
4
5

made to Jonah† the son of ‡Amathi, saying§ 2 "Arise and go into Nineveh, the great city,

come to be among his own servants—who spoke to the Jews who did not know Christ the son of God. *"The men of Nineveh will rise on Judgment Day with this generation and condemn it because they did penance at the preaching of Jonah. And behold one greater than Jonah is here"* [Matt. 12.41]. The carnal Jew is condemned by the believing world and perishes, unbelieving, even as Nineveh is doing penance.

¶And the word of the Lord was made: Seeing many things in the Spirit, as is the custom of a prophet, concerning these many things, he bursts forth into these words. 2

¶City: The world. So that the whole world might accept what the Jew despises. This [world] that God made as if a beautiful house so that he should be served by man, who, because he wandered away through pride, is called back to repentance.

¶Jonah, which means "dove," is sent to Nineveh, which is said to be splendid. Thus Christ, full of the Holy Spirit, is sent to the world, which is called in the Greek tongue "cosmos," that is, ordered and beautiful, because of the design of the Creator. Whence *God saw all the things that he had made, and they were very good* [Gen. 1.31]. Therefore the whole world praises him whom Israel despises so that

the humble man, having put down corrupting pride, might ascend into heaven by the Son of God descending.

¶Although Jonah, according to the interpretation, displays the figure of Christ himself, it is not necessary for us to strive to refer the whole sequence of the story to Christ by allegory, but only those things that are able to be understood clearly without the risk of interpretation. For just because the apostle says that in our first parents the sacrament of Christ and the Church is prefigured [Eph. 5.32], not all things that are

Fig. 2.2. Translation of the first page of the *Glossa ordinaria* on Jonah set in modern typeface, emulating the Rusch 1480/81 *editio princeps*. Originally published in McDermott, "The Ordinary Gloss on Jonah."

Moving into the interlinear gloss, we find lexical commentary on single words and names. The gloss above the name "Jonah" (gloss 3) reads, "Christ, over whom the Spirit in the appearance of a dove [appeared], who also is suffering on our behalf." The preface to the book has already told us that "Jonah" means dove, but here that meaning takes on an oblique relationship to Jonah's more direct allegorical correspondence to Christ. If we tease out precisely how this relationship is oblique, we will get a better sense of how the various sites of the page function together. In gloss 4 we are told that "Amathi" means "truth" because "God is truth." Like so many thousands of moments of interpretation in the *Glossa ordinaria*, this little gloss compresses an elaborate etymology that unfolds to prove Jonah's allegorical correspondence to Christ. It goes like this: Jonah is the son of Amathi; Amathi means truth; God is truth; therefore Jonah is the son of God; therefore Jonah corresponds to Christ, who is the true Son of God. Furthermore, the interlinear gloss on "saying," (gloss 5)—"the Father to the Son"—reminds us of Christ's baptism when the Father speaks to the Son. In the Gospel narratives, the Holy Spirit hovered over Christ in the form of a dove at Christ's baptism when the word of the Father came to him saying, "This is my beloved son, in whom I am well pleased" (Matt. 3:17). It is fitting, then, that the gloss on the word "saying" reads, "The Father to the Son." The word of the Lord that comes to Jonah allegorically corresponds to the word of the Father coming to the Son at his baptism. And in that Trinitarian tableau, the dove takes on the function of the Spirit. These associations send us back to the outer glosses 1 and 2, where the Spirit is revolving ideas in the mind of the prophet: for Jonah, the idea is to go to Nineveh and preach a forty days' fast, while for Jesus at his baptism, the idea is to go out into the wilderness and undergo a forty days' fast. Inner and outer gloss interact with the biblical text in such a way that no one of the three parts can convey its full meaning on its own.

In order to produce this rich exegesis, the glossator employs a knowledge of Hebrew, a form-critical hypothesis about the scene of composition, grammatical understanding of the function of conjunctions, intertextual verbal concordance between Old and New Testaments, and Christian allegory that assumes a mutually causal historical correspondence between Jonah and Christ and the two events of their prophetic vocations. This all adds up to a complex theological thought machine that depends on the physical layout of the page to lead readers from center to periphery, from main text to commentary, and back again.

Such lively allegorical thought has something in common with *Patience*'s energies, but not in a straightforward manner. Much closer to the mode of invention we find in *Patience* is another kind of gloss, that is, another of the many modes of commentary that make up the *Glossa ordinaria*. An interlinear gloss on Jonah 1:5 invents literal description in order to comment on the literal-historical sense of the text. The biblical text reads, "And the sailors were afraid, . . . and they threw the wares that were in the ship into the sea to lighten it of them." In case we were wondering why sailors would throw their cargo overboard, the Bible tells us that they did so to relieve the ship of its weight in a mighty tempest. But this is not enough for the glossator. Between the lines he adds, "So that it might leap more lightly across the waves."

This kind of gloss can be bewildering because it seems literally redundant. What does it add to our reading of the text? If we were completely ignorant of nautical physics, it might help us to understand the connection between a ship's weight and its ability to stay afloat. But surely that misses the point. It seems rather that the glossator takes the Bible's reason and converts it into a kinetic image. He takes the literal sense of the text and embellishes it with more literal detail purely for the sake of imaginative participation.

These inventive glosses are not always so redundant. Another interlinear gloss on the sailors' dumping of cargo adds a stroke of dramatic irony: "Thinking that the ship is weighed down by its customary freight, [the sailors] do not know that the entire weight is that of the fugitive prophet" (Jon. 1:5). Such a gloss establishes no allegorical correspondences; it serves no theological purpose. But it does participate in the making of narrative, in the invention of the literal sense of the story for the sake of that peculiar *Schadenfreudliche* pleasure-effect we call dramatic irony. Or again, a great tempest has been raised in the sea, and the interlinear gloss intensifies the sense of supernatural surprise by adding, "when just before everything had been calm" (Jon. 1:4). This glossator has a knack for detail, for that slight embellishment brings the scene to life. He likes to get in on the action. He likes to cooperate in the invention of a good work.

So does the *Patience*-Poet. Earlier I discussed how he amplified the Bible's single verse about the whale swallowing Jonah. Let us look closer at another amplification of that scene, in order to specify how the poet's particular mode of literal invention enables him to participate ethically in the same history of salvation. After musing on Jonah's bewilderment for eight lines, the poem circles back for another description, this time refracted through Jonah's perspective.

> For he knew vche a cace and kark þat hym lymped,
> How fro þe bot into the blober watz with a best lachched,
> And þrwe in at hit þrote withouten þret more,
> As mote in at a munster dor, so mukel wern his chawlez.
> He glydes in by þe giles thurȝ glaym ande glette,
> Relande in by a rop, a rode þat hym þoȝt,
> Ay hele ouer hed hourlande aboute,
> Til he blunt in a blok as brod as a halle;
> And þer he festnes þe fete and fathmez aboute,
> And stod vp in his stomak þat stank as þe deuel.
> Þer in saym and in sorȝe that sauoured as helle,
> Þer watz bylded his bour þat wyl no bale suffer.
> And þenne he lurkkes and laytes where watz le best,
> In vche a nok of his nauel, bot nowhere he fyndez
> No rest ne recouerer bot ramel ande myre,
> In wych gut so euer he gotz – bot euer is God swete.

(265–80)

This is narrative invention for the sake of participation, and it is a fascinating example of the bizarre descriptive and narrative detail that tropological invention can often produce. The narrator told his audience at the outset that he himself wants to learn patience to endure his material poverty: "syn I am put to a poynt that poverté hatte, / I schal me poruay pacyence and play me with boþe" (35–36). Now his own action of invention merges with Jonah's actions in the belly of the whale. The verb that describes Jonah's looking around down there—"layten"— literally means to illuminate, to shine. Here it is used figuratively, and we can imagine Jonah shining his glance around. But Jonah himself has no light; he is, as it says earlier, "waltering in derk" (151). While Jonah "laytes" (277) figuratively in one sense, the poet figuratively illuminates Jonah's darkness in another sense, describing visual, tactile, and olfactory details of the action. We see the whale *snatching* Jonah. Jonah *glides* through its mouth like a dust mote through a cathedral door, tumbling down an intestine like a road. The narrator cooperates with Jonah, supplying him with first-person impressions. As he anatomizes the whale's innards—gills, guts, stomach cavern, nook of the navel, mucus, digestive juices (he names all of these)—he effectively "fathmez aboute" (273) with an anatomical precision that Jonah could not have had himself. Poet and reader suffer the noxious muck vicariously, but with a kind of delight—a simultaneous taste for the sweetness of God—that exhibits the virtue of patience.

This delighted participatory suffering in part causes the literal details to proliferate. The logic of the alliterative line helps here. In order to make alliteration work, poets need synonyms on the tips of their tongues that produce the right sounds at the right part of the line. The poet needs to be able to say "slime" in a line that alliterates on *gl-* sounds, so he says "glaym" (269). Alliterative invention already has verbal proliferation built into it. Working in the other direction, a series of alliterating word choices can suggest further words—words that might even be literally redundant. In this line, "glaym" seems to produce "glet," and there is very little lexical difference between the two words: the poet might have said "slimy slime." Like the *Glossa ordinaria*, which produces redundancies in order to intensify or appreciate or heighten or ironize the effects of literal narrative, *Patience*'s alliterative logic amplifies the text not by interpreting it, but by cooperating with it to make more action, more detail, and more of a good work.

There is an analogy to salvation at work here. In the classical Augustinian doctrines of grace and virtue, every good work involves cooperation between the agent and God, who enables the agent to do the work by a gift of grace. In this transaction, no gift changes hands if the agent does not work with the gift that God has given in doing a good work. Thus the gift of grace does not exist until the agent does something with it, yet the gift of grace is always prior to the work it enables. The *Patience*-Poet's and the glossator's mode of participatory invention of literal detail follows a similar logic. In medieval Latin, *inventio* means both "to discover" and "to make." When the *Patience*-Poet eschews theological commentary in order simply to accept the gift of literal detail, he discovers that detail by making a new work, a cooperative invention that receives the grace of the literal sense in the same movement of further literary production. And that act of production, which the poet identifies as his attempt to "play me with [pacience]," constitutes a real historical event. It becomes part of the fabric of the same history in which the events of that ship and those sailors and that God-haunted prophet participated. And so, in the end, this act of literary invention according to the literal sense is also allegorical because it involves crucial events in the history of salvation. And it is tropological because it allows the narrator to "play" himself with patience.

When I assert that the *Patience*-Poet's and the glossator's inventions are allegorical, I mean that their own actions stand in a mutually causal relation to salvation history in much the same way that Jesus' resurrection participated in and embellished Jonah's emergence from the whale's belly. Emmanuel Lévinas proposed a similar metaphysics of texts in his philosophy of revelation. He famously equated the exegesis of the Hebrew Bible with ethics, for "it is as an ethical kerygma that the Bible is Revelation," that is, the opening up of the wholly transcendent, infinitely Other to human participation.[40] I turn to Lévinas not because he speaks for Middle English writers, but because he helpfully reorients our assumptions about the ontology of texts and what is at stake when writers read and readers write. Lévinas reports a rabbi who said that "the slightest question put to the schoolmaster by a novice constitutes an ineluctable articulation of the Revelation which was heard at Sinai. The individual person, unique in his historical position, is called upon: this means no less than that the Revelation requires History."[41]

Revelation requires history and individual people for its articulation. That is a good explanation of the kind of participatory invention

---

40. Emmanuel Lévinas, "Revelation in the Jewish Tradition," in *The Lévinas Reader*, ed. Seán Hand (Malden, MA: Blackwell, 1999), 207.

41. Ibid., 195.

we find in both the *Glossa ordinaria* and *Patience*. This invention presupposes a real metaphysical and historical continuum in which people and events synchronically depend on and touch upon each other, and texts are themselves meaningful events in which temporally far-flung people and communities can collaborate to make history and invent themselves by receiving the gift of others.

These might seem bold overtures for an argument about literal-historical exegesis, since we commonly imagine the literal sense as exegesis's destination *after* allegory. I do not dispute that the history of exegesis moved in this direction; the relative proportions of allegorical to philological commentary shifted drastically between, say, 1300 and 1700, even in mainstream Roman Catholic exegesis. But I am proposing that we reassess our understanding of how the literal sense in its various modes and literal-historical exegesis relate to the spiritual senses and theological exegesis. In what follows, I argue that Nicholas of Lyra, famous for championing the literal sense, understood the literal sense to be always already allegorical. Even for Nicholas, literal-historical exegesis can be more open to the spirit than often has been supposed. More importantly for literary history, I am arguing that if, as is commonly assumed, realistic description and literal detail as representational modes correspond to an exegetical preference for the literal sense, then the *Patience*-Poet's peculiar brand of realism is one that always already contains within it an allegorical impulse—which is one reason why the Jonah of *Patience* can be a comically real, sympathetic character and a figure of Christ at the same time.

Nicholas of Lyra, the Literal Sense of Scripture, and the Spiritual Sense of the Letter

I have argued that theories and practices of moral or tropological interpretation of the Bible could and did generate habits of literary invention that were not beholden to the recommendations of the rhetorical and homiletic traditions, and modes of literary ethics that were distinct from the discourses of moral theology and philosophy. Here I turn to the literal-historical interpretation of scripture, the "foundational"[42] exposition of "the way the words run"[43] and the "certain things done and undertaken . . . which themselves suggest other meanings to us."[44] A revolution in the theory of the literal sense of scripture took place in the fourteenth century, partly in reaction to the perception of a superfluous and indeed misleading accretion of scholastic interpretive apparatus that obscured the plain sense of the biblical text in its literary context.[45] Meanwhile, the site of the literal sense migrated from scripture's lexis, grammar, and syntax (according to some theorists) and its reference to salvation history (according to others) to the intention of the author. When the author's intention determined the literal sense, scripture, which had human and divine authors, could be understood as having

---

42. Writing circa 1330 in the second prologue to his *Postilla super totam bibliam*, Nicholas of Lyra remarks of prior theorists of exegesis, "All presume the literal sense as a kind of foundation." Nicholas of Lyra, "Second Prologue," *Postilla super totam bibliam*, in A. J. Minnis and A. B. Scott, eds., *Medieval Literary Theory and Criticism, c. 1100–c. 1375: The Commentary Tradition*, rev. ed. (Oxford: Clarendon Press, 1988), 268. Of course, the literal sense could also be figured as an exterior, the cover of a book, or the husk of a kernel, among other images.

43. Eugene Rogers translates Thomas Aquinas's "salva litterae circumstantia" (*De potentia* 4.1.c) as "preserving the way the words run." Rogers, "How the Virtues of an Interpreter Presuppose and Perfect Hermeneutics," 74. Lewis Ayres adopts the formulation to name his theoretical specification of the plain sense as the letter activated in a reading community: "The plain sense is 'the way the words run' for a community in the light of that community's techniques for following the argument of texts. The plain sense is, then, the sense that a text had for a Christian of the period versed in ancient [or medieval] literary critical skills." Lewis Ayres, *Nicaea and Its Legacy: An Approach to Fourth-Century Trinitarian Theology* (New York: Oxford University Press, 2006), 32.

44. Henry of Ghent, *Summae quaestionum ordinarium theologii* 16.7, in Minnis and Scott, *Medieval Literary Theory*, 258.

45. For a concise account of this development, see chapter 7, "The Literal Sense," in G. R. Evans, *The Language and Logic of the Bible: The Road to Reformation* (New York: Cambridge University Press, 1985), 42–65. For a more recent survey that takes into account the crucial issue of conflicting authorities, see Levy, *Reading the Scriptures*, 11–23.

two literal senses. Two authors produce two intentions, and God's intention can be very different from the human intention, as when God intends the words of David, "Thou art my son, this day have I begotten thee" (Ps. 2:7) to apply to the second person of the Trinity (cf. Acts 13:33). This can have the effect of distancing God's literal sense from the human literal sense in a way that a more traditional understanding of the allegorical sense did not.[46]

According to Henri de Lubac's history of medieval exegesis, the fourteenth century marked the tipping point for the disintegration of letter and spirit, of exegesis and theology. The *Postilla super totam bibliam* of the Franciscan Nicholas of Lyra (1270–1349) plays a prominent role in this declension narrative. Nicholas famously, in his theoretical prefaces to the *Postilla*, gave pride of place to the literal sense of scripture. Much later, humanists and reformers cited his soberly literal historical scholarship appreciatively, contrasting it, in Martin Luther's words, to the "beautiful harlot" of allegory.[47] To be sure, by the eighteenth century we can perceive, as Hans Frei argued, an increasing division between the historical sense of scripture and its theological import.[48] For some scholars it is possible to discern even in the fourteenth century, in Matthew Levering's words, a trend "leading to the autonomy of history from theology and thus to a problematic situation for theological exegesis."[49] But as I have argued elsewhere, Nicholas of Lyra was

---

46. On the conflicts the theory could occasion, see Karlfried Froehlich, "'Always to Keep the Literal Sense in Holy Scripture Means to Kill One's Soul': The State of Biblical Hermeneutics at the Beginning of the Fifteenth Century," in *Literary Uses of Typology from the Late Middle Ages to the Present*, ed. Earl Miner (Princeton: Princeton University Press, 1977), 20–48.

47. Cited in Brian Cummings, "Protestant Allegory," in *The Cambridge Companion to Allegory*, ed. Rita Copeland and Peter T. Struck (New York: Cambridge University Press, 2010), 177.

48. Frei, *Eclipse*.

49. Levering, *Participatory Biblical Exegesis*, 45. Levering, however, takes a more cautious line on Nicholas than de Lubac and other mid-twentieth-century scholars, remarking that Nicholas's "commentary is not far from what we found in Aquinas" (40). Levering's careful account of the consequences of

on the other side of this history, and his *Postilla* represents a vigorous and largely successful attempt to *reintegrate* biblical text, historical scholarship, and theological exegesis.[50] For this reason, among many others, new understandings of the literal sense in the fourteenth century did not necessarily distance God's intention from human intentions, nor did a renewed interest in the literal sense necessarily marginalize the spiritual senses.

Nicholas, who was hardly allergic to spiritual exegesis, consistently allegorizes and unfailingly offers a tropological exposition of every passage in the *Postilla moralis*, a companion to the *Postilla literalis*. In his commentary on Jonah, for instance, he reflects throughout on Jonah's allegorical correspondence to Christ, supplementing traditional glosses with lexical and theological readings from Rashi. His moral exegesis frequently draws on insights from the literal commentary, as when he identifies the meaning of Tharsis as "joy." Morally, Nicholas observes, the ship bound for "joy" that takes Jonah on board can be understood as people who take a traveling preacher into their home so that he might escape the delights of the world. Continuing the moral association with preaching, Nicholas claims that the great wind is the spirit of contrition roused by a good preacher showing people their sins, whereupon they are thrown into the sea of bitter penance, but do not drown because the fish, who signifies Christ, picks them up.[51] Even if he does not explicitly theorize it here, Nicholas is practicing a literal-historical exegesis that is thoroughly spiritual. His actual exegesis defies narratives that identify him as the pivot of a great shift away from spiritual exegesis and toward a literal-historical exegesis that is autonomous from theology.[52]

---

these developments in modernity helps us better to envision what repair might look like.

50. McDermott, "Henri de Lubac's Genealogy of Modern Exegesis."

51. Glosses on Jon. 1:3–4. I have consulted the *Postilla* printed in *Biblia latina cum Glossa ordinaria*, 6 vols. (Venice, 1603).

52. This point is made repeatedly by the fine studies of Nicholas's exegetical practice in Philip D. W. Krey and Lesley Janette Smith, eds., *Nicholas of Lyra: The Senses of Scripture* (Leiden: Brill, 2000).

Patience is an important text in this history because it exhibits a literary working out of what Christopher Ocker has identified as the fourteenth-century "integration of literal and spiritual meanings in exegesis."[53] The literal turn, he argues, did nothing to diminish spiritual exegesis among scholastics; rather, it shifted the theoretical locus of spiritual interpretation away from a universe of things outside the merely referential Bible and toward the language, the letter, of the Bible itself, by means of a new theory of "verbal signification" developed most comprehensively and influentially by Thomas Aquinas.[54]

> In the late Middle Ages, biblical readers tended to locate the experience of revelation in the text itself . . . ; but this included a tendency, seen in many commentaries, to put spiritual meaning in a literal framework. The distinction between literal and spiritual began to break down, which is to say scholars believed that the ability of the text to excite, to cause insight, and to overwhelm the reader with truth was intrinsic to the letter. The Bible became more like poetry.[55]

Ocker thus provides corroborating evidence for James Simpson's argument that, despite changing theories of the literal sense, two contrasting theories of how literal and spiritual exegesis relate, "one 'orthodox' and the other evangelical, run parallel across this entire period" of pre- and post-Reformation England.[56] In the fourteenth century, Aquinas's and Bonaventure's view "that spiritual meaning is intrinsic to the literal sense" took hold in a wide range of exegesis across Christian Eu-

---

53. Ocker, *Biblical Poetics*, 42. The next six paragraphs are adapted from McDermott, "Henri de Lubac's Genealogy of Modern Exegesis," 147–50.

54. Ocker, *Biblical Poetics*, 37–43.

55. Ibid., 73.

56. James Simpson, *Reform and Cultural Revolution: 1350–1547*, The Oxford English Literary History 2 (New York: Oxford University Press, 2004), 462.

rope.[57] "The verbal signs of scripture, and not the 'things' indicated by them, are revelatory—as words."[58]

This means that Robert Holcot, in a set of lectures on the Book of Wisdom (c. 1340–42), can read this Old Testament book as if its literal subject were the passion of Christ.[59] To Holcot, Wisdom 2:14, 16, 17, and 19 present intriguing difficulties that he explicitly labels "dubitaciones literales" (uncertainties about the literal sense), by which he means questions about whether the revelation of Christ was secret or given independently, and "just how much the persecuting Jews in the passion narratives knew of Christ's divinity—all allegorical speculations, pertaining to prophecy and to life in the church."[60] To these speculations, Holcot adds "figures," rhetorical embellishments that frame the moral sense of the text but do so in a way that exegetes of previous centuries would have recognized as allegorical. In his commentary on the literal sense of Wisdom 1:11 ("And spare your tongues of belittling, because dark speech will not go into the void"), Holcot understands speech as a figure of the Holy Spirit, and because the Spirit binds Father and Son in Trinitarian friendship, "dark speech" threatens friendship. He then brings forward examples from Martial, the *History of Charlemagne*, and the Bible to illustrate the ethics of friendship. Holcot's figures might seem allegorical to us and to many of his forbears, but he regards them as embellishing the literal sense.[61]

Holcot is engaged in the kind of figural and figurative elaboration of the literal on display in *Patience* in those moments when literal description expands to include oblique Christological allegory. I discuss such moments in more detail below. For both authors, these moral and Christological interpolations can harmonize with literal narrative or commentary because they understand language and history to be sites

---

57. Ocker, *Biblical Poetics*, 68.

58. Ibid., 40.

59. On the date and context of the lectures, see Hester Goodenough Gelber, *It Could Have Been Otherwise: Contingency and Necessity in Dominican Theology at Oxford, 1300–1350* (Leiden: Brill, 2004), 96–98.

60. Ocker, *Biblical Poetics*, 55.

61. Ibid., 54–55.

of equally powerful revelation. Indeed, they understand history and language to be continuous with each other, part of the same world, rather than related to each other merely by a system of reference. They write out of an assumption that "spiritual meaning is intrinsic to the literal sense and manifests, to the intellect, the organic continuity of history and creation."[62]

Because literal and spiritual senses are contiguous and mutually open to each other, the moral sense of a text is intrinsic to the literal sense. Consequently, "moral exegesis is a kind of replication of the literal" and "moral meaning elaborates historical experience."[63] This is not only because the plain sense of a text might be moral (as in the Beatitudes), but because history is always already moral by virtue of its status as "a theatre of divine action";[64] and, conversely, morality is always already historical because it ultimately concerns the itinerary of souls through the created world and its providential order of events on their way to participation in the life of God. On this understanding, poetry is ethical not only because of the particular relations that obtained between grammar, rhetoric, and philosophy in late medieval arts theory, as Judson Boyce Allen has demonstrated,[65] but also because the grammatically, rhetorically, and philosophically accessible literal sense always already implies tropology, understood not simply as a discourse of natural morality, but as a discourse of theological ethics that opens every historical moment to participation in Christ's life, death, and resurrection, and leads the soul to God.

Nicholas of Gorran offers an excellent illustration of how literal, moral, and tropological exegesis can function in tandem, all the while remaining historical and elaborating the literal sense. Nicholas is explaining how God's theophany in the burning bush is different from

---

62. Ibid., 42. Ocker is characterizing Bonaventure's exegetical theology. I argue for a similar understanding of the *De reductione artium ad theologiam* in chapter 1. Ocker's study is especially important for my broader argument because he demonstrates that such a view was fully operational and widely assumed in fourteenth-century exegesis (and well into the sixteenth century).

63. Ibid., 79.

64. Ibid., 80.

65. J. Allen, *The Ethical Poetic of the Later Middle Ages*, 3–66.

the disclosure of the divine nature in the normal experience of God's created effects. He makes this distinction in order to explain why the burning bush is called a "great vision." The commentary that follows is intended to clarify the literal sense of the text:

> *And he* [Moses] *saw that the bush burned, and it was not burned up,* in which is signified that through the flame of affliction the people were not consumed but rather were warmed [that is, encouraged]. Above in chapter 1[:12], "for as much as they [the Egyptians] oppressed, so much they [the Jews] multiplied and grew." Or in this it was signified that God, while existing amidst the Hebrew people in the bush, did not consume in them the thorns of sin, even though he would afflict them like a flame of fire through the oppression of the Egyptians. Or in this it is signified that a law was to be given to the people that would illuminate like a flame, and yet he would consume the thorns of sins by the fire of charity. *Therefore Moses said,* that is he deliberated with himself, *I will hurry,* namely to inquire, *and I will see this great,* that is shown of someone great, *vision,* the miraculous sign, *why the bush is not burned up.* Note that this vision is called great because of the greatness of the mystery. For the fire in the bush is the divinity [of Christ] in the humanity [of his physical body]. John 1[:14], "The Word was made flesh."[66]

The theophany of the burning bush differs from normal communication of God's nature in creatures because God intends it for "some particular person for the showing of some notable effect." This is why it can be called a "great vision." Moses is the particular person, and his historical circumstances—as a member of the enslaved Hebrews—specifies the "notable effect." Namely, the Hebrews' affliction in Egypt would not consume them, even though it would consume their sins. Nicholas tailors the tropological interpretation to the historical moment and assumes that the events of history have a fundamentally moral purpose.

---

66. Nicholas of Gorran, *Postilla super Exodum,* cited in Ocker, *Biblical Poetics,* 81.

In Nicholas's view, there is no gap between the historical and tropological meanings of the text.

We would have good reason, though, to question Nicholas's easy harmonization. Does he not import Christian theology into his tropological interpretation when he says that the Hebrews' sins will be consumed "by the fire of charity"? The lines immediately following the quoted passage leave no doubt: "For the fire in the bush is the divinity in the humanity. John 1[:14], 'the Word was made flesh.'" Yet even this explicitly Christological reading falls under the literal sense for Nicholas because Moses himself could understand the allegorical mystery: "And if it is asked whether Moses might have understood those mysteries, I respond: it is believed that he probably did, just as it is told of Abraham, John 8[:56], 'Abraham exulted that he would see my day,' etc. . . . And note that [God] named him twice [*Moses, Moses*] because he was summoned to a double understanding, namely spiritual and literal."[67] Because the historical Moses was capable of spiritual exegesis, a medieval Christian's allegorical reading of the burning bush is also literal because it coincides with the historical Moses' interpretation. And the moral of the story, which concerns the church's purification by charity through the fires of tribulation, can also be historical, because Moses' history is medieval Christians' history by virtue of their mutual participation in the same history of salvation.[68]

---

67. Ibid., 82.

68. In this respect, I think Ocker inaccurately characterizes Gorrans's reading as "atemporal" and accomplishing a "collapse of time" (*Biblical Poetics*, 81, 80). Far more accurate is his remark further on that "[w]ith the concurrence of historical wills came a particular experience of reading, one in which the reader is invited to return to the great sacred moments of the past and experience them in the present. Literal reading is empathetic. A textual past likewise elevates present experience; Christian beliefs and practices, especially the practice of penance, are ennobled by relocating them in the ancient history of Jews" (ibid., 86). Far from collapsing time, this empathetic literal reading reconfigures the specificity of each respective historical moment, and it is only by virtue of its attention to and preservation of historical difference that it is able to do so.

These exegetical principles, Ocker argues, gave rise to "a textual attitude" that Protestants continued, and that

> consisted of an association of spiritual or ultimate meaning with the literal sense, the communion of (divine and human) writers with (past and present) readers, and a sense of continuity between all religious writers and readers. This attitude assumed a continuity of meaning that extended subjectively and inter-subjectively outside the Bible. The correspondence of literatures, exegetical and doctrinal/dogmatic/philosophical, was based on a conviction of profound similarity, an aesthetic similarity of literatures, a shared biblical poetic. According to that poetic, the external world, and the literal text with it, was seamlessly joined to internal and divine truths in a late medieval reader's experience.[69]

This is a fascinating passage because we can see Ocker sliding from a rearticulation of historical theory and intellectual practice (the large majority of his book) to a description of belief to a statement about experience. Judging at least by the "textual attitude" we encounter in *Patience*, Ocker slides too easily from the intellectual practices of exegesis to poetics and the experiences to which poetry such as *Patience* gives us access. For *Patience* begins precisely at the *poynt* where the internal world conflicts with the external world, and poverty and adversity strain to the breaking point the seams joining divine truths and human experience.

Literal and Allegorical, Inner and Outer, Immanent and Transcendent in *Patience*

If the *Patience*-Poet has a literal imagination, then it is one that opens up the brute facts of linear history to the providential ordering of salvation history, with its meaningful intervals between corresponding

---

69. Ibid., 216.

people, things, and events. He can do this not because he can expect his readers to have an experience of the seamless ordering of history to salvation, but because the theology that underwrites the *Glossa ordinaria*'s inventive exegetical habits provides him with tools to reimagine story and history. He does this in part by dramatizing two related, potential conflicts in fourteenth-century exegetical theory: the conflict between the literal sense and the allegorical senses, and, within the theory of the *duplex sensus litteralis*, the conflict between the intentions of divine and human authors. The poet portrays Jonah's dilemma as a conflict between God's transcendent interests and Jonah's own immanent, historical exigencies. Jonah views God as an indifferent overseer, observing the field from a height, oblivious to the details of the world below. Jonah, meanwhile, responds to the literal details of the present moment, taking advantage of present circumstances to attain immediate satisfaction. God plays the allegorist to Jonah's literalist.

Patience adapts the theology of allegory to set up non-Christological correspondences, manipulating figures of heights and depths, sitting and walking, containment and release, ascent and descent to stage the argument not only between Jonah and God, but also between the literal sense and the spiritual senses—and so to reconcile them. The *Patience*-Poet's project, then, can be read as analogous to the fourteenth-century scholastic project to integrate literal and spiritual senses as well as human and divine authorship.

Details of events in the literal narrative of Jonah's story correspond to each other by analogies that owe something to the structure of mystical allegorical correspondences in salvation history. But first, consider those moments when the poet explicitly draws on allegorical exegesis of the Jonah story. Those moments are important, and I mention them here briefly by way of contrast, before returning to them later.[70] In the passage we have already examined, the remark that the whale's belly "stank as þe deuel. / Þer in saym and in sorȝe that savoured as helle" (274–75) recalls Jesus' own gloss on Jonah: "For as Jonas was

---

70. Most of the patently Christological moments in the poem are discussed in Malcolm Andrew, "Jonah and Christ in 'Patience,'" *Modern Philology* 70, no. 3 (1973): 230–33.

in the whale's belly three days and three nights: so shall the Son of man be in the heart of the earth [*in corde terrae*] three days and three nights" (Matt. 12:40; cf. Luke 11:29–32). Jesus reads Jonah Christologically, anticipating the fulfillment of Jonah's sojourn in the whale in his own descent to the depths of the earth, and now the *Patience*-Poet reads back into Jonah's story the common medieval identification of the *cor terrae* with hell. The "sign of Jonah" (Matt. 12:39) thus becomes the sign of Christ's sojourn in hell and resurrection after three days, and because of Jonah's associations with penance, it is a sign also for conversion: those who see the sign should heed Christ's preaching and do penance (Matt. 12:41). Then there is the Christological pun on *rode* (road or cross) with which the chapter opened (93–96). The prophet Jonah, it seems, cannot help being prophetic, and he does so at a moment of high dramatic irony, as A.C. Spearing notes: "By reminding us of the standard of which Jonah is so miserably falling short, the allusion serves to belittle him still further."[71] Jonah alternately prefigures and parodies Christ in his refusal to travel the *rode* of the *rode*.

The pun on *rode* relies on Christological allegory to achieve the effect of dramatic irony, but most of the poem's other allegorical moments do not invest their entire significance in allegory to achieve their effects. We read that the whale's belly "stank as þe deuel" (274), and we immediately take the colloquial remark as Jonah's refracted olfactory impression of the "glaym ande glette" (269). We need not follow the allegorical cue to Christ's descent to hell in order to gather the central effect of this passage, because even as the reference to the devil "positively encourages a wider perspective of significance," as Spearing observes, "this [perspective] is present, not as a hidden, unexpressed layer of meaning, but as part of the implication of an engrossing literal meaning."[72] That is, the poet's "realizing imagination," as Spearing calls it,[73] emulates the earthy expostulations of vulgar speech ("stank as þe deuel") at the same

---

71. Spearing, *The "Gawain"-Poet*, 87. On the contrast between Jonah and Christ as an occasion for dramatic irony, see Putter, *An Introduction to the "Gawain"-Poet*, 128–36.

72. Putter, *An Introduction to the "Gawain"-Poet*, 83.

73. Ibid., 55–65.

time as it validates the implied significance of the slang: that the fish might just *be the devil*, that Jonah might just *be in hell*, and all this by proleptic imitation of that prophet to the Gentiles "greater than Jonas" (Luke 11:32) who *did* (or *will*) descend to hell.

Like Langland, the *Patience*-Poet exploits the inventive potential of spiritual exegesis to produce a wide variety of effects in diverse signifying modes. He achieves perhaps his most virtuosic adaptations when he ratchets back the ambitions of Christological allegory in order to establish significant correspondences between people, things, and events within the primary history of the Jonah story (rather than reaching forward to the new dispensation inaugurated by Christ's life, death, and resurrection). In these moments, instead of unfolding Jonah's story out toward salvation history, he folds it in upon itself to create significant correspondences that work like mystical allegory, but never leave the literal-historical sense of the text.

This happens with particular care in the series of episodes in which Jonah is either the contained or the container, and these images of containment are related to vertical movement. The Vulgate Jonah is full of ascents and descents. Each descent means something different, but several entail containment. Jonah's descent to Joppa "away from the face of the Lord" (Jon. 1:3) merges into his descent into a ship ("he found a ship and went down into it" [1:3]), and Jonah further "went down to the inner part of the ship" (1:5). Going down means going inside. The Vulgate does not speak of Jonah descending to the fish—simply, "and Jonah was in the belly of a fish" (2:1). In this case, going inside means going down. Jonah himself says, "I went down to the lowest parts of the mountains" (2:7). Jonah thus identifies a fifth movement of descent: within the fish, he descends to the lowest parts of the earth, "into the deep, in the heart of the sea" (2:4). These descents toward containment maintain continuity and parallelism between the episodes of the Vulgate. Jonah, obeying his own will, stows away in the bowels of a ship. Later, compelled to submit to God's will, he is swept away in the bowels of a fish.

Patience flattens out these movements, eschewing the up/down, inside/outside binaries in favor of lexical and descriptive markers of continuity and parallelism. We never see Jonah going down into the hold of the ship, but when it is time to cast lots and the pilot "herȝed out of vche hyrne" every man on board (178), we learn that Jonah

... watz flowen for ferde of þe flode lotes
Into þe boþem of þe bot, and on a brede lyggede,
Onhelde by þe hurrok, for þe heuen wrache,
Slypped vpon a sloumbe-selepe, and sloberande he routes.

(183–86)

Patience pinpoints Jonah's location "in the interior part of the ship" (Jon. 1:3). He is, to be exact, lying on a board in the bottom of the boat, huddled next to the rudder-band.[74] This is the same rudder that was likely broken to pieces when "Þe bur ber to hit baft, þat braste alle her gere, / Þen hurled on a hepe þe helme and þe sterne" (148–49). The storm has "pooped" the ship, snapping the taut rigging and severing the connections between tiller and rudder.[75] As the sailors hustle about trying to jury-rig and bail the ship, Jonah finds a use for some broken gear; the pilot finds him asleep, perhaps with the *hurrok* for a pillow.[76] In realizing

---

74. *Hurrok* "probably denotes a rudder-band encircling the rudder to keep it in position." Andrew and Waldron, *The Poems of the "Pearl" Manuscript*, 193n185.

75. The danger of "being pooped abaft the beam" is vividly described by Stephen Maturin in Patrick O'Brian's sea story *H.M.S. Surprise*: "the real danger lay in a following wave striking the back of the ship such a buffet as to twirl it sideways to the wind, when it would lie down, receive the next wave broadside-on, and so be overwhelmed; hence the necessity for speed, for flying before the wind with all sail that could be set, and for steering with due attention, to outrun and avoid these blows. Yet they were to consider, that as the ship was exposed to the full force of the blast when it was on the top of the monstrous wave, so it was sheltered in the hollow some fifty feet below, where nevertheless the forward speed must be maintained, to enable the ship to be guided in the desired direction and to diminish the relative velocity of the ensuing wave; and that this necessarily called for a nice adjustment of the various sails and ropes in all their complexity." Patrick O'Brian, *H.M.S. Surprise* (New York: W. W. Norton, 1994), 172.

76. William Sayers speculates that the *hurrok* was a small nook in the hull of the ship, so Jonah might be huddled here as in the *hyrne* he finds in the whale. Sayers notes the Old Norse "term *hraukr* 'rick, small stack,' as exemplified in the compound *hrauktjald* 'a tent shaped like a hay-rick,'" and he suggests that "the image of a hay rick, the hay conceivably weighed down with lengths of turf or ropes with suspended stones, was inverted and used figuratively to describe the

this narrative, the *Patience*-Poet details not only the workings of the ship and Jonah's hiding place, but also the character traits that Jonah will display later on. Jonah delights in on-the-spot tactical maneuvers, whether he is "joyful . . . / þat þe daunger of Dry3ten so derfly ascaped" (109–10) when he embarks for Tharsis, or slobbering and snoring against a makeshift pillow. It is these descriptions of detail and Jonah's character that signal the correspondences between episodes in *Patience*, rather than the Vulgate's structural parallels.

Lexical markers and Jonah's tactical ingenuity signal continuity between the episodes of containment in the ship and in the whale's belly. After creeping about in the whale's guts looking for "rest" and "recoverer" (277–80), Jonah finally

> . . . hitte to a hyrne and helde hym þerinne,
> Þer no defoule of no fylþe watz fest hym abute;
> Þer he sete also sounde, saf for merk one,
> As in þe bulk of þe bote þer he byfore sleped.
>
> (289–92)

The pilot searching the ship had "her3ed out of vche hyrne" the boat's passengers, and now Jonah finds another *hyrne*, or nook, where he can stay safe and clean, just as he slept before in the boat. But now, instead of sleeping in the nook he has discovered by tactical ingenuity, he stays awake and turns to strategy, which in this story is another way to say that he turns to providence, "ay þenkande on Dry3ten, / His my3t and His merci, His mesure þenne" (294–95). The turn to theological contemplation prepares for the close translation of Jonah's prayer in the Vulgate, an extended meditation on the mystery of God's justice and

---

niche in the bottom of the ship, where the keel and floor timbers met the narrowing sides of the hull and stern and stern-post. This cube-shaped area with its rounded sides, at the very bottom of the vessel, would have been enclosed on all but one side, and thus have been a wet and dark hidey-hole." William Sayers, "Sailing Scenes in Works of the *Pearl* Poet (*Cleanness* and *Patience*)," *Amsterdamer Beiträge zur älteren Germanistik* 63 (2007): 146–47.

mercy that culminates in Jonah's concession to what even the animals believe, namely, that what God commands is good:

"Bot I dewoutly awowe, þat verray betz halden,
Soberly to do Þe sacrafyse when I schal saue worþe,
And offer Þe for my hele a ful hol gyfte,
And halde goud þat Þou me hetes: haf here my trauthe."

(333–36)

Jonah decides to consider good what God commands. That is, he transfers his evaluative focus from the emergent, contingent situation to the eternal, panoptic location of God's will. Here I adopt concepts from Michel de Certeau's theory of strategy and tactics. "Tactics," writes Certeau, "are procedures that gain validity in relation to the pertinence they lend to time—to the circumstances which the precise instant of an intervention transforms into a favorable situation."[77] Jonah's *modus operandi* thus far has been tactical. He has responded to an emergent crisis by doing whatever it takes to turn the situation to his advantage. The good has depended entirely on what seems good to Jonah in the moment. However, in his prayer in the whale's belly, Jonah vows to reorient his evaluative practices; henceforth, the good is whatever God commands.

The God's-eye norm of the good to which Jonah concedes is strategic. Outside of human time and space, in "His holy hous" (328), God can "give [himself] a certain independence with respect to the variability of circumstances." God's strategic approach to the good in history constitutes "a mastery of time through the foundation of an autonomous place" that affords him the "ability to transform the uncertainties of history into readable spaces."[78] Up to now, Jonah has acted in response to the uncertainties of history rather than to the readable spaces. As an interpreter of events, Jonah has responded to the literal-historical

---

77. Michel de Certeau, *The Practice of Everyday Life*, trans. Steven Rendall (Berkeley and Los Angeles: University of California Press, 1988), 38.
78. Ibid., 36.

sense as if there were no spiritual sense that reveals the gaps and dis-junctions of emergent situations as readable spaces. Where the biblical Jonah operates in stubborn refusal of the divine will, the Jonah of *Patience* is more distracted by the exigencies and particularities of the emergent situations in which the poet's realizing imagination has placed him. The Jonah of the Bible utters not a word in defiance of God's com-mand, but immediately rises up to "flee into Tharsis from the face of the Lord" (Jon. 1:2). The Jonah of *Patience* conjures up a detailed vision of violent emergency: "I com wyth þose tyþynges, þay ta me bylyue, / Pynez me in a prysoun, put me in stokkes, / Wryþe me in a warlok, wrast out myn yȝen" (78–80). While the biblical Jonah rebels against what he recognizes as God's providential plan, the Jonah of *Patience* re-acts primarily to the perceived dangers or pleasures of the moment, whether by fleeing to Tharsis, hiding in a *hyrne* in the bowels of a ship or a whale, or later on laughing and lounging in the shade of a woodbine (458, 461). Jonah reacts to the details provided by the poet's realizing imagination, rather than to God's strategic plan. The poem's elaboration of the literal sense facilitates Jonah's particular spiritual disposition. His chief flaw now is not so much disobedience—at least not at root—but immoderate attention to the letter of history, to the neglect of the spirit of history.

This is why, in his prayer in the whale, Jonah takes a pragmatic ap-proach to God's will: what God commands is good because God has the power to determine and sustain a particular version of what is good through strategic practices that consolidate God's autonomy in a place apart from the world. Instead of trying to discern the unity and con-sistency of God's will—the conditions under which justice and mercy might be reconciled—Jonah promises to consent unconditionally, to "'halde goud þat þou me hetes'" (336). He rests his appeal for rescue, in the two lines of this prayer that do not correspond to the Vulgate, not on God's mysterious reconciliation of justice and mercy, but on a tacti-cal opportunity: "Þou schal releue me, Renk, whil Þy ryȝt slepez, / Þurȝ myȝt of Þy mercy that mukel is to tryste" (323–24). Jonah projects his tactical approach onto God, arguing that while God's justice sleeps, he should seize the chance to exercise his mercy in order to resolve Jonah's immediate emergency. Such a wily approach is necessary to counter "the

'meschef' [484] of a dictatorial God," as Putter describes Jonah's re-
signed view of things.[79] In order to make this argument, Jonah adopts
the *Patience*-Poet's realizing imagination, letting the impulse toward realism personify God's attributes of justice and mercy and so introduce
contingency into the divine life. (Even in his deployment of personification allegory—often considered a nonrealistic mode—the *Patience*-
Poet achieves realizing effects.) In all of these adaptations of the Vulgate,
we can recognize a profound connection between narrative mode and
theological disposition. Narrative realism underwrites a kind of spiritual tactics on the part of Jonah. Jonah reacts to and exploits the contingent features of the story (of history) to the occlusion of providential
order and "readable spaces."

But Jonah's interpretation of events does not dominate the narrative
because the *Patience*-Poet builds another layer of complexity into the
story's realization, turning Jonah's emergent occasions into spaces readable by the poet, his readers, and, as we shall see, the king of Nineveh.
The perception of distance between these layers brings about the experience of dramatic irony, especially when Jonah is the one unwittingly
designing the correspondences that make the spaces between events
readable. When he announces God's message to the Ninevites, Jonah
threatens them with a fate similar to his own:

> "ʒet schal forty dayez fully fare to an ende,
> And þenne schal Niniue be nomen and to noʒt worþe;
> Truly þis ilk toun schal tylte to grounde;
> Vp-so-doun schal ʒe dumpe depe to þe abyme,
> To be swolʒed swyftly wyth þe swart erþe,
> And alle þat lyuyes hereinne lose þe swete."
>
> (359–64)

Like Jonah, who was "with a best lachched" (seized by a beast) (266),
the Ninevites will be "nomen" (seized) and brought to naught. Like
Jonah, who descended in the whale "to þe se boþem" (253), Nineveh will

---

79. Putter, *An Introduction to the "Gawain"-Poet*, 139.

fall to the ground and plunge deep to the abyss. Like Jonah, who was swallowed in "merk" (darkness) (291) by the whale, Nineveh will be swallowed by the dark (*swart*) earth. And just as Jonah lost all sweetness but God in the "glaym ande glette" of the whale's intestines, so will the Ninevites lose, with their lives, all sweetness.[80]

In delivering God's message of judgment, Jonah takes the events of judgment from his own past and projects them into the Ninevites' future. "The Ninevites are his people," Jim Rhodes notes, "insofar as they replicate his relationship to God."[81] Even though he does not announce his own story to Nineveh, he posits an analogy between himself and the Ninevites when he amplifies the Vulgate's laconic prophecy—"Yet forty days and Nineveh shall be destroyed" (Jon. 3:4)—with the figures of descent, enclosure, and loss of sweetness that define his own experience of judgment. His message and mode of invention are tropological: he preaches from the perspective of his own conversion for the sake of the Ninevites' conversion (whether he intends it or not), and in order to do so, he invents new work that inscribes his own identity into the general message of judgment.[82]

But because tropology never happens all by itself, because it is part of the allegorical mode, Jonah is also establishing allegorical correspondences between himself and the Ninevites. Jonah's allegorical readings are not Christological, but they function by the same logic of correspondence and analogy that undergirds Christian allegory. And despite Jonah's own wishes, this analogical mechanism forces open the anagogical sense of his message. If Jonah's descent corresponds to the Ninevites' impending doom, then Jonah's repentance and salvation from the whale must also correspond to a live option for the Ninevites. The events of the past (allegory) point to hope for the future (anagogy), pending right

---

80. The primary meaning of "swete" in this context would seem to be "life-blood" (*MED*, s.v. "swete" [n.(1)], a), but we are also surely meant to appreciate a secondary meaning, "sweetness" (*MED*, s.v. "swete" [n.(2)], 1a).

81. Jim Rhodes, *Poetry Does Theology: Chaucer, Grosseteste, and the Pearl-Poet* (Notre Dame, IN: University of Notre Dame Press, 2001), 118.

82. Compare Peace's song in *Piers Plowman* B.19/C.21, discussed in the last section of chapter 3.

action in the present (tropology). These correspondences are established, to be sure, between the events of the literal narrative. They do not need to be elevated spiritually by Christological interpretation in order to reveal their meaning. In fact, Christological interpretation would obscure their meaning. The tropological force of the correspondence between Jonah and the Ninevites depends on their common identity as sinners, which they do not share with Christ. So the complete message, which the king of Nineveh instantly grasps, is a tropological one that hinges on the right interpretation of past events and the proper reorientation of present action to correspond to a future possibility:

> "What wote oþer wyte may ȝif þe Wyȝe likes,
> Þat is hende in þe hyȝt of His gentryse?
> I wot His myȝt is so much, þaȝ He be myssepayed,
> Þat in His mylde amesyng He mercy may fynde.
> And if we leuen þe layk of oure layth synnes,
> And stylle steppen in þe styȝe He styȝtlez Hymseluen,
> He wyl wende of His wodschip and His wrath leue,
> And forgif vus þis gult, ȝif we Hym God leuen."
>
> (397–404)

Who knows whether God might forgive us if we give up our foul sins and peacefully walk in the path He walked in Himself?

Just as Jonah's allegorical reading opened up anagogical possibilities against his will, similarly the network of non-Christological correspondences between events in the literal narrative develops into Christological allegory. The king takes the point about repentance one step further than Jonah did. His confession here says nothing about conceding to God's view of the good; he takes that for granted. Nor does he merely promise to obey God's commands, as if God were only a lawgiver. Rather, the king seems to have access to a God who not only gives the law but follows it himself.

The Ninevite king's tropological invention recuperates other latent allegorical figures in the poem. When Jonah prophesies that Nineveh will plunge into "þe abyme" (362), he transposes the abyss from the sea—"in corde maris" (in the heart of the sea) (Jon. 2:4)—to "þe swart erþe" (363). Christ also transposes Jonah's abyss from sea to land in his surprising exegesis of "the sign of Jonah," when he prophesies for himself a descent "in corde terrae" (in the heart of the earth) (Matt. 12:40). Christ's sojourn in the heart of the earth issued in the harrowing of hell and the Resurrection of the Old Testament faithful; Nineveh's burial in "þe swart erþe" can only be averted by an analogous harrowing. The repentant Ninevites simulate Jonah's containment in the whale by donning sackcloth and fulfill his prophecy of burial in the earth by sitting in "a hep of askes" (380):

> Heter hayrez þay hent þat asperly bited,
> And þose þay bounden to her bak and to her bare sydez,
> Dropped dust on her hede, and dymly bisoȝten
> Þat þat penaunce plesed Him þat playnez on her wronge.
>
> (373–76)

The harrowing of the ship's pilot finally finds its soteriological fulfillment. The pilot "herȝed out of vche hyrne" the ship's passengers (178), and we have seen how "hyrne" links this episode lexically to Jonah's hiding place in the belly of the whale, which is bluntly compared to hell. Now, however, Jonah has figured Nineveh's impending doom in such a way that if they are to avert judgment, it will be by a kind of harrowing that rescues a throng of repentant sinners from an otherwise dire fate.

God accomplishes this harrowing by setting his figural argument on a pivot around the common term "heart." Jonah was in the heart of the sea; Christ will be in the heart of the earth. God recuperates this common term in his final speech to Jonah when he argues for the justice of his mercy toward the Ninevites:

> "And if I . . .
> . . . type doun ȝonder toun when hit turned were,
> Þe sor of such a swete place burde synk to My hert,
> So mony malicious mon as mournez þerinne."
>
> (505–8)

Here, near the end of the poem, we discover why the abyss is transferable from land to sea and from sea to land. The God who has proven himself "ly3tly a Lorde in londe and in water" (288) has a heart deeper than any abyss. The theme is familiar from the Psalms, as commentators on Jonah were quick to point out.[83] "Whither shall I go from thy spirit? or whither shall I flee from thy face? If I ascend into heaven, thou art there: if I descend into hell, thou art present" (Ps. 138:7–8). And in the depth of God's heart the city full of "vilanye and venym" (72) has turned into a "swete place" (507).

The God who reveals himself in *Patience*'s final speech dwells below. He is as much the God of the abyss as the God of the city, even a connoisseur of the city, appreciative of its sweetness. Such a God may be found in the Old Testament, and another Cotton Nero A.x. poem, *Cleanness*, remarks how "God as a glad gest mad god chere / Þat watz fayn of his frende, and his fest praysed" when Abraham hosts the Trinity at the Oaks of Mamre.[84] But it is the New Testament that fully develops the theology of a God who walks the *hodos*, the exemplary way or path, the God who claims, "I am the way" (John 14:6). Christ's way through the world is the way back to the Father. As a Wycliffite translation renders Christ's words, "Y stie to my fadir and to youre fadir, to my God and to youre God" (John 20:17).[85] The *Ormulum*, that prolix meditation on the life of Christ, speaks for much Middle English devotional and theological literature when it exhorts its readers, "foll3hesst tu . . . þatt stih Þatt Cristess þeoww birrþ foll3henn" (follow that path that Christ's virtuous manner of life must follow).[86] When the king of

---

83. The prologue to the *Glossa ordinaria* on Jonah comments, "So Jonah, having suffered something human, thought that he would flee from the sight of God, saying with David, *Where shall I go away from your spirit, and where shall I flee from your face?* [Ps. 138:7]." McDermott, "The Ordinary Gloss on Jonah," 427.

84. *Cleanness*, in Andrew and Waldron, eds., *The Poems of the "Pearl" Manuscript: "Pearl," "Cleanness," "Patience," "Sir Gawain and the Green Knight,"* ll. 641–42.

85. For the text of the Wycliffite Bible I have consulted the transcription available at Wesley Center Online, http://wesley.nnu.edu/biblical_studies/wycliffe/Joh.txt.

86. Robert Meadows White, ed., *The Ormulum* (Oxford: Oxford University Press, 1852), vol. 1, ll. 4914–15.

Nineveh proposes that the Ninevites "steppen in þe styȝe He styȝtlez Hymseluen" (402), we would not be wrong to hear a Christological tenor, a refrain encountered, *mutatis mutandis*, throughout writings on the *imitatio Christi*.

This incarnate God who walks through the world contrasts to the strategic God who "'syttes . . . on sege so hyȝe / In His glowande glorye'" (93–94), as Jonah grumbles, whose "elevation transfigures him into a voyeur" taking "voluptuous pleasure . . . in 'seeing the whole,' of looking down on, totalizing the most immoderate of human texts."[87] The king identifies a very different God, one who is capable of tactical adjustments, of changing his mind in response to emergent situations. This God and Jonah and the Ninevites

> are walkers, *Wandersmänner*, whose bodies follow the thicks and thins of an urban "text" they write without being able to read it. These practitioners make use of spaces that cannot be seen; their knowledge of them is as blind as that of lovers in each other's arms. The paths that correspond in this intertwining, unrecognized poems in which each body is an element signed by many others, elude legibility. . . . The networks of these moving, intersecting writings compose a manifold story that has neither author nor spectator, shaped out of fragments of trajectories and alterations of spaces.[88]

The Ninevite king rests his hope for mercy on the possibility that God is a tactical, not a strategic God. If this God is a walking God, to whose path the Ninevites' steps can correspond, then together they can follow an intersecting path "shaped out of fragments of trajectories and alterations of space." This is, in fact, how the message of repentance spreads through the city, for Jonah goes only one day's trip into the city that is three days' walk across, and only begins to preach once he has finished the day's walk:

---

87. Certeau, *The Practice of Everyday Life*, 92.
88. Ibid., 93.

Þat on journay ful joynt Jonas hym ȝede,
Er euer he warpped any worde to wyȝe þat he mette,
And þenne he cryed so cler þat kenne myȝt alle
Þe trwe tenor of his teme . . .

(355–58)

After Jonah preaches repentance to what must have been only a fraction of the population, his "speche" takes on a life of its own. "Þis speche sprang in þat space and spradde alle aboute, / To borges and to bacheleres þat in þat burȝ lenged" (365–66). But the message does not "elude legibility" because the God who walks among the people is also a God who sees from on high. The tactician is also a strategist at the same time. In order to change his mind he must be a tactician, but in order to forgive an entire people and avert the destruction of a great city, he must be a strategist. Indeed, his strategy is what makes his tactics possible.

The theological analysis of this problem offers up analogous terms. Considering "whether the will of God is changeable," Thomas Aquinas distinguishes between God's will with respect to first and final causes and God's will with respect to secondary causes:

And God wills both: that is, that in the order of the inferior cause a thing shall happen; but that in the order of the higher cause it shall not happen; or He may will conversely. We may say, then, that God sometimes declares that a thing shall happen according as it falls under the order of inferior causes, as of nature, or merit, which yet does not happen as not being in the designs of the divine and higher cause. Thus He foretold to Ezechias: "Take order with thy house, for thou shalt die, and not live" (Isaiah 38:1). Yet this did not take place, since from eternity it was otherwise disposed in the divine knowledge and will, which is unchangeable. Hence Gregory says (*Moral.* xvi, 5): "The sentence of God changes, but not His counsel"—that is to say, the counsel of His will.[89]

---

89. *Summa theologica*, I.19.7, ad 2.

In a way, God's immutability is what allows him to change his mind. Because "the counsel of His will" never changes, his sentence can change as much as it needs to in order to achieve the effects that his divine knowledge and will contemplate. Jonah knows this all too well, and he calls it "meschef": "'A, þou Maker of man, what maystery Þe þynkez / Þus Þy freke to forfare forbi alle oþer? / With alle meschef þat Þou may, neuer Þou me sparez" (483–85). In Jonah's opinion, God is a city planner and his totalizing view from high above threatens the people walking down below.[90] Unlike the king of Nineveh, Jonah cannot imagine a God who can both mete out mercy from above and walk the streets below.

Similar relations obtain between the literal sense of scripture and the allegorical senses of scripture; between the *Patience*-Poet's realizing imagination and his theological vision; between the poem's particular literal details and infinity.[91] This is why the *Patience*-Poet's realizing imagination can open up to allegory: secondary causation is not in competition with final causation. This could be in part what God and the narrator are getting at in the poem's peroration. The strategizing God affirms Jonah's tactical habits, claiming them for himself and redefining tactics, walking on the ground, as patience: "Be noȝt so gryndel, godman, bot go forth þy wayes, / Be preue and be pacient in payne and in joye" (524–25). God advises Jonah not to be angry, using a word with an Old Norse root meaning "storm, wind"—those forces of the sky that pay the ground no heed. Instead, Jonah should walk, perhaps still as he walked through Nineveh proclaiming the day of repentance, but perhaps not that at all. Perhaps the emphasis is on "þy," as in, "don't busy

---

90. See Certeau, *The Practice of Everyday Life*, 91–95.

91. Edward I. Condren's reading of the *Pearl*-manuscript's mathematical-theological designs bears out the same point: "Let us not be persuaded that the overall subject of the *Pearl*-manuscript is the felt life it portrays, or the human dilemmas it features. On the contrary, the manuscript continually forces readers to confront the very concept of infinity—not infinite power, or infinite love, but infinity itself." Edward I. Condren, *The Numerical Universe of the "Gawain"-"Pearl" Poet: Beyond Phi* (Gainesville: University Press of Florida, 2002), 41.

yourself with others' lives, but walk your own paths." In any case, he does not urge Jonah to follow the "wayes" of Christ, to "'steppen in þe styȝe He styȝtlez Hymseluen'" (402), as the Ninevite king put it. Jonah is already a type of Christ, however imperfect, without usurping Christ's prerogative to judge. Jonah can only be a type of Christ by going along his *own* ways if his allegorical correspondence to Christ is to maintain his individuality. And God's exhortation to him here seems to suggest just that. Jonah's story does not have to be subsumed under Christ's story in order for Jonah to prefigure Christ.[92] The literal Jonah can exist in all his realistic, comic, and sympathetic detail and still be cited by Christ, however many ages later, as a sign of the resurrection and the spread of the Gospel to the nations.

The Realizing Imagination after Humanism and Reformation

I have been arguing that *Patience* sustains the mutual interiority of the literal and allegorical senses of scripture and uses this exegetical relationship to think about how divine and human intentions might be reconciled. This dynamic—always susceptible to disintegration—came under increasing pressure in the sixteenth and seventeenth centuries for a variety of reasons. As Frei has observed,

> The unity of literal and figural [i.e., allegorical] reading depended, in the first place, on the coherence of literal or grammatical sense with historical reference. Secondly, it depended on the conviction that the narrative renders temporal reality in such a way that interpretive thought can and need only comprehend the meaning that

---

92. To this extent, I agree with Jim Rhodes that "Jonah should not be expected to act like Christ, nor should he be judged by that standard." J. Rhodes, *Poetry Does Theology*, 121. But precisely for that reason I do not think Jonah ever emerges as an exemplar of patience redefined as "a realization of the irreconcilability of the human will and divine imperative," as Rhodes goes on to argue (123).

is, or emerges from, the cumulative sequence and its teleological pattern, because the interpreter himself is part of that real sequence. When the identity of literal sense and historical reference is severed, literal and figural reading no longer belong together. Similarly, when the pattern of meaning is no longer firmly ingredient in the story . . . but becomes a function of a quasi-independent interpretive stance, literal and figural reading draw apart, the latter gradually looking like a forced, arbitrary imposition of unity on a group of very diverse texts. No longer an extension of literal reading, figural interpretation becomes a bad historical argument or an arbitrary allegorizing of texts in the service of preconceived dogma.[93]

Frei offers these remarks in a narrative of decline that follows the trend of disintegration up through the Reformation and into the nineteenth century. But Frei, Auerbach, and other genealogists of exegesis have not recognized that it is possible, even when literal and allegorical senses come apart, to sustain the realizing imagination so long as "the interpreter himself is part of that real sequence."[94] *Patience* confronts the pressures that Frei identifies and deploys a realizing imagination to address them, an imagination that tropologically circulates writer and reader through the history narrated, thereby constituting narrative and reading experience as real and really part of the history of salvation. Encountered in later biblical literature, this habit of literal-tropological invention points to an alternative path of continuity across the Refor-

---

93. Frei, *Eclipse*, 37.

94. Frei thinks that the disintegration of literal and figural reading happens after the magisterial Reformation, and the major turning point for him is not the Reformation but the Enlightenment (ibid., 37–40). Although I concur with Frei's placement of rupture beyond the late Middle Ages and Reformation, nonparticipatory, disintegrated exegesis was still an option for early radical reformers such as John Bale (as it was for medieval exegetes), as discussed in chapter 5. Continuity is to be found not in exegetical theory but in practices of reading and rewriting that maintain the present readers' involvement in the biblical world that constitutes narrative reality.

mation, even when theologians have mostly jettisoned the theoretical apparatus of fourfold exegesis.[95]

The book of Jonah provides an apt testing ground for these theories in the ages of humanism and Reformation because Jesus explicitly read "the sign of Jonah" allegorically and so required reforming critics of spiritual exegesis to grapple with the story's allegorical potential (Matt. 12:38–45, Luke 11:29–32). At the same time, despite its mythical narrative mode, the Jonah story was easily placed in the history of Israel and Near Eastern geopolitics by cross-referencing with Hebrew chronicle literature (2 Kings 14:25), and Jerome's commentary bristles with the kind of eyewitness historical detail that commanded European humanists' respect, if not credulity ("His grave is pointed out in one of the cities of Gath, in a hamlet that is at the second milestone on the road to Sepphoris").[96] Martin Luther and William Tyndale each published a vernacular, stand-alone translation of Jonah with paraphrasing commentary, and each uses the occasion to theorize about spiritual exegesis.[97]

---

95. For a full discussion of this argument, see chapter 5 on Reformation theories and practices of tropology.

96. McDermott, "The Ordinary Gloss on Jonah," 427. Jerome's impassioned argument about the precise botanical identity of the ivy or gourd in Jon. 4:6–7 became iconic of humanists' exacting philological standards, and this status is reflected by a prominent gourd hanging over Jerome's head in Dürer's famous woodcut of the saint's study. Peter W. Parshall, "Albrecht Dürer's St. Jerome in His Study: A Philological Reference," *The Art Bulletin* 53, no. 3 (1971): 303–5. Erasmus defended his own editorial and translation work against Edward Lee's attacks by comparing himself to Jerome in the debate over Jon. 4:6–7. Desiderius Erasmus, *Opera omnia Desiderii Erasmi Roterodami: Ordinis noni Tomus Quartus*, ed. Erika Rummel and Edwin Rabbie (Amsterdam: Huygens Instituut/Brill, 2003), 98.

97. Martin Luther, *Der Prophet Jona ausgelegt* (Augsburg, 1526); William Tyndale, *The Prophete Ionas with an Introduccio[n] before Teaching to Vndersto[n]de Him and the Right vse Also of All the Scripture, and Why It Was Written, and What Is Therin to Be Sought, and Shewenge Wherewith the Scripture Is Locked Vpp That He Which Readeth It, Can Not Vndersto[n]de It, Though He Studie Therin Never so Moch: And Agayne with What Keyes It Is so Opened, That the Reader Can Be Stopped out with No Sotilte or False Doctrine of Man, from*

Johannes Brenz explicates all four senses of the text, taking special care to reaffirm the historicity of the literal sense against "scoffing . . . wicked Ethnicke[s] [pagans]," the confirmation of which may be found in Jesus' typological reading of Jonah and the whale.[98] But it is Tyndale, whose prologue amplifies the Jonah story roughly by a factor of four, who has most in common with the *Patience*-Poet's habits of invention. And Tyndale's likely example for this kind of amplification was Erasmus, the inventor of humanist biblical paraphrase.

The genre of *Patience* had come to be known among humanists as paraphrase. Although medieval commentary had always employed paraphrase as its most pervasive rhetorical device,[99] humanists were the first to identify a distinct genre by that name. But it was Erasmus who seized on the newly defined genre and applied it to biblical narrative, associating his own practice with the early medieval Latin biblical poems of Juvencus and Arator.[100] Erasmus took to his newfound genre as eagerly as the audiences who made it the most widely circulated work in his lifetime. The editor of the New Testament's first critical edition remarked, "I would rather construct a thousand paraphrases than one critical edition."[101] As Mark Vessey and Hilmar Pabel have argued, Erasmus followed his master Jerome in employing paraphrase as a sophisti-

---

the *True Sense and Vderstondynge Therof*, Early English Books Online, 1475–1640 / 950:10 (Antwerp: M. de Keyser, 1531).

98. Like most reformers, Brenz prefers the language of "typology" to that of "allegory," and does not call his tropological and anagogical readings by those traditional terms. Johannes Brenz, *Newes from Niniue to Englande, Brought by the Prophete Ionas*, trans. Thomas Tymme, Early English Books Online, 1475–1640 / 523:07 (London: Henrie Denham, 1570), 26v–28v. Tymme translated Johannes Brenz, *Explicatio Ionae prophetae* (Frankfurt: Peter Brubach, 1566).

99. Rita Copeland, *Rhetoric, Hermeneutics, and Translation in the Middle Ages: Academic Traditions and Vernacular Texts* (New York: Cambridge University Press, 1991), 82–86.

100. Jean-François Cottier, "Erasmus's *Paraphrases*: A 'New Kind of Commentary'?," in *The Unfolding of Words: Commentary in the Age of Erasmus*, ed. Judith Rice Henderson (Toronto: University of Toronto Press, 2012), 28–30.

101. Cited in ibid., 30.

cated mode of literal commentary, according to which analysis of historical detail and authorial intention merge in service of spiritual and practical edification.[102] While Erasmus amplifies biblical narrative in many modes, like the *Patience*-Poet he frequently adds realistic and psychological detail that heighten readers' emotional and imaginative participation.

Other later works share this method of literal amplification that uses realistic detail to foster affective and imaginative participation by readers. Among paraphrases of Jonah, *Patience* stands out for its proliferation of concrete detail, but other works employ a realizing imagination to invent psychological realism, positing motivations where the Bible remains silent. The Wycliffite *Middle English Biblical Summary*, composed around 1390, surmises that "The lord vndurnymed [accused] [Jonah] of vnpacience."[103] It thus attributes a motive to God that I have not found in any other medieval commentary on Jonah besides *Patience*. In the *Middle English Metrical Paraphrase of the Old Testament* (c. 1400–1425), Jonah broods on the hillside waiting for Nineveh to be destroyed and mutters "in tene" about the fine weather, "þis fayr is fals, fully I fele."[104] William Tyndale imagines that

---

102. Mark Vessey, "The Tongue and the Book: Erasmus' *Paraphrases on the New Testament* and the Arts of Scripture," in *Holy Scripture Speaks: The Production and Reception of Erasmus' "Paraphrases on the New Testament,"* ed. Hilmar M. Pabel and Mark Vessey (Toronto: University of Toronto Press, 2002), 29–58; Hilmar M. Pabel, "Exegesis and Marriage in Erasmus' *Paraphrases on the New Testament*," in *Holy Scripture Speaks*, 175–209.

103. Robert Reilly, "A Middle English Summary of the Bible: An Edition of Trinity College (Oxon) Ms. 93," Ph.D. diss., University of Washington, 1966, 346–47. The *Middle English Biblical Summary* condenses the Jonah story, but it expands other narratives to amplify a certain affective realism, as Fiona Somerset has argued in *Feeling Like Saints: Lollard Writings after Wyclif* (Ithaca, NY: Cornell University Press, 2014), 179–202.

104. Michael Livingston, ed., *The Middle English Metrical Paraphrase of the Old Testament* (Kalamazoo, MI: Medieval Institute Publications, 2011), ll. 13987–88.

[w]hen Ionas had bene in te fishes bely a space and the rage of his conscience was somewhat quieted and swaged and he come to him selfe agayne and had receaued a lytle hope, the qualmes and panges of desperacion which went ouer his hert, halfe ouercome, he prayed . . .[105]

Tyndale pursues a deft psychological realism in order to give an example of "the right use" of scripture.[106] That right use involves approaching scripture "so that thou fele in thyn hert" your failure to live up to the law and the mercy and patience of God filling your heart with love. That emphasis on right feeling is one that Fiona Somerset has identified as a hallmark of the *Middle English Biblical Summary* and related Lollard writings. The author of *MEBS* invents emotional and psychological detail that "requires readers," as Somerset puts it, "over and over, to position themselves in salvation history, between stories of the past and prophecies of the future in an uncertainly positioned, aspirational here and now."[107] Tyndale's efforts to teach his readers to do the same, as well as his paraphrastic method of instruction, are consistent with both Middle English biblical verse and Erasmian paraphrase. While Tyndale explicitly rejects traditional fourfold exegesis as papistical, "chopologicall" nonsense, he nevertheless counsels a "right use" of scripture that shares with medieval tropology the imperative to apply scripture to one's own life:[108]

That is that thou first seke out the law, what god will haue the to doo, interpretinge it spiritually with out glose or coueringe the brightnesse of Moses face . . . and thou must washe all thy good dedes in christes bloude, ther they can be pure and an acceptable sacrifice vn

---

105. Tyndale, *The Prophete Ionas*, fol. B.4r–B.4v.

106. Ibid., fol. C.1r.

107. Somerset, *Feeling Like Saints*, 183.

108. William Tyndale, *The Obedyence of a Christian Man and How Christen Rulers Ought to Gouerne*, Early English Books Online (London: William Hill, 1548), 112r.

to God, and must desire god the father for his sake, to take thi dedes aworth and to pardon þe imperfectenesse of them, and to geue the power to doo them better and with moare feruent loue.[109]

Like medieval tropologists, Tyndale distinguishes between works that are naturally good and works that participate in God's plan of salvation through the grace of "moare feruent loue." Of course, Tyndale radically departs from the sacramental economy that medieval Catholicism understood as the necessary means of participation. But he compensates for the loss of one kind of participation with the practice of a "feeling" participation in scripture, for which purpose he amplifies the book of Jonah with literal detail.

A similar intention animates Thomas Lodge and Robert Greene's treatment of Jonah in their play, *A Looking Glasse for London and England* (c. 1590). The play comprises a series of moral vignettes in preconversion Nineveh. At the end of each scene, the prophet Hoseah comes on stage extradiegetically and preaches a short homily, using the foregoing scene as an *exemplum* to hold the mirror of vice up to modern-day London. Some of the vignettes muster substantial emotional strength through a compelling psychological realism. Unlike Hoseah, Jonah enters into the play within the diegesis, and his story is developed with the same psychological realism as the other plots. The play's realizing imagination also amplifies the literal sense of the Jonah story. Returned safely to land, the captain of Jonah's ship tells of the storm with a nautical realism comparable to that of *Patience*—though overlaid with a classicizing high style:

> Then scantled we our sailes with speedie hands,
> And tooke our drablers from our bonnets straight,
> And seuered our bonnets from the courses,
> Our topsails vp, we trusse our spritsailes in[.]

The climax even indulges in alliterative anachronism:

---

109. Tyndale, *The Prophete Ionas*, fol. C.1r–C.1v.

The steersman pale and carefull holds his helme,
Wherein the trust of life and safetie laie,
Till all at once (a mortall tale to tell)
Our sailes were split by Bisas bitter blast,
Our rudder broke, and we bereft of hope.[110]

These realizing flourishes are possible only because Jonah is part of the story, not standing off to the side commenting on the action, like Hoseah. Jonah's participation in the play's plot makes the meaning of his story a meaning that derives from narrative, from experience, and, for the audience, from the feeling of sharing in his experience. The literal sense, with all its amplified realizing details, elicits feelings in the audience that help them to participate in the story, not just to judge its morals, as the Hoseah character does in his moralizing soliloquies. In Tyndale's prologue and in *A Looking Glasse*, readers and audience should participate especially in the conversion part of the story. To this end, both amplify the elements of the story dealing with conversion. Tyndale focuses his invention on Jonah's anguished prayer in the belly of the whale, while *A Looking Glass* dwells on the Ninevites' repentance, adds a final conversion for Jonah as he cheerfully goes off to preach a "mercie day" in Nineveh, and concludes with an address to the audience, inviting them to join in with an "Amen."[111] In each of these acts of paraphrastic invention, the human author's intentions are brought into harmony with those of the divine author, effecting in literary practice the kind of conversion commended to the audience. As human and divine intentions correspond, tropologically motivated invention of literal detail invites the affective equivalent of the *Looking Glasse* audience's participatory "Amen."

In the next two chapters I approach Reformation tropologies by way of *Piers Plowman* in order to map out two related problematics that emerge with particular poignancy in the sixteenth century. Chapter 3

---

110. Thomas Lodge and Robert Greene, *A Looking Glasse for London and England*, ed. George Alan Clugston (New York: Garland, 1980), 188.
111. Ibid., 224, 231–32.

identifies in *Piers Plowman* a theory of tropological making that conceives of writing as ethical action. Chapter 4 then inquires how such writing relates to the sacramental economy, the church's official means of participation in the history of salvation. Langland's answer is that tropological invention can itself be a form of sacramental satisfaction, which also suggests a related question, explored at the end of chapter 4: What becomes of penitential invention in the Reformation, when the Roman Catholic Church's sacramental system goes into eclipse?

3

"Beatus qui verba vertit in opera"

Langland's Ethical Invention

I can conceive him (like his own visionary William) to have been sometimes occupied in contemplative wanderings on Malvern Hills [. . .].
Sometimes I can descry him taking his staff, and roaming far and wide
in search of manners and characters; mingling with men of every accessible rank, and storing his memory with hints for future use. I next
pursue him to his study, sedate and thoughtful, yet wildly inventive,
digesting the first rude drafts of his Visions, and in successive transcrip-
tions, as judgment matured, or invention declined, or as his observations
were more extended, expanding or contracting, improving and sometimes perhaps debasing his original text.
—Thomas Dunham Whitaker, *Visio Willi de Petro Plouhman* (1813)

History and allegory may conflict at the point where the individual
human's free will seems to collide with providence, as in the relationship
between a historical figure of the Old Testament (Jonah) and his

An earlier version of chapter 3 appeared as "'Beatus qui verba vertit in opera':
Langland's Ethical Invention and the Tropological Sense," in *Yearbook of Langland Studies* 24 (Turnhout: Brepols, 2010), 169–204.

allegorical fulfillment in the New Testament (Jesus). The *Patience*-Poet, as discussed in the previous chapter, resolved this conflict between old and new by configuring allegorical likeness according to the logic of tropological invention, wherein Jonah's unique history can fit God's plans only when Jonah makes it his own and goes his own way. The present chapter applies this logic to two other relationships of figure and fulfillment: the literary relationship between source text and translation or commentary, and the ethical relationship between an exemplar and action patterned on the exemplar. By investigating how *Piers Plowman* handles these relationships of model and copy, this chapter articulates a tropological theory of literary invention in which originality and creativity—in the modern sense of those values—can be a function of fidelity to a source text or exemplar. This new approach to *Piers Plowman* provides a vantage point from which to reassess the ethical status of writing in *Piers Plowman*, an argument that I develop further, and link to sacramental participation, in the next chapter. In addition to pursuing a local argument about the interpretation of *Piers Plowman*, then, this chapter offers demonstrative evidence for my contention in chapter 1 that rhetoric and moral philosophy cannot account for certain aspects of literary ethics. Here, tropological theory reveals a mode of invention that has been obscured by rhetorical criticism and pre- and postmodern philosophical ethics.

WILLIAM LANGLAND HAS NEVER NEEDED A CHARLES MUSCATINE to rescue him from critical exaggerations of his originality. Whereas Muscatine's *Chaucer and the French Tradition* proposed to debunk the "post-Victorian . . . notion of Chaucer's 'revolt' from 'outworn' convention,"[1] Langland, to one of his most important Victorian-age readers, J. J. Jusserand, was largely oblivious to—not in conflict with—classical

---

1. Charles Muscatine, *Chaucer and the French Tradition: A Study in Style and Meaning* (Berkeley and Los Angeles: University of California Press, 1957), 3, 4.

and recent continental poetic traditions.[2] When it comes to originality and that sprightliness of creative thought that the Victorians called "invention," Langland appears an anomaly, at least viewed alongside Chaucer. There is little evidence of his striving with agonistic, paternal literary traditions against which one might assess originality. But at the same time, readers throughout the nineteenth and twentieth centuries remarked on his lively knack for invention.[3] Readers have always found Langland to be just as inventive as Chaucer. The critical challenge has been to explain how both can be so inventive, despite their drastically different habits of invention and disposition to their sources.

Anne Middleton's assessment of the critical heritage nearly three decades ago is still true today, although with some important qualifica-

---

2. "Never, assuredly, would it occur to our visionary [Langland] that when approaching the threshold of God's paradise, the thing to say is: 'Apollo! Now that the hour has come for the last of my tasks, fill me with the breath of thy inspiration' [Dante, *Paradiso*, 1.1.13–15]." J. J. Jusserand, *"Piers Plowman": A Contribution to the History of English Mysticism*, trans. M. E. R. (London: T. Fisher Unwin, 1894), 211.

3. Whatever attention Langland has enjoyed beyond English literary studies has been sustained in large part by a sense—right or wrong—that he was particularly *inventive* of innovative social and cultural configurations. Even when Langland was taken as the Ricardian *vox populi*, he was deemed "eminently original." George P. Marsh, *The Origin and History of the English Language and of the Early Literature It Embodies*, rev. ed. (New York: Charles Scribner's Sons, 1892), 296. David Matthews observes that Charles Dunham Whitaker, cited in the epigraph, characterizes Langland "as a protomodern poet" in much the same way that Renaissance and Victorian writers talked about Chaucer. David Matthews, *The Making of Middle English, 1765–1910* (Minneapolis: University of Minnesota Press, 1999), 91. And as the mouthpiece of the *commune*, "the man in whom Catholic faith and national feeling are fused in a single flame," Langland has struck modern readers such as Christopher Dawson as one-of-a-kind, productive of some rare and protomodern vision. Writing in 1953, Dawson not only finds Langland more inventive than Chaucer, but also opposes Langland's "realism," by which he implies modernity, to Chaucer's "classicism." Christopher Dawson, "The Vision of *Piers Plowman*," in *Medieval Essays* (Washington, DC: Catholic University of America Press, 2002), 207, 214.

tions: "*Piers Plowman* yields to 'sources and analogues' study little trace of its immediate *literary* antecedents and possible models: it appears that what Chaucer called 'alle poesie' played little part in Langland's conception of his 'making.'"[4] However many quotations, images, or topoi we might identify, they always stand in oblique relation to the poem, functioning less as "background" or "source" than as fodder for a remarkably fecund organic process that incorporates, metabolizes, and transforms them into something new.[5] In this respect, Langland's "invention" seems closer to the modern sense of the word, with its emphasis on original creation, than to classical rhetoric handbooks' stress on the discovery of ready-to-hand *materia* that need only be disposed and possibly amplified or otherwise turned—and all of this in a poem whose *modus agendi* often is that of commentary, ostensibly the most derivative of inventional habits.[6]

---

4. Anne Middleton, "Introduction: The Critical Heritage," in *A Companion to Piers Plowman*, ed. John A. Alford (Berkeley and Los Angeles: University of California Press, 1988), 19–20, my emphasis. We have suffered no shortage of work on *Piers Plowman*'s literary antecedents, especially on the genre of dream visions. But this type of criticism often ends up in an apophatic mode, calling our attention to similarities between Langland and other poets only to identify Langland's ever greater dissimilarity. See, for example, David Aers, *Piers Plowman and Christian Allegory* (London: Edward Arnold, 1975), 42–51, and John Burrow, *Langland's Fictions* (Oxford: Clarendon Press, 1993), 6–27, 113–18; both argue for Guillaume de Deguileville's influence on Langland, while drawing sharp contrasts between de Deguileville's heavy-handed, static allegories and Langland's "imaginatively powerful and satisfactory" disposition of dreams and salvation history (Aers, *Piers Plowman and Christian Allegory*, 102).

5. Compare Mary Carruthers's exemplary remark about the meaning of *Dowel*: "No outside source can possibly tell us what the word really means; the concept is being created by the text of the poem itself." Carruthers, *The Search for St. Truth*, 20.

6. Recent scholarship has made up for the paucity of literary models primarily by mining the rhetorical and homiletical traditions for clues to Langland's craft of thought. As early as 1963, A. C. Spearing noted how some of the *artes praedicandi* envisioned the kind of free invention apparent in Langland's "willingness to conceive of better beginnings and impose them on the emerging

If *Piers Plowman* is "a commentary on an unknown text," then it is a remarkably inventive one.[7] But since Rita Copeland's study of the creative potential of commentary, this should not surprise us.[8] And we have learned from Mary Carruthers to interpret monastic meditational and exegetical theories and practices as crafts of rhetorical invention.[9] So Langland's harnessing of scriptural and liturgical commentary habits, like Piers's yoking of the four exegetical "stottes" (plow horses), should make sense to us as a productive means to "tulye [cultivate] treuthe" and *verba Scripturae vertere in opera*—to turn the words of scripture into ethical and literary works, as Liberum Arbitrium proposes in passus B.15/C.16, citing St. Bernard of Clairvaux.[10] Langland's habits of tro-

---

structure of the work," as D. Vance Smith more recently observed. D. Smith, *The Book of the Incipit*, 73; Spearing, "Verbal Repetition in *Piers Plowman* B and C." See also Elizabeth Salter, *"Piers Plowman": An Introduction*, 2nd ed. (Cambridge, MA: Harvard University Press, 1969), 24–57; and A. C Spearing, *Criticism and Medieval Poetry* (New York: Barnes and Noble, 1964), 68–95. In some of the earliest research on medieval rhetorical theory as literary theory, Judson Boyce Allen suggests that *Piers Plowman* is a "book about its own making . . . a text in which the *modus agendi* [the mode of making] and the *forma tractatus* [the structure of the work] are the same." J. Allen, *The Ethical Poetic of the Later Middle Ages*, 92–93. Smith elaborates on this point in *The Book of the Incipit*, 104–6.

7. Morton W. Bloomfield, *"Piers Plowman" as a Fourteenth-Century Apocalypse* (New Brunswick, NJ: Rutgers University Press, 1962), 32.

8. Copeland, *Rhetoric, Hermeneutics, and Translation in the Middle Ages.*

9. See Carruthers, *The Craft of Thought* and *The Book of Memory*.

10. For the scene of plowing scripture, see C.21.262–73a and the section "The Allegory of the Cultivation of Scripture" in chapter 1. "'*Beatus*,' saith seynt Bernard, '*qui scripturas legit / Et verba vertit in opera* emforth his power'" (C.16.222–23). Cf. B.15.60–61: "'*Beatus est*', seiþ Seint Bernard, '*qui scripturas legit / Et verba vertit in opera* fulliche to his power.'" The closest biblical reference is Rev. 1:3: "Beatus qui legit et qui audiunt verba prophetiae et servant ea quae in ea scripta sunt" (Blessed is he that readeth and heareth the words of this prophecy: and keepeth those things which are written in it). Skeat compares Bernard's Epist. 201.3, which I cite at greater length: "Memento etiam voci tuae dare vocem virtutis. 'Quid illud', inquis? Ut opera tua verbis concinant, immo verba operibus, ut cures videlicet prius facere quam docere" (Remember also to

pology extend beyond an imagined conversion of the will to influence even his own acts of composition. In *Piers Plowman*, tropology does not work as an exegetical key to unlock the ethical secrets of the text; rather, habits of tropological *interpretation* translate into habits of tropological *invention*. On this reading, Langland is concerned not only with readers' ethics and the ethics of reading, but also with the ethics of invention: with habits that make writing itself meaningful action and submit the invention of new literature to the high standard of the "law of love."[11]

---

give your voice the tone of virtue. Why is that? you say. So that your works might chime with your words, or even better your words with your works, so that you might first clearly undertake to do what you teach). Bernard of Clairvaux, *Epistolae*, ed. Jean Leclercq and Henri Rochais, vol. 8, Sancti Bernardi opera (Rome: Editiones Cistercienses, 1977), 60. In the Bernardian *Tractatus de ordine vitae et morum institutione*, we find, "Beatus qui divinas Scripturas legens, verba vertit in opera" (Blessed is the one who, reading the divine scriptures, turns words into works) (PL 184:566c). See John A. Alford, "Some Unidentified Quotations in *Piers Plowman*," *Modern Philology* 72, no. 4 (1975): 396. But even this Bernardian text seems to be a direct quotation of the seventh-century *Liber scintillarum* ("De lectionibus"), a florilegium on the vices and virtues that attributes the remark to Jerome, and which appears in the eleventh-century London, British Library, MS Royal 7.C.IV with interlinear Old English translation. See Defensor Locogiacensis, *Liber scintillarum*, ed. H. M. Rochais, CCSL 117 (Turnhout: Brepols, 1957), 81.12; and E. W. Rhodes, *Defensor's "Liber Scintillarum," with an Interlinear Anglo-Saxon Version Made Early in the Eleventh Century*, EETS, o.s., 93 (London: N. Trübner, 1889), 218. A search of the Corpus Christianorum on Brepols.net Library of Latin Texts, Series A, does not reveal similar phrases in the works of Jerome, pseudo-Jerome, or Jerome's translations of Origen. Alford also cites Pseudo-Chrysostom: "Verba enim, quae non convertuntur ad opus, arena sunt spargibilis" (For words that are not converted into work are scattered like sand) (PG 56:746).

11. Another title for this chapter could be "Will as Writer," which would echo James Simpson's important inquiry into the ethics of interpretation, "Desire and the Scriptural Text: Will as Reader in *Piers Plowman*," in *Criticism and Dissent in the Middle Ages*, ed. Rita Copeland (New York: Cambridge University Press, 1996), 215–43. There Simpson argues that Langland "often represent[s] Will, as the human will, as a readerly model being moved from within the text, and being moved through his encounter with scriptural texts" (219).

Tropological theory is particularly helpful in this context because we currently do not have adequate theories to explain how Middle English writing can seek harmony with its literary and ethical models and simultaneously strike readers as "wildly inventive."[12] According to the Roman theorists in Copeland's account of translation-as-invention, *Piers Plowman* would have to displace its sources in order to be truly inventive, yet Langland has no intention of doing so. And according to some recent theories of exemplarity as a mode of ethical literary invention, *Piers Plowman*, in order to achieve the characteristic aesthetic of Middle English exemplary texts, would have to "invalidate the very norms [it] invoke[s]."[13] These theories assume that to be creative, an author must violently overthrow a model or break a law.[14] They consequently risk occluding habits of literary and ethical invention that are not motivated by competition and, rather than displacing their models, instead seek to harmonize with them.

Piers Plowman invites us to rethink these assumptions—not only for medieval literature but also for prevailing theories of literary invention and ethics. When Jacques Derrida meditates on the conditions of invention by reading Cicero, he appreciates the great orator's inventiveness in disguising the violence of his own invention.[15] For Derrida,

---

This chapter looks within the text not primarily for models of interpretation but for models of invention.

12. William Langland, *Visio Willi de Petro Plouhman*, ed. Thomas Dunham Whitaker (London: J. Murray, 1813), vi.

13. Elizabeth Allen, *False Fables and Exemplary Truth in Later Middle English Literature* (New York: Palgrave Macmillan, 2005), 23. Allen is glossing Wolfgang Iser, *The Act of Reading: A Theory of Aesthetic Response* (Baltimore: Johns Hopkins University Press, 1978), 218–25.

14. Or in the words of Derek Attridge, one of our most incisive theorists of invention and ethics in modernity, "To be original . . . is to create something that marks a significant departure from the norms of the cultural matrix within which it is produced and received." *The Singularity of Literature* (New York: Routledge, 2004), 35. This view of originality is common because it holds true for so much literature, especially modern literature.

15. See Jacques Derrida, "Psyche: Invention of the Other," trans. Catherine Porter, in *Psyche: Inventions of the Other*, ed. Peggy Kamuf and Elizabeth Rottenberg (Stanford, CA: Stanford University Press, 2007), 1:1–47.

nothing less than the appearance of the absolute Other—the first condition of ethics—is at stake. The Other cannot appear unless all norms and expectations are shattered. If this is true, then rhetorical invention always implies ethics—an insight that has recurred in studies of literary ethics over the past two decades. With the rise of the "new ethics" in literary studies, we have become open to literary moments where a genuine encounter with the Other might occur, so long as "ethics" does not involve specific moral injunctions. Yet Emmanuel Lévinas argues that "only the ritual law of Judaism" with its "austere discipline that strives to achieve . . . justice . . . can recognize the face of the Other."[16] Does genuine invention break *this* law, too? Do Dowel, Dobet, and Dobest threaten the invention of the Other?

While Langland does not require us to pit one high theorist against another, he does invite us to notice that Cicero does not have a monopoly on ancient theories of invention. We find different theories of invention in the Jewish tradition, with its strong emphasis on law as a fruitful and empowering grace, and in the Christian tradition, with its Trinitarian model of how to think about likeness and difference at the same time. In Langland's hands, these traditions also give us a vital link between rhetoric (the words we invent to get people to do things) and ethics (the responsible action we actually undertake). We can inquire about Langland's "ethical invention" only if we are willing to entertain the notion that invention extends beyond rhetoric to action. For Langland, rhetoric and hermeneutics are incomplete without an active response, just as in exegetical theory it is not enough to perceive by allegorical interpretation that the gift of tongues at Pentecost recapitulates and redeems the confusion of tongues at the Tower of Babel; we must proceed to tropological interpretation, taking the event to include ourselves, and kneel to sing a hymn of praise in unity with our fellow Christians. Even the best-intentioned rhetorical inventions are preethical, and they will come to naught if not borne out in a *praxis* that copies in action what the invention modeled in words and ideas. At the

---

16. Emmanuel Lévinas, "A Religion for Adults," in *Difficult Freedom: Essays on Judaism*, trans. Seán Hand (Baltimore: Johns Hopkins University Press, 1990), 18.

same time, Langland is striving to conceive and practice a kind of writing, of making, that will count as action, and he draws on tropological theory to do so. For tropology is never simply an analysis of one text, but rather an invention of another—fruitful activity, acted out in production of new literature, even of profane literature.[17]

My argument in this chapter is cumulative, but throughout it traces what are most helpfully thought of as model-copy relationships: the play of similarity and difference between literary or ethical models and the texts and patterns of action that derive from those models. In Langland's poetics of exemplarity, likeness between model and copy does not obliterate the copy's freedom, individuality, or originality. Because they are not in competition, the copy's adherence to the model can actually intensify its individuality. For this reason, the classical account of rhetorical invention as a competition for mastery between generations needs to be supplemented with noncompetitive models of invention in order to understand Langland's irenic relationship to his literary and intellectual sources. In Langland's treatment of Pentecost, the literary centerpiece of this chapter, we see how a literary text can conserve its biblical and liturgical models, yet nevertheless invent previously unseen phenomena. Medieval theories of biblical exegesis provide the fullest articulation of how this happens because they emphasize the continuity between rhetoric, interpretation, and action, and because they rest on a robust doctrine of analogy that allows readers and writers to copy the Bible as a model even as they participate in the history of salvation by inventing previously unforeseeable phenomena. But before I propose that tropological theory can best articulate Langland's ethical invention, we need to see how the discourses of exemplarity and classical rhetoric give alternative but overlapping accounts of ethics and invention.

Exemplarity at Pentecost

At perhaps the climax of *Piers Plowman*, Will and his guide Conscience show up at the scene of Pentecost just as the Holy Spirit is descending

---

17. I am grateful to Ashley Faulkner for this felicitous way of putting it.

on the apostles. Langland gives us a mere sketch of the Acts narrative: "... and thenne cam, me thouhte, / Oen *spiritus paraclitus* to Peres and to his felawes. / In liknesse of a lihtnynge a lyhte on hem alle / And made hem konne & knowe alle kyne langages" (C.21.200–203). These details suffice to import the episode from Acts into Will's dream as a live, inter-active *exemplum* continuous with Conscience's sermon on the economy of salvation, which paused just two lines earlier. As *exempla* go, this one is especially participatory; it is an extreme case of an *exemplum* "set in a pragmatic situation that is inconclusive and demands a decision."[18] In-deed, Will, distinctly perceiving the action's inconclusiveness, has to nudge Conscience and ask for an interpretation: "Y wondred what þat was and wagged Consience" (C.21.204). And the situation certainly de-mands a decision, exacted by Conscience's none-too-subtle command, "Knele now ... and yf thow canst synge, / Welcome hym and worschipe hym with *veni creator spiritus*" (C.21.209–10). As befits an *exemplum*, the coming of the Holy Spirit opens up a range of meanings even as it closes down the range of proper action.[19]

Yet the Pentecost narrative as it occurs in Acts is not originally an *exemplum*; it only becomes one by a complex process of translation, beginning with the collation of eye-witness accounts and developing through Greek manuscript recensions, Old Latin translations, Jerome's Vulgate, evolving theological exegesis, Middle English oral paraphrases in sermons, and finally, Langland's rendering here. These translations form the backstory to any exemplary citation of scripture. Not only does this *exemplum* invite an audience's interpretation and response—

---

18. Karl-Heinz Stierle, "Story as *Exemplum—Exemplum* as Story: On the Pragmatics and Poetics of Narrative Texts," in *New Perspectives in German Lit-erary Criticism: A Collection of Essays*, ed. Richard E. Lange and Victor Amacher, trans. David Henry Wilson (Princeton: Princeton University Press, 1979), 398. Stierle is commenting on Dante's use of *exempla*.

19. "The nature of the *exemplum*," according to J. Allan Mitchell, "is to be open-ended or expansive with respect to the meaning of the moral terms, and closed or reductive when it comes to determining action." J. Allan Mitchell, *Ethics and Exemplary Narrative in Chaucer and Gower* (Rochester, NY: D. S. Brewer, 2004), 19. On the historical development of *exempla* away from the purpose of motivating determinative action, see Stierle, "Story as *Exemplum*."

that is, not only does it posit inventive activity as its final cause—but it also presumes a prior history of invention. I mean this in a very modern way: this *exemplum* was not just discovered in and excised from Acts, then plopped into *Piers Plowman*, "isolated from a context and placed in a new context," as J. D. Lyons characterizes early modern *exempla*.[20] Rather, it had to be *made into* an *exemplum*. *Exempla* like this one are just as much made as they are found. But it is easy to miss this point. The collections of *exempla* that were made in the later Middle Ages, if interpreted as the natural habitat of *exempla*, can belie the vibrant novelty that the mode is able to convey even as late as *Piers Plowman*.[21] At Pentecost with Will and Conscience as they join "many hundret" in singing the "Veni Creator Spiritus," we are quite far from an exemplarity that pretends to transcendent moral authority, regardless of its local context.[22] Langland desires no such thing. Granted, the meaning of

---

20. J. D. Lyons, *Exemplum: The Rhetoric of Example in Early Modern France and Italy* (Princeton: Princeton University Press, 1989), 31.

21. One of the greatest "*exempla* collections" of the age, John Bromyard's *Summa praedicantium*, displays the two competing tendencies of *exempla*. On the one hand, it presents itself as a collection or encyclopedia of *exempla* alphabetically organized by topic and cross-referenced. On the other hand, potted *exempla* are few and far between, interspersed amidst densely associative, analogical meditations that deploy concrete, "exemplary" situations to speculate on the mysteries of vice, virtue, and the human and divine natures. The preacher on deadline would be hard-pressed to follow, much less re-create, the series of agile analogies that get Bromyard from here to there. See John Bromyard, *Summa praedicantium*, 2 vols. (Venice, 1586), available online at www .archive.org. For the subfield-changing argument for the historical complexity of the *exemplum*'s narrative simplicity, see Larry Scanlon, *Narrative, Authority, and Power: The Medieval Exemplum and the Chaucerian Tradition* (New York: Cambridge University Press, 1994), 25–36.

22. Elizabeth Allen argues that the exemplary mode is "ostensibly dedicated to the fantasy that, if a story can remain unchanged as it is imported into a new set of circumstances, then so too can its meaning be fixed, transcending time and place, and that it can thereby perpetuate clear and immutable social and moral principles as well." E. Allen, *False Fables*, 21. On this view, the exemplary mode is disingenuous in its pretensions to authority (because its authority is not *actually* clear and immutable). Scanlon's account of exemplary authority

Pentecost does transcend time and place—hence Will's apparent time travel—but not in order to achieve an absolute identity across the temporal, situational, and perspectival lines that might otherwise separate author and reader, source text and translation, or model and copy. The *exemplum* of Pentecost connects Will's and the readers' time to the early church, allowing them to participate in Pentecost, but without collapsing the two times. Will's bewilderment—"Y wondred what þat was" (C.21.204)—signals his and the reader's persistent sense of distance and difference from what is happening, even as he gets to take part.

Indeed, an animating doctrine of Pentecost is that unity does not necessarily entail identity and that difference does not preclude likeness—and never less so than in the Trinity, which is really only first given, in its full economic manifestation, at Pentecost. Nicholas of Lyra can thus report in his own words "what the Gloss says here: The apostles were not only speaking and understanding every language, but while they themselves spoke in one language (whatever that was), all of those listening, however different their languages, understood by the power of God in their own language (whatever that was)."[23] The Pentecostal vision of unity amidst diversity accentuates humans' individuality. Far from promoting "the fantasy of moral imitation . . . as . . . the creation of an exact correspondence between the two versions,"[24] Pentecostal unity as imagined in *Piers Plowman* assumes a diversity of

---

better fits Langland's exemplary mode in the Pentecost episode. *Exempla* such as this do not make claims to transcendent authority; rather, they "persuaded by appealing to heroic figures and *auctores* the audience *already* venerated. This appeal was never static because it was precisely the capacity to produce moral authority which the figures being appealed to embodied" (Scanlon, *Narrative, Authority, and Power*, 33, my emphasis). The Holy Spirit, Piers, and his "felawes" embody the capacity to invent moral authority and to invent actions in accord with these morals.

23. Nicholas of Lyra, *Postilla super totam bibliam*, vol. 4 (Strasburg, 1492). Cf. Bede's citation of Gregory of Nazianzus by way of Rufinus on Acts 2:6 in Bede, *The Venerable Bede: Commentary on the Acts of the Apostles*, trans. Lawrence T. Martin (Kalamazoo, MI: Cistercian Publications, 1989), 30.

24. E. Allen, *False Fables*, 21.

tongues without assuming primal conflict between the One and the Many. A Wycliffite can thus write, "it is licly þat þes pilgrimes conseyveden þe same langage þat þei knewen moost of alle, and þe witt of þis langage; and so ech man hadde his owne miracle, and God movede apostlis as he wolde. And þis figuride oonesse of herte."[25] Pentecostal translation intensifies individuality while at the same time fostering "oneness"; each man could have his own miracle because, although he experienced the same Holy Spirit as every other man, his experience was not in competition with the others'.

Medieval cultural discourses, including literature, were often concerned with the translation of authority in order to conserve or assimilate ideological, symbolic, religious, and political power. These competitive objectives, however, are not the only factors that motivated translation or governed the relationships between religious or literary models and copies.[26] Never complacent about linguistic and cultural disparities, Langland seeks to reconcile his culture's heteroglossia in what Katherine Zieman, drawing on the theory of choral communities, has called heterophony, "the experience of different voices sounding in unison."[27] At Pentecost Langland imagines a harmony of the many servant voices conforming to the voice of their master, the Holy Spirit, even as they achieve their individuality—points to which I will return near the end of this chapter.

Competitive Invention in Classical Rhetoric

In *Rhetoric, Hermeneutics, and Translation in the Middle Ages,* Copeland demonstrates how medieval exegetes of classical literature assimilated the *auctoritas* of classical texts to their own rhetorical performances of

---

25. Thomas Arnold, ed., *Select English Works of John Wyclif* (Oxford: Clarendon Press, 1871), 2:307.

26. For an example of genuinely political translation motivated by power and competition, see Lynn Staley, *Languages of Power in the Age of Richard II* (University Park: Pennsylvania State University Press, 2005), 75–164.

27. Katherine Zieman, *Singing the New Song: Literacy and Liturgy in Late Medieval England* (Philadelphia: University of Pennsylvania Press, 2008), 160.

commentary, serving their "master" texts, but also supplanting them.[28] The analogy of master and servant derives from classical rhetorical theory, and its recognition of hierarchical power relations is apt. Copeland identifies a centuries-long struggle for primacy among the disciplines, waged in a competition between the discourses of grammar, rhetoric, and commentary. The key distinction is between "primary translations," which "exhibit a close alliance with the aims and methods of exegetical practice, and like exegesis define their purpose in terms of service to a source text," and "secondary translations," which "derive their essential methods and motive from exegesis, but . . . define themselves . . . through rhetorical models of invention, that is, discovery of one's own argument or subject out of available topics or commonplaces."[29]

Copeland also demonstrates that translation and commentary are fundamentally practices of invention, even of creative originality. Cultural rivalry with Greece leads Roman translators to opt for an agonistic theory of imitation. The inheritance of a Greek literary tradition incites "a historical agenda of conquest and supremacy through submission, or in Horace's famous words, 'Graecia capta ferum victorem cepit et artis / intulit agresti Latio' (captive Greece captured the savage victor and brought the arts into rustic Latium)."[30] For Horace and the subsequent *Ars poetriae* tradition that was so influential in medieval poetics, the copy's inventive difference from the model, not its lineal continuity, comes to constitute its excellence. "Horace proposes a theory of rhetorical imitation where the force of invention intervenes between model and copy, just as Quintilian remarks that 'nothing grows from imitation alone.'"[31] While translation always to a certain extent preserves the text or culture translated, what is valued in the translation may be the copy's competitive striving to displace the model text. For the Roman rhetorical theorists, likeness to the model is the norm, and

---

28. Copeland, *Rhetoric*, 3. An early and more theoretically explicit version of this argument appears in Rita Copeland, "The Fortunes of 'Non Verbum pro Verbo': Or, Why Jerome Is Not a Ciceronian," in *The Medieval Translator*, ed. Roger Ellis (Wolfeboro, NH: D. S. Brewer, 1989), 15–35.

29. Copeland, *Rhetoric*, 6–7.

30. Ibid., 31, citing Horace, Epistle 2.1.156.

31. Ibid., 29.

difference is a desirable departure by which copies attain to individuality, vitality, and excellence.

This distinction holds true enough for the classical rhetorical traditions, and it goes a long way toward explaining how Chaucer and, to a lesser extent, Gower vie with their classical forbears and literary contemporaries in order to "make it new" and assimilate *auctoritas* and originality to their own texts. But the only model of invention by translation and commentary that Copeland explores is the classical rhetorical model animated by generational competition between model and copy. The question remains open whether literature motivated by *non*competitive exegesis, "in service to a source text," cannot be just as inventive as, say, Chaucer's *Legend of Good Women*, the featured text of Copeland's discussion of Chaucer.[32]

The Pentecost episode in *Piers Plowman* gives us just one reason to theorize a literary ethics that can explain how a product of invention might be noncompetitive, nontotalizing, "original," and ethically demanding all at the same time. Too often Copeland's early work on translation is cited as a comprehensive account of medieval literary translation and its potential for rhetorical invention. The master-servant model that

---

32. Ibid., 184–203. In essays on devotional writing, Atsushi Iguchi has proposed alternatives to Copeland's models for understanding vernacular difference from Latin sources: "Copeland's theoretical framework of medieval vernacular translation, based on those writers who . . . are conscious of what they are doing in the vernacular in contestation with Latin, is not directly applicable to devotional translation, where the chief aims are replicative. . . . In such a context, the subversive aspect of translation is less apparent." In what could be seen as a dilation of Copeland's category of "primary translation," Iguchi accounts for difference between model and copy in devotional translations in terms of the "new purposes, different effects and, as often as not, . . . different audience," rather than competition to displace the model. Atsushi Iguchi, "Translating Grace: The *Scala Claustralium* and *A Ladder of Foure Ronges*," *Review of English Studies* 59, no. 242 (2007): 661. See also Atsushi Iguchi, "The Visibility of the Translator: The *Speculum Ecclesie* and *The Mirror of Holy Church*," *Neophilologus* 93, no. 3 (2009): 537–52. In my view, Langland is much more innovative than the devotional texts on which Iguchi focuses, so that neither Iguchi's expanded category of primary translation nor Copeland's category of secondary translation is adequate to *Piers Plowman*.

structures translation and commentary *in the rhetorical tradition* from at least the time of Horace down to Chaucer and Gower is not the only way of construing the relationship between text and commentary, but it has dominated scholarship on the topic.[33]

Model and Copy: The Image on the Coin

Langland's conception of ethical and rhetorical invention, though reliant on the classical rhetorical topos of the imprinted coin, construes the relationship between model and copy differently by introducing the element of false intentions in the politically charged practice of counterfeiting:

> Me may now likene lettred men to a loscheborw [counterfeit coin]
>   oþer worse
> And to a badde peny with a gode printe:
> Of moche mone þe metal is nauhte
> And ȝut is þe printe puyr trewe and parfitliche ygraue.
> And so hit fareth by false cristene: here follynge [baptism] is trewe,
> Cristendoem of holy kyrke, the kynges marke of heuene,
> Ac þe metal þat is mannes soule of many of this techares
> Is alayed with leccherye and oþer lustes of synne
> That god coueyteth nat þe coyne þat crist hymsulue printede
> And for þe synne of þe soule forsaketh his oune coyne.
> Thus ar ȝe luyþer [wicked] ylikned to lossheborwe sterlynges
> That fayre byfore folk prechen and techen
> And worcheth nat as ȝe fyndeth ywryte and wisseth þe peple.
>   (C.17.73–85)

---

33. Take, for example, Douglas Kelly's blanket statement about literary translation: "infidelity to source, and thus unfaithful translation, is what we must expect and, in all its intertextual implications, what we must look for and study." "The *Fidus interpres*: Aid or Impediment to Medieval Translation and *Translatio*," in *Translation Theory and Practice in the Middle Ages*, ed. Jeanette Beer (Kalamazoo, MI: Medieval Institute Publications, 1997), 58.

Like *lossheborwes*—the counterfeit English coins imported from the
Low Countries (or Luxembourg, as the name suggests)[34]—the souls
of false Christians are alloyed with sin, so that, although they bear
the image of Christ impressed in baptism (*follynge*), God refuses to
recognize them as legal tender. By contrast to later Lancastrian discourses of counterfeiting, which rhetorically linked the crime to heresy
and treason, Langland is more concerned here with everyday moral or-
thopraxis than with orthodoxy. But the discourse of true and counterfeit coinage activates a symbolic complex not easily contained: "between
seeming and being, outer and inner, counterfeit and real, material and
ineffable, heretical and orthodox, illegitimate and legitimate."[35]

Langland's awareness of this semiotic richness is reflected in his revisions between the B and C texts, where the theory of imitation evolves
from concerns about rhetoric to concerns about ethics. In B, Anima
counsels "alle cristene to conformen hem to charite" (B.15.344). Where

---

34. Lusshebournes were counterfeit English pennies manufactured from
cheap alloys in the Low Countries to piggyback on the strength of the English
coinage, on which Edward I built one of the most reliable monetary systems
in Europe. Edward III's Statute of Treasons of 1352 makes counterfeiting "the
king's . . . money" an offense of the same gravity as plotting his death or vi-
olating his wife since it "extends to our lord the king and his royal majesty."
A. R. Myers, ed., *English Historical Documents*, vol. 4, *1327–1485* (London: Eyre
and Spottiswoode, 1969), 403. See Diana Wood, *Medieval Economic Thought*
(New York: Cambridge University Press, 2002), 127–28. For other treatments
of the image of God and the image of the coin in *Piers Plowman*, see Barbara
Raw, "Piers and the Image of God in Man," in *"Piers Plowman": Critical Ap-
proaches*, ed. S. S. Hussey (London: Methuen, 1969), 143–79; and Margaret E.
Goldsmith, *The Image of "Piers Plowman": The Image on the Coin* (Cambridge:
D. S. Brewer, 1981).

35. Paul Strohm, *England's Empty Throne: Usurpation and the Language
of Legitimation, 1399–1422* (New Haven: Yale University Press, 1998), 146.
Strohm does not discuss *Piers Plowman*, and his case study of William Carsewell's confession of counterfeiting involves a kind of counterfeiting different
from the racket run in the Low Countries. Instead of passing off cheap metals
as real coins, Carsewell claimed to have been recruited by the outlawed Lollard
John Oldcastle to melt down silver clippings from genuine coins and to cast
them as groats with the proper markings.

C locates the corruption of the coin in "false cristene" who have received the mark in baptism, B does not mention baptism and locates the "defaute" in the discrepancy between the "fair speche" of "som folk now" and their actual failure to love (B.15.347, 351): "Boþe lettred and lewed beþ alayed now wiþ synne, / That no lif loueþ ooþer, ne oure lord as it semeþ" (B.15.354–55). According to this theological anthropology, baptism imprints the soul with the image of God, making it a Christian soul. The Christian then bears out the image in "fair speche," rhetorically conforming to the image of God. As in the sequence of the incarnation, where the Logos exists first only as Word but then takes on flesh, the rhetorical image of God precedes the deeds that incarnate the word of God in an ethical life.

The C text further develops the movement from rhetoric to ethics, explicitly drawing on invention theory. Bad clergy now take the brunt of the criticism in the C text, and they are at fault not just because of common hypocrisy, but because they "fayre byfore folk prechen and techen / And worcheth nat as ȝe fyndeth ywryte" (C.17.84–85). Hypocritical clergy elevate the hypocrisy of the "lewed" in B to a sin made graver because they practice it in the institutionally authorized rhetorical office of the preacher. Not only do they fail to match actions to words, but they also betray the *character* impressed on them in ordination, the "particular imprint on the soul, which indicates that those in holy orders are marked off to perform certain spiritual functions."[36]

The ethical errors of the clergy therefore follow from rhetorical errors, namely, errors of invention. Scripture, what is "ywryte," supplies ample models and topics both for speaking and action. These preachers apparently find the material sufficient for the invention—the *finding* (C.17.85)—of elaborate sermons, but insufficient for the invention of works. They do not act according to what they discover written and what they invent homiletically. The hypocritical preachers manage to interpret and invent according to the ethical sense of scripture, but their

---

36. Alastair Minnis, *Fallible Authors: Chaucer's Pardoner and Wife of Bath* (Philadelphia: University of Pennsylvania Press, 2008), 67. On the moral responsibility of preachers, see 36–54.

invention realizes only its rhetorical potential without proceeding to practical ethical invention, the invention of actions. Because their invention is not an invention of works, Liberum Arbitrium observes, it cannot persuade and they fail truly to teach the people ("nat . . . wisseth þe peple" [C.17.85]). Liberum Arbitrium's analysis suggests that interpretation and rhetorical performance are irreducibly ethical; if invention is not borne out in practice, even its rhetorical dimension will come to naught.

For Langland, then, the goal of rhetorical invention is rhetorical imitation, which should issue in practical, concrete ethical imitation. Because of original sin, the model and the copy are originally different. Baptism restores—indeed, perfects—the similarity between model and copy. But sin persists, and even with the clear imprint of baptism, the total form of the soul, the complete image, remains different from the model. Thus difference between model and copy is the norm, and similarity is a desirable departure from the norm. People achieve excellence by closing the gap between model and copy.

This logic of invention and imitation should be familiar from the cult of the saints and the theology of Christ's and Mary's exemplarity that animates much late medieval monastic piety and transfigures the agonistic violence of classical rhetoric as a positive, reconciling force. Horace's violent images of invention come strikingly close to twelfth-century Cistercians' and Carthusians' images of sin, as Caroline Bynum describes them, only with the goals reversed: "fragmentation, rupture, assertion of one's differentness from the image of God that one is in the process of becoming. The idea of Christ as nursing or pregnant mother is for Cistercians one among a host of images that articulate a process of return through love of others to true dependence, a return made possible by the breaking of false dependence on the difference and otherness of the world."[37] Whereas for Copeland's Romans, "the force of

---

37. Caroline Walker Bynum, *Jesus as Mother: Studies in the Spirituality of the High Middle Ages* (Berkeley and Los Angeles: University of California Press, 1982), 166.

invention intervenes between model and copy,"[38] for Langland the force of invention should conform the copy to the model. And while this relationship is figured by Horace with the violent imagery of battle, in the later medieval discourse of the imitation of Christ, as expressed in the devotion to the Sacred Heart and in theological explanations of the stigmata, the wounds of Christ "were regarded as places of refuge, spiritual remedies, and wells or fountains of life, pity, mercy, comfort, grace."[39] That is, the copy conforms to the model by suffering violence, but this violence is seen as salutary and reconciling rather than as martial and hegemonic. If invention does indeed entail violence, why should we not understand it as the violence of repair, instead of rupture?

The "violence of repair" could suggest one path for thought about Langland's own chronic revisionism, here on display in the transition from B to C. Humans may achieve excellence by closing the gap between model and copy, but *Piers Plowman* never depicts life with the gap closed. This is not to say that Langland avoids imagining rightly ordered lives and communities; rather, he reserves visions of fulfillment for his most allegorical moments, one of which I discuss at the end of this chapter when I raise the question of how Langland's anagogical imagination relates to his tropological imagination. Besides issues of eschatological fulfillment, there are other reasons why copies will never be *the same* as their models. In kinship models, for instance, the child will never be *the same* as its father or mother, no matter how close the resemblance. D. Vance Smith has shown how, in the genealogy of sin that *Piers Plowman* traces through the curse of Cain, human paternity threatens to displace divine paternity, positing "an irredeemable gap

---

38. Copeland, *Rhetoric*, 29.

39. Giles Constable, *Three Studies in Medieval Religious and Social Thought: The Interpretation of Mary and Martha, the Ideal of the Imitation of Christ, the Orders of Society* (New York: Cambridge University Press, 1995), 225. This represents a further application to bodily suffering of an enduring interpretation of imitation as the reconciling participation in Christ's divinity and the closing of the gap between humans' intact *imago Dei* and their obliterated ethical and ontological likeness (*similitudo*) to God. On participation, see 150–55 and 164–65; on ethical and ontological image and likeness, 166–68.

between material making and divine creation."[40] Other gaps, however—such as the gap between God's being and human beings—are built into creation and so are not in need of redemption or violent recuperation.[41]

Tropology and the Ethics of Making

For texts such as *Piers Plowman*, we need a more supple theory of invention and exemplarity than a dyadic account according to which imitation produces alterity, not sameness. If I am right that the rhetorical traditions, as they have been used to explain Middle English literary invention, cannot provide such an account, then perhaps other intellectual resources will serve us better. I suggest that we turn to the highly developed theories of ethics and invention that emerge from the theology and practice of biblical exegesis and overlap with homiletic theory.

In 1215 the Fourth Lateran Council intervened in debates about the relationship between nature and grace by succinctly defining the analogy of being in terms that should be familiar: "One cannot note a similarity between Creator and creature—however great—without having to note an ever greater dissimilarity between them."[42] The doctrine of analogy expressed here carefully secures the transcendence of the abso-

---

40. D. Smith, *The Book of the Incipit*, 138; on paternity and beginnings, 113–38.

41. See the final section in this chapter, "The Invention of Peace."

42. This formulation is Erich Przywara's, translated by John R. Betz in Betz, "Beyond the Sublime: The Aesthetics of the Analogy of Being (Part One)," *Modern Theology* 21, no. 3 (2005): 374. For Przywara's work on analogy, which has inspired a new wave of creative work on the analogy of being in philosophical theology, see Erich Przywara, *"Analogia entis": Metaphysics: Original Structure and Universal Rhythm*, trans. John R. Betz and David Bentley Hart (Grand Rapids, MI: William B. Eerdmans, 2014). The Lateran IV formulation occurs in a defense of Peter Lombard's Trinitarian definitions against Joachim of Fiore's criticisms: "inter creatorem et creaturam non potest similitudo notari, quin inter eos maior sit dissimilitudo notanda." Heinrich Denziger and Adolf Schönmetzer, eds., *Enchiridion symbolorum, definitionum et declarationum de rebus fidei et morum* (Barcinone: Herder, 1973), 806.

lutely other God, while allowing creaturely participation in and imitation of God. Such a dynamic, tensile theory of analogy can contemplate the sameness and difference entailed in every invention without reducing literary and ethical action to a zero-sum economy of struggle between old and new, model and copy.

Such a theory can help us understand a peculiar aspect of readers' responses to exemplary texts: while readers are often inspired to convert words into works, they seldom do exactly what their models did. Some kind of translation occurs between the represented action and the action readers feel inspired to perform. The theology of exegesis helps to explain how this happens because, in Gilbert Dahan's words, "it is the passage from the letter to the spiritual or mystical senses that sets in motion the mechanisms of *translatio* [transfer of meaning]."[43] In the exegetical theory of Bonaventure, for example, the translation of a text (or any created datum) into a reader's ethical action is built into the fabric of creation itself: "Because the way to God is through faith, hope, and love, every creature is a suggestion of what we should believe, expect, and do. And parallel to this, there is a threefold spiritual meaning: the allegorical concerning what we should believe, the anagogical concerning what we should expect, and the moral concerning what we should do, for love leads to action."[44] But every imitative action, as Lateran IV insists, evinces an ever greater dissimilarity from the model for the action—not because imitation subverts the model, but because the model itself transcends any possible likeness it inspires. Like Gregory of Nyssa's Moses, who chases after the back of God for all eternity, the nearer the copy approaches its model, the farther it finds it has to go.[45]

---

43. Dahan, *L'exégèse chrétienne*, 55.

44. Bonaventure, *Collations on the Six Days*, 13.11.

45. "Certainly whoever pursues true virtue participates in nothing other than God, because he is himself absolute virtue. Since, then, those who know what is good by nature desire participation in it, and since this good has no limit, the participant's desire itself necessarily has no stopping place but stretches out with the limitless." Gregory of Nyssa, *The Life of Moses*, trans. Abraham J. Malherbe and Everett Ferguson (New York: Paulist Press, 1978), Prol. 7.

Imitation does indeed produce alterity, but it also produces sameness—or, more accurately, correspondence. The challenge of interpretation is not to determine whether ethical inventions reflect literal or figural modes of interpretation, but to discover how—since invention is never the *same*—to be sensitive to the diverse renditions that models undergo as they are reinvented in unforeseeable copies. In other words, saints in hagiographies and literary characters such as Will and Conscience are not just models, but models of how to be copies. Built into these texts is the understanding that ethics is always translation, and translation always entails invention. Texts such as *Piers Plowman* give examples or represent models of people struggling to turn words into works, inspired not merely by responsibility to the Other but by the very specific possibility of participation in the history of redemption on the way to contemplation of a God who is always ever greater.

The theory of tropological interpretation can help us attend to these translations in at least two important ways. First, tropology helps us to see writing as ethical action. If Liberum Arbitrium is right about the blessedness of the one who turns words into works, then Langland can defend his practice of making because writing qualifies as labor, as *opera*. Imaginatif, sometimes a critic of literary making, approves Spirit-inspired copying: "Althouh men maden bokes God was here maystre / And seynt spirit þe saumplarie and said what men sholde write" (C.14.46–47). He imagines the making of the Bible in a monastic scriptorium, where God (the Father) superintends the scribal work and the authors of scripture copy from the "saumplarie" (the copytext) that is the Holy Spirit. Imaginatif uses the image to prove a point much larger than the inspiration of the Bible, namely, that books are an appropriate and necessary medium for knowledge of God: "For as a man may nat se þat misseth his yes, / No more can no clerk but if hit come of bokes" (C.14.44–45). It is noteworthy that Imaginatif does not here defend the teaching office of the church, *sacra doctrina*, philosophy, or even learning in general. Instead he defends "bokes," which metonymically comprehend all disciplines, even the "makyng" he earlier criticized.

Bonaventure draws an analogy between the two terms of Imaginatif's metonym—the Bible and "bokes"—dividing all the arts on analogy to the four senses of scripture. All knowledge concerned with practical action falls under the tropological sense of scripture. And he extends the analogy according to Aristotelian causal analysis: everything relating to efficient causation (which corresponds to practical action) also falls under the tropological sense. For example, in the mechanical arts, the allegorical sense corresponds to the "mediating similitude" the maker has in mind; the tropological sense to the manner, quality, and activity of making; and the anagogical sense to the delight in the finished product.[46] Bonaventure can thus "reduce"—lead back—all making to the divine illumination of scripture because all making already proceeds from the same source as scripture. Imaginatif, who has accused Will of meddling with makings,[47] can approve of a kind of making that can be led back to scripture by an analogical reduction. Tropological making, then, is not merely writing about ethical themes or even for the purpose of inspiring ethical action, but a habit of invention that translates idea into action with a "reductive" momentum leading back to scripture and (at the same time) forward toward full correspondence with its model, toward the soul's mystical union with God and the church's fulfillment in the kingdom of heaven. That is to say, tropological making happens between the letter of scripture (the literal sense), the truth of salvation history (the allegorical sense), and their eschatological fulfillment (the anagogical sense).

Second, tropological theory helps us recognize those moments when Langland specifies ethical action and the good as, precisely, participation in Christian salvation history as made available in the Bible, the liturgy, and the sacraments. For example, Christ's exemplarity is given a tropological cast when it becomes the means by which the disciples on the road to Emmaus recognize him:

> Cleophas ne knewe hym nat þat he Crist were
> For his pore parail and pilgrimes clothes
> Til he blessed here bred and brake hit hem bitwene.

---

46. Bonaventure, *Saint Bonaventure's "De reductione artium ad theologiam,"* 12–14.

47. "þou medlest þee wiþ makynges" (B.12.16).

So by his werkes thei wisten þat he was iesu
Ac by clothyng they knewe hym nat, so caytifliche he ȝede.
And al was ensample, sothly, to vs synfole here
That we sholde be low and louelich and lele vch man til oþer
And pacient as pilgrimes for pilgrimes are we alle.

(C.12.124–31)

Cleophas and his companion recognize Christ not by his words or appearance, but by his works. This is "al" an example—first to the disciples in Emmaus who recognized Christ by his actions, and then to "vs synfole here," who must recognize Christ in poverty, meekness, and love, so conforming ourselves to his pilgrim ethic. The "here" has a deictic function, locating the example's intended audience in the present place and time, and by those coordinates identifying the reading subject as the hermeneutical object of Christ's ethical intentionality.

This hermeneutics requires conversion. The poverty that is commended as a good at the end of the quotation actually distracts the disciples from Christ's identity at the beginning of the episode, requiring their interpretive conversion along the way. In order to do the good, they have to recognize the good, and in order to do that, they have to interpret Christ's poor rags as signs of his divinely humble identity. But the interpretation is not complete until Christ *acts*, making himself known in the breaking of the bread: "So by his werkes thei wisten þat he was iesu." The act allows the disciples to read the situation aright, and when they do so, they (and perhaps we) discern a call to be "low and louelich . . . and pacient as pilgrimes."

In Luke's telling of the story, their act of interpretation results in their conversion: they turn back from Emmaus and return to Jerusalem, where Jesus had already instructed the disciples to wait. This literal turn is a reminder of why early Christians appropriated the classical definition of tropology (dealing with turns of phrase, figures of speech) to name the ethical sense: the Greek root *tropos* means both "turn" and "way of life." This moral use of *tropologia* was a Christian innovation, for in classical rhetoric the root was taken much less literally; our modern sense of a trope as a "turn of phrase" is nearly identical to the ancient usage. In the words of Robert of Melun, "*Tropologia* means speech that turns (*sermo conversivus*), because it designates a deed of such a sort that it is necessary for us to be converted to it with respect to the establishment of moral edification."[48] Alan of Lille, in perhaps the most widely known etymology of the later Middle Ages, significantly draws his example of tropology from the life of Christ: "It is called tropology when through some act it is understood what we ought to do; whence also it is called tropology as if [it were] a word turned toward us, like this: by Christ having his hands affixed to the cross, it is signified that we ought to restrain our hands from the guilt of sin."[49]

On the road to Emmaus, Christ gives the example of the ideal unity of interpretation and invention, having himself "expounded to them in all the scriptures the things that were concerning him" (Luke 24:27). Christ presents himself as the ideal copy of the Old Testament model (the Law), but at the same time he reverses the relationship, establishing himself as the model in which Law and Love are summed up. As *Piers Plowman's* subsequent discourse on poverty suggests, the same Christ who rightly expounds the scriptures becomes the prototypical exemplar of poverty. Mary herself was "a puyre pore mayde and to a pore man ywedded" (C.12.135), copying the model of her son.

For Langland, it is not enough to see Christ, or even to hear him interpreting scripture Christologically; Christians must also be enabled

---

48. Cited in de Lubac, *Medieval Exegesis*, 2:129.

49. He continues, "*Tropus* means conversion. It is also a figure, as when a word is converted from its proper meaning, whence the phrase, 'it is said *tropica*,' that is, figuratively." (Tropologia dicitur . . . quando per aliquod factum intelligitur quod a nobis sit faciendum; unde et tropologia dicitur quasi sermo conversus ad nos, ut per hoc quod Christus habuit manus affixas cruci significatur quod manus debemus cohibere a reatu peccati. Tropus dicitur conversio. Est etiam figura quando dictio a propria significatione convertitur, unde locutio dicitur tropica, id est figurativa.) Alan of Lille, *Distinctiones dictionum theologicalium*, s.vv. "tropologia" and "tropus," in PL 210:981a–b. On the migration of this etymology from early lexicons into the homiletic aids and sermons of the later Middle Ages, see Riccardo Quinto, "Peter the Chanter and the 'Miscellanea del Codice del Tesoro' (Etymology as a Way for Constructing a Sermon)," in *Constructing the Medieval Sermon*, ed. Roger Anderson (Turnhout: Brepols, 2007), 33–81.

by the Spirit to practice spiritual exegesis on the scriptures themselves and invent "in our own tongues the wonderful works of God," which is what Luke says of the glossolalic apostles at Pentecost (Acts 2:11). The ethical invention modeled in *Piers Plowman*, then, should be considered tropological because it situates ethical activity—especially Langland's activity of making *Piers Plowman*—between the Christian-historical narrative of allegorical or figural reading and the mystical union of the anagogical sense. Tropological invention is a pilgrim invention, always underway between doctrine and fulfillment, between model and perfected copy, and realized only in "low and louelich and lele" relations "vch man til oþer . . . for pilgrimes are we alle" (C.12.130–31). That is, tropological invention according to *Piers Plowman* situates the ethics of alterity within a dynamic, circulating movement between moral law, free action, and final goods.

Ethical Invention and the Event of Beginning

How do final goods rate in a lifetime of chronic revision? On the one hand, there is the Langland who revises in a dogged, faithful pursuit to understand and experience the ultimate goods of the Christian faith that are "out there."[50] On the other hand, there is the Langland whose search for St. Truth is an "exploration" without "a fixed, previously known referent," in which "the concept is being created by the text of the poem itself."[51] Surely Langland invents both by transcendent and immanent impulses.[52] But we have more trouble understanding how final goods, how ethical teleologies, can coexist with free invention, free action, and the ethics of alterity. Literature involves, in Derrida's words,

---

50. Along these lines, I appreciate how Pamela Raabe argues for the coherence of Langland's project and the attainability of faithful understanding and final goods in *Imitating God: The Allegory of Faith in "Piers Plowman" B* (Athens: University of Georgia Press, 1990).

51. Carruthers, *The Search for St. Truth*, 10, 20.

52. Raabe and Carruthers both recognize this, each in her own way.

"the invention of the other."[53] In his influential account, invention is an ethical act, first, because it requires breaking the norm; second, because it allows the Other to come into view, and, as Lévinas teaches, "access to the face [of the Other] is straightaway ethical."[54] But the origin of this encounter with the Other is, tellingly, an act of inventive violence: "An invention always presupposes some illegality, the breaking of an implicit contract; it inserts a disorder into the peaceful ordering of things, it disregards the proprieties."[55]

In the so-called "new ethical theory," the conflict that Derridean invention imposes between the Same and the Other orders the social ethics of literature.[56] As his work has been digested and applied by literary theorists, Derrida stands for an agonistic ethic of reading in which literature facilitates ethical experience when "[t]he reader experiences the free play of his or her imagination as produced through a power struggle with a social other . . . who, in turn, binds him or her."[57] For proponents of the new ethics within literary studies, literature invents ethical experience when it troubles "certainty by an apprehension that comes through surprised feeling,"[58] and when it upsets the rigid absolutes of morality with the contingencies and irresolvable tensions of (the new) ethics.[59]

---

53. See Derrida, "Psyche."

54. Emmanuel Lévinas, *Ethics and Infinity*, trans. Philippe Nemo (Pittsburgh: Duquesne University Press, 1985), 85.

55. Derrida, "Psyche," 1.

56. For a survey of the "new ethics" in literary studies, see Dorothy J. Hale, "Aesthetics and the New Ethics: Theorizing the Novel in the Twenty-First Century," *PMLA* 124, no. 3 (2009): 896–905. On the first wave of the new ethics, see Lawrence Buell, "In Pursuit of Ethics," *PMLA* 114, no. 1 (1999): 7–19.

57. Hale, "Aesthetics and the New Ethics," 902.

58. Ibid., 903.

59. J. Allan Mitchell contrasts "the immanent particularity of ethical practices or patterns of behavior (Hegelian *Sittlichkeit*) and normative rules of morality regulating behavior (*Moralität*)" in order to argue that "ethics is situated in the factical event prior to congealing into abstract morality." *Ethics and Eventfulness in Middle English Literature* (New York: Palgrave Macmillan, 2009), 24.

But this distinction between an underdetermined, immanent, non-teleological *ethics* and an absolute, extrinsic, teleological *morality* smuggles in a Kantian opposition between heteronomy and autonomy that may only awkwardly be applied to the concrete moralities we encounter in *Piers Plowman*. For a poem in which a central character is a personified Conscience, a simplistic opposition between loving, open-ended concern for the Other and the prescriptive morality of law will not suffice. "Hoso lyueth in lawe and in loue doth wel," counsels Wit, adducing matrimony as a prime example of love for others, but also warning married couples, "worcheth nat out of tyme" (C.10.203, 288). The "lawe" forbids "loue" during menstruation and pregnancy. Is this a paradox? Wit does not think so. He does not admit a choice between autonomous practical reason and heteronomous natural law; loving couples must use their practical reason to cooperate with and participate in the natural and moral laws governing fertility, with the understanding that their love and their offspring (their inventions) will be the better for it.

This ethical conception is underwritten by what Rémi Brague, intending to short-circuit the heteronomy-autonomy binary, calls "cosmonomy," according to which "it is in fact the insertion into the cosmos that enables the moral subject to be truly himself, to be truly an *autos*. This conformity in no way consists in bending to an exterior law, an other (*heteros*). . . . It is only our insertion into the *kosmos* where it is most fully itself . . . that confers authentic freedom upon us."[60] According to Wit, men and women are most fully and freely able to exercise their love when they reserve "bedbourde" (bed play) for the right "tyme" (C.10.288–91). Just as a copy need not displace its model in order to be freely itself, the law of creation is not in competition with creaturely becoming.[61]

---

60. Rémi Brague, *The Wisdom of the World: The Human Experience of the Universe in Western Thought*, trans. Teresa Lavender Fagan (Chicago: University of Chicago Press, 2003), 153.

61. In Brague's phrase, "human action [is] in phase with cosmological realities." Rémi Brague, *The Law of God: The Philosophical History of an Idea*, trans. Lydia G. Cochrane (Chicago: University of Chicago Press, 2007), vii.

At Pentecost, Will and Conscience are inserted into one of those points where the *kosmos* is most fully itself, a signal event in the history of salvation. By sleight of dream and the *ductus* of Conscience's sermon, they achieve what Margot Fassler identifies as the goal of Victorine sequence hymns: "to draw the singing clergy into the world of the primitive Christian church."[62] But however primitive this intense experience of cosmonomy might be, the old does not efface the new. Will's subjective perspective—"and thenne cam, me thouhte, / Oen *spiritus paraclitus*" (C.21.200–201)—tethers readers to the *now*, even as he assimilates himself to the *then*. Just as the Wycliffite exegesis of Pentecost envisions the simultaneous diversity of language and unity of understanding, so Langland's treatment of this episode conserves the new and the old, the model and the copy. The "Creator Spirit" comes "in liknesse of a lihtnynge" and "ouerspradde[s]" the apostles "in fuyres liknesse," counterintuitively adopting the role of copy to his creatures' models, as the language of likeness suggests (C.21.202–5).

Similarly, Langland casts the episode in the likeness of the Acts narrative, but in doing so he also invents it. Exploiting the combinatory, imaginative privileges of a maker, Langland makes a quasihistorical etiology of the invention of the church and part of the liturgy.[63] The scene is both interpretive—encountering a historical "source" that comes before it—and inventive. Langland represents an act of literary-liturgical invention even as he himself innovates. In the interpretive mode, like the bystanders in the Acts narrative who "wondered . . . 'what meaneth this?'" (Acts 2:12), Will "wondred what þat was and wagged [nudged] Consience" to interpret the tongues of fire; Conscience explains their meaning as the "*spiritus paraclitus*," whose name is Grace

---

62. Margot Fassler, *Gothic Song: Victorine Sequences and Augustinian Reform in Twelfth-Century Paris* (Cambridge: Cambridge University Press, 1993), 269.

63. On imagination as a combinatory faculty, see Alastair J. Minnis, "Langland's Ymaginatif and Late-Medieval Theories of Imagination," *Comparative Criticism* 3 (1981): 71–103. For an excellent discussion of Langland's imagination, including a survey of relevant research, see Michelle Karnes, "Will's Imagination in *Piers Plowman*," *Journal of English and Germanic Philology* 108, no. 1 (2009): 43–53.

(C.21.204–8). And in the inventive mode, with the "many hundret" they can kneel—"Knele now"! (C.21.209)—and sing the song of praise, a response to the Holy Spirit's advent.

Here we glimpse the invention of the *Veni creator spiritus*—a Pentecost sequence hymn—at the foundation of the liturgy, which Langland envisions simultaneously with the foundation of the church. *En masse*, as if at Mass, the crowd kneels and creates a hymn of praise to the Spirit of creation. As if inspired like Peres's "felawes" (201), who instantaneously "knowe alle kyne langages" (203), Will and the congregation find that they know a hymn in the language of the church, that is, the universal language, Latin.[64] The hymn preexists their singing—or so Conscience presumes—but it could not have preexisted Pentecost. They sing it for the first time, but it comes before them, or comes to them, ready-made. They invent it because they discover it, and they discover it in singing it. The hymn is a gift, but no less, for that, an invention.

Read in light of Derrida's analysis of invention, the Holy Spirit breaks through the horizon of history to reinterpret the Jewish holiday, thus inventing a new event that issues in a call—signaled by the *incipit* of the hymn "*Come* Creator Spirit"—with which the nascent church responds by its own participatory "come." Invention of the other breaks through history as an *event*, the event of a call, to which the inventor

---

64. Fiona Somerset has recognized a similarly demotic use of Latin in the B-prologue, where MS F prefaces Latin lines from a summa for preachers with, "Thanne cryeden alle þe comonys with o voys atonys" (B.Prol.143). This line asserting lay unity takes the form of a Latin leonine hexameter, melding conventions from both languages and "accomplish[ing] on the level of form the assertion of commonality, exchange, or even fusion between Latin and the vernacular that . . . is foregrounded by the passage's insistence that the 'commune' speaks a 'vers of latyn.' . . . There is no firm boundary between Latin and English . . . : words or phrases may be used effectively by both the fully fluent, and those with the most limited functional literacy." Fiona Somerset, "'Al þe comonys with o voys atonys': Multilingual Latin and Vernacular Voice in *Piers Plowman*," *Yearbook of Langland Studies* 19 (2005): 135–36. What Somerset identifies from a sociolinguistic perspective Langland approaches theologically in the Pentecost episode, addressing the pneumatological and ecclesial conditions under which linguistic unity and diversity need not conflict.

answers, "*come in.*"[65] Here the ethical comes into view: how to say "come" and to answer the call of the other.[66] But can Derrida's construal of the event of invention comprehend Langland's invention? If Langland's invention does not disturb the peace but *makes* it, and if the highest aim of his copies is to conform to their models, then either *Piers Plowman* is an "invention of the same"—limiting itself to the realm of the possible, inventing only what already exists, and so, in effect, inventing nothing and foreclosing the advent of the other—or we need to question whether Derrida's account of invention is comprehensive enough. In Derrida's thought, because "invention of the other" is predicated on the impossible, invention structured on a model-copy relationship can only be "invention of the same." Invention of the other must always involve the overthrow of all models and so it must always involve some kind of originary violence. In Derrida's terms, the event of invention must interrupt every possible horizon (every possible model). But what if the event comes before all horizons, if the copy precedes the model? This is the crucial question that Jean-Luc Marion has introduced to phenomenology, and it opens a perspective on Langland's invention and ethics not afforded by the new ethical theory.[67]

---

65. "This invention of the entirely other is beyond any possible status; I still call it invention, because one gets ready for it, one makes this step destined to let the other come, *come in.* . . . To get ready for this coming of the other is what can be called deconstruction. . . . To invent would then be to 'know' how to say 'come' and to answer the 'come' of the other." Derrida, "Psyche," 39.

66. The possibility of the other's call is implied by the temporality of texts. Because a text is also an event, it participates in the event-ness of history. "Never does an invention appear, never does an invention take place, without an inaugural event. Nor is there any invention for the future of a *possibility* or of a *power* that will remain at the disposal of everyone. Advent there must be, because the event of an invention, its act of inaugural production . . . must be valid *for the future* [l'avenir]." Ibid., 5–6.

67. A brief genealogy of Marion's innovation in phenomenology might run as follows: Edmund Husserl limited phenomenality—what it is that phenomenology studies—to what appears to consciousness. Martin Heidegger redefined phenomenality to include all beings and Being. Marion further stretches phenomenality to define it as anything that shows itself, effectively

In the phenomenology of agonistic invention, invention is violent because it breaks a "horizon," a prior condition of possibility. But Marion sidesteps violence by sidestepping horizons. In Marion's thought, the event of invention does not interrupt horizons; rather, it happens, or *comes*, without horizon or before any horizon. The event is always a gift, a phenomenon that comes without being called, before there is even language with which to call: "The gifted does not have language or *logos* as its property, but it finds itself endowed with them—as gifts that are shown only if it regives them to their unknown origin."[68] In a similar manner, Will and the crowd at Pentecost are endowed not with just any language of praise, but with the sequence hymn that, at least in the liturgies of York and Hereford, accompanied the procession of the gifts of bread and wine, the works of human hands, to the altar before the Eucharistic canon.[69] They give the gift of the hymn back to its origin, the

---

conceptualizing the phenomenon before or without any horizon. Thus mental states that have no existence, such as boredom or expectation, as well as phenomena without being (understood as *ens commune*), such as God, would now be objects of phenomenological inquiry. For the original maneuver in this direction, see Jean-Luc Marion, *God without Being: Hors Texte*, trans. Thomas A. Carlson (Chicago: University of Chicago Press, 1991). A helpful conspectus of the "religious turn" in phenomenology is Kevin Hart, "Introduction," in *Counter-Experiences: Reading Jean-Luc Marion*, ed. Kevin Hart (Notre Dame, IN: University of Notre Dame Press, 2007), 1–54.

68. Jean-Luc Marion, *Being Given: Toward a Phenomenology of Givenness*, trans. Jeffrey L. Kosky (Stanford, CA: Stanford University Press, 2002), 288. In Marion's work, the language of "the given" and "givenness" take over the conceptual work that "event" performs in Derrida's thought. It may be that the concepts are interchangeable in the most fundamental issues of phenomenology, such as the definition of phenomenality and the possibility of phenomena without being. At some crucial moments, especially when speaking of temporality, Marion crosses into the language of event, and at these moments his thought is completely consistent with other moments when the language of gift dominates. See, for example, ibid., 131–39.

69. Stephen A. Barney, *The Penn Commentary on "Piers Plowman,"* vol. 5, *C Passūs 20–22; B Passūs 18–20* (Philadelphia: University of Pennsylvania Press, 2006), 132.

Creator Spirit, who, as the hymn says, swells the neck with speech.[70] But does this not cancel out the singers' originality? "How can anything be the origin of what it must take as its own premise?" asks Jean-Louis Chrétien.[71] How can makers possibly bear out the work of the Holy Spirit so that neither are they merely Spirit-*possessed* ("These men are full of new wine" [Acts 2:13]), nor does their making conflict with and eventually displace the Spirit's agency?

Marion answers this question by differentiating between sameness and correspondence. For Marion, as for Derrida, the structure of the event is one of call and response. But Marion inverts the order: although the call (or the gift) is absolutely prior to the response, the response is phenomenologically prior because "only the response performs the call, and the gifted renders visible and audible what gives itself to it *only by corresponding to it* in the act of responding."[72] While in Derrida invention is predicated on rupture, Marion bases invention on correspondence. The response's correspondence to the call, what Derrida might call its "sameness," is not an optional choice (as the invention of the same is for Derrida), but the very condition of the call showing itself at all. How, then, does Marion escape the tyranny of the same? He does so just as Langland does: by refusing the dichotomy of likeness and difference. The given, for Marion, is like Langland's *spiritus paraclitus*: its single source "in liknesse of a lihtnynge" (C.21.202) in a single movement "ouerspradde hem alle" (C.21.206) in order to produce the diversity of "alle kyne langages" (C.21.203). Since all that one has (the grace

---

70. "Sermone ditans guttura" (l. 12). The possessives in the first stanza underscore the Spirit's intrinsic cooperation with human creativity: "Veni creator, spiritus, / Mentes tuorum visita, / Imple superna gratia, / Quae tu creasti pectora" (Come, Creator Spirit / Visit your minds, / Fill with supernal grace / The hearts you have created) (ll. 1–4). Guido Maria Dreves, ed., *Hymnographi Latini: Lateinische Hymnendichter des Mittelalters*, vol. 2, Analecta hymnica Medii Aevi 50 (Leipzig, 1907; repr. New York: Johnson Reprint Company, 1961), 193–94.

71. Jean-Louis Chrétien, *The Call and the Response*, trans. Anne A. Davenport (New York: Fordham University Press, 2004), 5.

72. Marion, *Being Given*, 288, my emphasis.

of the Holy Spirit) has been given, and the given only appears when the gifted one makes it appear in a response ("Veni, creator spiritus!"), the call and the response (the given and the gifted) always correspond without ever being the same because the response is always a completely new, unforeseen event. "[The call] shows itself only if the gifted *converts* it into a phenomenon (responsal) where from now on it has a visibility."[73] We find here in Marion the fundamental tropological movement that Liberum Arbitrium expresses in the words of Bernard: "'*Beatus . . . qui . . . verba* vertit *in opera*'" (Blessed is the one who *converts* words into works) (C.16.22–23). The call (the text) never shows itself, is never activated (was never a call at all), unless it first receives a response in the form of *conversion* into a new action, an event, a phenomenon. And while that phenomenon is nothing more than the call of the Holy Spirit made audible in choral response, it is also nothing less than a completely new, previously impossible, unforeseeable phenomenon.

The Pentecostal image of ideal model-copy relationship—reconciling individual to communal voice, Latin to vernacular, local parish to universal church—breaks down in subsequent action. Beginning with Grace's sermon on the crafts, where the vagaries of daily economic life defy a neat summary according to medieval estates theory, the breakdown culminates in the capitulation of the Barn of Unite to vicious complacency. The only reason we should not read this collapse as the undoing of the work's cumulative ambitions is that *Piers Plowman*'s vision of ethical invention is not necessarily a vision of ethical progress. Indeed, as Nicolette Zeeman has observed, "although the poem has its visionary climax, it does not cease to produce narratives of failure, rebuke, suffering and desire."[74] As the gap between model and copy reopens, as the Christian community disintegrates, and as Piers disappears from the narrative, the resultant lack instigates desire, which translates into more writing, more passūs, or, at the end of the work, into Conscience's new quest for Piers, presumably "solicit[ing] the reader to

---

73. Ibid., 299, my emphasis.
74. Nicolette Zeeman, *"Piers Plowman" and the Medieval Discourse of Desire* (New York: Cambridge University Press, 2006), 263.

enter into this process."[75] *Piers Plowman*'s ultimate beginning shifts the onus of invention onto the reader, joining "the reader with the text's 'I' and carr[ying] an imperative of performance, a demand that this text ... be embodied and put into action."[76] This imperative, I suggest, is best considered as *tropological* because instead of taking the form of a raw command, it invites readers to participate in a narrative that has been represented (allegorically) as salvific. Just as allegorical interpretation recognizes Christ in the Old Testament history of Israel's redemption, and just as, by a tropological interpretation, readers depart daily from Egypt in their own personal Exodus, so *Piers Plowman* invites its readers to participate in its salvific narrative (copied from the biblical model) and to invent new beginnings.[77]

Such an account of invention as the response to a tropological imperative allows us to elaborate D. Vance Smith's explanation of how invention begins "in the act of living itself. A well-ordered life, an exemplary life, constructs the mind as a well-ordered place in which to store the knowledge acquired to live properly. It is for this reason that the Middle Ages connects poetry with ethics."[78] And it is for this reason that *Piers Plowman* begins again and again, seeking to make up for the brute reality that, as Marion puts it, "the responsal will always be suspected of having poorly or partially identified the call, of not having perfectly accomplished its injunction, of not having exhausted all its possibilities. . . . Each advance remains a beginning, and the responsal never finishes

---

75. Ibid., 19.

76. Nancy Bradley Warren, "Incarnational (Auto)biography," in *Oxford Twenty-First Century Approaches to Literature: Middle English*, ed. Paul Strohm (New York: Oxford University Press, 2007), 380.

77. The daily recapitulation of Israel's history is a prominent tropological theme. For example, the Pseudo-Remigius writes, "For that which was prefigured there once is fulfilled in each believer at the end of the age by means of the Church's daily mournings; for Israel departs from Egypt daily, when one of the faithful spiritually departs from this world." *In Psalmos* [113], PL 131:721a; cited in de Lubac, *Medieval Exegesis*, 2:359n42.

78. D. Smith, *The Book of the Incipit*, 68.

beginning (like desire)."[79] Langland's new beginnings emerge (more often than not) from a desire to keep the law, not to break it, as Derridean invention would have it. But these beginnings are not oblivious to Derridean invention. Indeed, Conscience sets out on his ultimate quest at the end of passus B.20/C.22 not only "to seke Peres the Plouhman," but so that friars, who currently "for nede flateren / And countrepledeth me," might have an alternative "fyndynge" (C.22.383–84)—a term with ethical as well as inventive connotations. The Wycliffite Bible translates the Latin *adinventio* in Wis. 14:12 as "finding," meaning the source or root or beginning of an ethical disposition: "The bigynnyng forsothe of fornycacioun is the outseching of maumetis, and the finding of hem is corupcioun of lyf."[80] When Conscience seeks a "fyndynge" for the friars, Langland means not just an endowment but a better mode of ethical invention.[81] Conscience, poised at the beginning of his final journey, desires to respond to the call issued at Pentecost, to undertake the responsibility and let the call manifest itself. He hopes his new beginning will create, in turn, other calls that in their inevitable inadequacy will demand interpretation and invention, forming a circuit for what Marion has called the "invention of heretofore unseen phenomena."[82] To revise Liberum Arbitrium's citation of Bernard: blessed is the one who converts these words into heretofore unseen phenomena.

If allegory, according to Augustine of Denmark, deals with the content of belief, and anagogy with the substantial fulfillment of things hoped for, then tropology fittingly falls between them, measuring and traversing the distance between ideas and their fulfillment.[83] The ethical imperative to invent words and actions, to enact ideas, occurs in the gap

---

79. Marion, *Being Given*, 303.

80. J. Forshall and F. Madden, eds., *The Holy Bible . . . by John Wycliffe and His Followers*, 4 vols. (Oxford: Oxford University Press, 1950). Cited in *MED*, s.v. "finding," 3b.

81. For the meaning of endowment, see *MED*, s.v. "finding," 5c.

82. Jean-Luc Marion, "'Christian Philosophy': Hermeneutic or Heuristic?," in *The Visible and the Revealed*, trans. Christina M. Gschwandtner (New York: Fordham University Press, 2008), 74.

83. For Augustine of Denmark's quotation, see ch. 1, note 8.

between copy and model. Langland, for this reason, is never in danger of succumbing to the Joachite heresy, which holds that the New Testament fulfillment of the Old Testament types would in turn be fulfilled—and superseded—in a new Age of the Spirit inaugurated by St. Francis. The "spiritual" Franciscans, by reading their own age as the anagogical referent of biblical prophecy, especially the Apocalypse of John, collapsed the tropological sense into the anagogical sense. No longer was human activity to be thought of as an ethical passage between the doctrine of the church (allegory) and the Parousia (anagogy); rather, they believed that right now, immediately, they, the spiritual Franciscans, were making the kingdom of heaven on earth.[84] It is true that for Langland and orthodox exegetes the tropological age corresponds to the age of the church (a correspondence Langland signals in the Pentecost episode), but *Piers Plowman* leaves no room for Joachim of Fiore's premillennial Age of the Spirit. Langland everywhere rejects such triumphalism, replacing progress, in the Joachite sense, with making—that paraliturgical craft, the practitioners of which live hand to mouth and have no place to lay their heads. If Langland apologizes for making by "short-circuit[ing] the binary opposition between clerical and lay performance and identity," then Will's notoriously unsettled, unbeneficed, and economically uncertain clerical identity, as described in the C.5 *vita*, corresponds to an equally unstable, nonprogressive form of making.[85]

So there is certainly validity in reading *Piers Plowman* as a poem generated out of the gap between model and copy, reinforced by an eschatology that stubbornly insists on the *not-yet* of the church's exilic experience. We can even, in a certain sense, name this mode of invention tropological, observing that tropology, so necessary in this earthly

---

84. Lawrence M. Clopper notes "how profoundly different Langland's historical scheme is from Joachist ones." *Songs of Rechelesnesse: Langland and the Franciscans* (Ann Arbor: University of Michigan Press, 1997), 279. For a discussion of the Joachite heresy in the context of exegetical theory, see Nicholas of Lyra, *Nicholas of Lyra's Apocalypse Commentary*, ed. Philip D. W. Krey (Kalamazoo, MI: Medieval Institute Publications, 1997), 1–30; and de Lubac, *Exégèse médiévale*, 4:325–67.

85. Zieman, *Singing the New Song*, 177.

sojourn through the *saeculum*, will be obviated in the Parousia when, according to one strand of eschatology, faith and hope obtain their object and words and works become coterminous in creation's perfectly fulfilled participation of the creator's pure and simple act of self-donation.[86] But *Piers Plowman* also envisions invention generated by successful fidelity of a copy to its model, and this anagogical mode of invention, as it could be called, deserves further explication.

The Invention of Peace

Langland imagines the closing of the gap between model and copy in the debate between the Four Daughters of God, where their reconciliation in songs of praise achieves in the poem's narrative what Christ's sacrifice and resurrection have achieved off-stage. I turn to this episode as a counterpoint to Nicolette Zeeman's powerful exploration of how *Piers Plowman* sublimates frustrated desire in a discourse constituted by the failures of theology and systematic thought in general, in order to "hint at the presence of a divinity whose workings are veiled but who can still be glimpsed in the interstices of events."[87] To be sure, the reconciliation of the Daughters of God could be read as yet another of "the 'episodic' narratives of the poem," where "what appears to be progress always leads directly back to reiterative experiences of failure, rebuke, and loss."[88] This climax of B.18/C.20 is followed in quick succession by the Pentecost episode and the prompt collapse of the church. But these vicissitudes never actually cancel out the Daughters' reconcili-

---

86. This would be according to the predominant Western Christian understanding of the Parousia as an infinitely satisfying repetitive stasis, rather than the Eastern vision of an infinite or "epectatic" progress further into the divine life. In the view I elaborate below, Langland's eschatology leans to the East, and it is quite possible to imagine Langlandian anagogical invention, if not tropological invention, in heaven. For a recent articulation of the Western version of eschatology contrasted to the Eastern, see Griffiths, *Decreation*, 21–28.

87. Zeeman, *"Piers Plowman" and the Medieval Discourse of Desire*, 36.

88. Ibid., 18.

ation; it remains a beacon of hope, which is not necessarily the same thing as desire.[89] Although Langland spends much of the poem in the tropological mode (especially passūs B.8–13, where Zeeman situates her study), tracing and retracing "a recurring beneficial pattern operating in creation according to which human desire can be turned, through a natural experience of sin and suffering, to good,"[90] he also sustains an anagogical mode through B.18–19/C.20–21. By placing this vision of eternal reconciliation in hell and imagining it as a debate, Langland can maintain the gaps and tensions that drive *Piers Plowman*'s plot and thematic development. At the same time, he is able to demonstrate *in literary terms* how the gap between model and copy might be closed. In Peace's final reconciliation with her sisters, the logic of exemplarity does not function merely as an ethical theory that submits public and private rhetoric to the normative practices of baptism and conversion, as in the counterfeiting passage. Here the logic of exemplarity also underwrites Langland's disposition of wisdom traditions, scripture, and liturgy, as he inventively converts them into verse and, at times, song. Peace closes the gap between model and copy by an act of literary invention. In Peace's invention of a reconciling song, Langland depicts how the gap between model and copy might be closed—and why "closure" does not adequately describe the new beginnings opened up by ethical invention.

When Peace "piped . . . of poesie a note" to resolve the soteriological dispute over justice and mercy among the Four Daughters of God, she cites the most exemplary of texts, a proverb from the easiest section of the *Liber parabolarum*, a standard elementary Latin "textbook": "*Clarior est solito post maxima nebula phebus; / Post inimicicias Clarior est & Amor*" (C.20.451a–b). She then translates and amplifies the distich:

---

89. Zeeman distinguishes between Will's fearful desire of despair and "tentatively positive" desire of hope (ibid., 226; see also 85–89), but hope as an infused theological virtue "is not a passion, but a habit of the mind" (Thomas Aquinas, *Summa theologica*, II-II.17.1, ad 1).

90. Zeeman, *"Piers Plowman" and the Medieval Discourse of Desire*, 19. On the network of interpretive and inventive ethics I am associating with tropology, see especially 173–87; 201–26.

"Aftur sharpe shoures," quod pees, "most shene is þe sonne;
Is no wedore warmore then aftur watri cloudes;
Ne no loue leuore ne leuore frendes
Then aftur werre and wrake when loue and pees ben maistres.
Was neuere werre in this world ne wikkedere enuye
That loue, and hym luste, to lauhynge ne brouhte;
And pees thorw pacience alle perelles stoppeth."

(C.20.452–58)

Although the *Liber parabolarum* or *Parabolae* is probably the work of Alan of Lille, it did not circulate under his authority; instead, it gained widespread adoption as part of a primary-education curriculum bundle that modern scholars refer to as the *Auctores octo* or *Liber Catonis*, the "Catoun" that Chaucer's John the carpenter "knew nat" (I.3227).[91] The "poesie" Peace cites had currency not as the clerkly wisdom of classical antiquity, nor as the work of a theological pioneer of the late twelfth century, but as a school text that nearly every young pupil across western Europe learned by "memorizing the text so that it entered into his very bones."[92] The distich seems indeed to have become part of Peace, for when she goes on to amplify the text in English, she makes it a song about the divine attribute she personifies, peace. Peace obviates competition with her model because she has already assimilated it to herself,

---

91. Chaucer, *The Canterbury Tales*, I.3227. See Alan of Lille (Alano di Lilla), *Liber parabolarum (Una raccolta di aforismi)*, ed. Oronzo Limone (Lecce: Congedo Editore, 1993). The distich that Peace cites is ll. 33–34 (also edited in PL 210:579–94c). The *Liber parabolarum* is translated and introduced in Ian Thomson and Louis Perraud, eds., *Ten Latin Schooltexts of the Later Middle Ages* (Lewiston, NY: E. Mellen Press, 1990), 283–325. On the ethical evolution of the primary curriculum, see Nicholas Orme, *Medieval Schools from Roman Britain to Renaissance England* (New Haven: Yale University Press, 2006), 98–105, which cites the fourteenth-century statutes of the university of Oxford that instructed schoolmasters "to teach only 'morals or metaphors or honest poetry'" (100).

92. Jill Mann, "'He Knew Nat Catoun': Medieval School-Texts and Middle English Literature," in *The Text in the Community: Essays on Medieval Works, Manuscripts, Authors, and Readers*, ed. Jill Mann and Maura Nolan (Notre Dame, IN: University of Notre Dame Press, 2006), 42.

so that her song can express both the model and her own invention in a seamless development. Her copy (translation, amplification) has the difference that her identity is now central to the theme of the proverb, but this extends the proverb's vitality rather than confuting it.

Peace's song is a kind of autobiography, describing her own role in the reconciliation of conflict, and inscribing her identity into a traditional proverb that previously spoke only allegorically of peace. At the same time, her song actively consolidates the peace toward which the entire episode has worked. She speaks it or sings it in dialogue with her sisters, Righteousness, Truth, and Mercy—and it was their original disagreement that opened the episode to conflict. Her invention is very much her own; it is extremely innovative, but it works to confirm and renovate, rather than to surpass, the elementary wisdom that children learn from parents and teachers. The success of Peace's song depends, then, not only on her conformation to the model inculcated through a primary school text, but on the grown-up's confirmation by experience that what she was taught as a child is indeed still true. As Jill Mann aptly remarks, "one of the best things about the Redemption is finding out that one's schoolbooks are true."[93] If Peace had aimed in her poetics of invention to outdo and displace her model, she probably could have succeeded—indeed, an eleventh-century grammarian rated the *Liber Catonis* "tin" or "lead" on an aesthetic scale, far below the gold of Virgil and silver of Plautus.[94] Instead, Peace's invention is oriented not toward rivalry but toward action, toward securing the happiness of reconciliation.

At the same time, Peace's vision of reconciliation runs on comparatives: reconciliation ushers in not only brightness, warmth, friendship, and laughing, but comparatively *more* brightness, warmer weather, dearer friendship, and more laughing. The new peace surpasses whatever détente obtained before "werre and wrake," just as the personified Peace's amplification of "Cato's" distich goes beyond the original. To close the gap between model and copy, to supply the object of desire

---

93. Ibid., 66.

94. Ibid., 49, citing Harry F. Reijnders, ed., "Aimericus, Ars Lectoria," *Vivarium* 9 (1971): 119–37; *Vivarium* 10 (1972): 41–101, 124–76.

(Zeeman), to reconcile individual to communal in choric heterophony (Zieman)—none of these anagogical operations in *Piers Plowman* halts the poem's momentum or forecloses its possibilities or effaces its previous exertions. At this moment of reconciliation, Peace and *Piers Plowman* do not require a catastrophe in order to go on singing. Instead, they can enter the register of praise with Truth, who sings the liturgy's highest canticle, "*te deum laudamus*" (C.20.465). Reconciled and already partaking of Easter joy, "Til þe day dawed thes damoyseles caroled" (C.20.467). Only Will's waking—not some further fall—silences their strains. While any illusions of modern liberal progress disintegrate over the following two passūs, this anagogical vision remains intact.

If *Piers Plowman* owes its multiplying beginnings and episodic pulse to "a distinctive dynamic of failure, rebuke, and renewal," as Middleton, Smith, and Zeeman have argued, it also envisions more beginnings and more writing on the other side of reconciliation.[95] If Langland's primary mode of invention is tropological, always struggling to convert ideas into words and words into actions, always situated *between* ideal and fulfillment, then he also has a secondary anagogical mode. That is, sin and its consequent suffering and lack are not the only spurs to desire; frustration and sublimation are not the only psychic causes of invention. Especially where *Piers Plowman* rises to the register of praise, it reveals a positivity that is the source even of its negativity.

This is in part, I think, what Smith is getting at in his meditation on Langland's *via negativa* when he writes, "It is precisely because negation has a kind of presence, because it continues to do something, that the poem's theory of reference is so complex."[96] Driving every pseudo-

---

95. Zeeman, *"Piers Plowman" and the Medieval Discourse of Desire*, 22. See Anne Middleton, "Narration and the Invention of Experience: Episodic Form in *Piers Plowman*," in *The Wisdom of Poetry: Essays in Early English Literature in Honor of Morton W. Bloomfield*, ed. Larry Dean Benson and Siegfried Wenzel (Kalamazoo, MI: Medieval Institute Publications, 1982), 91–122; and D. Smith, *The Book of the Incipit*, 82–86.

96. D. Vance Smith, "Negative Langland," *Yearbook of Langland Studies* 23 (2009): 48.

Dionysian negation is an affirmation of negation.[97] But while many moments of academic disputation and theologizing seem to display Langland's investment in the apophatic tradition, he is at least equally invested in the complementary discourse of analogy—not only logical and grammatical analogy of the kind Smith illuminates in *The Book of the Incipit*, but the analogy of being.[98] The soul journeys to God by analogy because analogy is a created good, the fitting means by which the soul is led back to God. The soul encounters the "ever-greater dissimilarity" from God in every creaturely similarity as a step toward union with God rather than as frustration and failure.

We must distinguish between moral failures, disorders, and frustrations, on the one hand, and, on the other, the analogical intervals across which humans approach God. Although Smith is attuned to the affirmations involved in pseudo-Dionysius's and Thomas Aquinas's *triplex via*, "failure" is the word that rings out at key moments throughout his discussion of apophaticism.[99] But as Aaron Riches has argued, Thomas recruits the pseudo-Dionysius in order to splice together "the cataphatic-*exitus* and apophatic-*reditus*" in a third movement beyond cataphaticism and apophaticism, the movement of union by which the created

---

97. That is why, as Smith points out, the pseudo-Dionysius follows up his rigorously apophatic *Mystical Theology* with *The Divine Names* (ibid., 55).

98. D. Smith, *The Book of the Incipit*, 157–70. Smith does argue that Langland's analogical extension of grammatical relation to metaphysical relations "discloses his attempts to anchor human and divine institutions in stable beginnings" (*The Book of the Incipit*, 170). But the *analogia entis* is quite a different animal from a foundationalist "great chain of being" because the epectatic "ever greater dissimilarity" slips anchors and destabilizes beginnings.

99. "Within Studie's critique of theology . . . is an affirmation of a negative way, an affirmation of the necessity and inevitability of the failure of systematic thought. . . . We discern the causes of things in the failure of the terms we use to designate them: their failure to designate both the referent that would give their phenomenal nature substance and real existence *and* to designate their likenesses to each other in ways that would verify their own existence is a failure to designate their ultimate likeness to the divine nature. . . . The failure of Theology continues . . . where the poem returns to the necessary failure of theology to comprehend beginnings." D. Smith, "Negative Langland," 54–56.

soul participates in God's likeness through its own difference.[100] In this third way, "the otherness of the creature—its difference—becomes integral to how it participates in God and how it analogously signifies God's goodness."[101] That is to say, the ever greater dissimilarities that all naming encounters, and to which Langland is so sensitive, need not frustrate and need not result in failure. It is not calamitous that the gap between model and copy never closes, nor is the "gap" always a constitutive lack, a guilt that gets sublimated into mystical desire, as Freudian or Lacanian theory would have it.[102] We can discern a positive momentum of *reductio* in the episodes of Pentecost and Peace's song, and even of Conscience's final, hopeful quest. The final passus has plenty of ethical and institutional failure, to be sure, but the gap between tropological making and anagogical fulfillment retains an analogical interval that invites hope. The next chapter explores the reasons for that hope in Langland's identification of tropological invention with sacramental satisfaction.

---

100. Aaron Riches, "Being Good: Thomas Aquinas and Dionysian Causal Predication," *Nova et Vetera: The English Edition of the International Theological Journal* 7, no. 2 (2009): 476.

101. Ibid., 468.

102. Zeeman, *"Piers Plowman" and the Medieval Discourse of Desire*, 31–37.

4

Practices of Satisfaction and *Piers Plowman*'s Dynamic Middle

I have argued that tropology elevates ethics from questions of right and wrong and virtuous habits to participation in the life of God. The best tropological commentary, then, would be a life that participates in God. Christianity has historically offered three chief sites for God's intensive presence and availability to participation: the human heart, understood as the seat of the soul and the affections; divinely revealed scripture, which is coterminous with the Word, the second person of the Trinity; and the sacraments of the church. These three sites converge in the Mass, which commences with the *sursum corda*, the lifting up of hearts to the Lord, and comprises the liturgy of the Word and the liturgy of the Eucharist. In this chapter I read *Piers Plowman*'s liturgically structured passūs B.18–19/C.20–21 as tropological commentary on scripture, with the narrated Mass and Holy Week liturgies functioning as commentary and Will's writing of his dream functioning as tropological invention. In these episodes, including the Pentecost episode discussed in the previous chapter, Will enters a visionary experience of biblical history

An earlier version of chapter 4 appeared as "Practices of Satisfaction and *Piers Plowman*'s Dynamic Middle," *Studies in the Age of Chaucer* 36 (2014): 169–207.

through the liturgy and engages in truly participatory exegesis. This exegesis ultimately takes the form of tropological invention when Will wakes up and writes what he has dreamed. Langland links this writing to the sacramental economy by characterizing it as satisfaction, the third part of penance that is both a prerequisite to receiving communion and also an important way to receive the grace of the sacraments. If the best tropological commentary is a life, Langland seems to say, then it is a life lived in continual circulation through the sacraments of penance and Eucharist—not primarily in the brief moments of confession or the affective disposition of contrition, but in the positive, productive, joyful acting out of satisfaction as a means of participation in biblical history. For Langland, then, literature does not just *represent* scripture and sacramental life; it can also be a direct participation in both and, indeed, the means by which the one connects to the other. Biblical poetry can *be* sacramental satisfaction. If poetry can satisfy, then satisfaction stands a chance to cross the Reformation divide, along with tropological invention, even as the penitential system is dismantled.

Satisfaction in a Secular Age

Ian McEwan's novel *Atonement* seems to end with the scene of its invention, the moment its fictional author, Briony Tallis, begins to write the book we have just read. She writes in order to exonerate her sister's lover, the man she has fatefully and wrongly accused of rape, before his conviction in the court of law can irreversibly ruin his life: "She knew what was required of her. Not simply a letter, but a new draft, an atonement, and she was ready to begin."[1] It turns out that the story we have read was meant to set the legal record straight and restore justice. However, the book does not end there. It begins again on a new leaf, where Briony confesses, now in the first person, that the people she injured had died long before they could enjoy the relatively happy reunion narrated in the previous thirty pages. Briony has been revising her story, her confession,

---

1. Ian McEwan, *Atonement* (New York: Doubleday, 2001), 330.

for fifty-nine years, always too late. Her decision to write a happy ending came late in life and seemed to her the only way to satisfy the "love of order" that inspired her to write as a girl and that "shaped the principles of justice."[2] "As long as there is a single copy," Briony writes near the real end of the book, "a solitary transcript of my final draft, then my spontaneous, fortuitous sister and her medical prince survive to love."[3] Briony has to settle for giving literary immortality to those she has wronged because literature by her definition cannot atone. "There is no one, no entity or higher form that [the novelist] can appeal to, or be reconciled with, or that can forgive her."[4]

Atonement's ending registers Briony's grief not only for unreconciled sin, but also for the loss of a cosmos in which a sinner can make satisfaction even if the injured party cannot forgive. Even as Briony recognizes the medieval distinction between satisfaction directed to God and legal satisfaction, or restitution, directed to an offended party, her quandary is particularly modern. She stands near the extreme end of a history of satisfaction: after Gratian and Peter Lombard had formalized it as one of the three parts of penance;[5] after Thomas Cranmer's prayer book had obviated human practices of penance on account of Christ's "full, perfect, and sufficient sacrifyce, oblacion, and satysfaccyon";[6] after the Roman Catholic Church introduced the confessional box, signaling "the decay of the idea that sin was a social matter";[7] after both sacred

---

2. Ibid., 7.

3. Ibid., 371.

4. Ibid.

5. See Joseph Goering, "The Scholastic Turn (1100–1500): Penitential Theology and Law in the Schools," in *A New History of Penance*, ed. Abigail Firey (Leiden: Brill, 2008), 219–37.

6. Church of England, *The Boke of the Common Praier and Administratio[n] of the Sacramentes and Other Rytes and Ceremonies of the Churche, after the Vse of the Churche of Englande* (Worcester, England: John Oswen, 1549), 161r, Early English Books Online.

7. John Bossy, "Practices of Satisfaction, 1215–1700," in *Retribution, Repentance, and Reconciliation: Papers Read at the 2002 Summer and 2003 Winter Meeting of the Ecclesiastical History Society*, ed. Kate Cooper and Jeremy Gregory (Woodbridge, Suffolk: Boydell Press, 2004), 111. See also John Bossy, "The

and secular "institutionalizations of charity" evacuated the practices and languages of satisfaction of their efficacy;[8] and after the modern subject tamed truth so that it could no longer transfigure the self or give subjectivity.[9] Whereas Martin Luther merely disrupted medieval complacency about the sufficiency of sacramental satisfaction, the fictional Briony Tallis is desperately certain that nothing can ever satisfy.

It is tempting to read Briony as a figure for modern failures of acknowledgment, recognition, and communal reconciliation, alienated by at least one epoch from the medieval school of forgiveness, the penitential system in which the living and the dead practiced the social grammar of reconciliation.[10] Briony rightly grieves. Too late, Briony! Too late for a tribunal, too late for a confessional, too late for God.

"Is't not too late?," asks a sixteenth-century Lutheran doctor, hoping it might not be.

"Too late," says the Evil Angel.

"Never too late," says the Good Angel, "if Faustus will repent."[11]

Social History of Confession in the Age of the Reformation," *Transactions of the Royal Historical Society (Fifth Series)* 25, no. 1 (1975): 29–33.

8. Ivan Illich, *The Rivers North of the Future: The Last Testament of Ivan Illich*, ed. David Cayley (Toronto: House of Anansi Press, 2005), 175–200. Illich's arguments are best appreciated in the haunting recordings of the radio series produced by Cayley, "The Corruption of Christianity: Ivan Illich on Gospel, Church and Society," *Ideas* (Toronto: Canadian Broadcasting Corporation, 2000).

9. "If we define spirituality as being the form of practices which postulate that, such as he is, the subject is not capable of the truth, but that, such as it is, the truth can transfigure and save the subject, then we can say that the modern age of the relations between the subject and truth begin when it is postulated that, such as he is, the subject is capable of truth, but that, such as it is, the truth cannot save the subject." Michel Foucault, *The Hermeneutics of the Subject*, ed. and trans. Frederic Gros (New York: Palgrave Macmillan, 2005), 19.

10. See Sarah Beckwith, *Shakespeare and the Grammar of Forgiveness* (Ithaca, NY: Cornell University Press, 2011), 20–33.

11. Christopher Marlowe, *The Tragedy of Doctor Faustus, B-Text*, in *Doctor Faustus and Other Plays: A Text*, ed. David Bevington and Eric Rasmussen (New York: Oxford University Press, 2008), 2.3.75–78. Quotations are from the play, attributions are mine.

Briony might not have a good angel to turn to, but Marlowe's post-penitential drama reveals how her despair presumes a certain periodization of history and structure of time. "Behold, now is the acceptable time," Paul wrote, "now is the day of salvation," but Briony's window of opportunity for effective satisfaction has passed, and she lives and writes after the "now," after religion.[12] Briony subscribes, then, to a subtraction story of secularization, according to which modernity is what remains after religion has dwindled away.[13] To be modern means to come after religion and its trappings, to live—if now is the day of salvation—after the now. It is always too late, even if she wants to repent.

In this chapter I seek to postpone and assay the consequences of such a foreclosure by allowing several medieval, early modern, and contemporary voices to speak about satisfaction alongside one another and to challenge each other. This method of depicting a speculative, transhistorical conflict is designed not so much to narrate a shift in religious forms as to illuminate beliefs about, and practices of, satisfaction. These new vantages grant, in turn, a new perspective on *Piers Plowman* as a key text in the history of satisfaction and as a poem structurally as well as authorially invested in writing for the sake of satisfactory participation in salvation history. This chapter shifts, then, from the logic and practice of tropology to its use, that is, to its efficacy within the economy of salvation as administered by the institutional church.

---

12. 2 Cor. 6:2.

13. On subtraction narratives, see Charles Taylor, *A Secular Age* (Cambridge, MA: Belknap Press, 2007), 569–79. I find Taylor's critique of subtraction narratives compelling. However, from the perspective of medieval religious history, Taylor tends toward the opposite error by imaginatively adding to the Middle Ages a surplus of faith sufficiently robust to sustain all of modernity's subtractions and still persist. While not reductively Weberian, Taylor's account also avoids the reason for continuity that most religions themselves give: that God continues to exist and work in the lives of humans and their institutions. This exaggeration occurs mostly in chapter 1, "The Bulwarks of Belief." For more cautious accounts of medieval faith and practice, see 90–95. For an alternative account of medieval belief, explicitly contrasted to Taylor's, see Steven Justice, "Did the Middle Ages Believe in Their Miracles?," *Representations* 103 (2008): 1–29.

My larger argument about the history of satisfaction in late medieval and early Reformation literary culture centers on a major point of disagreement among *Piers Plowman*'s readers across the centuries, namely, how to understand the work as a whole in light of the apparent failures that dominate its ending. Like Briony's story and the larger story of satisfaction's demise, *Piers Plowman* suggests glum conclusions. The poem ends in disaster, with the total corruption of the church and the undoing of the penitential self as the pitiful Contrition abandons his own allegorical essence and "clene for3ete to crye and to wepe" (C.22.369). No wonder some of the poem's best readers have identified failure as its chief engine of invention and closure.[14] Yet I argue in this chapter that Langland designs the poem to reframe failure within a history of salvation in which Christians can participate sacramentally to redeem failure, especially by penitential satisfaction.[15] Satisfaction, then, not failure itself, motivates the poem's inventive impulse. Langland conceives of sacramental and literary satisfaction not as the termination of a discrete penitential sequence (contrition, confession, satisfaction), but as an ongoing, open-ended habit of beginning again and making good ends. Tropological invention is certainly not the only means of performing such satisfaction, but it is Langland's primary means. And tropological invention is also the means by which Protestant writers can persist in satisfaction after traditional penance has fallen under suspicion.

---

14. See my discussion of failure in the final section of chapter 3, "The Invention of Peace," as well as Middleton, "Narration and the Invention of Experience"; D. Smith, *The Book of the Incipit*, 82–86; D. Smith, "Negative Langland"; and Zeeman, *"Piers Plowman" and the Medieval Discourse of Desire.*

15. For a reading of the ending as dominated by the pattern of failure, rebuke, and loss, see Zeeman, *"Piers Plowman" and the Medieval Discourse of Desire*, 263–83. "For a brief phase, the poem's protagonists are all 'patient' enough to allow the redemption to happen. It is doubly notable, therefore, that a narrative of failure reappears again at the end of the poem. . . . Once more Piers is gone. Once more Conscience departs. Such narratives of denial and loss have shaped the poem since its inception, and it is no surprise that one more such narrative brings the poem to its famously gaping close" (283). Zeeman's book ends here.

In support of these claims, I interpret both formal and historical evidence and demonstrate how the two kinds of evidence support each other.[16] Formally, *Piers Plowman* employs chiastic structures to resist purely linear reading and to reinscribe patterns of failure into larger histories of redemption. I will identify chiastic structures at work locally in alliterative patterning and more broadly in the plot of the poem, especially the visionary and liturgical climax where the dreamer Will witnesses and participates in the signal events of salvation history: Christ's passion, descent to hell, resurrection, ascension, and Pentecost. Historically, *Piers Plowman* develops a currently underappreciated, capacious understanding of penitential satisfaction. Drawing on late medieval penitential liturgy and literature and on the work of historians of penance, I retrieve an understanding of satisfaction according to which writing a poem such as *Piers Plowman* can constitute a work of mercy and therefore count as sacramental satisfaction. These two kinds of evidence are linked by *Piers Plowman*'s unique announcement of its writtenness in the midst of its most significant chiastic structure. When the dreamer Will announces that he woke up and wrote what he had dreamed, he does so in the context of penitential participation in the history of salvation through liturgy. Will's dream of that history merges with the real-time Holy Week liturgies. If Will and William Langland are writing as an act of penitential satisfaction, then they occupy what may seem a strange place in the medieval economy of salvation, standing

---

16. While I am adducing two kinds of evidence for this argument— formal and theological-historical—a third type of evidence could further support the argument for the importance of Langland's writing from the middle, namely, evidence of *Piers Plowman*'s order of composition and revision, though I do not have the space to develop the relationship here. For an argument from the evidence of revision that Langland's making is essentially penitential, see Alan J. Fletcher, "The Essential (Ephemeral) William Langland: Textual Revision as Ethical Process in Piers Plowman," *Yearbook of Langland Studies* 15 (2001): 61–84. My analysis here suggests that Fletcher should shift his focus from contrition to satisfaction. I discuss the potential for corroboration with Lawrence Warner's hypotheses about *The Lost History of Piers Plowman* in note 106 below.

outside the clerically controlled sacrament of penance, yet also seeking that sacrament's benefits. The central part of this chapter, then, seeks to make that place seem less strange and to articulate how Langland's questionable vernacular making both stands outside clerical sacramental authority and also stakes a claim to being legitimate *lele labour* as a penitential practice.

If we can understand Langland's writing as satisfactory, we can better appreciate the failures and successes of penance in the late Middle Ages, and better recognize practices of satisfaction across the Reformation that narratives of decline and loss tend to overlook.[17] *Piers Plowman's* eschatological vision of hope and satisfaction beyond personal and institutional religious failure challenges Briony Tallis's self-binding temporality, her *post*-apocalyptic sense of belatedness that rebukes hope and occludes present help. The poem also challenges Faustian histories of the Reformation and modernity—not necessarily those that register loss and shed a contrite tear, but those that, less than halfway through the play, say, "*Consummatum est*" (*Doctor Faustus* 2.1.74) and so see devils holding down repentant hands and cannot see the angels there all along.

The history of modernity within which we necessarily practice criticism and historiography is not yet finished and likely holds many surprises. We do not know its end, and therefore we do not know how "late" we really are. If the age of reform had its unintended consequences, as Brad Gregory has argued, it also had its unrealized intentions and multiple futures—futures that may not yet even have arrived.[18]

---

17. I include some of the most influential of these narratives in notes 7, 8, and 9 above. For an approach to continuity and change similar to mine, see Katherine C. Little, "Transforming Work: Protestantism and the *Piers Plowman* Tradition," *Journal of Medieval and Early Modern Studies* 40, no. 3 (2010): 497–526.

18. Brad S. Gregory, *The Unintended Reformation: How a Religious Revolution Secularized Society* (Cambridge, MA: Belknap Press, 2012). This admirably ambitious work tells multiple overlapping, and at times conflicting, stories about the origins of modernity, marshaling an impressive array of primary and secondary texts to do so. Taken as a whole, the book wields tremendous and

This chapter is designed to recognize some of those futures by studying practices of satisfaction not only over a long duration of literary and religious texts, but in the manifold permutations, returns, and possibilities inscribed in the texts themselves and in the futures they collaborate in inventing. The next section looks closely at two forms of permutation and return in *Piers Plowman*, a text that resists simple linear reading toward an ending. Instead, it invites readers to layer their interactions with it, repeatedly returning to certain structural "middles" that produce the meaning of the poem more than its actual ending does.

Chiasmus and *Piers Plowman*'s Dynamic Middle

For all the attention that has fruitfully been lavished on the forms and energies of beginning and ending in *Piers Plowman*, it is a surprisingly centripetal poem. To be sure, the center does not hold. But the poem begins again so many times because it is constantly trying to return to a center of gravity. That center is the incarnation of Christ, as Cristina Maria Cervone has argued in her study of "Incarnational poetics" in Middle English poetry. "In making the hypostatic union so central to the work that form does, an Incarnational poetic encourages a process of thought that comes back again to that good and fundamental beginning. In all of these poems, . . . the Incarnation is the pivot point around which thought and form coalesce."[19] In *Piers Plowman*, the incarnation

---

nuanced explanatory power. Yet its powerful method prevents it from treating its primary texts as more than markers of historical developments. The book must perforce move on with its arguments; it cannot linger with a text, respond to its recursive invitations, or tease out its multiple possible futures in disparate communities of interpretation. This book that illuminates the sources and contours of modern pluralism cannot itself give a good account of the plural possibilities of its primary texts. (I am grateful for a conversation with Will Revere in which he articulated this perspective.) *Piers Plowman* stands at the center of the present book because it is a text that invites its readers to return, revise, and layer their responses, as its reception history bears out.

19. Cervone, *Poetics of the Incarnation*, 208.

comprises a narrative structure of exit and return, of the Son's descent from the Father into human flesh and ultimately the region of the dead, and of his ascent by way of the resurrection to the right hand of the Father in heaven. That narrative structure provides a template for humanity, which fell from grace in Adam and Eve, suffered death, but through Christ can rise again and ascend not only into heaven but even into union with the triune God. As the patristic dictum puts it, "God became man that man might become God."[20] This famous saying absorbs the symmetry of the narrative structure of the incarnation into its syntactic structure, producing the poetic figure of chiasmus. And Langland employed metrical, syntactic, and narrative chiasmus to give *Piers Plowman* an incarnational form that directs readers' attention repeatedly back to the middle, the place of salvific exchange between God and humanity.

Modern literary scholars have been cautious about chiasmus on historical and methodological grounds. Historically, there has been little evidence of conscious chiastic patterning by literary writers, although new research in recent years has begun to change that assessment.[21] Methodologically, the fear is that once you start looking for chiasmus, you see it everywhere. I use the term advisedly, with due historical caution. I employ the term *chiasmus* to name an array of parallel and concentric reversals or reciprocity, from syntactical arrangements grouped in medieval rhetorical manuals under the figure *commutatio*, to larger structural patterns that reflect the semantic symmetry that David Howlett has noted as one mark of "biblical style" in early medieval writings

---

20. Cf. Athanasius, *De incarnatione Dei Verbum*, in *Select Writings and Letters of Athanasius, Bishop of Alexandria*, ed. Archibald Robertson, Nicene and Post-Nicene Fathers, 2nd ser., vol. 4, ed. Philip Schaff and Henry Wace (Grand Rapids, MI: William B. Eerdmans, 1953), 54.3.

21. On chiastic structure in medieval meditative theology and poetry, see Robert McMahon, *Understanding the Medieval Meditative Ascent: Augustine, Anselm, Boethius, and Dante* (Washington, DC: Catholic University of America Press, 2006), 36–42. For a study of chiasmus based on late medieval and early modern mnemonic culture, see William E. Engel, *Chiastic Designs in English Literature from Sidney to Shakespeare* (Burlington, VT: Ashgate, 2009).

such as St. Patrick's *Confessio*.[22] Langland's chiastic effects depend on a complex interplay of line-level chiasmus, larger structural chiasmus, and conceptual or narrative chiasmus as found in the basic Christian plot of creation, fall, incarnation, and redemption.

Medieval poetics and rhetoric hardly register the term *chiasmus* (it became popular only with Renaissance rhetoric).[23] More common are the terms *isocolon, antimetabole, commutatio,* and *annominatio*. In the widely cited definition of the *Rhetorica ad Herennium, commutatio* "occurs when two discrepant thoughts are so expressed by transposition that the latter follows from the former although contradictory to it."[24] In this strict sense, *commutatio* must occur at the sentence or line level, where two opposing ideas are expressed using the same root word or words. But such a line can still express larger chiastic structures, even plot structures, as in, "that was tynt thorw tre, tre shal hit wynne" (C.20.143). In this line, the plot of salvation history and its central events of winning and losing revolve around a tree—or two trees: the tree of life in the Garden of Eden and the tree of the cross on Golgotha. I therefore speak of chiasmus as an umbrella term to describe the wide array of symmetrical, reciprocal, or concentric parallelisms and antitheses that Langland deploys not only in his rhetoric but also in his disposition of salvation history and the events that constitute the plot of *Piers Plowman*, in his marking of topographical ascents and descents, and in the various metrical balancing tactics he enlists to create a range of effects

---

22. See Saint Patrick, *Liber Epistolarum Sancti Patricii Episcopi*, ed. David R. Howlett (Dublin: Four Courts Press, 1994); and David R. Howlett, *British Books in Biblical Style* (Dublin: Four Courts Press, 1997).

23. Medieval awareness of the Greek *chiasmos* comes across primarily in the figure of *isocolon*. See Heinrich Lausberg, *Handbook of Literary Rhetoric: A Foundation for Literary Study*, ed. David E. Orton and R. Dean Anderson (Leiden: Brill, 1998), 322.

24. *Rhetorica ad Herennium* 4.28.39. In Harry Caplan, trans., *Ad C. Herennium: De ratione dicendi (Rhetorica ad Herennium)* (Cambridge, MA: Harvard University Press, 1964), 324.

with his alliterative lines.[25] While one can appreciate the methodological objection that once we start looking for chiasmus, we find it everywhere, it is significant that in the case of *Piers Plowman*, we do not find chiasmus everywhere. We find it in strategic places, in the middles to which Langland wants us to return in our meditative reading habits, and especially in the middle on which this part of the chapter focuses, a middle between two episodes dominated by the figure of Christ's cross.

Chiasmus has long been associated with the cross. The term derives from the Greek letter χ (*chi*) because chiasmus involves a crossing of elements in a symmetrical array. The crossing may be expressed as *abba* or, in diagram form:

Early Christians associated the letter *chi* with Christ; the *Chi Rho* Christogram, derived from the first two letters of the Greek *Christos*, predated the cross as the central Christian symbol. New Testament scholars have found chiasmus to be an essential rhetorical structure of the Gospels, especially John.[26] *The Dream of the Rood* anchors structural chiasmus with single-verse chiasmus, such as, "Rod wæs ic aræred. Ahof ic ricne cyning" (As a cross was I raised up | lifted I the mighty king).[27] Beyond

---

25. For an even more capacious understanding of chiasmus, anchored in pre-Socratic thought and formal logic, see Patrick Lee Miller, *Becoming God: Pure Reason in Early Greek Philosophy* (New York: Continuum, 2011), 1–42.

26. See John Breck, *The Shape of Biblical Language: Chiasmus in the Scriptures and Beyond* (Crestwood, NY: St. Vladimir's Seminary Press, 1994).

27. Michael Swanton, ed., *The Dream of the Rood* (Manchester: Manchester University Press, 1970), l. 44. "This line . . . divides the active Christ from the passive one and the passive cross from its active role. It also bisects the four portions of the narrative so that they form a chiasmus, the central juxtaposed scenes depicting the dual acts of Christ ascending the cross and of the cross raising Christ and being pierced by the nails, the framing scenes being on the one side the enemies raising the cross and on the other side the friends taking

the line level, cruciform symmetries structure many Middle English meditative lyrics, such as "The Four Leaves of the Truelove," which conveys a cross-patterned homily on the saving love embodied in the flower truelove and Christ's form "spred on a Crosse," or Thomas of Hales's "Love Rune," with its cryptic inscription of the sign of the cross at the precise numerical center of the hermetic *roune*.[28] In *Piers Plowman*, deep within the incarnation's narrative chiasmus, Mercy sets the dream's larger structure on a pivot around the cross in a line-level chiasmus: "And that was tynt thorw tre, tre shal hit wynne" (C.20.143). At the end of the same passus Will exhorts his wife and daughter to participate in an Easter Sunday liturgy that involves creeping to the cross and kissing it. The next passus begins with a dream of Christ, dressed in Piers's armor, bearing a cross. It is to these particular crosses and this chiastic crossing that Langland draws our recursive, meditative attention. These crosses are particularly poignant because they frame the first explicit announcement of the poem's writtenness, which allows us to understand how the work of writing relates to the cross by means of penitential liturgy.

To appreciate how and why Langland creates intense chiastic effects in this part of the poem, we first need to step back and consider what is going on in the larger plot of Will's dreams. The pivotal first line of C.21 is also the first line of the *Vita de Dobest*, the final movement of the poem as rubricated in most B and C manuscripts. The line is situated between two passūs comprising vivid dreams of biblical-liturgical action. They begin with Will alienated from community, going along "ylike a lorel al my lyf tyme" (C.20.3), and they end with the church, the king, and the commons alienated from each other. The plot of the two

---

down Christ and burying the three crosses." Carol Braun Pasternack, "Stylistic Disjunctions in 'The Dream of the Rood,'" *Anglo-Saxon England* 13 (1984): 178.

28. Susanna Greer Fein, ed., "The Four Leaves of the Truelove," in *Moral Love Songs and Laments* (Kalamazoo, MI: Medieval Institute Publications, 1998), l. 199. Fein argues that Hales's line 100—"Est and west, north and suth!"—"may be meant to invoke the sign of the Cross and thereby sanctify the rune. . . . If this interpretation is correct, the line is integral to the cryptic, runic nature of the poem" (41n100).

passūs progresses from spiritual dryness and disorder to intense liturgical and visionary participation in the events of Holy Week and Pentecost, and back again to spiritual dissolution.[29] More immediately, Will
wakes and writes between two liturgies involving the cross. At the end
of passus 20, six lines earlier, Will urges his wife and daughter to "'arise
and go . . . crepe to þe croes on knees and kusse hit for a iewel'"
(C.20.470–71). Then at the beginning of passus 21, seven lines later, Will
falls asleep in the middle of Mass and dreams "That Peres þe plouhman
was peynted al blody / And cam in with a cros before þe comune peple"
(C.21.6–7). It is fitting and significant that this chiastic structure—with
writing in the middle framed on either side by liturgical devotion—
should depend on the cross and, as we shall see, Langland's distinctive
theology of the cross. In the next section I develop an understanding of
how Langland's use of chiasmus in the alliterative line performs a theological argument about Christ's passion and frames the signal moment
when Will wakes and writes. Then, in the following section, I take up
the question of what it means, given this framing, to wake up and write.

Alliterative Chiasmus and Langland's Theology of the Cross

The standard alliterative long-line is notably unbalanced. Like *Piers
Plowman* itself, the end of an alliterative line swerves away from the
prior pattern of alliteration: *aa|ax*. But Langland was able to enlist the
alliterative line to produce a wide variety of effects, including balance
and symmetry, as Macklin Smith has demonstrated in his studies of
Langland's "balancing tactics."[30] These tactics include line-level allit-

---

29. The significance of this liturgical, penitential, and Eucharistic setting
for the poem's central problems cannot be overstated. For an appreciation of
how penance and Eucharist finally and fittingly support each other here, see
David Aers, *Sanctifying Signs: Making Christian Tradition in Late Medieval England* (Notre Dame, IN: University of Notre Dame Press, 2004), 29–51.

30. Macklin Smith, "Langland's Alliterative Line(s)," *Yearbook of Langland Studies* 23 (2009): 190–93. I rely also on Smith's correspondence and un-
published papers, including Macklin Smith, "Chiastic Form in *Piers Plowman*"

erative meter as well as chiastic "frames" established by interlinear alliteration. Smith demonstrates that alliterative stress can perform the
function that polyptoton—deploying a word or form of the word twice
to different effects—performs in standard *commutatio*.[31] Instead of re-
peating the same words in reverse order to express opposed thoughts,
those thoughts can be opposed or apposed by different, yet alliterating,
words. This is precisely what occurs at C.21.14.

Here, Conscience tells Will that his vision of Piers "peynted al
blody" and bearing a cross at Mass "Is Crist with his croes, conquerour
of Cristene" (C.21.14). This "enriched" line, with its *aa|aa* alliterative
patterning, is the closest that Langland usually comes to alliterative chiasmus in a single line, but it nevertheless capitalizes on the full potential
for symmetry that the four-beat line bears.[32] The chiastic alliterative
structure can invite speculation about conceptual chiasmus: in what
ways might the inner and outer full staves, when paired, produce effects
of symmetry, balance, antithesis, or parallelism? A. V. C. Schmidt notes
the line's "heavily emphatic enriched fourth lift growing, as it were, out
of the root *Crist* planted as the (anticipated) first *k* lift."[33] Taking the
"commutative property" of this alliterative *commutatio* even further,
"Crist" and "Cristene" can be interchangeable in the economy of salvation as a consequence of the identity that obtains between the inner alliterating terms, "croes" and "conquerour." Christ is the conqueror and

---

(presented at the Forty-Fourth Annual International Congress on Medieval
Studies, Kalamazoo, MI, 2009); and Macklin Smith, "Balancing Tactics in *Piers
Plowman*" (presented at the Fifth International *Piers Plowman* Conference, Ox-
ford, England, 2011). I am grateful for permission to cite this work.

31. See Lausberg, *Handbook of Literary Rhetoric*, 288–92.

32. I use A. V. C. Schmidt's terminology, which indicates that the line alliterates as usual on the first three lifts and then enriches or "fills" the final lift
of the b-verse with another alliterating syllable. A. V. C. Schmidt, *The Clerkly
Maker: Langland's Poetic Art* (Cambridge: D. S. Brewer, 1987), 32. There are
only ten *ab|ba* lines in *Piers Plowman* B, but three of them do not map onto the
stress pattern. See Tomonori Matsushita, ed., *A Glossarial Concordance to William Langland's "The Vision of Piers Plowman," the B-Text* (Tokyo: Yushodo
Press, 1998), 3:700.

33. Schmidt, *The Clerkly Maker*, 47.

belongs to all Christians ("conquerour *of* Cristene"), and by commutation these properties apply also to the cross: it is a conqueror, it belongs to all Christians, and they conquer under its sign. Because the cross is the conqueror, Christ and Christians are *at one*; through the atonement humanity completes the second half of the great patristic chiasmus, "God became man that man might become God."[34] Through the crossing of Christ's passion, humanity crosses back to its original *telos* of participation in the divine life.

The line's chiastic argument does not merely recapitulate, however neatly and heuristically, Chalcedonian Christology.[35] It also chiastically substantiates the claims in the previous passus that the cross completes the incarnation. C amplifies the argument of B that God "bicam man of a mayde . . . to se þe sorwe of deying" (B.18.213–14) with the even bolder claim that God's knowledge was incomplete without experiencing human death and suffering: "Ne hadde god ysoffred of som oþer then hymsulue / He hadde nat wist witterly where deth were sour or swete" (C.20.217–18). The omniscient God could not have proper knowledge of death without becoming a human. The line's chiastic structure ab-

---

34. Athanasius, *De incarnatione*, 54.3.

35. The Council of Chalcedon's (451) articulation of the hypostatic union depended on the notion of *communicatio idiomatum*, the exchange of attributes between Christ's divine and human natures, expressed in Leo the Great's influential "Tome" written in 449: "Thus in the whole and perfect nature of true man was true God born, complete in what was His own, complete in what was ours. And by 'ours' we mean what the Creator formed in us from the beginning and what He undertook to repair." Leo the Great, "Letter 28," in *Leo the Great, Gregory the Great*, ed. Charles Lett Feltoe, Nicene and Post-Nicene Fathers, 2nd ser., vol. 12, ed. Philip Schaff and Henry Wace (Buffalo, NY: Christian Literature Publishing Co., 1895), 40. Langland elaborates the anthropological consequences of the hypostatic union in terms of consanguinity. As Christ says during the Harrowing of Hell, "Ac to be merciable to man thenne my kynde hit asketh / For we beth brethrene of bloed" (C.20.417–18). This is significant in Will's dream because Christ bearing the cross not only wears Piers's armor, but is "al blody," with the blood covering and presumably making indistinguishable what is Christ and what is Piers.

sorbs and focuses reverberations from these bold soteriological overtures elsewhere in the poem, illustrating Smith's argument that

> the occasional crisscross patterns in *Piers Plowman* communicate *extra*, higher meanings at play in—or over—the course of this complex, recursive, experiential, messy, and pervasively imbalanced poem. . . . Langland . . . seems to have theorized his frames and symmetries, using them to suggest Providential forms and even . . . to describe God's essence and agency. In other words, Langland also theorizes chiasmus, translating it, as it were, from rhetoric into theology, via poetics.[36]

This particular line in fact transposes the thematic chiasmus of salvation history into an alliteratively chiastic line, thus translating theology into poetics. The soteriological commutation of "Crist" and "Cristene" across the middle terms of "cross" and "conquerour" contributes to the larger centripetal force of the Holy Week liturgy as it bears out the chiastic structure of incarnation and redemption centered around the triumphant defeat of the crucifixion and descent into hell. Such a grand defeat can result in triumph only thanks to the hinge-like properties of the incarnation, which can be expressed poetically in a line of chiastic alliteration. The normative alliterative line is unbalanced (*aa|ax*), just as defeat does not normally balance itself out with victory. Yet for those rare defeats that result in victory there are rare balanced and chiastic alliterative lines. This one functions as a hinge mechanism for the poem's entire plot, opening onto the victory of the cross and transferring the benefits of that victory to those in need of salvation.

On the other side of the chiastic fold between passūs 20 and 21, another alliteratively balanced line binds repentant sinner to saving God across their asymmetrical relationship. As we have seen, upon waking from his dream of the harrowing of hell, Will exhorts his wife and daughter, Kitte and Calote, "Arise and go reuerense godes resureccion / And crepe to þe croes on knees and kusse hit for a iewel" (C.20.470–71).

---

36. M. Smith, "Chiastic Form in *Piers Plowman*," 1–2.

The first line of Will's exhortation could hardly be more imbalanced thematically. The *a*-verse's imperatives put Kitte and Calote in a passive, penitential position even as the *b*-verse comprises God's greatest action. Yet chiastic, contrapuntal alliteration[37] yokes the two halves together, facilitating commerce between penitent sinners and glorified God. Three full staves alliterating on [r] are counterpointed with a secondary alliteration on [g] in the *a*-verse and a corresponding, stressed [g]-syllable in the *b*-verse position normally reserved for the key-stave: "'A*r*ise and go *r*eu̯erense | *g*odes resu*r*eccion'" (*a[b]a|ba*).[38] The following line amplifies this exhortation, identifying the object of reverence as the cross, which stands in for "godes resureccion," thus converting the instrument of death into the sign of life.

Langland's contemporaries might have appreciated a similar translation in the liturgical chronology, for although the ceremony of creeping to the cross was occasionally observed on Easter morning, it was much more commonly associated with Good Friday. Whichever practice was familiar to Langland's readers, the Easter morning veneration of the cross renders the instrument of defeat the sign of victory, not only by carrying it across the cosmic reversal of the harrowing of hell on Holy Saturday, but also by making the cross available to penitents for participation. For the victory of the cross can only be complete when sinners repent, take up their crosses, and follow Christ—when their rising and going alliterates in counterpoint, as it were, with God's own resurrection. In this sense, the line's highly anomalous absence of a key-stave invites alliterative participation. God ("godes") occupies the key position, alliterating only with the secondary, unstressed, human-oriented

---

37. Schmidt, *The Clerkly Maker*, 62–67.

38. This is a rare line indeed, one that the standard typology would not admit if scanned *aa|xa*. ("The minimum requirement of metricality is that two full staves must appear in the *a*-verse and the first stave in the *b*-verse must be full." Hoyt N. Duggan, "Notes toward a Theory of Langland's Meter," *Yearbook of Langland Studies* 1 [1987]: 43.) Nor does "godes" here submit to the distinction between full, mute, and blank staves. It cannot be full since it does not alliterate on the primary [r] sound. It cannot be mute since it has stress. And it cannot be blank since it *does* alliterate on the secondary [g] sound.

"go" of the *a*-verse. Whereas the key-stave normally "unlocks" the primary alliterative pattern of the *a*-verse, here what it reveals about the *a*-verse is the urgency of human agency, the tropological imperative that makes every "go" in the Gospels faintly echo with Jesus' exhortation, ". . . and do thou in like manner" (Luke 10:37). To "go" in this line is to alliterate with "godes," and so to participate in "godes resureccion."

The two chiastic, crucicentric lines just analyzed frame with a rough symmetry the clearest signal in all of *Piers Plowman* that Will and William Langland are self-consciously making a public literary artifact. At the middle of this crucicentric middle, at the middle of the chiastic fold between passūs 20 and 21, between cross and cross, Will says, "Thus y wakede and wrot what y hadde ydremed" (C.21.1). In this line, writing—"wrot"—is situated directly between waking and dreaming; it is in fact the numerical center of the line's nine words. Will enjoys one of his precarious, always interstitial waking moments eight lines after waking and just four before falling asleep again. This middling site of writing becomes, in turn, a frame in its own right, reappearing in similar form at the end of the passus to bracket the poem's climactic vision of the resurrection's communal consequences.

Critics have gravitated to this juncture between C.20 and 21 (B.18 and 19) as a site of heightened interpretive vision even as the poem proceeds to its irresolute ending. Morton W. Bloomfield writes, "In a profound sense, the powerful scene of the Harrowing of Hell is the true end of the poem, of the quest for Christian perfection which this poem exemplifies."[39] But the poem does not end with B.18/C.20 in any of the extant manuscripts. If the quest for Christian perfection from the ethical-soteriological crises of the "fair feld ful of folk" (C.Prol.19) culminates in B.18/C.20, then the final two passūs mirror that development in reverse, declining from the perfect unity of Pentecost to the ruin of Holy Church. This plot of fall-to-redemption and redemption-to-fall bears a broadly chiastic pattern. Thus, Anne Middleton notes "the latent similarities, a pattern of cyclical return, of theme and form that joins the beginning to the end of the poem, markedly enhancing a broad

---

39. Bloomfield, *"Piers Plowman" as a Fourteenth-Century Apocalypse*, 125.

chiastic symmetry between the two opening visions and the two post-Resurrection visions that conclude both long forms of the poem."[40] Middleton recognizes that something happens around the beginning and ending of *Piers Plowman* that keeps the beginning and ending from fully determining the work's *ratio*. Beginning and ending do not map onto the work's first and final causes, and they can give a misleading sense of its formal and efficient causes. I have focused on the literary form of chiasmus as a formal cause that refuses the determinations of beginning or ending. The centripetal force of chiasmus invites a new critical perspective on *Piers Plowman*, one that reads middles as at least equally productive of its *sentence* as its beginnings and ends. If Bloomfield and Kathryn Kerby-Fulton's early work read Langland through his endings, and Anne Middleton and D. Vance Smith read him through his beginnings, then I am arguing for a reinvigorated focus on the middle.[41]

My argument about the chiastic middle where Will wakes and writes hovers around the end of *Piers Plowman*. But other structural and thematic middles earlier in the poem—from its numerical midpoint to Will's middle age to the theological middle of the incarnation—have prepared for this late, crucicentric middle. This late middle is particularly significant because it dilates the most prevalent middle in the poem, the incarnation, and makes it available to literary and sacramental participation. Will wakes and writes between two penitential liturgies—one in waking life, one in a dream—that involve the incarnation and the cross. Because Will and his wife and daughter are here able to participate in the drama of the incarnation, this chiastic middle consummates the dozen or so visionary, metaphoric, and figural accounts

---

40. Anne Middleton, "Acts of Vagrancy: The C Version 'Autobiography' and the Statute of 1388," in *Written Work: Langland, Labor, and Authorship*, ed. Steven Justice and Kathryn Kerby-Fulton (Philadelphia: University of Pennsylvania Press, 1997), 269.

41. Bloomfield, *"Piers Plowman" as a Fourteenth-Century Apocalypse*; Kathryn Kerby-Fulton, *Reformist Apocalypticism and "Piers Plowman"* (New York: Cambridge University Press, 1990); Middleton, "Narration and the Invention of Experience"; D. Smith, *The Book of the Incipit*. Middleton also reads from the end in her essay "Making a Good End."

of the incarnation earlier in the poem.[42] I call this middle "dynamic" because it is not anchored to a point in the sequence of reading or of composition. Rather, this incarnational and crucicentric middle bears a centripetal force that draws the poem's acts of invention and the readers' acts of interpretation back to it. And because this middle becomes a middle by virtue of readers' recursions to it in their own lives of sacramental participation in crucicentric satisfaction, it dynamically moves outside the text. This movement beyond the text is of course tropological, but it is so in various respects, depending on the frame of participation. Readers can encounter the crucicentric middle in the Bible's passion narratives, in *Piers Plowman*'s narrative poetry, in liturgy, and in the small, daily sufferings they endure as their own way of the cross. The variety of tropologies entails diverse forms of participation in a range of ontological registers.

This particular crucicentric middle stands out for its framing of the poem's writtenness and for its connection of writing to penitential liturgy and therefore to satisfaction. Because this middle comes near the end, it concerns *novissimis*: the poem's internal eschatology, its hope for an ending, and its anagogical *ratio* of invention, according to which, as the Latin term suggests, last things entail new things, new hopes. By chiastic patterning, Langland draws the focus that is normally due a poem's ending away from the actual ending, reorienting it to a site at the middle of the ending where Will participates intensely in the salvific work of doing well. Writing in the middle is important for Langland because it becomes the chief activity by which Will does well. The writer and the readers might do well beyond the poem in countless ways, but writing is the most appropriate form of labor by which to model doing well in a literary work.[43] Making *Piers Plowman* performs the work of penance

---

42. On some of these figural and metaphoric middles, see Cervone, *Poetics of the Incarnation*, chapter 5: "'He is in the mydde point': Poetic Deep Structure and the Frameworks of Incarnational Poetics," 159–208.

43. John But recognizes this when he "thoroughly identifies the 'profitable werkes' that enable Will to end well the 'lyf . . . ordeyned for the' with the lifelong ambitions and literary project of the poet whose work he respects." Middleton, "Making a Good End," 246.

that Langland goes out of his way to articulate in considerable detail. Langland renders Will's writing as one kind of satisfaction, namely, as the literary way to fulfill the "silent middle term" of Truth's laconic pardon, the assurance that mercy abounds for sinners who repent.[44] This broaches a new perspective on tropological invention. So far in this book we have seen how tropology works ethically and how a prominent strand of tropology presupposes a participatory metaphysics of history, but we have not yet witnessed participation happening in any mode other than virtue, imagination, and affect. Now Langland's penitential, crucicentric framing of the poem's invention carries tropology into a new participatory mode, the sacramental. So it becomes especially urgent to understand what it means, in Langland's literary milieu and in the context of the poem thus far, to say, "I waked and wrot."

What Does It Mean to Say, "I woke up and wrote"?

Up to the point of Will's announcement that he woke up and wrote, Will has been identified as someone who writes only three times in the A- and B-texts combined, and not at all in C. The A-text represents Will as a copyist in the service of merchants.[45] When Imaginatif accuses Will in B of meddling with making "bokes" to "telle men what dowel is, dobet and dobest boþe," Will does not deny the charge (B.12.16–22b). Later in B, Will worries that priests "wol be wrooþ for I write þus" (B.15.489). On the whole, as Wendy Scase has observed, "there is only sporadic internal conceptualization of the poem as a written text."[46]

---

44. Traugott Lawler, "The Pardon Formula in *Piers Plowman*: Its Ubiquity, Its Binary Shape, Its Silent Middle Term," *Yearbook of Langland Studies* 14 (2000): 117–52.

45. "Þanne were marchauntis merye; many wepe for ioye, / And yaf wille for his writyng wollene cloþis; / For he copiede þus here clause þei couden hym gret mede" (A.8.42–44).

46. Wendy Scase, "Writing and the Plowman: Langland and Literacy," *Yearbook of Langland Studies* 9 (1995): 127.

The waking and writing scenes that bookend B.19/C.21 therefore stand out for their literary self-consciousness and participate in a rich, late medieval tradition of waking and writing in dream visions. Will hears bells in his dream that wake him up to a scene of composition similar to the dreamer's in Chaucer's *Book of the Duchess*:

> Ryght thus me mette, as I yow telle,
> That in the castell ther was a belle,
> As hyt hadde smyten houres twelve.
> Therwyth I awook myselve
> And fond me lyinge in my bed;
> And the book that I hadde red,
>
> . . . .
> I fond hyt in myn hond ful even.
> Thoghte I, "Thys ys so queynt a sweven
> That I wol, be processe of tyme,
> Fonde to put this sweven in ryme
> As I kan best, and that anoon."
> This was my sweven; now hit ys doon.[47]

Chaucer's dreamer describes his waking, his reflections on his dream, and his resolution to write it down in rhyme. The last line of the poem indicates that what we have just read constitutes the work the dreamer set himself to do when he awoke from his dream.

As in many medieval dream visions, Chaucer and Langland both "focused attention on a human experience clearly linked to literary process, and the reader of a dream vision was prepared for a poem that, examining the dream experience, might also examine its own status as poetry."[48] Like Chaucer, Langland indicates the two waking moments

---

47. Geoffrey Chaucer, *The Book of the Duchess*, in *The Riverside Chaucer*, ed. Larry D. Benson, 3rd ed. (Boston: Houghton Mifflin Company, 1987), ll. 1321–24.

48. Steven F. Kruger, *Dreaming in the Middle Ages* (Cambridge: Cambridge University Press, 1992), 135.

on either end of B.19/C.21 as prompts to writing. But Langland's scenes of waking composition differ from Chaucer's and those of most other medieval dream visions in that they do not neatly conclude the poem. Will's writing functions as more than a frame that links dreaming to literary process. Writing here constitutes part of the plot, part of Will's spiritual and ethical itinerary.

Langland's momentary etiology of the poem's invention also pointedly avoids the didactic rhetoric of some prophetic dream visions, in which dreamers are called to make known certain teachings and judgments to the powers that be.[49] In *Mum and the Sothsegger*, the beekeeper evinces none of Imaginatif's caution about making when he exhorts the dreamer,

> "Loke thou write wisely my wordes echone;
> Hit wol be exemple to sum men seuene yere here-after.
> . . . .
> And make vp thy matiere, thou mays do no better.
> Hit may amende many men of theire misdeedes.
> Sith thou felys the fressh lete no feynt herte
> Abate thy blessid bisynes of they boke-making."[50]

The beekeeper places the vision in the tradition of political counsel books, the various "mirrors of princes" that convey wisdom to the powerful so that they may "amende . . . theire misdeedes" and solve the problem of disordered action by supplying right knowledge. The beekeeper betrays a naïvely Platonist anthropology, according to which agents

---

49. On prophetic and apocalyptic visionary vocations and their significance in *Piers Plowman*, see Richard K. Emmerson, "The Prophetic, the Apocalyptic, and the Study of Medieval Literature," in *Poetic Prophecy in Western Literature*, ed. Jan Wojcik and Raymond-Jean Frontain (Cranbury, NJ: Fairleigh Dickinson University Press, 1984), 40–54.

50. "Mum and the Sothsegger," in Helen Barr, ed., *The "Piers Plowman" Tradition: A Critical Edition of "Pierce the Ploughman's Crede," "Richard the Redeless," "Mum and the Sothsegger," and "The Crowned King"* (London: J. M. Dent, 1993), ll. 1268–69, 1278–81.

must only know the good in order to do it, while the work as a whole expresses a satirist's cynicism about the likely impact his truth-telling will have on society. The dreamer awakes confident that his visions were "nedeful and notable for this newe world, / and eeke plaisant to my pay for thay putten me reste / Of my long labour and loitryng aboute" (1295–97). But instead of writing down his dream, the narrator proceeds to unpack "a bagge" of "poyse," "Of vice and of vertue fulle to the margyn" (1343, 1344, 1346), and these fragments of satire and moral allegories ramble on for four hundred inconclusive lines. Since he never directly links his dream to the invention of the foregoing lines, they merge into the rag-tag collection of "poyse." As A. C. Spearing puts it, "ultimately the dream has been used as an excuse for the collapse of literary form into a mere catalogue."[51] Unlike B.19/C.21 of *Piers Plowman*, the poem *Mum and the Sothsegger* fails to incorporate the invention of the poetry and the act of writing into a plot of ethical and spiritual development. This may be why "boke-making" remains for the beekeeper an unambiguous good: writing never promises to take on the responsibility of sacramental penance.

Guillaume de Deguileville's *Pèlerinage de la vie humaine* comes closer to the liturgical context of waking and writing in B.19/C.21. Like the bells at the end of B.18/C.20, liturgical bells also wake de Deguileville's dreamer, inspiring him to write down his dream:

Algates up I ros me and to Matines I wente, but so tormented and weery I was þat I mihte nothing doo þere. My herte I hadde so fichched to þat I hadde met þat me thouhte, and yit do, þat swich is þe pilgrimage of dedliche man in þis cuntre, and þat he is ofte in swich periles—and þerfore I haue sett it in writinge in þe wise þat I mette it.[52]

51. A. C. Spearing, *Medieval Dream-Poetry* (Cambridge: Cambridge University Press, 1976), 166.

52. Avril Henry, ed., *The Pilgrimage of the Lyfe of the Manhode* (New York: Oxford University Press, 1988), 1:174. On Langland's awareness of and indebtedness to de Deguileville, specifically in the waking moments, see

Like Will at the start of B.19/C.21, the dreamer of the *Pèlerinage*, when he wakes up, promptly goes to church, however reluctantly, and has trouble concentrating on the prayers because the dream has wearied him and still demands his affective attention. He had so affixed his heart to what he had dreamed that he perceived its profound affinity to waking life: "me thouhte . . . þat swich is þe pilgrimage of dedliche man in þis cuntre." To "sett" the dream "in writinge" cements the connection between dreamlife and waking life and renders the dream available to others' participation.

Will's writing also opens his dream to others' participation, but in a mode more closely united to penitential liturgy in the intricate Holy Week and post-Resurrection plotting of passūs B.18–19/C.20–21. As Míceál Vaughan and Raymond St.-Jacques have established, the intricate plot of these passūs follows the Holy Week liturgies by quoting from and alluding to them.[53] The Holy Week and Pentecost liturgies set the itinerary for Will's progress through the scenes of redemption history, with Conscience as his guide. Along the way, Will participates in these quasi-historical events by making liturgical acts of devotion, such as kneeling at the coming of the Holy Spirit. When, upon waking from his dream of the Four Daughters of God, Will sends his wife and daughter to "go reuerense godes resureccion / And crepe to þe croes on knees and kusse hit for a iewel" (C.20.470–71), he is inviting them to participate in the drama of redemption he has just witnessed in his dream. They are to participate liturgically by creeping to the cross and kissing it, a practice so integrated into penitential culture that it was treated simultaneously as an expression of contrition and work of satisfaction in the thirteenth-century Constitution of Giles of Bridport, bishop of Salisbury and codifier of the Sarum Use: "Let no one presume on Eas-

---

Barney, *The Penn Commentary on "Piers Plowman,"* 5:104–5; and Burrow, *Langland's Fictions*, 113–18.

53. Míceál F. Vaughan, "The Liturgical Perspectives of *Piers Plowman* B, XVI–XIX," *Studies in Medieval and Renaissance History* 3 (1980): 87–155; Raymond St.-Jacques, "Conscience's Final Pilgrimage in *Piers Plowman* and the Cyclical Structure of the Liturgy," *Revue de l'Université d'Ottawa* 40, no. 2 (1970): 210–23; and Raymond St.-Jacques, "Langland's Bells of the Resurrection and the Easter Liturgy," *English Studies in Canada* 3, no. 2 (1977): 129–35.

ter Day to approach the Body of Christ unless he has first confessed and adored the cross."[54] The liturgical context of this waking interlude draws all prior and subsequent episodes into its orbit—just as the Triduum encompasses and reframes the entire Christian liturgical year. Whatever comes beyond this point will necessarily have to refer back to the centrality of the cross and the penitential participation by which the cross effects salvation. By signaling the writtenness of the poem at this theologically pivotal moment of the work, Langland unites his work of making to a penitential practice of satisfaction. Will's writing in the waking state corresponds to the textually encoded liturgical actions of kneeling and creeping to the cross. Langland connects this marker of invention, of written labor, to the penitential liturgy of devotion to the cross and to the sacrament of the Eucharist by placing the first explicit acknowledgment of the poem's writtenness in the chiastic fold between two liturgies.

Sacramental Penance and Literary Satisfaction

Having situated the writing of *Piers Plowman* within a theologically significant chiastic patterning that unites the work of writing the poem to the work of penitential liturgy, I now turn to the evidence from historical theology concerning practices of satisfaction. Langland invests a great deal in these formal dynamic middles, perhaps because he is chiefly concerned with the lives of the spiritual middle class, the *mediocriter boni* who have not given themselves over to evil, nor reached the state of perfection, but who must repent and rely on God's mercy if they are to make it to heaven.[55] Truth's pardon, the poem's most succinct soteriological statement, assigns those who do good to heaven and those who do evil to hell, leaving the vast middle category of sinners who

---

54. Henry John Feasey, *Ancient English Holy Week Ceremonial* (London: Thomas Baker, 1897), 120. Here adoration of the cross is the fitting expression of contrition and satisfaction, the other parts of penance in addition to confession.

55. See Constable, *Three Studies in Medieval Religious and Social Thought*, 342–60.

repent for further explication.[56] This middle category is vast indeed, for the Christian life, even the life of a saint, requires continuous conversion. It is always lived in and from the middle, *in via*.[57] Traugott Lawler has demonstrated how Langland articulates this middle option throughout the poem, especially in revisions from the B to the C text.[58] Peace and Mercy carry the day in their debate with Truth and Righteousness (B.18/C.20) precisely because Christ's mercy extends to sinners who repent, and extends to them for the sake of their salvation. Lawler sum-

---

56. The pardon that Truth gives to Piers comprises two lines of Latin from the Athanasian Creed, "*Et qui bona egerunt ibunt in vitam eternam; / Qui vero mala in ignem eternum*" (C.9.286a–b). A priest who is looking on glosses the Latin, "do wel and haue wel, and god shal haue thy soule / And do yuele and haue euele and hope thow non oþere / Bote he þat euele lyueth euele shal ende" (C.9.290–92).

57. As Alan Fletcher has argued, drawing on evidence of Langland's practice of revision from version to version, "if the *conversio morum* and its socially desirable by-products were to be sustained, contrition must ever be renewed. It was not a once-off event. And such ongoing contrition is necessarily a project that only a fluidly adaptive text is likely to succeed in enabling: a continuing *conversio morum* requires a coextensive *conversio textus*; it demands an ongoing, restless adaptation, a re-making by and in the agents of its manufacture. Writing, and the unending business, until death, of repenting and doing well in the real world, may for Langland have been reciprocal activities, and this reciprocity, I would suggest, yields another way of accounting for why he was drawn repeatedly back to his poem. His repeated acts of 'making' may in themselves have embodied a moral venture as much as they indulged some guiltily self-absorbed pleasure in the writing of poetry." Fletcher, "The Essential (Ephemeral) William Langland," 67–68.

58. Lawler, "The Pardon Formula in *Piers Plowman*," 128–31. Lawler adduces evidence from emphatic C-text revisions, such as this amplification of Repentance's prayer on behalf of the repentant *commune*:

> "What tyme we synnefole men wolden be sory
> For dedes that we han don ylle dampned sholde we ben neuere
> Yf we knowlechede and cryde Crist þerfore mercy:
> *Quandocumque ingemuerit peccator omnes iniquitates eius non recordabor
>   amplius.*"
>
> (C.7.145–47a)

marizes the soteriology thus: "if to do penance is to do well, and to do well is to enter eternal life, then those who sin but do penance will enter eternal life."[59]

Langland identifies the public penitential work of *Piers Plowman* by drawing on the pastoral theology of satisfaction in all its diversity. Penitential practices and theology figure prominently in *Piers Plowman*. Patience explicitly rehearses the conventional penitential theology—"*Cordis contricio* cometh of sorwe of herte / And *oris confessio* cometh of knowlechyng and shrifte of mouthe / And *operis satisfaccio* for soules paieth and alle synnes quyteth" (C.16.29–31). Satisfaction remains largely undefined in *Piers Plowman*, and its conventional tripartite analysis as prayer, fasting, and almsgiving does not readily correspond to the work many readers understand the poem to be doing. Scholars have given much more attention to confession because this part of the sacrament clearly corresponds to the poem's narrative of failure.[60]

----

59. Ibid., 140.

60. Of the three parts of penance, confession has received the most attention in studies of *Piers Plowman*. Its first lines signal that the work involves confession. The narrating "I" reflects back on another time from a particular moral vantage, one from which the "werkes" of his past seem "vnholy" (C.Prol.3). The Londe of Longynge episodes, especially, can be read as the extended confession of error. Vaughan argues that *Piers Plowman* "is one man's confession of mouth, his contrite narration of his past life of sleeping, of misunderstanding, ignorance, and sin, from which he finally 'gan awake.'" Míceál F. Vaughan, "'Til I gan awake': The Conversion of Dreamer into Narrator in *Piers Plowman* B," *Yearbook of Langland Studies* 5 (1991): 191. See also Vaughan, "Liturgical Perspectives," 87–101. John Bowers doubts whether Will has the requisite contrition to make a good confession, arguing that his sleepiness in the early passūs represents a slothful disposition that resists contrition. John M. Bowers, *The Crisis of Will in "Piers Plowman"* (Washington, DC: Catholic University of America Press, 1986), 61–77. Katherine C. Little leaves the poem's penitential work to one side to focus on its critical function, arguing that "Langland's portrait of confession [in B.5] underlines the magnitude of the task of reform as well as 'some misgivings' about it." Katherine C. Little, *Confession and Resistance: Defining the Self in Late Medieval England* (Notre Dame, IN: University of Notre Dame Press, 2006), 27. For a consideration of the poem's lived theology of penance ordered toward reconciliation, see Rachael Deagman,

But three themes from the pastoral literature on satisfaction complicate and enrich an understanding of satisfaction as prayer, fasting, and alms-giving, and illuminate how Langland understands satisfaction.

First, one aspect or "part" of satisfaction is contrition for and recol-lection of past sins *in prayer*, apart from and subsequent to auricular confession to a priest. As the Good Samaritan tells Will, "sorwe of herte is satisfaccion for suche þat may nat paye" (C.19.604). The fourteenth-century preaching manual *Fasciculus morum* suggests the narrative quality of prayerful satisfaction: "Therefore, the words of the Psalm apply well to these and others who thus grieve for their sins: 'I will re-count to you all my years,' and so forth; add: the years I have spent in vain endeavors, for which I have held the eternal years in my mind which I have lost with their glory, and therefore I have kept them firmly in my contrite mind."[61] This kind of contrite recollection *as satisfaction* could describe much of what readers of *Piers Plowman* have typically and problematically treated as confession. To understand *Piers Plow-man*'s narratives of failure as confession is problematic because auricu-lar confession must be made to a priest, and so any analysis of *Piers Plowman* in terms of confession has had to use an analogy to confes-sion, rather than the sacrament itself. If we understand the narratives of failure as satisfaction, we can see how Will within the poem and Wil-liam Langland as author could both be performing the work of satisfac-tion by recounting "the years I have spent in vain endeavors."

Second, by the fourteenth century the category of "almsgiving" had greatly expanded to include all the corporal and spiritual works of mercy, with the latter including "to teach the uneducated, give counsel to people who are in doubt, console the sorrowing, correct the sinner, forgive those who offend, support those who are burdened, and pray for all."[62] The meaning of "alms" is similarly dilated in *Piers Plowman*,

---

"The Formation of Forgiveness in *Piers Plowman*," *Journal of Medieval and Early Modern Studies* 40, no. 2 (2010): 273–97.

61. Siegfried Wenzel, ed., *Fasciculus morum: A Fourteenth-Century Preacher's Handbook*, trans. Siegfried Wenzel (University Park: Pennsylvania State University Press, 1989), 525.

62. Ibid., 529.

where the *lorelles* who do not want to help Piers plow his half-acre pray that his grain will multiply, in exchange for his "Almesse þat ȝe ȝeuen vs here" (C.8.133). The material alms Piers might give the *lorelles* are later transfigured into the fruits of his scriptural plowing, as the seeds of virtues that he plants grow into good deeds (C.21.258–75). Likewise, *Fasciculus morum* turns the parable of the sower and the seed to consider satisfaction by almsgiving: "Next you must . . . put on it some soil that is rich and fertile, called *marl* in English, which is true and just penance for this and that sin. And then let us sow the seed of good works."[63] Alms-deeds, understood to include all the spiritual and corporal works of mercy, resist the privatization of satisfaction. Satisfaction by alms is oriented toward the person or community offended, making it a public action rather than a private transaction of the kind satirized throughout *Piers Plowman*, the "pryue payement" that Friar Flatterer accepts from Contrition at the low point of the final passus (C.22.364). Furthermore, the works of mercy prominently include edification, counsel, and fraternal correction. *Piers Plowman* is full of such works of mercy, and therefore the writing of the poem constitutes the work of "alms" as penitential satisfaction.

Third, *Piers Plowman* holds a mechanistic understanding of penance up to critique, promoting instead what I call open-ended satisfaction. Priests from at least the thirteenth century onward frequently imposed, in addition to a specific penance, this general penance as part of the absolution: "May whatever good you do and suffering you endure be for the remission of your sins."[64] Thomas Aquinas praised this

---

63. Ibid., 549.

64. This is the rubric as it was eventually formalized after Trent in the penitential rite of Paul V: "Passio Domini nostri Iesu Christi, merita beatae Mariae Virginis, & omnium Sanctorum, & quicquid boni feceris & mali sustinueris sint tibi in remissionem peccatorum, augmentum gratiae, & praemium vitae eternae." *Rituale romanum Pauli Quinti* (Rome, 1636), 48–49. The exact wording varies in pre-Tridentine sources. Relevant to England is this rubric for absolution in the Sarum Pontifical: "Passio Jesu Christi, merita beatae Mariae, et omnium sanctorum, et totius ecclesiae catholicae, quicquid etiam boni feceris et mali sustinueris pro dilectione Dei et proximi, cedant tibi in remissionem istorum et aliorum peccatorum tuorum, in augmentum gratiae, et praemium

penance for its psycho-spiritual sensitivity, noting that the debt of sin is often so great that a fittingly heavy penance would extinguish the small flame of contrition. Better, he thought, "that the priest should tell the penitent how great a penance ought to be imposed on him for his sins; and let him impose on him nevertheless something that the penitent could tolerably bear." Then if the penitent does more good beyond the penance, those works will avail for the remission of sins because the priest has endowed them with the expiatory power of the keys.[65] By 1614 this general penance was enshrined in the mandatory Roman penitential rite, but it was in widespread use in the late Middle Ages.[66] This

---

vitae aeternae." William Maskell, ed., *Monumenta ritualia ecclesiae Anglicanae: or, Occasional Offices of the Church of England According to the Ancient Use of Salisbury, the Prymer in English, and Other Prayers and Forms*, vol. 1 (London: W. Pickering, 1846), 228.

65. Thomas Aquinas, *Quaestiones de quodlibet*, n.d., quodlibet III, q. 13, art. 1, http://www.corpusthomisticum.org. This quodlibetal question, composed during Thomas's second regency in Paris, 1268–72, is the earliest record of the rubric I have found, besides the Sarum use (see previous note). Thomas suggests that the rubric is already in widespread use: "These things which he does beyond the expressed command more greatly receive the power of the expiation of present sins from that general imposition that the priest says: *May whatever good you do be for the remission of your sins.* So it is praiseworthy that many priests became accustomed to saying this—although they do not have the greater power to grant remedy against future sin; and insofar as such satisfaction is sacramental in this case, it expiates already committed sins by the power of the [office of the] keys."

66. The rubric seems to have become more closely united with routine absolution and more widely used over the course of the fourteenth and early fifteenth centuries. The Sarum Pontifical, which likely has its roots in the early thirteenth century, gives this rubric in the context of the reconciliation of excommunicates (see note above). In *Pupilla oculi* (1385), an influential manual for priests, John of Burgh, chancellor of the University of Cambridge, assumes that the rubric is being used regularly for the penance of lay communicants. He remarks that "after the imposition of the specific penance, priests are accustomed to say, 'May whatever good you do be for the remission of your sins,'—and this practice is extremely praiseworthy." John of Burgh, *Pupilla oculi* (Strasburg: Schott, Knobloch, and Götz, 1516), xl, available online through Gateway Bayern, http://gateway-bayern.de. The Middle English verse adap-

meant that when wisely applied, the three parts of penance did not constitute a closed sequence with a discrete beginning and end, confined to the parish church during the obligatory annual shrift in Holy Week, but rather permeated all of life, since every good work and every suffering could avail for the remission of sins.

Piers Plowman is not the only fourteenth-century example of writing as an alms-deed, a spiritual work of mercy in an open-ended, lifelong practice of satisfaction. The Middle English translation of Robert of Gretham's Anglo-Norman *Miroir* "envisions a non-sacramental instructional fellowship, probably corresponding to that 'spiritual work of mercy' which enjoins one to counsel the sinful."[67] According to Richard Rolle's *Form of Living*, alms-deeds involve "nat only to gyf pouer men met or drynke, bot for to . . . enfourme ham how þay shal do þat ben in poynt to perisshe."[68] *Piers Plowman* is, if nothing else, an effort to "enforme" those who will someday face death "how þay shal do" by making of the phrase a question and enacting the search for its answer in the quest for Dowel, Dobet, and Dobest. Rolle's penitent can "enfourme ham how þay shal do" by "clennesse . . . in hert, in mouth, and in werke," three spheres of the spiritual life that continuously interact in "honest occupacioun and profitable," and in "litelle . . . speche." The economy of speech Rolle envisions cannot be achieved until "þi hert be stablet in þe

---

tation of *Pupilla oculi*, John Mirk's *Instructions for Parish Priests* (c. 1400), includes the rubric in Latin as an intrinsic part of the absolution, with no comment on its laudability. See John Mirk, *Instructions for Parish Priests*, ed. Gillis Kristensson (Lund: Gleerup, 1974), 162–63. To situate the mainstream adoption of this rubric in the broader historical development of penance, see Henry Ansgar Kelly, "Penitential Theology and Law at the Turn of the Fifteenth Century," in *A New History of Penance*, ed. Abigail Firey (Leiden: Brill, 2008), 239–98.

67. Hanna, *London Literature, 1300–1380*, 191. Hanna offers an extensive discussion of how the Middle English *Mirror* extends this responsibility to lay people (176–202), finally associating the practice of "kenn[ing] it about" with "neighborhood religious corporations" such as that in St. Peter's, Cornhill, probably Langland's parish church (199–202).

68. Richard Rolle, *The Form of Living*, in *Richard Rolle, Prose and Verse*, ed. S. J. Ogilvie-Thomson, EETS, o.s., 293 (Oxford: Oxford University Press, 1988), 13.

loue of Ihesu, so þat þe þynke þat þou lokest euer on hym [Christ], wheþer þou spek or noȝt." This means that the task Holy Church enjoins on Will—"Lere hit thus lewed men . . . : / Than treuthe and trewe loue is no tresor bettre" (C.1.135)—might constitute a work of satisfaction, an "almes dede" of "clennes of mouth," but not without great travail and habituation: "Bot such a grace may þou noght haue in þe first day, bot with longe trauaille and gret bisinesse to loue, and with custume."[69] To do well in such work will require lifelong practice.

Rolle's immediate audience was the anchoress Margeret Kyrkeby, but his conception of *clene speche* as a lifelong work of satisfaction extends to the project that Nicholas Watson finds him sharing with Dante: "to engage in complex processes of reinterpretation of their lives and writings in order to present them as patterned in meaningful ways . . . creating retrospective patterns where none were before."[70] As Watson notes, the evangelistic goals of such a project require author and literary persona to overlap, connecting the subjectivities and work of invention inside the poem to the work of an author outside the poem, thus rendering the fictive material real and publicly available for use and participation.[71] Anne Middleton has also recognized that "the visionary duration of Will's life, the making of the poem that records it, and a life of penitential self-knowledge through confession are . . . rendered synonymous."[72] This obliquely autobiographical connection causes the

---

69. Ibid.

70. Nicholas Watson, *Richard Rolle and the Invention of Authority* (New York: Cambridge University Press, 1991), 267.

71. Compare, in a nonsacramental but intensely ethical framework, Gower's similar disposition: "his persona is a (fictive) moral agent within the artful world of the text, but is also identified as the producer of the text, and therefore is a (real) moral agent in the political world. In this sense, Gower's various personae model the relationship between making and acting, and also model various relationships to both the social world and philosophical knowledge." Matthew W. Irvin, *Poetic Voices of John Gower: Politics and Personae in the Confessio Amantis* (Suffolk: D. S. Brewer, 2014), 4.

72. Anne Middleton, "William Langland's 'Kynde Name': Authorial Signature and Social Identity in Late Fourteenth-Century England," in *Literary*

internal, fictional work of the poem, Will's quest, and, eventually, his writing to participate in the external work of its invention, composition, and disposition: William Langland's work of satisfaction, understood as a lifelong project to "kenne it aboute" (C.1.88) "how þai sall do"—in Rolle's terms—by "clennes of mouth."[73]

Rolle's and Langland's shared sense of the lifelong, open-ended nature of satisfaction anticipates the expansion of the absolution rubric in Mirk's *Instructions to Parish Priests* (c. 1400) to emphasize just this aspect of satisfaction. Mirk integrates the "whatever good you do" rubric with the traditional absolution and makes explicit what was only implied in earlier versions of the rubric: "may all the good deeds which you have done *and will do up to the end of your life* be for the remission of these and all your other sins."[74] Langland approaches the relationship between penance and Dowel, Dobet, and Dobest from this open-ended perspective on penance, this sense of satisfaction as ongoing and potentially imbuing all of life.[75] The poetry's representational mode absorbs the form of the sacrament. The writing of the poetry can then become a means of enacting the sacrament of penance, of doing well for the remission of sins.

This relationship between what I have called the internal and external work of the poem intensifies the tropological hermeneutical circle,

---

Practice and Social Change in Britain, 1380–1530, ed. Lee Patterson (Berkeley and Los Angeles: University of California Press, 1990), 60.

73. Rolle, *The Form of Living*, 13.

74. Mirk, *Instructions for Parish Priests*, 163 (my emphasis). The full rubric after the traditional absolution reads, "Ista humilitas et passio domini nostri ihesu christi / et merita sancte matris ecclesiae, et omnes indulgencie / tibi concesse, et omnia bona que fecisti et facies vsque / in finem vite tue, sint tibi in remissionem istorum et / omnium aliorum peccatorum tuorum. Amen" (162–63).

75. Larry Scanlon has recognized this dynamic in the B.5 pageant of the seven deadly sins, where the penitential "discourse this piece of poetry draws on offers no moment where semiosis stops. Langland's personifications of penitential discourse are drawn into an endless signifying loop by the requirement of doctrines no less than by their poetic complexity." Larry Scanlon, "Personification and Penance," *Yearbook of Langland Studies* 21 (2007): 1–29.

and it provides a rationale for the continuations of *Piers Plowman* discussed in chapter 1. In most cases, when the reader is the tropological agent, the text sends the reader outside the poem to fulfill the tropological imperative. But in the present case, William Langland the writer is the tropological agent, and so when the tropological imperative prompts him to make satisfaction, it sends him back to the writing of the poem. Because *Piers Plowman* itself envisions satisfactory writing, readers such as John But, R. H., and the Protestant clergyman Stephen Batman could interpret its tropological imperative as a call to participate in the poem's invention as a means of doing well. The title page that Batman designed for his "antique" manuscript of *Piers Plowman* presents it as a pastoral book about the cultivation of scripture, and both its epigraph and brief continuation frame it as an evangelical work. By commending *Piers Plowman* to his contemporaries, as his title page and continuation do, Batman also undertakes evangelical work—a work of mercy, in penitential terms.[76] But Batman's terms are not penitential terms, at least not in the Roman Catholic sense. What, then, are the options for satisfaction by tropological invention in the new theological world that Batman inhabited?

Making Satisfaction across the Reformation

If we wanted an image of a pivotal juncture between Langland's practice of making satisfaction, Conscience's tears in the final passus "for the failure . . . of the penitential system,"[77] and Briony Tallis's authorial despair

---

76. On Batman, see the last section of chapter 1, "Tropological Reception of *Piers Plowman*."

77. Nicholas Watson, "*Piers Plowman*, Pastoral Theology, and Spiritual Perfectionism: Hawkyn's Cloak and Patience's Pater Noster," *Yearbook of Langland Studies* 21 (2007): 116. Watson labels this interpretation of Conscience's cries as "Lutheran" or more generally "post-Reformation," and, after interrogating the post–Lateran IV "pastoral project" and its failures, he concludes that "even in crisis, Langland's commitment to the universalism of the pastoral project remains unshaken." As evidence, he turns to the chiastic passages that have occupied much of this chapter: "the sacrament of the Eucharist survive[s] untouched, given renewed emphasis by Will's reintegration with the church

over the impossibility of atonement, we might turn to Sir Thomas Wyatt's *A Paraphrase of the Penitential Psalms*, probably written in the wake of a revision of penitential theology by the 1536 *Articles about Religion* (commonly known as the Ten Articles). In passages of connecting commentary, as well as in the Psalm paraphrases themselves, Wyatt dwells on the incommensurable difference between God and man, and on the impossibility of satisfying the infinite debt not only of David's grave sins but of any sin whatsoever.

> But when he weigh'th the fault and recompense,
> He damn'th his deed and findeth plain
> Atween them two [David and God] no whit equivalence
> Whereby he takes all outward deed in vain
> To bear the name of rightful penitence,
> Which is alone the heart returned again
> And sore contrite that doth his fault bemoan,
> And outward deed the sign of fruit alone.
>
> (ll. 648–55)[78]

---

through the Mass in passūs 18–19, as he experiences the life and death of Christ and lives the same events liturgically in his waking life (especially B.18.427–33, 19.1–4)" (117). According to my reading here, *Piers Plowman* embraces and transcends penitential "failure," absorbing it in the ongoing life of sanctification and satisfaction, not only for individuals, but for the corporate church as well—a topic for another book. Langland's understanding of open-ended satisfaction, as I have developed it here, resists Watson's understanding of the meaning of pastoral and institutional failure in *Piers Plowman*. The poem is not just a critique of a failed project, nor a desperate act of hope predicated on an overrealized eschatology (ibid., 96). Rather, it contributes to the pastoral project and articulates an eschatological horizon in which the failures of the institutional church must constantly be repaired and atoned for in a penitential quest for union with the crucified Lord. The pastoral project is not a progressive nor an apocalyptic project, and therefore need not be abandoned when it does not succeed in effecting or witnessing an "imminent transformation of the world" (ibid.). To attribute a phrase of Protestant coinage to Langland, *Ecclesia semper reformanda est* (the church must always be reformed).

78. Sir Thomas Wyatt, *A Paraphrase of the Penitential Psalms*, in *The Complete Poems*, ed. R. A. Rebholz (Harmondsworth: Penguin, 1978). Line numbers are cited in the text.

Wyatt's suspicion of the "outward deed" echoes the 1536 *Articles'* emphasis that works cannot of themselves merit anything: "not as though our contrition, or faith, or any works proceeding thereof, can worthily merit or deserve to attain the said justification."[79]

Reading both of these texts from the perspective of later developments in radical Puritan thought, James Simpson notes that for Wyatt's David, "nothing but grace, or God's unprovoked, unmerited gift, defines the relation between sinner and God . . . . Grace, in this account, renders the virtuous accretions of the individual life entirely redundant, or at best a 'sacrifice.'"[80] To be sure, certain strains of English theology would develop in this direction, and Thomas Cranmer's *42 Articles* of 1552 would exclude penance from the sacraments, grouping it among those practices "grown partly of the corrupt following of the Apostles," leaving only the "dominical" sacraments of Baptism and Eucharist.[81] Yet the 1536 *Articles*—the same formulas to which Wyatt's *Paraphrase* apparently responds—include penance in the triad of sacraments "instituted of Christ in the New Testament as a thing so necessary to man's salvation, that no man which after his Baptism is fallen again, and hath committed deadly sin, can, without the same, be saved, or attain everlasting life."[82] While the 1536 *Articles* consider that the sinner "hath no works or merits of his own, which he may worthily lay before God, as sufficient satisfaction for his sins,"[83] they emphatically endorse practices of satisfaction that might as well find their place in a medieval Catholic penitential manual:

---

79. *Articles about Religion, Set out by the Convocation, and Published by the King's Authority,* in Charles Lloyd, ed., *Formularies of Faith Put forth by Authority during the Reign of Henry VIII* (Oxford: Oxford University Press, 1856), 12.

80. Simpson, *Reform and Cultural Revolution,* 324.

81. Gerald Lewis Bray, *Documents of the English Reformation, 1526–1701* (Cambridge: James Clarke, 2004), 299.

82. *Articles about Religion,* in Lloyd, *Formularies,* 8.

83. Ibid., 9.

all men truly penitent, contrite, and confessed, must needs also bring forth the fruits of penance, that is to say, prayer, fasting, alms-deeds, and must make restitution or satisfaction in will and deed to their neighbour, . . . and also must do all other good works of mercy and charity, . . . or else they shall never be saved.[84]

In the political welter of subsequent decades, the 1536 *Articles*' palpable tension between the real social consequences of sin, the gratuitousness of salvation, and penitential cooperation with grace in works of satisfaction would appear to have been no more than "a careful, if finally incoherent, compromise between radical and conservative views."[85]

But Langland's practices of satisfaction—performed as contrite, questing, and edifying works of mercy—suggest another view on Wyatt's penitential poetic, a view from which the 1536 *Articles* appear surprisingly coherent. Langland's careful development of the relationship between doing well, poetic making, and sacramental satisfaction finds an echo in Wyatt's penitential poetics. For David's contrite heart does more than just feel contrition; it "doth his fault bemoan" (l. 654), not only in acknowledgment of wrongdoing but in recognition and announcement of God's mercy, to "lere[n] hit thus lewed men" (C.1.135) in Holy Church's terms: "Sinners I shall into thy ways address, / They shall return to thee and thy grace sue" (ll. 486–87). Wyatt's David echoes the penitential manuals' understanding of edification as a work of mercy because medieval penitential theology was itself derived in part from the penitential Psalms—a salutary reminder that reformist preference for scripture often did not effect a rupture with tradition, which was also based on scripture. Although Wyatt interjects his own concern about outward show—"But thou delights in no such gloze / Of outward deed as men dream and devise" (ll. 498–99)—he also uses the Psalm that would become the Book of Common Prayer's morning canticle to work out how deeds, and especially his own public, poetic practice of satisfaction,

---

84. Ibid., 10–11.
85. Simpson, *Reform and Cultural Revolution*, 324.

can constitute authentic "sacrifice." The key is God's grace cooperating within him to generate deeds that God can accept outwardly:

> Thou must, O Lord, my lips first unloose,
> . . . .
> Make Zion, Lord, according to thy will,
> Inward Zion, the Zion of the ghost.
> Of heart's Jerusalem strength the wall still.
> Then shalt thou take for good these outward deeds
> As sacrifice thy pleasure to fulfil.
> Of thee alone thus all our good proceeds.
>
> (ll. 494, 503–8)

Wyatt takes pains to parse outward show and inward true contrition because he keenly perceives the danger of what Sarah Beckwith has called "the mind's retreat from the face" in early modern England—the widening gap between personal belief and collective uniformity, between private dissent and public allegiance, between authentic religion and perfunctory rites, and between the invisible and the visible church.[86] For Wyatt's David, sin is the name for this retreat, and insofar as it is a retreat from the face of God, the remedy for sin is to be healed and strengthened from inside out—not just inside.[87] Sin has not lost its public dimension, nor has reconciliation.[88]

---

86. Beckwith, *Shakespeare and the Grammar of Forgiveness*, 20–33.

87. On the same issue of inner and outward actions, Erasmus believed, according to Jennifer Herdt, that "To imitate exemplary virtues—the charity of Christ and the saints—is not to do something merely 'external'; to honor and admire exemplary virtue without imitating it is." Jennifer A. Herdt, *Putting on Virtue: The Legacy of the Splendid Vices* (Chicago: University of Chicago Press, 2008), 109. Where Wyatt could differ—and where Herdt locates a fatal development in early modern ethical theory—is on the capacity of outward deeds to effect inward change. For Erasmus, "what is 'exterior,' what appears, can shape what is 'interior,' the character of our hearts" (109).

88. As Simpson remarks, in David's efforts to reconcile himself with God, we can also perceive Wyatt's suit to regain Henry VIII's favor. While the analogy renders "the relationship between [temporal] lord and servant . . . massively

The radical Protestant Robert Crowley, who edited, glossed, and printed three editions of *Piers Plowman* B in 1550, seems to have concurred.[89] To be sure, he identifies Lady Mede's ability to finagle cheap grace as "the fruites of Popish penaunce," and he labels as "the olde satisfacion" Lechour's preposterous rehab plan to "drynke but wiþ þe duck" for seven years of Saturdays.[90] But despite Crowley's periodization, he aligns the Protestant present with Langland's deeply conventional critique of penitential abuses, revealing a fundamental continuity between the two authors' reforming impulses. And at what is perhaps *Piers Plowman*'s most "Catholic" moment, when Christ entrusts the office of the keys to a very Petrine Piers (B.19.182–90), Crowley's only gloss actually intensifies the penitential logic of *redde quod debes*, by which "hath Pierce power . . . / To bynde and unbinde, both here and els where / And assoylen menne of all synnes" (fol. 106v). In the margin adjacent to this controversial Catholic claim, Crowley notes, "Pierces pardon is, þai that thou oweste."[91] While the gloss could seem subtly to redirect the passage toward purely juridical restitution, Crowley elsewhere chimes in with

---

disproportionate," it also presents Wyatt's work of poetry as satisfaction for his offenses. Simpson, *Reform and Cultural Revolution*, 327.

89. See R. Carter Hailey, "'Geuyng Light to the Reader': Robert Crowley's Editions of *Piers Plowman* (1550)," *Papers of the Bibliographical Society of America* 94 (2001): 483–502; R. Carter Hailey, "Robert Crowley and the Editing of *Piers Plowman* (1550)," *Yearbook of Langland Studies* 21 (2007): 143–70; Sarah A. Kelen, *Langland's Early Modern Identities* (New York: Palgrave Macmillan, 2007), 26–36; Little, "Transforming Work," 508–13.

90. Robert Crowley, ed., *The Vision of Pierce Plowman, nowe the seconde tyme imprinted by Roberte Crowlye . . . Whereunto are added certaine notes and cotations in the mergyne, geuyng light to the Reader*, Early English Books Online, 1475–1640 / 122:19 (London: Robert Crowley, 1550), fols. 12v, 21v.

91. Scanlon cogently surmises that "Crowley tolerates the ecclesiological claims because . . . Langland is poetically extending Catholic authority and not simply affirming it, and because as the passus continues he will use this poetic extension to demonstrate that virtuous social action is an imperative of individual conscience." Larry Scanlon, "Langland, Apocalypse, and the Early Modern Editor," in *Reading the Medieval in Early Modern England*, ed. Gordon McMullan and David Matthews (New York: Cambridge University Press, 2007), 69.

Patience's commentary on David's penitential Psalm 32 to affirm that "Satisfaction kylleth sinne" (fol. 73r; B.14.95–6).[92] Crowley's sideline cheer for satisfaction might bespeak uneasiness about the efficacy of auricular confession, but in no way does it resonate with the interiorization and privatization of sin and forgiveness that Langland and Crowley both see as threats to authentic Christian living.

That the discourses of sacramental and literary satisfaction were alive and well in the early Reformation should not surprise us. As historian Thomas N. Tentler has remarked,

> The polemics of the Reformation and confessional age were bitter and prolonged precisely because the opposing parties agreed on fundamentals: that there must be ecclesiastical rites of expulsion and reconciliation, dogmatic theological formulas and causal explanations of the justification of sinners, a comprehensible psychological description of the experience of that forgiveness, and belief in the eternal consequences of the success or failure to "achieve" that forgiveness.[93]

Martin Luther may have been driven to desperation by the impossibility of ever fully making satisfaction for his sins, but once he rediscovered grace through faith, lifelong repentance turned from bane to boon, the very way of the cross, as the opening salvo of the 95 Theses attests:

1. Our Lord and Master Jesus Christ, when He said *Poenitentiam agite*, desired that the whole life of the faithful be penance.
2. This saying cannot be understood concerning sacramental penance, i.e., confession and satisfaction, which is administered by the priests.

---

92. "And satisfaction seketh oute the rote, and both sleeth and voydeth / And as it never had ben, to nought bringeth dedly syn" (fol. 73r).

93. Thomas N. Tentler, "Postscript," in *Penitence in the Age of Reformations*, ed. Katharine Jackson Lualdi and Anne T. Thayer (Burlington, VT: Ashgate, 2000), 240–59.

3. Yet he means not only interior [penitence]; indeed, interior [penitence] is nothing, unless one outwardly performs manifold mortifications of the flesh.[94]

Langland's understanding of open-ended satisfaction, as I have developed it here, would make a very intriguing gloss on Luther's second thesis. One scandal of Truth's pardon—"Dowel and have well and God shal have thy soul"—is that it seems to elide the penitential system, as does Luther's second thesis. But the dynamic middle of *Piers Plowman*, saturated both with sacramental penance and the grace of faith, absorbs the penance administered by priests into a much larger picture, the "whole life of the faithful" living the *evangelium crucis*, Luther's mark of the authentic Christian life.

Lutherans were not the only Protestants who exhibited affinities with Catholic penitential practices. Later English Reformed writers stressed lifelong sanctification as the participation in the life and death of Christ. Granted that hardline Calvinist election soteriology could seem to obviate a Christian's growth in holiness, pastoral practice in many branches of the Reformation cultivated a lively and robust sense of how the good a Christian might do, or the suffering he or she might endure, could avail for saving participation in Christ.[95] As Deborah Shuger argues, many Tudor Protestants believed that "the road to heaven

---

94. "1. Dominus et magister noster Iesus Christus dicendo 'Penitentiam agite &c.' omnem vitam fidelium penitentiam esse voluit. 2. Quod verbum de penitentia sacramentali (id est confessionis et satisfactionis, que sacerdotum ministerio celebratur) non potest intelligi. 3. Non tamen solam intendit interiorem, immo interior nulla est, nisi foris operetur varias carnis mortificationes." Martin Luther, *Disputatio pro declaratione virtutis indulgentiarum*, Project Wittenberg, http://www.projectwittenberg.org/.

95. Peter Lake characterizes the "ordo paenitendi" of the moderate Puritan Abdiel Ashton as an open-ended experience by which "God always employed the faults of his children to their ultimate spiritual advantage, since each lapse provided the occasion for a fresh turning to God through a recapitulation of the processes of repentance. . . . Not only was Christ responsible, through his sacrifice on the cross, for our freedom from the imputation of sin, he was also the moving force in our gradual liberation from our own sins, in the process of

is paved with good works."[96] Where Catholic and Protestant could most readily disagree was on the possibility of what Catholics called condign merit—whether good works performed by grace could avail for a soul's salvation—and on the necessity of the priestly office.[97] But all believed on the basis of biblical evidence that good works and sufferings would at least receive rewards in heaven (e.g., Luke 6:23, 35).

By arguing that we should recognize continuities in the practice of efficacious satisfaction as open-ended growth in holiness characterized by works of mercy, literary or otherwise, I do not mean to occlude the many convolutions of penitential practice and theology wrought by the cultural revolutions of the late medieval and early modern periods.[98] Nevertheless, if we are to understand penance as a sacrament, or tropology as participation with God, then we cannot reduce their history to the mere sum of variable practices and discourses. One brief example from recent history suggests how we might consider a changing phenomenon such as satisfaction to exceed the range of vision of social and intellectual history.

The *Joint Declaration on the Doctrine of Justification* (1999) was the fruit of ecumenical dialogue between the Roman Catholic Church and

---

sanctification." Peter Lake, *Moderate Puritans and the Elizabethan Church* (New York: Cambridge University Press, 1982), 164–65.

96. Debora Shuger, "The Reformation of Penance," *Huntington Library Quarterly* 71, no. 4 (December 2008): 561. Shuger likens Edmund Spenser's penitential theology to Langland's, noting how Una entrusts the Redcross Knight "to the care of Mercy, who guides him to a 'holy hospital' where 'seven beadmen that had vowed all / Their life to service of high heaven's King' instruct the knight in the seven works of mercy, so that 'Mercy in the end his righteous soul might save.' Here, as in Langland, this saving mercy is at one and the same time the righteous soul's own mercifulness and the mercy of God extended to the merciful; the syntax insists upon the interlacings of human and divine initiative" (561).

97. For a good example of this argument, see Thomas More, *The Confutation of Tyndale's Answer*, in *The Complete Works of St. Thomas More*, ed. Louis Martz et al., 15 vols. (New Haven: Yale University Press, 1963–97), 8.1:90–91.

98. For an appreciation of these changes that emphasizes rupture, see Thomas N. Tentler, *Sin and Confession on the Eve of the Reformation* (Princeton: Princeton University Press, 1977), 345–70.

the main historical branches of the Reformation that has been taking place seriously since at least the 1960s. In it, Lutherans and Catholics "confess together" that even after baptism,

> the justified must all through life constantly look to God's unconditional justifying grace . . . and are not exempt from a lifelong struggle against the contradiction to God within the selfish desires of the old Adam (cf. Gal 5:16; Rom 7:7–10). The justified also must ask God daily for forgiveness as in the Lord's Prayer (Mt. 6:12; 1 Jn 1:9), are ever again called to conversion and penance, and are ever again granted forgiveness. . . . We confess together that good works—a Christian life lived in faith, hope and love—follow justification and are its fruits. When the justified live in Christ and act in the grace they receive, they bring forth, in biblical terms, good fruit.[99]

Absent from this formulation is agreement on the function of the office of the keys, and the declaration avoids explicit discussion of the distinction between temporal and eternal *poena* and *culpa*.[100] Nevertheless, it recognizes as common to both traditions a fundamental sense of penance as an ongoing, open-ended practice of good works as a way of participating more fully in Christ. The framers of the declaration refuse to paper over the Reformation-era disagreements; the mutual "condemnations are still valid today and thus have a church-dividing effect."[101] But neither side thought it too late to move toward reconciliation. Nor are the declaration's "binding decisions" the end, for the church is still *in via*, "on the way to overcoming the division . . . toward that visible unity

---

99. Lutheran World Federation and the Catholic Church, *Joint Declaration on the Doctrine of Justification*, 1999, 4.44, 4.47. http://www.vatican.va/.

100. For a modern Lutheran's very "Catholic" view of the office of the keys in early Lutheranism, see David Yeago, "The Office of the Keys: On the Disappearance of Discipline in Protestant Modernity," in *Marks of the Body of Christ*, ed. Carl E. Braaten and Robert W. Jenson (Grand Rapids, MI: William B. Eerdmans, 1999), 95–122.

101. *Joint Declaration*, Preamble.1.

which is Christ's will."[102] The *Joint Declaration* was subsequently ratified by the World Methodist Federation and has been widely acknowledged as valid by Anglicans.[103]

The principle of continuity on which these bodies based their agreement was not primarily a convergence of social practices or a hindsight equivocation of intellectual discourses. Rather, they understood themselves to be enhancing the incomplete "visible unity" of the universal church, which receives its coherence only from the future, from the promised end of Christ's high-priestly prayer "ut sint unum" (John 17:11)—that all may be one. For the ecclesial bodies on both sides of this agreement, the phenomenon of sacramental penance appears fully only when seen in eschatological perspective. The churches can recognize satisfaction and its attendant works and mortifications as an essential part of the Christian life because they are revealed in Christ, whom the churches hold to be continuously present in his extended body, the church universal—though not with the fullness that will be manifest in the kingdom of heaven. As Paul writes, Christians are "always bearing about in our body the mortification of Jesus, that the life also of Jesus may be made manifest in our bodies" (2 Cor. 4:10). So it is finally the Pauline logic of the always-present but not-yet-fulfilled body of Christ, rather than historical agreements, that underwrites the *Joint Declaration*'s agreement about lifelong, open-ended satisfaction as growing participation in the life of Christ.

---

102. Ibid., Preamble.4, 5.44. The decisions shed significant "new light": "the doctrinal condemnations of the 16th century, in so far as they relate to the doctrine of justification, appear in a new light: The teaching of the Lutheran churches presented in this Declaration does not fall under the condemnations from the Council of Trent. The condemnations in the Lutheran Confessions do not apply to the teaching of the Roman Catholic Church presented in this Declaration" (5.41).

103. On Anglican agreement, see R. William Franklin, "A Model for a New Joint Declaration: An Episcopalian Reaction to the Joint Declaration on Justification," in *Justification and the Future of the Ecumenical Movement*, ed. William G. Rusch (Collegeville, MN: Liturgical Press, 2003), 37–38.

This example suggests that inquiry into religious continuity across Renaissance and Reformation should not function primarily on a logic of conservation versus loss, though it certainly involves those dynamics. Rather, in the self-understanding of the churches on either side of the Reformation, God and the human, united in Christ, are the dual principles of continuity. A history that does not enter sympathetically into this self-understanding is capable of measuring greater or lesser degrees of change in social practices and intellectual discourses, but not of seeing continuity in the way the communities it studies see it.

To read *Piers Plowman* from its dynamic, crucicentric middle, where loss and gain hang in the balance, refreshes the temporality of penance so that even in its dismal final passus it is not too late to cry after grace. The crucicentric middle ensures that even failure can be turned to satisfaction. Piers may end up a "presence-become-absence" by the end of the poem, but that ending is not the poem's "conclusion."[104] Conscience's quest might seem endless, doomed to failure because he seeks to endow the very religious orders that brought ruin to the penitential system and the pastoral project commenced in 1215.[105] But as Conscience sets off on his new search for Piers, crying after Grace, he and his readers know much more than they did back in the fair field full of folk. They know where to look. In his new quest, Conscience knows to seek again the dynamic middle where the search for Dowel, Dobet, and Dobest prompts continual repentance and renewal in the sacraments and fosters growth in holiness, and where Piers's life of *lele labour* merges with Christ's life lived unto death for humanity.[106]

---

104. Aers, "Langland on the Church," 73. For a close reading of the final passus's penitential crisis that concurs with Aers and lends detail to my argument here, see Deagman, "The Formation of Forgiveness in *Piers Plowman*," 90–94.

105. Aers, "Langland on the Church," provides the most comprehensive account of the final passus's institutional and sacramental failures as well as the various ecclesial options.

106. These poetic and theological considerations stand to gain intriguing support from Lawrence Warner's proposal that the B-text as we know it acquired its final two passūs from the C-text. Warner gives us a scenario in which

How else could the poem end, when the principle of continuity that will leap across the Reformation intact, the only available goal for Conscience to seek after at the end of *Piers Plowman*, is a Pauline figure of the church as the suffering body of Christ, both conquered and conqueror in the doubled illumination of eschatological hope?

> ... Peres þe ploughman was peynted al blody
> And cam in with a cros before þe comune peple
> And riht lyke in alle lymes to oure lord iesu.
>
> . . . .
>
> Quod Conciense and knelede tho, "this aren Peres Armes,
> His colours and his cote armure; ac he þat cometh so blody
> Is Crist with his croes, conquerour of Cristene."
>
> (C.21.6–8, 12–14)

Piers or Christ?, Will asks. The answer is both, in chiastic relation to each other. At the beginning of Will's dream, Piers looks "riht lyke" the Lord Jesus in his physical appearance, "in alle lymes," while in Conscience's response, Christ looks like Piers in the visible marks of identity, his arms and insignia. Here the chiastic relation formally enacts the *commercium divinum* of the hypostatic union by which God and humanity enter into the eternal mutuality reflected in the patristic dictum,

---

Langland sits for some years on the satisfactory, heavenly conclusion of B.18, and then adds a new ending that includes both the clearest realization of ecclesial unity in this world in the Pentecost scene of C.21 *and* the crisis of dissolution in C.22. This new ending resituates the previous ending as an intermediate phenomenon. The addition of the final two passūs then would render the old conclusion as the middle term, the balancing point for the chiastic structure I have been exploring here. In other words, by reinventing *Piers Plowman*'s ending, Langland would simultaneously introduce open-ended irresolution *and* embed the anagogical climax of the work in the middle. And if he was indeed undertaking such ambitious additions and revisions, then it is highly significant that instead of unraveling the conclusion of B.18, Langland left the reconciliation of the Four Daughters of God and his Easter morning waking intact. See Lawrence Warner, *The Lost History of Piers Plowman: The Earliest Transmission of Langland's Work* (Philadelphia: University of Pennsylvania Press, 2011).

"God became man that man might become God." The dictum finds an image in Piers, but becoming happens in the search, in the crying after grace, in the open-ended work of satisfaction. *Piers Plowman* ends with an open-ended quest and a cry:

> "By Crist!" quod Consience tho, "y wol bicome a pilgrim
> And wenden as wyde as þe world rennet
> To seke Peres the Plouhman . . ."
> And sethe he gradde [cried, prayed] after grace tyl y gan awake.
> (C.22.380–82, 86)

Conscience's cry and prayer echo across epochs, down to Marlowe's Faustus and even to McEwan's Briony: it is still not too late; now is the acceptable time. Langland's open-ended, recursive practice of satisfaction speaks to at least part of Briony's grief, witnessing that writing can participate in atonement. Perhaps, if atonement requires a God in which to participate, and that God does not exist, then Briony is still right that her writing cannot atone. But then it is not a matter of being too late. Periodization will not put to rest the question of faith.

5

Tropology Reformed

Scripture, Salvation, Drama

The Reformation consolidated a broad shift in the late Middle Ages toward the valorization of the literal sense of scripture. Reformers saw themselves shattering an ossified tradition of allegorical extravagance, aided by groundbreaking philological techniques and a historical consciousness that brought the words and deeds of the Bible into intimate proximity. "Back then," Luther remarked in 1532,

> I used to allegorize everything, even the toilet, but later on I reflected on the histories and thought how difficult it must have been for Joshua to fight with his enemies in the manner reported. If I had been there I would have shit my pants out of fear. It was not allegory, but it was the Spirit and faith that inflicted such havoc on the enemy with only three hundred men. Jerome and Origen—God forgive them!—promoted the practice of seeking only allegories. In all of Origen there is not one word about Christ.[1]

---

1. Cited in Raymond Andrew Blacketer, *The School of God: Pedagogy and Rhetoric in Calvin's Interpretation of Deuteronomy* (Dordrecht: Springer, 2006), 225.

Characteristically twisting medieval terminology, Luther contrasts the dead letter of allegory to the life-giving literal sense of "Spirit and faith." The spirit of the text comes through meditation on the historical sense, activated by a focus on realistic detail that recalls the *Patience*-Poet's scatalogizing imagination. As Luther's own exegesis shows, the triumph of the literal sense hardly entailed the death of spiritual exegesis. As for Nicholas of Lyra—whom Luther now lauds, now excoriates—a return to the literal sense could open the airways for the breath of the spirit to fill scripture once again.[2] As we saw in chapter 2, the literal-historical sense was capacious enough to contain the spiritual senses.

Reformation polemics against allegory therefore tend to obscure the continuity of spiritual exegesis.[3] Although the literal turn has been amply documented, scholarship has tended to assume that this was a turn *away* from spiritual exegesis, rather than to investigate the consequences of this turn for the spiritual senses. In the first part of this chapter I pursue one strand of this investigation: the curious prominence—indeed priority—of tropological exegesis in the early Reformation, a period often associated with obsessive attention to the literal sense. After exposing the soteriological stakes of tropological exegesis for Calvin and Luther, I turn to Thomas More and William Tyndale, who rehash the debate but, perhaps surprisingly, nearly converge in their tropological concerns. That is because both are influenced by Erasmus, in whom we find a participatory sense of scripture continuous with medieval understandings of tropology. What becomes of this tropological habit when Erasmus is adopted as an icon of reform by

---

2. See McDermott, "Henri de Lubac's Genealogy of Modern Exegesis."

3. "Indeed, the acceptance or rejection of traditional exegesis on the part of a given Reformer becomes increasingly unpredictable as one moves away from the great debates of the Reformation to examine the vast array of passages in Scripture that played no particular role in doctrinal controversy. And even in the case of texts lying at the heart of sixteenth-century debate, the tradition is surprisingly nuanced." Richard A. Muller, "Biblical Interpretation in the Era of the Reformation: The View from the Middle Ages," in *Biblical Interpretation in the Era of the Reformation: Essays Presented to David C. Steinmetz in Honor of His Sixtieth Birthday*, ed. Richard A. Muller and John Lee Thompson (Grand Rapids, MI: William B. Eerdmans, 1996), 17.

Protestant royalty in England? Nicholas Udall's preface to his and his associates' translation of Erasmus's *Paraphrases* on the New Testament fashions King Edward VI as a tropological reader. The young king's historical purpose reveals one way in which Protestant theology and practices of piety sought a means of participation in the biblical story of salvation.[4] But this participation could take many forms—apocalyptic, propagandistic, martyrological—as Martin Bucer's theoretical considerations of drama and the actual drama of the Edwardian court suggest. The martyrological mode is realized in the life and dramatic writings of John Careless, a radical reformer who also happened to be an ardent player in Coventry's famous biblical cycle. The figures and texts studied in this chapter reveal a wide range of tropologies in Reformation England, some of which were continuous with Catholic practices and some of which persisted in unresolved tension with more traditional theology.

John Calvin: Tropology Untheorized

Like many reformers, John Calvin eschewed the language of fourfold exegesis, but his sermons on Deuteronomy (1555–56) necessarily interpret Israel's covenant in the light of Christ and convert obsolete observances into relevant inspirations to piety. God's commandment to keep the Sabbath holy does not apply literally to Christians, since "al the things that were figured in those shadowes, are accomplished in [Christ]."[5] But at the same time, "God intended to giue a rule that should indure for

---

4. In this chapter and the next, I use the term "Protestant" as noun and adjective to refer to all branches of ecclesial dissent from the Roman Catholic status quo. I use lowercased terms "reformer," "reformist," and so on, to refer to proponents of religious reform, whether Catholic or Protestant. I use uppercased "Reformed" to refer to the Calvinist tradition.

5. John Calvin, *The Sermons of M. Iohn Caluin vpon the Fifth Booke of Moses Called Deuteronomie Faithfully Gathered Word for Word as He Preached Them in Open Pulpet*, trans. Arthur Golding, Early English Books, 1475–1640 / 199:02 (London: Henry Middleton for George Bishop, 1583), 201–2. I am in-

euer. Therefore let vs not thinke that the thinges which Moses speaketh of the Saboth day, are needelesse for vs." Indeed, Hebrews 4 "applyeth the thinges that were spoken of the Saboth day, to the instruction of the Christians and of the new Church." Because the image of God in us has been defaced by sin, it can only be restored if we "fashion our selues lyke to our God and to yeelde to his will, and to inquire of his workes: that wee may doe the lyke." God himself gave us an example by resting on the seventh day of creation. In our efforts to conform to the image of God, we strive to enter not the literal but the "spiritual Saboth or rest" all the time. However, God provided the figure of the Sabbath day to show us that we will never have complete rest in this life; "there will alwayes be somewhat worthie of blame in vs." While our sins should humble us and cause sorrow and true repentance, nevertheless "ought we on the other side to be ye more moued & quickened vp to goe forward."[6] As an aid to this perseverance and growth in holiness, the church actually does observe the Sabbath on Sunday. And though its observance does not abide by the strict statutes of Deuteronomy, the church follows the literal "order" of the Sabbath as a day designed "to exercise the faithfull in the seruice of God": no work, no play, no gossip, but leisure for Bible study, prayer, praise, listening to sermons, and communal ministry of the sacraments and confession of the faith.[7]

Calvin must seek beyond the literal sense of the Sabbath command-ment not because it is obscure, but because its relationship to the new covenant is one of shadow to fulfillment. However, the Christian fulfill-ment of the law elevates rather than abrogates the literal sense. Calvin recruits the historical sense tropologically, interpreting the Sabbath's li-turgical "order" as guidelines for Christian behavior that will foster growth in holiness. He also reaches an anagogical insight about the at-tenuated experience here below of the spiritual rest promised in heaven. Without trafficking in the traditional exegetical language of letter and

---

debted to the excellent discussion of Calvin's Sabbath exegesis in Blacketer, *The School of God*, 171–200.

6. Calvin, *Sermons vpon Deuteronomie*, 203.

7. Ibid., 204–5.

spirit, still less of fourfold exegesis, Calvin operates in continuity with more traditional practices of spiritual exegesis.[8]

But while Calvin can recognize objects of belief and hope in the shadows of the old law, his aversion to speculative interpretation keeps him fixated on the historical sense of Old Testament narrative. The details of Old Testament history then become primarily pedagogical; they provide occasions for Christians to recognize God's will in history and to submit themselves affectively to his will in the present. Christians might recognize that the stone tablets of the Decalogue prefigure the "true" covenant of grace, but Moses' preparation and inscription of the tablets remains tropologically potent. Just as Moses had to polish the stones to make them smooth tablets amenable to inscription, so must our hearts be made docile to receive the writing of the new law of grace.[9] In Calvin's exegesis of the Old Testament, spiritual interpretation remains necessary, but it must always work through the literal sense and nearly always for moral edification. If there is innovation here, it may be identified more accurately in Calvin's predilection for tropology than in his attention to the literal-historical sense, which he shared with both his late medieval predecessors and his contemporaries.[10]

---

8. "Once it has been seen that Calvin consistently understood the 'literal' meaning of Old Testament prophecies of the kingdom to be not only the reestablishment of Israel after the exile but also the establishment of the kingdom in the redemptive work of Christ, the furtherance of the kingdom in the reform of the church in the sixteenth century, and the final victory of the kingdom in Christ's second coming, it can also be seen that the 'literal' meaning of the text, for Calvin, held a message concerning what Christians ought to believe, what Christians ought to do, and what Christians ought to hope for. This paradigm seems suspiciously familiar. . . . It asks that the exegete move past the rather bare grammatical meaning of the text to doctrine, morality, and hope—in short, from littera to *credenda, agenda,* and *speranda.*" Muller, "Biblical Interpretation in the Era of the Reformation," 11.

9. Calvin, *Sermons vpon Deuteronomie,* 421–23. See Blacketer, *The School of God,* 220–29.

10. "Calvin's critical interests extended to questions of authorship, historical, background, philology, and rhetoric. Yet he never allowed such questions to dominate his exegesis, which had as its constant goal the edification of

Martin Luther: Tropology as Theology

While Calvin practiced tropological exegesis without articulating a theory of spiritual interpretation, tropological theory gave Martin Luther a methodological fulcrum on which to leverage his early theological insights about faith and justification. However, the pressure Luther exerted on the tropological sense transformed it from a mode of scriptural interpretation into a theological principle at work in every encounter with the word of God. The transformation began in his 1513–15 *Dictata* on the Psalms, which come down to us in a rich set of autograph lecture notes and extended glosses, or *scholia*, in the margins of Luther's Psalter. Luther would not arrive decisively at his revolutionary position on justification for another five or so years, but in these early lectures the exegetical foundations of that theology can be discerned.[11]

Luther begins his transformation of spiritual exegesis by identifying *doctrina* with the moral sense of scripture. Commenting on the prefatory verse of Psalm 59 (60), Luther glosses the intended purpose of the Psalm—"ad docendum"—as "for the sake of teaching morally" (*moraliter instruendum*).[12] Assuming the etymological relation of *doceo* to *doctrina*, he goes on to explain why he specifies teaching as *moral* teaching. "For the moral sense is called 'doctrina' in scripture. Rom. 15[:4]

---

the church. The story of the migration of ancient Semites was interesting to Calvin, less out of historical curiosity than out of a sense of its place in the unfolding of God's plan for the redemption of the world." David C. Steinmetz, "John Calvin as an Interpreter of the Bible," in *Calvin and the Bible*, ed. Donald K. McKim (New York: Cambridge University Press, 2006), 288.

11. Brian Cummings, *The Literary Culture of the Reformation: Grammar and Grace* (New York: Oxford University Press, 2002), 57–101; Gerhard Ebeling, "Die Anfänge von Luthers Hermeneutik," *Die Zeitschrift für Theologie und Kirche* 48 (1951): 172–230; Alister E. McGrath, *The Intellectual Origins of the European Reformation*, 2nd ed. (Malden, MA: Blackwell, 2004), 159–66.

12. *Luther Bibel* (1545): "zu lehren." Luther uses the Septuagint numbering of the Psalms. In discussing Luther, I give the modern (Hebrew) numbering in parentheses. Available online at www.biblegateway.com.

'For what things soever were written were written for our learning [*doctrinam*].'"[13] If Chaucer played on the ambiguity of *doctrina* in the late Middle Ages to excuse his more profane tales, Luther here constrains its meaning to a single sense, ruling out the sense traditionally associated with allegory, the *credenda* or theological truths to which the Christian intellect ought to assent.[14] For now, the moral sense fully occupies the semantic space of *doctrina*. "And therefore the tropological sense is the ultimate and principle intention in scripture."[15]

In more expansive comments prefaced to Psalm 77 (78), Luther theorizes the relationship of tropology to the other spiritual senses. "We have often said that the tropological is the primary sense of scripture, and, when this has been expressed, the allegorical and anagogical and particular applications of contingent events follow easily and of their own accord."[16] The tropological sense gains priority because it is the condition of any authentic encounter with the Word. The letter kills universally, but the Spirit gives life only personally, in what Gerhard Ebeling has characterized as an existential encounter.[17] Tropological reading allows us to receive scripture as *pro nobis*, Luther's dative cry of passive dependence on God's promises. Only then can the *credenda* of allegory and the *speranda* of anagogy truly mean anything.

Luther evacuates the theological domain of *doctrina* and replaces it with tropology only to drive out the competition and eventually reoccupy it, granting theology sole proprietorship. He accomplishes this by

---

13. "Quaecumque enim scripta sunt ad nostram doctrinam scripta sunt." *Luther Bibel* (1545): "Was aber zuvor geschrieben ist, das ist uns zur Lehre geschrieben." Martin Luther, *D. Martin Luthers Werke*, ed. J. F. K. Knaake et al., Kritische Gesamtausgabe (Weimar: Böhlau, 1883–), 3:335; hereafter cited as *WA* by volume and page number.

14. "For oure book seith, 'Al that is writen is writen for oure doctrine,' and that is myn entente." Geoffrey Chaucer, *Canterbury Tales*, X(I).1083.

15. Luther, *WA*, 3:335.

16. Martin Luther, *Luther's Works*, ed. Jaroslav Pelikan et al. (Saint Louis and Philadelphia: Concordia and Fortress, 1955–), 11:12; hereafter cited as *LW* by volume and page number; *WA*, 3:531.

17. Ebeling, "Die Anfänge von Luthers Hermeneutik," 226–30.

identifying tropology with faith. The lengthy Psalm 77 (78) is a fitting place for this theoretical discussion because it rehearses Israel's experience of God's saving power. The primary objects of interpretation in this Psalm are therefore God's works, which may be divided into the works of creation, the spiritual works of the people of Israel, and the works of redemption. Each of these kinds of work may then be submitted to fourfold understanding—literally, as performed personally in Christ; tropologically, in the soul against the flesh; allegorically, in the church's struggle against evil in the world; and anagogically, in heaven and hell.[18] The diversity of works and spiritual senses multiplies the agents of the works, but all of these works remain God's works. How can this make sense, if diverse agents are performing the works? Here Luther performs a *reductio ad fidem*, shifting the question away from agency and tracing the action back to the source of its energy, which is faith. "God's work [*opus*] and His strength [*virtus*] is faith. This makes people righteous and produces all virtues; it chastises, crucifies, and weakens the flesh, so that it should not have its own work or strength but that the work of God should be in it. And thus it saves and strengthens the spirit. But when this happens, then all who do this become God's work and God's strength allegorically"—that is, they participate in the salvation-historical struggle against evil. "And so the church is God's work and strength."[19] Whenever scripture prompts righteous action, that is, whenever it is read tropologically, read in such a way that the reader responds to the tropological imperative, then it is faith at work; the reader is reading faithfully. This is why Luther considers tropology the primary sense of scripture. The reader must read faithfully, tropologically, in order for any of the other senses of scripture to be activated as Gospel—even the literal sense. The other senses follow after the tropological sense because everything related to salvation must follow after faith. "The tropological

---

18. *LW*, 11:12; *WA*, 3:532. In the three kinds of work we can hear echoes of the varieties of tropology discussed in chapter 2. For Luther, tropology is diversified according to the kind of work interpreted tropologically. So natural tropology, for example, is attuned to the works of God in creation.

19. *LW*, 11:12–13; *WA*, 3:532.

good is faith and its works, and from this by itself arises the allegorical good, that is, the body of Christ, namely, those who cling to the Lord until the coming glory, the anagogical good."[20]

While it would later become possible to kick out the ladder of four-fold exegesis under his mature *theologia crucis*, Luther's careful attention to tropological theory performs powerful conceptual work in his early Psalms lectures and the overlapping Romans lectures of 1515–16. As Brian Cummings has argued, Luther's early Psalms exegesis is often intertwined with his developing thought about justification in Romans, especially Romans 1:17: "Iustitia enim Dei in eo revelatur ex fide in fidem sicut scriptum est iustus autem ex fide vivit" (For the justice of God is revealed therein, from faith unto faith, as it is written: The just man liveth by faith). The *Dictata* and *scholia* of this period reveal "an intricate network in Luther's reading: Paul quoting the Psalm [31 (32)], Augustine quoting Paul and the Psalm alongside each other; and Luther himself interpreting both Psalms and Paul through the medium of Augustine in a succession of commentaries and treatises in a variety of enveloping contexts. Each time Luther drives his reading back to Romans 1:17 in clinching conclusion."[21]

Cummings analyzes the intricate *theologia grammatica* at work in these passages, but Luther also consistently relies on tropological theory to harmonize the Pauline Gospel with the ancient Jewish prayers. In his *scholia* on the crucial Psalm 31 (32), which Paul discusses at length in Romans 4, Luther explains why the Psalm is titled "Eruditio David" (the learning or understanding of David).

> "Understanding" in the holy scriptures takes its name more from the object than from the power, contrary to its use in philosophy. For the understanding is the thought or awareness of the sense of

---

20. *LW*, 11:13; *WA*, 3:532.

21. Cummings, *Literary Culture of the Reformation*, 96. Cummings is working within a long tradition of scholarship on the Psalms *Dictata* and the origins of Luther's theological breakthrough. Of special significance for his argument as well as mine is Ebeling, "Die Anfänge von Luthers Hermeneutik."

Christ, about which the Apostle in 1 Cor. 1 and 2 teaches excellently, because "the Wisdom we speak of is hidden in mystery, which none of the princes of this world knew" [1 Cor. 2:7–8]. It is, briefly, nothing other than the wisdom of the cross of Christ, which is foolishness to the Gentiles and a scandal to the Jews, namely to understand that the son of god became incarnate and was crucified and died and rose again for our salvation.[22]

But Luther recognizes that he cannot simply superimpose Paul's theology onto the title of Psalm 31. To support this reading, he goes to Psalm 31:9, which urges, "do not become like the horse and the mule, who have no understanding [*intelligentia*]." "Considered tropologically, the sense therefore is: Because the Jews became like horses and mules, among whom there is no understanding of faith [*intellectus fidei*], therefore they are not able to approach God."[23] Luther grounds his Pauline reading of the Psalm in a tropological interpretation. That such a move can be considered authenticating, rather than simply an act of *eisegesis*, depends entirely on the theory that the tropological sense is the primary and ultimate sense of scripture.

These tropological circulations between the Psalms and Paul crystallize in the *scholia* on Psalm 71 (72), in which Luther immediately states that "'judgment' and 'justice' in the Scriptures of the old law are very rarely taken literally concerning the future, but very frequently—or truly, always—according to tropology and morals and Allegory."[24] Luther then pursues the tropological reading vigorously not because he needs to convert Old Law into New Law—any of the spiritual senses will bring Old Testament references into the future (the present)—but because the tropological sense is designed to circulate agency, to convert the action of one subject into the action (or passion) of another. When we read that God judges, we should understand, tropologically, that God "condemns the works of the flesh and the world." But the more

---

22. *WA*, 3:176.
23. Ibid.
24. Ibid., 3:461–62.

important tropological move occurs when those who cling to God by faith adopt God's judgment and consider their own works as vile and abominable. In this judgment consists true humility, and to the truly humble God gives his grace. Therefore "judgment" is "most frequently understood this way in scripture. So 'justice' tropologically is the faith of Christ. Rom. 1[:17]: 'The justice of God is revealed therein,' etc."[25] Only the faith of Christ working in the sinner can enable him to adopt God's judgment for his own. But the Father recognizes his Son's faith, now appropriated tropologically as the soul's own, as justice, and converts his judgment into mercy. By a tropological conversion, then, God's judgment is our salvation. Luther thus arrives at his revolutionary interpretation of Romans 1:17 by means of tropology with the crucial translation of "iustitia Dei" into "fides Christi."

Twenty years later, in his Galatians commentary, Luther has left behind the language of tropology to work entirely within an understanding of the literal sense as the "theological sense" that reveals the gospel of salvation by grace through faith.[26] Where before tropology had negotiated the relationship between divine and human action, now Luther has explicitly theorized a theological, as opposed to philosophical, account of action:

Therefore "doing" [facere] is one thing in nature, another in philosophy, and another in theology. In nature the tree must be first, and then the fruit. In moral philosophy "doing" means a good will and right reason to do well; this is where the philosophers come to a halt. . . . Therefore we have to rise higher in theology with the word "doing," so that it becomes altogether new. For just as it becomes something different when it is taken from the natural area into the moral, so it becomes something much more different when it is transferred from philosophy and from the law into theology. Thus it has a completely new meaning; it does indeed require right

---

25. Ibid., 3:462–63; the same collocation recurs on 3:466.
26. On the prehistory of the *duplex sensus litteralis* and the contrast between the *sensus logicus* and *sensus theologicus*, see Froehlich, "'Always to Keep the Literal Sense in Holy Scripture Means to Kill One's Soul.'"

reason and a good will, but in a theological sense, not in a moral sense, which means that through the word of the Gospel I know and believe that God sent his son into the world to redeem us from sin and death.[27]

Although Luther has abandoned the language of fourfold exegesis, the turn that he made using tropological theory remains intact. That turn pivoted on the traditional recognition that tropology exceeds moral philosophy in its comprehension of ethics because it grasps the soteriological momentum of human actions as they participate in the history of redemption. The major difference between Luther and this tradition is the conditions of participation. Before, the history of redemption was, as it were, outside or to the side of one's normal position in a fallen world, and so one had to join in with it by doing the works of charity and taking part in the sacraments. For Luther, though, it is the presence or absence of faith—that is, of Christ—*for you* that determines whether or not your actions, however pious, are participating in the history of redemption. In both systems, the initiative belongs to God, and the work is ultimately God's work. But the cooperative dimension of tropology, activated in the circulatory push and pull of interpretation and invention, has been rejected in Luther's rigorous reduction to grace, which leaves only God's action and humanity's passion. The intertextual tensions and spiritual-exegetical complexities that animated Luther's early struggles with Paul through the Psalms have given way to a post-exegetical dialectic of law and gospel that cannot tolerate the cooperative vision of human and divine agency that the early tropological investigations had afforded.

More vs. Tyndale: Tropological Realism vs. Tropological Inspiration

Thomas More's and William Tyndale's monumental disagreement— carried on in voluminous detail and at a voluble rhetorical pitch in More's *Dialogue Concerning Heresies* (1529), Tyndale's *Answer to More*

---

27. *LW*, 26:262; *WA*, 40.1:410–11.

(1531), and More's massive *Confutation of Tyndale's Answer* (1532 and 1533)—exudes mutual frustration over exegetical practice. While More's explicit rhetoric concerning biblical interpretation traffics in Tyndale's own terminology of plainness and clarity, his fundamental critique of Tyndale's exegesis turns on tropology. More's critique emerges most fully in a disagreement over whether David's sins concerning Bathsheba imperiled his salvation. Like so many of the loci in the More/Tyndale debate, this one is chosen not only for its doctrinal content but for its resonance with popular practices of piety. The David and Bathsheba story formed the backdrop for the Penitential Psalms, which remained for Protestants key texts for imagining holy repentance in lieu of Catholic understandings of penance. Tyndale rejected a Catholic rendering of Christ's command "poenitentiam agite" as "do penance," but he followed Luther in affirming the centrality of *repentance* in the Christian life, and translated Matthew 4:17 as "Repent, for the kingdome of heven is at honde." The sins for which David had to repent were vividly replayed in illustrations of the Penitential Psalms in countless Catholic and Protestant Psalters and instruction manuals.[28] When they meditated on the Penitential Psalms and the narrative of David's grave sins, Christians were invited to adopt David's first-person position, a practice to which a wealth of early modern English verse renderings of the Psalms attests.[29] This merger of life narratives was less exemplary than tropological, ordered as it was to repentance for the sake of salvation rather than to virtue. But in this distinction between virtue and repentance—between two different kinds of fruit of a spiritual encounter with the Word—lies an elusive convergence of More's and Tyndale's understandings of tropology.

---

28. Clare Costley King'oo, *Miserere Mei: The Penitential Psalms in Late Medieval and Early Modern England* (Notre Dame, IN: University of Notre Dame Press, 2012), 25–61.

29. Hannibal Hamlin, "Piety and Poetry: English Psalms from Miles Coverdale to Mary Sidney," in *The Oxford Handbook of Tudor Literature, 1485–1603*, ed. Mike Pincombe and Cathy Shrank (New York: Oxford University Press, 2009), 203–21.

If tropology raises the question, *What should I do?*, then there are three kinds of answers I might entertain. First, I might discover suggestions about a specific course of action in a present occasion in my life. Or I might come away with a principle, such as love of neighbor, which I will then look for an opportunity to put into action. Or I might, as in the case of reading a Penitential Psalm, discover a universal action commended, without a specific occasion.

Do penance, repent: this form of the tropological imperative calls for the third category of response, an action that More and Tyndale both agree is a necessary part of salvation. The just man (More) or the elect man (Tyndale) repents of sin. His repentance is felt in contrition and enacted in works that both writers consider the fruits of charity.[30] But the tropological imperative of Psalm 51, or any of the Penitential Psalms, is not to do this or that good work, to yield this or that fruit, but rather to undertake repentance, "poenitentiam agite." And the work of repentance happens in the context of salvation—either as a supernatural entailment of election (Tyndale) or as a necessary return to the state of grace (More).

David's test case reveals much about Tyndale's and More's relative positions because both can agree on David's salvation—More by the church's authority, and Tyndale because scripture records that God elected David to salvation (cf. Ps. 65:4). For More, David is a saint because he repented of deadly sin. But for Tyndale, David's faith given in the grace of election preserves him from damning sin. Tyndale reasons that "in all that longe tyme from the adultery of Bethsabe vntyll the prophet Nathan rebuked hym, he had not loste his faith nor his loue vnto the laws of god, no more then a man loseth his wyttes whyle he is a slepe."[31] As Tyndale's observation makes clear, the nature and status of

---

30. "Nowe yf thou have true faythe so seyst thou the excedynge and infynyte love and mercy which god hathe shewed the frely in Chryst: then must thou nedes love agayne: and love cannot but compell the to worke." Tyndale, *The Obedyence of a Christian Man*, fol. 81r.

31. More, *The Confutation of Tyndale's Answer*, in *Complete Works*, 8.1:534. Because More quotes Tyndale at length, it is convenient to cite this work for both authors for the present purposes.

David's repentance depends on the status of his salvation during the time he was sinning with Bathsheba.

More offers both a tropological reading of David's story of repentance and a theoretical account of how David interprets God's word tropologically. He observes that Tyndale's tropology is ordered exclusively to salvation, and not also to action. For Tyndale, David's repentance consists solely in the revival of his "feeling faith" and not in the penance and prayer he undertakes in response to God's rebuke through Nathan.[32] As we have seen in previous chapters, the ambit of the tropological sense ranges from literal moral instruction to salvific participation in the story of redemption. And for the master of tropology Gregory the Great—whose *Moralia in Iob* was a prized text of Thomas Cranmer[33]—tropological reading at its best circulates the literal morality and history of scripture through the reader's life as a means to salvation and to a lived meditation on the promises of heavenly peace apprehended in the anagogical sense. Tyndale limits this range to soteriological meanings alone, and by divorcing sinful actions from eternal consequences, he renders David's relationship to his own salvation nonparticipatory, or at best somnambulic.

More finds this opinion alarmingly amoral.[34] During this period of sleepwalking, David's actions manage not to participate in his salvation;

---

32. For Tyndale's distinction between "hystorycall fayth" and "felynge fayth," see ibid., 8.2:742–43; for More's critique of the distinction, see ibid., 8.2:816–29.

33. Cranmer owned two heavily annotated copies of the *Moralia*. See David Gordon Selwyn, *The Library of Thomas Cranmer* (Oxford: Oxford Bibliographical Society, 1996), 38. However, English reformers such as John Foxe and Matthew Parker tended to view Gregory as an early corruptor of pristine Christianity. See Jean-Louis Quantin, *The Church of England and Christian Antiquity: The Construction of a Confessional Identity in the 17th Century* (New York: Oxford University Press, 2009), 78–79.

34. As would the Epitome of the Formula of Concord (1577): "We also reject and condemn the dogma that faith and the indwelling of the Holy Ghost are not lost by wilful sin, but that the saints and elect retain the Holy Ghost even though they fall into adultery and other sins and persist therein." "The Epitome of the Formula of Concord," *The Book of Concord: The Confessions of the Lutheran Church*, 2008, sec. 4.3, http://bookofconcord.org.

they cannot touch his election to eternal life. Tyndale's version of the Pauline split self—"Finally yf I do that I wolde not then is it not I that doo it but synne that dwelleth in me doeth it" (Rom. 7:20, Tyndale Bible)—enables the self committing sin not to have eternal consequences, while the elect, righteous self waits like a sleeping body to come to its senses and carry on with the life of the blessed. But More's critique ventures beyond morality to David's status as one of the great authors and interpreters of God's word. Having minimized David's willful complicity in his sin, More argues, Tyndale gives us an astoundingly deaf and blind David. When Tyndale's David hears the prophet Nathan speaking God's word to him, his response can be tropological only insofar as he repents of his sleep-sins. Any subsequent reformed behavior, on Tyndale's account, must be ascribed to his faith, instilled by election, not to a response to God's word.

But the evidence, More contends, suggests that David's repentant actions directly respond to God's word of rebuke in hope that he can change the verdict that Bathsheba's child must die and the plague will remain with his line forever. "And yet was not David out of hope," More writes, "wyth other penaunce (whyche he hadde leuer sustayne) to purge and redeme that punisshement to / and therfore fasted and prayed to saue the chylde, vntyll the tyme that it was dede in dede."[35] David's repentance is not just a matter of revived feeling, but of specific actions that respond to God's word for the sake of his son's temporal salvation, the well-being of the people of Israel, and ultimately his own eternal salvation. And God responds. While the child by Bathsheba does die, God removes the plague. David's confession, recorded in Psalm 51, and his acts of repentance prompt God to "translate thy synne that was, from deadly to venyall / that is to wyte the punysshment from eternall to temporal."[36] More is concerned that Tyndale's univocal tropology renders him a bad reader, deaf to God's own charge that David "synned so deadly, that he sinfully despysed bothe goddes lawe and god hym selfe therwyth."[37]

---

35. More, *The Confutation of Tyndale's Answer*, in *Complete Works*, 8.1:541.

36. Ibid., 8.1:540.

37. Ibid., 8.1:541.

It would be only partly true, however, to say that Tyndale's doctrine of election forces him to sever the ethical from the soteriological dimension of tropology. In fact, his understanding of tropology emerges on its own from his theology of scripture. In Tyndale's theology, a true encounter with the word of God in scripture ignites the elect reader and induces repentance not just once, but over and over again in a life nourished daily by reverent scriptural study.[38] The Christian encounters scripture in this way through "felynge fayth." The Holy Spirit inscribes the Christian heart with an indelible feeling, like the sense-memory of having been burned.[39] It follows that an authentic reading of scripture must involve a feeling encounter rather than just a "historical" encounter.

In *The Obedyence of a Christian Man* (1528), Tyndale sets out to discredit "the four senses of scripture," but in fact develops an equally supple theology of exegesis that embraces the spiritual modes of reading traditionally named allegory and tropology—despite a mischievous jab at the Papists' "chopologicall sense."[40] The reader who comes to scripture with feeling faith will find comfort, moral edification, and supernatural virtues that will "strength thy fayth" and "feare the from euell doynge."[41] Although Tyndale insists that only the literal sense of scripture is valid, "God is a spirite and all his wordes are spirituall. His litter-

---

38. Compare this to Cummings's analysis of the intimate union of life and scripture reading that Luther posited: "Luther . . . offers to replicate in his readers the reformatory powers he attributes to his own experience of reading. . . . 'Thought, study, reflection' is precisely Luther's subject, and the location of his subjectivity, not at all trivial but a primary part of 'life in the most comprehensive sense of the word.' In the pattern of his conversion his reading becomes his life." *Literary Culture of the Reformation*, 63.

39. Tyndale contrasts feeling faith to historical faith using the analogy of a mother who tells her child not to put his finger in the fire because it will burn him. He will believe her because he trusts her, "but as sone as I had put my finger in the fyre I shulde haue beleued not by the reason of her, but wyth a felynge fayth so that she coulde not haue persuaded me afterward to the contrary." More, *The Confutation of Tyndale's Answer*, in *Complete Works*, 8.2:742.

40. Tyndale, *The Obedyence of a Christian Man*, fol. 112r.

41. Ibid., fol. 113v.

all sence is spirituall, and all his wordes are spirituall."[42] Conflating the exegetical literal and spiritual senses, Tyndale draws a far more important distinction between the two theological senses of letter and spirit, that is, law and gospel: the former accuses us of sin while the latter promises mercy and life.[43] But this spiritual sense does not just convey the theological content of Christ's saving mercy (it is not, in a more traditional understanding, just allegorical, that is, teaching what ought to be believed). The spirit of the Gospel is also active in the lives of those who encounter it with a feeling faith. The spiritual sense of scripture "quickeneth your hertes and geveth you life and lust, and maketh you to do of loue and of your owne accorde without compulcion, that which the lawe compelled you to do, and dampned you because ye could not do with loue and lust and naturally."[44] By the ongoing power of the Holy Spirit, the Bible makes present to today's readers Christ's preaching not only as a historical record, but also "wyth power and spyryte that maketh a man fele and knowe and worke to."[45] So the works of charity are the fruits of a saving encounter with Christ in scripture, animated by feeling faith.

Tyndale is describing not a once-for-all conversion, but an ongoing, habitual encounter with scripture. As Thomas Cranmer would later write in the Book of Homilies (1547), "These bokes [of the Bible] therfore, ought to be much in our handes, in our eyes, in our eares, in oure mouthes, but moste of all, in our hartes. For the scripture of God is the heauenly meate of our soules."[46] Cranmer could even call scripture "a

---

42. Ibid.

43. "For the letter (that is to say the lawe) kylleth: but the spirite geveth lyfe (that is to saye the spirite of god whiche entereth your hertes when ye beleve the glad tydynges that are preached you in Christe)." Ibid., fol. 113v.

44. Ibid.

45. More, *The Confutation of Tyndale's Answer*, in *Complete Works*, 8.2:743.

46. Thomas Cranmer, *Certayne Sermons, or Homelies Appoynted by the Kynges Maiestie, to Be Declared and Redde, by All Persones, Vicars, or Curates, Euery Sondaye in Their Churches, Where They Haue Cure*, Early English Books Online, 1475–1640 / 48:03 (London: Rychard Grafton, 1547), fol. A4v.

sure, a constant, & a perpetuall instrument of saluacion."[47] While Tyndale's doctrine of election would cause him to balk at this formulation, he conceived of the good works "quickened" by scripture as a means of participating more fully in the life of what Paul called the "newe man" (Eph. 4:24, Tyndale Bible).[48] Christ, who "is al in al thinges to them that beleue, and the cause of al loue," transforms the ecclesial and social polity so that any good work is done by him and to him.[49] To do good works, then, is not to participate individually in Christ for the sake of salvation from hell—God's unmerited election took care of that—but to participate communally in the body of Christ for the sake of *life*.[50] Although Tyndale rules out rewards for good works, then, he maintains a robust understanding of how the Christian participates in the life of Christ through the reading of scripture—a reading that animates the moral life. In his revision of tropological theory, Tyndale restricts tropological interpretation to a recognition of the need for repentance and the promise of mercy. But once the Christian has repented, habitual encounters with scripture motivate her to do works of charity freely. Rather than a tropological imperative, Tyndale identifies a tropological inspiration. And when the Christian works charitably in Christ, she participates fully in the new life Christ promised her. This life of tropological inspiration, then, fulfills anagogy. No mystical ascent or ascetic ecstasy is required to reap the fruits of anagogy: they are realized in the moral life.

Had he seen fit, then, Tyndale could have responded to More in these terms. He could have given an account of David's acts of moral conversion that would appreciate their liveliness as movements of "feeling faith" in response to God's word coming to him through the prophet

---

47. Ibid.

48. Tyndale, *The Obedyence of a Christian Man*, fol. 104r.

49. Ibid. "In Christ there is neyther french nor english: but the frenchman is the englyshmans owne selfe" (fol. 103v).

50. Compare the prominent ecclesiological, communal dimension of Erasmus's tropological exegesis, detailed in Friedhelm Krüger, *Humanistische Evangelienauslegung: Desiderius Erasmus von Rotterdam als Ausleger der Evangelien in seinen Paraphrasen* (Tübingen: J. C. B. Mohr, 1986), 134–40.

Nathan. Tyndale could share More's sense of *how* David responded to God tropologically, even if he must reject More's contention that David's tropological invention cooperated in his salvation.

Erasmus and Udall: Vernacular Tropology

Sixteenth-century proponents of biblical translation often cited Erasmus's lyrical desideratum in *Paraclesis* (1516): "I wold desire that all women shuld reade the gospell and Paules epistles / and I wold to god they were translated in to the tonges of all men / So that they might not only be read / and knowne / of the scotes and yryshmen / But also of the Turkes and sarracenes."[51] Archbishop Thomas Cranmer would echo Erasmus's praise of vernacular scripture in his prologue to the first officially promulgated English Bible.[52] But historians of the translation debates have often overlooked the tropological motivations of Erasmus, Cranmer, and many early proponents of the English Bible. They advocated translation so that common people could be formed by scripture. Erasmus imagines a plowman as immersed in scripture as a Benedictine monk, able to "singe a texte of the scripture at his plowbeme."[53] He wishes that "all the communication of the christen shuld be of the scripture / for in a maner soch are we oure selves / as oure daylye tales are." When people know and love scripture, it can permeate daily intercourse. Cranmer likewise conceives the sequence of biblical formation as one of hearing, learning, and teaching—"though not wyth his mouth, yet with his lyvynge and good example; which is suer the moost lyuely

---

51. Desiderius Erasmus, *An Exhortation to the Diligent Studye of Scripture, Made by Erasmus Roterodamus. And Tra[n]slated in to Inglissh. An Exposition in to the Seventh Chaptre of the First Pistle to the Corinthians*, Early English Books Online, 1475–1640 / 39:05 (Antwerp: Hans Luft, 1529).

52. Thomas Cranmer, *The Byble in Englyshe . . . Apoynted to the Vse of the Churches*, Early English Books Online, 1475–1640 / 129:02 (London: Rychard Grafton, 1540).

53. Erasmus, *Exhortation*, fol. 6r.

and effecteuouse forme and manner of teaching."[54] Erasmus and Cranmer wanted common people to be able to read the Bible not so much to *know* scripture as to *practice* it. And it was possible, they believed, to teach the word of God through action. The word would come to life not in the bare text itself, nor simply by being understood, but in scripture-saturated lives.

While reformers would come to disagree on the soteriological function of the lived word, the tropological sense of scripture took on such central importance in Reformation hermeneutics that a modern Reformed theologian has characterized the era as "the triumph of tropology."[55] Erasmus's influence in this regard, especially in the English context, is hard to overestimate.[56] Although his new Greek edition and Latin translation of the New Testament disrupted medieval biblical scholarship, his marriage of critical method with pious motives proved compelling to scholars in reformist and traditional camps alike. Erasmus also modeled for a new, Bible-obsessed age how to turn the words of scripture into literary works. His *Paraphrases in Novum Testamentum* was a sixteenth-century bestseller and, according to Erasmus himself,

---

54. *The Byble in Englyshe*, fol. +3v.

55. Peter J. Leithart, *Deep Exegesis: The Mystery of Reading Scripture* (Waco, TX: Baylor University Press, 2009), 13–15; for a broader overview, see McGrath, *The Intellectual Origins of the European Reformation*, 150–64.

56. As the English Reformation developed, Erasmus's influence became ever more oblique. Although many early reformers were inspired by him, the loyally Catholic Erasmus soon could not function directly as a source of evangelical or Reformed theology. Instead, he is called upon as a modern authority analogous to the patristic authorities such as Augustine and Chrysostom, whom reformers tended to invoke for argumentative leverage. "Erasmus did not represent mainstream English Protestantism, but rather . . . his legacy became a counterpoint to the emerging dominance of Calvinist theology within English religious culture." Gregory D. Dodds, *Exploiting Erasmus: The Erasmian Legacy and Religious Change in Early Modern England* (Toronto: University of Toronto Press, 2009), 3. It is therefore through the *Paraphrases* and its model of scriptural participation that Erasmus may have had the greatest, most direct long-term influence.

his greatest hit.[57] The English translation of the *Paraphrases* on the Gospels and Acts had the force of the Tudor and Elizabethan states behind it. Edward VI's royal injunctions of 1547 charged every parish to obtain, in addition to a Great Bible, "the Paraphrasis of Erasmus also in English upon the Gospels, and the same set up in some convenient place . . . whereas parishioners may most commodiously resort unto the same, and read the same." Curates were charged not to discourage "authorized and licensed" persons from reading both books.[58] Although Mary Tudor proscribed many books promoted during the Edwardian reforms, she pointedly did not prohibit the *Paraphrases* (or the Great Bible).[59] Elizabeth I revived Edward's royal injunction in 1559, adopting much the same language but striking out the caveat that the reader must be "authorized and licensed," and requiring curates to purchase for themselves the *Paraphrases* on the entire New Testament, not only the Gospels.[60] The extant evidence suggests that the publication campaign and its enforcement were successful, that "the *Paraphrases* was widely purchased and used, that it was instrumental in making the New Testament in English available and known to clergy and people, and that it was the chief means by which Erasmus was claimed for the English reformed church."[61] In all of these injunctions, the *Paraphrases* is conceived of as a means of edification in tandem with the Bible itself, which is commended not simply as a book to know, but as "the very lively word of

---

57. "All good people agree in declaring that there is no book from which they have taken more fruit than they have from my *Paraphrases*." Cited in Cottier, "Erasmus's *Paraphrases*," 33.

58. Walter Howard Frere and William Paul McClure Kennedy, eds., *Visitation Articles and Injunctions of the Period of the Reformation* (London, New York: Longmans, Green & Co., 1910), 2:117–18.

59. John Craig, "Forming a Protestant Consciousness? Erasmus' *Paraphrases* in English Parishes, 1547–1666," in *Holy Scripture Speaks: The Production and Reception of Erasmus' "Paraphrases on the New Testament,"* ed. Hilmar M. Pabel and Mark Vessey (Toronto: University of Toronto Press, 2002), 327.

60. Frere and Kennedy, *Visitation Articles*, 3:10, 13–14.

61. Craig, "Forming a Protestant Consciousness?," 335.

God, and the special food of man's soul, that all Christian persons are bound to embrace, believe and follow, if they look to be saved."[62]

The *Paraphrases*' precise relationship to "the very lively word of God" remains ambiguous in part because of Erasmus's own expansive theology of scripture. Erasmus held a kerygmatic view of the Gospel. In reading the New Testament, one encounters or experiences through the words of scripture an essential way of being that Erasmus called "philosophia Christi."[63] This kerygma is best encountered in the Bible itself, which is infinitely rich, but it can also be expressed in other works. In the prologue to the *Paraphrase on Matthew*, Erasmus wishes for a lively catechetical instrument to help introduce lay people to the Gospel, "a summary of the Christian faith . . . a mixture, taken not from the shallow pools of human literature, but from Gospel sources, from apostolic writings, from the Apostles' creed."[64] This summary could take many forms, and he approves of "comedies now performed in some churches (to my mind something not altogether bad) about Christ rising and ascending into heaven, and about the sending of the Holy Spirit."[65] Although he never says so explicitly, it seems that Erasmus desired his *Paraphrases* to serve a similar purpose, a purpose for which the Edwardian and Elizabethan injunctions enlisted the work.

Edward VI promulgated the English *Paraphrases* when he was nine years old, and the first volume appeared the next year, 1548.[66] The Gospels and Acts paraphrases had been translated between 1543 and 1545 at the behest of his father Henry VIII's final queen, Catherine Parr, by a royal team including the queen herself, Princess Mary, and moderately

---

62. Frere and Kennedy, *Visitation Articles*, 2:118.

63. The notion of "philosophia Christi" is most pointedly developed in Erasmus, *Exhortation*.

64. Desiderius Erasmus, *Paraphrase on Matthew*, ed. Dean Simpson, Collected Works of Erasmus: New Testament Scholarship 45 (Toronto: University of Toronto Press, 2008), 19. This prologue was not included in Udall's English editions.

65. Ibid., 21.

66. Desiderius Erasmus, *The First Tome or Volume of the Paraphrase of Erasmus upon the Newe Testamente*, ed. Nicholas Udall, Early English Books Online, 1475–1640 / 1772:01 (London: Edwarde Whitchurche, 1548).

reformist clergy, presided over by Nicholas Udall.[67] Udall's lengthy preface addressed to the boy king—a twenty-three-page mirror of princes built on the model of Erasmian paraphrase—weaves a tapestry of allegorical, tropological, and anagogical correspondences from the Old and New Testaments and Edward's own royal history. Allegorically, Henry VIII recapitulates the careers of King David and King Josiah. As Henry's son, Edward is called tropologically to imitate his father, but also allegorically to fulfill the roles of the boy David, slaying the papist Goliath, and the boy Josiah, delivering the lost law of God to the people. He is also to fulfill Solomon's role by building the church his father had envisioned. Anagogically, "the Englishe Michaell Kinge Henry" had already "cast the dragon [of Rev. 12:7–9] that olde Serpente and his Aungels oute of Englande," so now Edward must restore the City of God in his realm.[68] Edward can tropologically participate in this restoration, just as Joshua led Israel into the promised land after Moses died. Udall exhorts him "to sette us Englishe men in the lande of Canaan which is the sincere knoweleage and the free exercise of Goddes moste holy Woorde."[69] What precisely constitutes God's word remains ambiguous. Repeatedly, Udall speaks of "Scripture and other dyvine workes in the vulgare tongue." He never separates the two types of literature, and so while he clearly identifies Erasmus's *Paraphrases* as a "setting forth" of scripture, his more theoretical statements always use this dual category that allows the *Paraphrases* to creep back toward the category of Bible.[70]

---

67. E. J. Devereux, "The Publication of the English Paraphrases of Erasmus," *Bulletin of the John Rylands Library* 51 (1969): 348–67.

68. Desiderius Erasmus, *The First Tome or Volume of the Paraphrases of Erasmus vpon the Newe Testament Conteinyng the Fower Euangelistes, with the Actes of the Apostles: Eftsones Conferred with the Latine and Throughly Corrected as It Is by the Kinges Highnes Iniunccions Commaunded to Be Had in Euerie Churche of This Royalme*, ed. Nicholas Udall, 2nd ed., Early English Books Online, 1475–1640 / 2057:01 (London: Edward Whitchurch, 1551), fol. 4r; all citations to *Paraphrases* are from this second, revised edition.

69. Ibid., fol. 6r.

70. Ibid., fol. C5r.

The ambiguity makes sense in light of Erasmus's tropologically inclined theology of scripture, which locates the text of the Bible in a circuit formed also by the events of salvation history, the life of Christ, and
the lives of Christians. The *Paraphrases* are designed to integrate their
readers (and their author) into that circuit. It is this emphasis on living
into the story of scripture that leads Erasmus to regard the tropological
sense as the primary spiritual sense of scripture.[71] Situating him in the
rhetorical tradition, Mary Jane Barnett has observed that "in Erasmus's
work, the concern for practical application becomes paramount."[72] But
this ideal is not simply an intensification of a standard rhetorical desideratum, a hallmark of Renaissance humanism. Instead, Erasmus's
model for practical application is the fusion of words and works in Jesus'
life. As Friedhelm Krüger has demonstrated in considerable detail, the
theological—not rhetorical—inspiration for Erasmus's mode of invention in the *Paraphrases* is the idea that "the teaching and life of Christ
form a perfect unity."[73] "The teaching of Christ is the acts of Christ collected in words. And conversely, the words of Christ are nothing other
than the explanation of his deeds."[74] To write a paraphrase, then, is to
work on the model of Christ himself, whose "entire *behavior* is but a
paraphrase of his *teaching*."[75] Likewise, the Christian reads scripture in
order to encounter Christ and participate in his life. In the *Ratio verae
theologiae*, a treatise included in the prefatory materials of the 1518
Novum organum, Erasmus exhorts, "Let this be your first and only goal,
your prayer, your sole objective: that you be changed, that you be seized,

---

71. McGrath, *The Intellectual Origins of the European Reformation*, 150.

72. Mary Jane Barnett, "Erasmus and the Hermeneutics of Linguistic
Praxis," *Renaissance Quarterly* 49, no. 3 (1996): 545.

73. Krüger, *Humanistische Evangelienauslegung*, 144; on Erasmus's tropological exegesis generally, which "quantitatively stands far to the foreground"
compared to the other senses, see 131–50.

74. Manfred Hoffmann, *Erkenntnis und Verwirklichung der wahren Theologie nach Erasmus von Rotterdam* (Tübingen: Mohr, 1972), 99; cited in Krüger,
Humanistische Evangelienauslegung, 133.

75. Krüger, *Humanistische Evangelienauslegung*, 142.

that you be inspired, and that you be transformed into what you are learning."[76]

The word of God lives in the works of Christians, including the literary work of a Gospel paraphrase. And every Christian life is itself a Gospel paraphrase:

> Nothing is said there [in the Gospels] that does not pertain to each of us; nothing is done there that is not done in our lives on a daily basis—less obviously, to be sure, but more truly. Christ is born in us, nor is there a lack of Herods, who try to kill the infant still fragile and suckling. Christ grows and develops through the stages of life. He cures every kind of disease, if only a person implores his aid with confidence. He does not reject the lepers, or the demoniacs, or those unclean with a flow of blood, or the blind, or the lame. No defect of mind is so foul, so incurable, that he does not take it away, if we say to him with sincerity: "Jesus, son of David, have mercy," and "Lord, if you will, you can make me clean." He even raises the dead to life. He teaches, he terrifies, he threatens, he coaxes, he consoles.[77]

Faith is the virtue by which the Christian can examine his own life and hear Christ teaching in it. Udall's preface to Edward VI models a way for the boy-king to see Christ's work in his own life story. Udall comes alongside Edward just as Christ came alongside the disciples on the road to Emmaus, an episode to which Erasmus devoted eight percent, or about thirty folio pages, of his *Paraphrase on Luke*, which occupies 368 folio pages in the 1552 edition.[78] As Christ unfolds the scriptures to the distraught disciples, he urges them not only to consider the prophecies of the Old Testament, but also "diligently [to] compare

---

76. Cited in ibid., 133n16.

77. Erasmus, *Paraphrase on Matthew*, 16. This lengthy preface "To the Pious Reader" is not included in Udall's edition.

78. Jane E. Phillips, "On the Road to Emmaus: Erasmus' Paraphrase of Luke 24:27," *Erasmus of Rotterdam Society Yearbook* 22 (2002): 69.

the writing of the prophetes with the thinges whiche ye have seen wrought and dooen."[79] Christ interprets the Old Testament allegorically, but he connects the figures to the disciples' own experiences, drawing the despairing story they told him—"howe thei had clene cast awai al hope"—into the larger, truer story of redemption.[80] By a tropological turn, allegory becomes consolation. Udall, too, seeks to console, and the continuities he establishes between Old Testament heroes, Edward's parents, and the young king keep alive the dead parents' memory even as they argue a providential rationale for their absence.[81] God took Henry out of this world before his work was complete so that Edward might not reign "in a careless supinitie, but in a perpetuall exercise of all princely vertues, that ye mighte consummate and finishe suche regall enterprises as he begonne."[82] Udall commends to Edward conduct that will fulfill his allegorical potential. To act rightly is to live into the allegory. What may have been a heavy burden of expectation for the nine-year-old Edward nevertheless expresses Erasmus's ideal of Christian conversion.

Martin Bucer: Dramatic Tropology

In late 1548, after receiving Udall's preface, Edward began work on his own anti-papist apocalyptic treatise. Around the same time he received a play created for and starring the boy king himself: Bernardino Ochino's *A Tragoedie or Dialoge of the Vniuste Vsurped Primacie of the Bishop of Rome, and of All the Iust Abolishyng of the Same.*[83] In the same year,

---

79. Erasmus, *Paraphrases*, fol. 387r.

80. Ibid., fol. 382r; cf. Mark Vessey, "The Actor in the Story: Horizons of Interpretation in Erasmus's *Annotations on Luke*," in *The Unfolding of Words: Commentary in the Age of Erasmus*, ed. Judith Rice Henderson (Toronto: University of Toronto Press, 2012), 67–68.

81. Erasmus, *Paraphrases*, fols. 5r–6r.

82. Ibid., fol. 6r.

83. Bernardino Ochino, *A Tragoedie or Dialoge of the Vniuste Vsurped Primacie of the Bishop of Rome, and of All the Iust Abolishyng of the Same*, trans.

Martin Bucer, a personal guest of Archbishop Cranmer and a refugee from Strasbourg religious politics, envisioned a very different kind of tropological drama in his *De regno Christi*, a blueprint for the reformed Christian kingdom that he hoped Edward would establish. Part theo-political treatise, part public policy white paper, *De regno Christi* sketches an ambitious reform program that conceives of government, law, and ecclesiastical polity as supporting structures in the larger domain of a human culture whose goods are fulfilled only in a community of evangelical charity—the kingdom of Christ. Touching on issues ranging from poor relief, the penal system, and higher education to the wool trade, hotel standards, and conspicuous consumption, Bucer's project of social engineering assumes that legislation can only support prior cultural formation, "for men do not accept law and observe it consistently . . . unless they are first instructed and convinced that the law is salutary for them."[84] The kingdom of the world can govern with "beatings, whippings, prisons, exile," but secular administration will yield a happy society only if first "those who have wandered from the way of salvation . . . are led back to it with the chains of repentance, under the impulse of only the word and the Spirit."[85] But it is not enough to print bibles and preach in church. The old religion worked through all areas of culture, and so must the new. Therefore culture—education, music, sports, public preaching, and drama—forms the core of Bucer's reform program, fostering a wide array of edifying communal activity and, especially, opportunities to activate the impulse of Word and Spirit.

To appreciate how Bucer conceived of biblical drama in the kingdom of Christ, it helps to understand how the Bible functioned in his theology and intellectual method. Among the magisterial reformers who did not inspire movements named after them, Bucer was the most productive and immediately influential. Known across Europe as a

---

John Ponet, Early English Books Online, 1475–1640 / 327:10 (London: N. Hill for Gwalter Lynne, 1549).

84. Martin Bucer, *De regno Christi*, in *Melanchthon and Bucer*, ed. Wilhelm Pauck (Philadelphia: Westminster Press, 1969), 269.

85. Ibid., 181.

skilled—perhaps too skilled—theological diplomat, he contributed to a series of ecumenical efforts to find common ground among reforming movements. His theological congeniality and intellectual dexterity owe a great deal to his early passion for Erasmian biblical culture—a combination of piety and learning that a 1518 encounter with Luther turned to evangelical, reforming ends. In addition to his work as architect of a reformed church in Strasbourg and beyond, Bucer enjoyed, according to John Calvin, the "special credit of devoting himself to the interpretation of Scripture with more dedicated exactitude than anyone of our time."[86] Unlike Calvin, he never wrote a systematic theology, and unlike Luther, he was never driven by a single insight, unless it was the primacy of the encounter by faith with Christ the Word in scripture. Through this encounter he worked out theological controversies, absorbed the most recent philological research, and found homiletical material. The organization of his commentaries often reflects their multiplicity of purpose. The commentary on John, for example, treats each pericope first by paraphrase, then by annotation (philological and theological), and then again by "observations" of a homiletical, practical nature. His theological style in other works bears out this form.[87] "The true theology," he wrote, "is not theoretical or speculative, but active and practical. Its goal is to do likewise, that is, to live a life conformed to God [deiformem]."[88]

Much of that activity in Bucer's own life was dedicated to commentary on scripture. In Calvin's judgment, Bucer's powers of invention were so great that "he does not know how to stop writing."[89] However that may be, Bucer thought of any form of evangelism as a tropological

---

86. Cited in D. F. Wright, "Martin Bucer," *Dictionary of Major Biblical Interpreters* (Downers Grove, IL: InterVarsity Press, 2007), 248–49.

87. "Bucer's theological stance is fundamentally characterized by the shunning of all speculation and by the turn to a practical biblical piety (*Bibelfrömmigkeit*)." Johannes Müller, *Martin Bucers Hermeneutik* (Gütersloh: Gütersloher Verlagshaus G. Mohn, 1965), 135.

88. Martin Bucer, *Enarratio in Evangelion Iohannis (1528, 1530, 1536)*, ed. Irena Backus, Martini Buceri Opera Omnia 2 (Gütersloh: Mohn, 1988), 433.

89. Cited in Wright, "Martin Bucer," 249.

participation in the work of the Apostles. "Whoever wants to imitate the Apostles and teach salubrious things from Scripture in the church should tell about all the wonderful things God has done among his people. From this, faith will be strengthened and the love of God enkindled."[90] The exegesis of scripture cannot remain simply the explication of knowledge, nor even simply a proclamation of the Word that incites a saving experience of the law/gospel dialectic, as certain Lutheran sects believed.[91] It must also retell and reimagine narrative as it elucidates. In so doing, it can edify the church in two ways. The people and deeds of scripture can be examples of good and evil, occasions to "persuade to

---

90. Bucer, *Enarratio in Evangelion Iohannis*, 153.

91. The latter option, promoted by a sect the Book of Concord calls the Antinomians, reduces faith to an experience of the law/gospel dialectic and scripture to an occasion for that experience. As James Simpson has remarked, such a theology "produces not an account of historical unfolding and progressive revelation but a sequence of moments, each of which replays the same intense drama." James Simpson, *Burning to Read: English Fundamentalism and Its Reformation Opponents* (Cambridge, MA: Harvard University Press, 2009), 185. But this understanding of law and gospel was not the only nor the most prevalent option, not even for Lutherans. The Formula of Concord (1577) considers precisely this reductive option and rejects it, noting that "law" and "gospel" must be understood in two senses, one dialectical-theological and the other narrative-historical, which embraces "the entire teaching of Christ, which he presented in his teaching ministry, as did his apostles in theirs." Robert Kolb and Timothy J. Wengert, eds., *The Book of Concord: The Confessions of the Evangelical Lutheran Church*, trans. Charles Arand et al. (Minneapolis: Fortress Press, 2000), 500. That "entire teaching" ultimately consists of deeds as well as words, including the deeds that comprise the history of the Old Testament: "For the descendants of the dear patriarchs like the patriarchs themselves continually remembered that human beings had been originally created by God righteous and holy and had transgressed God's command through the deception of the serpent and had become sinners. . . . They also comforted and consoled themselves through the proclamation of the seed of the woman that was supposed to trample upon the head of the serpent and through the proclamation of Abraham's seed, 'in which all the nations of the earth shall be blessed,' and of David's son, who was to restore the kingdom . . . who was 'struck down for our sins' . . . through whose wounds we have been healed." Ibid., 585–86.

all honest things and most powerfully dissuade from inhonest things."[92] But beyond this merely exemplary form of didacticism, the Holy Spirit inspires a more participatory form of edificiation, one that is properly tropological. The saints of the Old Testament were rendered "partakers [*participes*] of Christ," and we can share in their blessings through Christ when we "recognize a certain similitude and shadow and so by translation [Gal. 4:24] adapt—by analogy [*cum proportione*]—those things which were written about them to our own affairs. This is *allegorein kai tropologein*[:] . . . in considering those things we might be edified [*doceamus*]."[93] The tropological translation or adaptation that Bucer describes is made possible not in the order of representation, as a conceptual comparison of like with like (what Thomas Aquinas calls equivocation), but in the order of being, "according to the relation of a creature to God as its principle and cause," that is, "according to analogy or proportion."[94] Bucer's hermeneutic in this regard is squarely Thomist.

> "He is the Word through whom all things were made" [Jn. 1.3] and will be restored. Therefore whatever at all is or is done in the world refers in its own way to the Word and has the Word within it, and therefore the pious mind, having been stirred up by the Spirit, can rise up to contemplation [*cognitionem*] of the Word. And things that happened to the people of God for their education in salvation contain an even more certain image of the Word.[95]

It is possible to speak of Old Testament narrative in terms of mere exemplarity, as a humanist might praise the plays of Terence or histories of Sallust for displaying vice and virtue, and Bucer approves of this kind of moral reading. But here and elsewhere the history of Israel matters for him in a different way, as the providential unfolding of God's plan for humanity's redemption in Christ. And through Christ, in whom all

---

92. Bucer, *Enarratio in Evangelion Iohannis*, 153.
93. Ibid., 145.
94. Thomas Aquinas, *Summa theologica*, I.13.5.
95. Bucer, *Enarratio in Evangelion Iohannis*, 142.

the faithful partake, people in different ages participate together in edification as a communal project. "For that saying of the Lord, 'What I say to you, I say to all' [Mk. 13:37], is true of the entire scripture."[96] While Bucer recognizes the value of merely exemplary tropological interpretation of scripture, he favors a full-fledged tropological participation in salvation history.

These two options in Bucer's biblical hermeneutic help to frame his discussion of drama in *De regno Christi*, where any edifying drama is approved, but only biblical drama is considered in full-fledged tropological terms. Bucer turns to drama in a section on "honest games" (*ludi honesti*) within a broader discussion of labor and markets. His remarks have often been noted in surveys of dramatic theory for how they reduce the classical "distinction between comedy and tragedy to the simple difference between representation of everyday happenings as opposed to extraordinary actions."[97] But Bucer's novel theorization of tragedy and comedy goes further. While he condones plays as a salubrious form of necessary leisure time, they may edify in two ways: comedy by treating of moral themes directly and tragedy by treating history under the aspect of divine providence. Biblical material suits both genres, and Bucer himself sketches the plots for several biblical plays, devoting an extended treatment to the comedy of Isaac and Rebekah. "From this story can be described the pious solicitude of parents in seeking religious marriages for their children; the good faith and efficiency of reputable servants; . . . the character of the girl, a really modest person, and also humane and hospitable."[98] Biblical tragedies can also display exemplary behaviors, but they are set apart from biblical comedies by "events which turned out contrary to what was expected, which Aristotle calls reversal."[99] Bucer baptizes the *Poetics* by reframing *peripeteia* in a providential view of history. If *metanoia* (repentance) names the logic of providential history, then *peripeteia* is its dramatic counterpart. And Bucer,

---

96. Cited in Müller, *Martin Bucers Hermeneutik*, 142n46.

97. John N. King, *English Reformation Literature: The Tudor Origins of the Protestant Tradition* (Princeton: Princeton University Press, 1982), 275.

98. Bucer, *De regno Christi*, 350.

99. Ibid., 351.

who likes to echo Paul in saying that "the kingdom of God is founded on power [*virtus*], not on talk,"[100] identifies the *action* of reversal, rather than moral themes, as tragedy's chief ethical motivator:

> Since all such things [reversals] have so wonderful a power [*vim*] of confirming faith in God and enkindling a desire and love for God and likewise an admiration of piety and righteousness, . . . how much more does it befit Christians to derive their poems from these things, in which they can represent the great and illustrious plans, efforts, characters, emotions, and events of mankind.[101]

Viewed in the framework of salvation history, all human action is seen as a kind of turning, either in "the horrible fear of God's judgment" or in "a joyful trust in God and his promises."[102] But rather than flattening history into a series of dialectical conversion moments, Bucer's theory of tragedy retains a tropological tension and circulation among the spiritual senses of scripture: the letter of history in all its variegated "plans, efforts, characters, emotions"; the Gospel that elicits belief; and the promise of eternal salvation. Bucer's is not a strong version of tropological participation, but it does situate ethics within the drama of salvation while retaining history as a necessary, and unfinished, dimension of salvation.[103] Bucer therefore refuses to reduce the senses of scripture to allegory (unlike Luther's reduction of tropology to the law/gospel dialectic) or to anagogy (as could Udall's post-apocalyptic sense of living beyond the end of history). This tropological balance keeps ethics from shrinking to individual morality even as it keeps theology from narrowing to the question of individual salvation. And its dramatic set-

---

100. Bucer, *Enarratio in Evangelion Iohannis*, 433.

101. Bucer, *De regno Christi*, 351.

102. Ibid.

103. For a strong version of tropological participation in drama, see the discussion in the section "Mirror of Drama, Mirror of Scripture: A Prologue to a French Passion Play" in the next chapter on the parasacramental exchange among actors, audience, and biblical persons, particularly as articulated by Arnoul Gréban.

ting would keep scriptural discourse a common and public, rather than subjective and private, form of textuality.[104]

The Boy King and the Dragon: Apocalyptic Tropology

Udall's preface to Erasmus's *Paraphrases* invited Edward VI in the most exciting terms to take up his father's fight against "the huge sevenfolde headed draguon" of the Roman church.[105] Udall was not the first to compare Edward to Josiah, but he enriched the comparison with exegetical thoroughness and a dramatic imagination far surpassing the mild exhortations that Cranmer addressed to the new Josiah at his coronation.[106] The unfolding drama of the apocalypse enkindled the young king's imagination, fanned no doubt by his evangelical tutors. As noted above, Edward began work on his own anti-papist apocalyptic treatise in late 1548, after receiving Udall's preface and around the time he received Ochino's *Tragoedie*, composed expressly for himself.[107] Ochino, who had found refuge in England through the same channels as Bucer,

---

104. In this, Bucer's intentions resonate with what Adrian Streete has characterized as Elizabethan drama's "effort to maintain an avowedly *public* form of engagement with scripture, one where verbal and ideological interrogation of the biblical text takes place at a *communal* level." Adrian Streete, "Introduction," in *Early Modern Drama and the Bible: Contexts and Readings, 1570–1625,* ed. Adrian Streete (New York: Palgrave Macmillan, 2012), 15.

105. Erasmus, *Paraphrases,* fol. 4r.

106. Thomas Cranmer, *Remains,* ed. Henry Jenkyns (Oxford: Oxford University Press, 1833), 2:118–20.

107. For the argument that Edward used the play, before it was published, in his own composition, see Diarmaid MacCulloch, *The Boy King: Edward VI and the Protestant Reformation* (Berkeley and Los Angeles: University of California Press, 2002), 26–30; on the circumstances of the play's composition and extended discussion, see Stephen Alford, *Kingship and Politics in the Reign of Edward VI* (New York: Cambridge University Press, 2002), 100–115; Michael Wyatt, *The Italian Encounter with Tudor England: A Cultural Politics of Translation* (Cambridge: Cambridge University Press, 2005), 91–94.

composed a tragedy that fits Bucer's own definition of the genre. It handles, in Bucer's words, "events which turned out contrary to what was expected, which Aristotle calls reversal."[108] Its subject, however, is not biblical but apocalyptic. The expectations are set in the first scene by the conspiracy of Satan and Beelzebub "to attempt [the early church's] ouerthrowe by arte, policie, diligence, crafte, subteltie, gyle, and prodition [betrayal]."[109] Their plot calls for the invention of Antichrist, in the person of the "ambicious, and craftie" Boniface III, who in 607 "obteyned of Phocas the Emperour by suttill trayne the dignitie of a Pope."[110] Satan invents Antichrist so that Antichrist might invent the papacy. Looking down from heaven on the subsequent abominations of the papistical church, Christ circa 1527 explains that he has bided his time to "make his glory more notable."[111] Echoing the rationale for the incarnation rehearsed in biblical literature in the "parliament of heaven" tradition, Christ determines that "the measure is full," that humanity has suffered enough, and he sends the angel Gabriel to inspire Henry VIII with the idea that the pope just may be the Antichrist.[112] A long disputation among Henry, a papist, and Cranmer yields to the final tableau, in which Edward proclaims his intention "to pursewe the famouse enterprise of oure moste famouse father, and not onely to plucke vp by the rootes, and vtterlye banishe out of our kingdome the name of Antichrist and his Iurisdiction: but also clearely to purge ye mindes of oure subiectes from all wycked idolatry, heresie, and superstycyon, and suche lyke deuelishnes as by hym was brought in."[113] The Lord Protector advises him to use the sword of the scriptures to behead the Antichrist, as David had beheaded Goliath. While the *Tragoedie* draws on the conventions of

---

108. Bucer, *De regno Christi*, 351.
109. Ochino, *A Tragoedie*, fol. A4v.
110. Ibid., fol. Aa.1r.
111. Ibid., fol. X.3v.
112. Ibid., fol. X.4r. The "parliament of heaven" tradition began in England with Robert Grosseteste's *Chasteau d'Amour*, found virtuosic expression in *Piers Plowman*, and was popularly represented in the late fifteenth and early sixteenth centuries in the N-Town Parliament of Heaven play.
113. Ibid., fol. Cc.1r.

mirror-for-princes plays such as *Magnyfycence*, which John Skelton wrote for Edward's young father, the *Tragoedie*'s investment in Edward's peculiar history and vocation sets it apart.

The evidence that Edward may have played himself in a production of the *Tragoedie* is tantalizingly suggestive, and consistent with his tutors' and advisors' efforts to enlist him tropologically in the apocalyptic history they saw unfolding in their own time. That Edward performed in court plays is nearly certain. After the death of Henry VIII, the Revels Office remained under the energetic mastership of Thomas Cawarden and in the early years of Edward's reign busily produced entertainments at a pace and expense consistent with the reign of Henry.[114] Revels Office records attest to costumes being made for a king character on at least three occasions, one of them explicitly for Edward himself, and two of them for plays with anti-papal themes, indicated by orders for "albes surplices and heade clothes" and other recognizably Catholic garb.[115] While the costuming for recorded revels is not consistent with the *Tragoedie*'s cast of characters, Edward was certainly viewing and quite probably acting in anti-papal plays that involved a king in the years 1548–51, when Ochino wrote and shared the *Tragoedie* with Edward and eventually published it.

One of these plays, performed for Shrovetide 1549, called for the "makyng of a dragon of vij heades with all necessaries to hit."[116] Blending Udall's vivid evocation of "The huge sevenfolde headed draguon" of Rome with polemical material likely similar to Ochino's *Tragoedie*, the play's prop list in Revels Office records links it to a wider background of Reformation religious drama.[117] The Catholic costumes and cast of characters are also found in the records of Cambridge school

114. W. R. Streitberger, *Court Revels, 1485–1559* (Toronto: University of Toronto Press, 1994), 180–204.

115. Albert Feuillerat, ed., *Documents Relating to the Revels at Court in the Time of King Edward VI and Queen Mary (the Loseley Manuscripts) Edited with Notes and Indexes* (Louvain: A. Uystpruyst, 1914), 39; Streitberger, *Court Revels, 1485–1559*, 182–83, 185.

116. Feuillerat, *Documents*, 39.

117. Erasmus, *Paraphrases*, fol. 4r.

drama. The "Lord in Christmas" appointed at St. John's College for 1548 commanded three large chests of props and costumes, including two devils' coats with horns, a miter, various rich clerical gowns, and two dragons. The Lord of those yuletide revels, Thomas Lever, would soon become the rigorously reformist master of the college, would preach to Edward near his death, and, in Elizabeth's reign, would preside as chief religious authority in Coventry over the latest performances of biblical drama.[118] The Cambridge where Bucer composed *De regno Christi* was already an active center for drama, including reformist plays such as Thomas Kirchmeyer's Latin *Pammachius*, which shared with Ochino's *Tragoedie* and Bale's *King Johan* an apostate bishop of Rome who colludes with Satan to corrupt Christianity.[119] That the producers of school and court drama of the time deemed miters, albs, devils' outfits, and dragons essential to their work reveals a common apocalyptic imaginary. But depending on the performance context, this type of drama can be understood to seek quite different, though not necessarily contradictory, results. At Cambridge, apocalyptic reformist drama disseminated a set of ecclesiastically revolutionary ideas and polemical topoi to win the feisty hearts and minds of the youthful elite. But at Edward's court, performed for or even by Edward, the same anti-Catholic drama could anticipate a tropological response. Yet the tropology of such a play would entail a quite different object of participation than the plays of the old religion it sought to correct.

As I discuss in detail in the next chapter, what made the drama of the medieval biblical plays tropological was that the audience could participate in the represented drama of salvation by doing good works in their own lives, lives that were ordered to salvation by means of sacramental participation. When Edward hypothetically acted in Ochino's

---

118. Alan H. Nelson, ed., *Records of Early English Drama: Cambridge* (Toronto: University of Toronto Press, 1989), 1:159–62; I am developing the network of biographical and material culture relationships sketched by Paul Whitfield White, *Drama and Religion in English Provincial Society, 1485–1660* (New York: Cambridge University Press, 2008), 74–76.

119. On "militant protestantism" and drama at Cambridge, see P. White, *Drama and Religion*, 109–14.

Tragoedie or in the other lost apocalyptic dramas, his playing would have followed a logic similar to that of the medieval biblical plays, but with a crucial difference. Whereas Catholic cycle plays mediated between biblical history and the sacramental economy of salvation, Ochino's drama mediates between apocalyptic history and the destiny of the Tudor regime. By these transpositions, Udall and Ochino hardly promote an advanced political theology that would substitute nation for church and exchange heavenly ends for the proximate goods of the *saeculum*. Rather, this Edwardian drama unfolds always in the context of a cosmic battle that in turn plays out in the providential plans of God, in which the English nation and the Tudor monarchy have been elected to special parts. Edward is encouraged to live into this cosmic story, and indeed into his own salvation, not only by being the Tudor king but also by wielding the sword of the Gospel to bring light to his people. For the ultimate intended audience, the prince himself, these plays are tropological in the fullest sense. Eschewing an evangelical view of conversion that would flatten history, Ochino's play depends on a deep sense of the unfolding of providential history—for its target audience and chief participant, Edward.[120] And so these court plays cannot be considered simply propaganda, although as Paul Whitfield White has documented, Bale, Foxe, and others explicitly considered drama as propaganda, and "professional players . . . were perceived . . . as disseminators of Protestant doctrine working in conjunction with the ministries of preaching and publishing to advance the Reformation."[121] The propagandists themselves are engaged in a form—perhaps a cruder form—of Langlandian tropological making, a work of mercy to instruct the ignorant and correct the erring.[122] By possibly acting, or at least appearing as a character, in Ochino's play, Edward does not avail himself of the church's

---

120. On evangelical flattening of history, see Simpson, *Burning to Read*, 184–221.

121. Paul Whitfield White, *Theatre and Reformation: Protestantism, Patronage, and Playing in Tudor England* (New York: Cambridge University Press, 1993), 42–66, quote at 45.

122. See chapter 4, especially the section "Sacramental Penance and Literary Satisfaction."

reconciling grace in an act of ongoing, open-ended sacramental satisfaction, but he does participate for the sake of his own, and his nation's, salvation.

Tropological Drama as Propaganda

Even for the orchestrators of this dramatic propaganda, drama's overlap with liturgy and its involvement in the unfolding providential history of the Reformation rendered it more than just a neutral medium for spreading the gospel of reform. A memo to Henry VIII about reform and propaganda, titled "A Discourse Touching the Reformation of the Lawes of England" (c. 1537–42), captures a sense of synergy between drama's capacity for representation (good for propaganda) and its openness to participation (good for religious and political liturgy). Its author, Richard Morison, would later serve as host to Ochino in London while he was writing the *Tragoedie*, and the two became good friends.[123] In the "Discourse," a coldly pragmatic attitude toward dramatic activity combines oddly with a typological argument from the ceremonies of ancient Israel. In his capacity as one of Thomas Cromwell's propaganda agents, Morison advises the king not to outlaw plays, minstrelsy, processions, and books in English, but to use them so that the truths of the Reformation might be "daily by all meanes opened inculked and dryven into the peoples heddes."[124] Morison is more pragmatic than cynical. The man who argues elsewhere in the "Discourse" that laws should still be written in Latin because lawyers are used to working with Latin recognizes the pragmatic value of custom, and he compares popular culture to an unpleasant physic for a "sicke comenwelthe." But Morison is not satis-

---

123. The relevant passage is edited in Sydney Anglo, "An Early Tudor Programme for Plays and Other Demonstrations against the Pope," *Journal of the Warburg and Courtauld Institutes* 20, no. 1/2 (January 1, 1957): 176–79; on the Morison-Ochino connection, see Anne M. Overell, *Italian Reform and English Reformations, c. 1535–c. 1585* (Abingdon, UK: Ashgate, 2008), 49.

124. Anglo, "An Early Tudor Programme," 178.

fied with his arguments from pragmatism, and he must also appeal to biblical evidence, where it turns out that propaganda does not exhaust the purpose of play and game. When Morison turns to the Old Testament, he finds that God desires sacrifices of praise and thanksgiving expressed in festive and dramatic culture. Since God commanded Israel to celebrate the Passover in "perpetuall memorye" of the Exodus, "is it not convenyant and most meete that yerely for ever, in memorye that our savyour christe, by his Moses, your magestie, hathe delyvered us out of the bondage of the most wicked pharao of all pharaos, the bysshop of Rome, . . . we kepe a solempne feaste thereof, to geve god laude and thankes therfore?" When Morison turns to the practices of the reformed church, he discovers standing precedent for the liturgical ordering of time that had long contributed to the paraliturgical character of religious drama, performed as it was for church feasts. If priests and bishops annually beat the bounds in a processional liturgy to "savegard ther rightes and tythes, . . . how moche more ought ther be an yerely tyme appoynted partely to teache and preache the usurped power of the bisshoppe of Rome."[125] Plays and processions might be expedient means of propaganda, but they are also appropriate responses to the work of God in history, not only because they *express* thanksgiving and memorialize those works, but also because, as the term "convenyant" suggests, they fit in with the actions of the people of God across salvation history.

Paul Whitfield White has observed that "for the Reformation dramatist, the thesis or argument conveyed to the audience takes precedence over 'story' and 'character.'"[126] But for Morison and other apologists for the Tudor Reformation, the story and characters are essential to the argument, which is ultimately an argument about the history of salvation. Morison imagines plays and processions that are primarily concerned with England's history, understood as an important chapter in providential history. That history pits the character of King Henry VIII, typologically recapitulating the victories (and occasional weaknesses) of King David, against the bishop of Rome, the Antichrist.

125. Ibid.
126. P. White, *Theatre and Reformation*, 75.

Morison, however, can appreciate the fittingness of liturgical drama without espousing a participatory understanding of salvation history. Reformed theologies presented a spectrum of thought about how liturgy, paraliturgical play, and history are related to each other. Maximally, when English evangelicals stage a procession memorializing the victory of the Gospel over the pope, they are responding to God's works with praise and thanksgiving on analogy to the Church of England's Eucharist. Minimally, they are obeying God's extremely pragmatic Old Testament exhortations to "remember all the way which the Lord thy God led thee" (Deut. 8:2), and in so doing they are imitating, but not participating with, all the people of God who have celebrated the Passover in the past. However Morison might have understood this kind of dramatic activity theologically, his propagandistic intentions serve his theological intentions. If there is any need for propaganda, the need will be discovered by the study of scripture, and propaganda will serve to build up the kingdom of God. For plays such as Morison envisioned and John Bale produced, then, "catechesis" might be a better term than "propaganda," however much they contributed to England's political theology and served the ends of a rapidly expanding state.

John Careless and Coventry Drama: Tropological Martyrdom

White has traced an intriguing path from the Revels Office of Edward VI and the dramatic activity in Edwardian Cambridge to the Elizabethan Coventry Play, one of the longest-lasting civic biblical dramas in England. The same Thomas Lever who was staging anti-papist plays at Cambridge with casts and props similar to those in Edward's court became, in the 1560s and 1570s, "Coventry's leading religious authority and champion of Puritan reform."[127] White argues that Lever's authority as archdeacon of Coventry put him in a position to support the Coventry Play at a time when other local authorities were suppressing their antique biblical drama. In 1567, Matthew Hutton, dean of York Minster,

---

127. P. White, *Drama and Religion*, 74.

found the York Play unreformable, "Disagreinge from the senceritie of the Gospell."[128] A year later Coventry's own Hocktide play celebrating victory over the Danes was suppressed. But Coventry's biblical plays continued, even thrived. Many, if not all, of the Coventry pageants had been revised, some in 1535, others early in Elizabeth's reign. These Corpus Christi pageants, "the most famous of their kind in England," drew crowds "from far and wide" through the 1560s and 1570s.[129] The memory of the play's economic stimulus motivated several attempts to resurrect it, and lingered into the middle of the seventeenth century, when William Dugdale reported, "I have been told by some old people, who in their younger years were eye-witnesses of these *Pageants* so acted, that the yearly confluence of people to see that Shew was extraordinary great, and yielded no small advantage to this City."[130] The popularity of the play and its proximity to Stratford have prompted many critics to suggest that Shakespeare might have seen the cycle in his youth.[131] Entertaining two speculations at once, then, it is possible to imagine that protection by a hot reformist Cambridge dramatist preserved the Coventry Play long enough for a young Shakespeare to see it and learn from its "incarnational aesthetic" to create drama as "an embodied art form" and "ritualistic display."[132] Thanks to the ministrations of a Reformation

---

128. Alexandra F. Johnston and Margaret Rogerson, eds., *Records of Early English Drama: York* (Toronto: University of Toronto Press, 1979), 1:353.

129. R. W. Ingram, "Fifteen Seventy-Nine and the Decline of Civic Religious Drama in Coventry," *Elizabethan Theatre* 8 (1982): 114; Sir William Dugdale, *The Antiquities of Warwickshire Illustrated from Records, Leiger-Books, Manuscripts, Charters, Evidences, Tombes, and Armes: Beautified with Maps, Prospects and Portraictures*, Early English Books Online, 1641–1700 / 182:03 (London: Thomas Warren, 1656), 116.

130. Dugdale, *The Antiquities of Warwickshire*, 116. Dugdale attributed the pageants to the Grayfriars "before the suppression of the Monasteries."

131. In Beatrice Groves's careful formulation, "it is widely accepted that it is at least probable that Shakespeare caught the local expression of England's rich heritage of religious drama." *Texts and Traditions: Religion in Shakespeare, 1592–1604* (Oxford: Clarendon Press, 2007), 38; with discussion and documentation concerning Coventry in particular, 36–41.

132. Ibid., 36–59; quotes at 41, 59.

propagandist, Shakespeare might have absorbed, as Helen Cooper has argued, "that element of enactment—of subordinating the word to the deed, supplementing speech with embodiment" that his plays share with the medieval stage.[133]

These speculations would expose a sharp irony if only they revealed hot reformers like Lever wincing theologically from the recoil of rashly conceived multimedia propaganda. But as White has demonstrated in the case of Coventry, a hotbed of reform could cultivate biblical, "incarnational" drama as a "point of consensus" in the negotiations between an emergent Protestant culture and persistent traditional affinities.[134] The embodied, enacted medium in which the Bible came to life could be a major attraction to a reformer such as Lever. As Jennifer Waldron has argued, "Far from dismissing the significance of bodily participation in either religious ritual or theater, the hotter Protestants were the most interested in securing divine sanction for bodily actions."[135] Waldron's attention to a reformed theology of the body indicates one way in which Reformation-era appreciation of drama could go beyond the desire for consensus that White has identified as a motive for religious drama's persistence.

Yet another motive for Protestant religious drama, the desire to encounter scripture, participate in it, and turn its words into works, is demonstrated by the career and virtual martyrdom of Coventry's most famous player, John Careless. As Careless scripts his own martyrdom in letters to fellow prisoners, he echoes the language of the Coventry pageants and patterns his actions after the plays' objects of persecution and figures of hope.

---

133. Helen Cooper, "Shakespeare and the Mystery Plays," in *Shakespeare and Elizabethan Popular Culture: Arden Critical Companion*, ed. Stuart Gillespie and Neil Rhodes (London: Arden Shakespeare, 2006), 19; on the peculiarity of a play that "*acted its action*," see Cooper, *Shakespeare and the Medieval World* (London: Methuen Drama, 2010), 48–51.

134. Paul Whitfield White, "Reforming Mysteries' End: A New Look at Protestant Intervention in English Provincial Drama," *Journal of Medieval and Early Modern Studies* 29, no. 1 (1999): 122.

135. Jennifer Waldron, *Reformations of the Body: Idolatry, Sacrifice, and Early Modern Theater* (New York: Palgrave Macmillan, 2013), 11.

Careless was arrested with three other men for "lewd and sediciouse behaviour" on All Hallows Day, 1553, a charge that anticipates Mary's injunction two years later that would ban "playing of Enterludes . . . concerning doctrine in matters now in question."[136] Imprisoned for two years, first in Coventry and then in the King's Bench in London, Careless corresponded with a network of hot reformers, many of whom awaited trial or execution. Careless's personality and evangelical disposition emerge from his twenty-two letters and his own account of his deposition, copies of which must have been smuggled out of prison and delivered into the hands of John Foxe for inclusion in his *Actes and Monuments*. As White has noted, Careless complicates "our stereotypical image of an early Protestant martyr," combining "deeply felt Protestant piety . . . with an evident commitment to playing."[137] While in the Coventry jail, Careless "was there in such credite with his keeper, þat vpon his worde he was let out to play in the Pageant about the City with other his companions. And that done, keeping touch with his keeper, he returned agayne into prison at his houre appointed."[138] Given that he had no way to prepare for that year's Corpus Christi play, Careless must have been a seasoned performer.[139] Because he likely did not perform with his own guild, the Weavers—his name appears nowhere in their thorough, well-preserved records—he must have been valued for his theatrical acumen, not just for fraternal bonds.[140]

---

136. R. W. Ingram, ed., *Records of Early English Drama: Coventry* (Toronto: University of Toronto Press, 1981), 569; John Foxe, *The Unabridged Acts and Monuments Online* (Sheffield: HRI Online Publications, 2011) (1583), 1408, http://www.johnfoxe.org.

137. P. White, "Reforming Mysteries' End," 123.

138. Foxe, *Actes and Monuments* (1583), 1944.

139. Careless had already been moved to London before this performance, and so must have been returned to Coventry jail at a certain point prior. See Ian Lancashire, ed., *Dramatic Texts and Records of Britain: A Chronological Topography to 1558* (Toronto: University of Toronto Press, 1984), 119; P. White, "Reforming Mysteries' End," 141n2.

140. Ingram, *Records of Early English Drama: Coventry*, 562–63.

Beyond a penchant for theatrical imagery, which other critics have remarked,[141] Careless's letters suggest that he was deeply formed by the devotional language and dispositions of his native city's traditional religious drama. The two extant pageants of the Coventry cycle—treating the nativity, massacre of the innocents, the presentation of the child Jesus at the Temple, and the boy's examination by the doctors of the Temple—deal with persecution, faithful witness, and mutual comfort, themes of special interest to the imprisoned Careless. As Ritchie Kendall has argued, radical Protestants frequently modeled their own trials and sufferings on those of Christ.[142] Careless also imitates Christ, but the model for his imitation is as much the Christ of the Coventry pageants as he is the Christ of the Gospels. Before the King's Bench, Careless claims direct inspiration by the Holy Spirit, like the Coventry boy Jesus before the doctors at the Temple, but unlike the biblical Christ.[143] Careless's intimate forms of address to his correspondents—"Ah my deare hart and most louing brother" (1945); "My most sweet and loving brethren" (1947); "Ah mine owne hartes" (1948); "O my deare and faithfull sister" (1949)—echo the language of mutual comfort used by Anna and Simeon as they prepare for imminent death and hope for news of the promised Messiah. "O feythefull frynde and louer dere," Simeon addresses Anna, relating to her the prophecies whose hope they nourish together (231). Anna asks her "olde frynde in God" to pray for her, and Simeon's exhortation to pray without ceasing (256–57, 270–76) re-

---

141. P. White, "Reforming Mysteries' End"; Ingram, *Records of Early English Drama: Coventry*, 569.

142. Ritchie D. Kendall, *The Drama of Dissent: The Radical Poetics of Nonconformity, 1380–1590* (Chapel Hill: University of North Carolina Press, 1986).

143. Foxe, *Actes and Monuments* (1583), 1944. The boy Jesus before the doctors at the Temple likewise deflects facetious barbs with an extrabiblical claim to divine inspiration: "Syris, the Whoole Goste in me hath lyght / Thatt my powar ys to preyche, / And of the Godhed most of myght, / Most perfettly here ma I teche." "The Weavers' Pageant," in Pamela M. King and Clifford Davidson, eds., *The Coventry Corpus Christi Plays* (Kalamazoo, MI: Medieval Institute Publications, 2000), ll. 911–14. Hereafter cited in the text by line number.

sounds in Careless's valedictory refrain, "pray, pray, pray" (1946, 1948–50, 1955, 1957). Simeon's call to prayer, says Anna, "Inwardely gladyth me in my hart" (260). These mutual admonitions comfort both friends in holiness and sustain their hope. Careless extends and receives similar forms of comfort. To his wife Careless writes, "it reioyceth my poore hart to heare . . . that you do oftentimes vse to repeate this godly saying: The Lordes wil be fulfilled" (1946). Simeon, speaking in the presence of his "Fryndis" (270), makes a similar act of resignation: "But asse thow wolt, Lorde, all thyng mvst be" (285). Careless could plausibly have derived these ideas from the Bible, but the expressions themselves share an intimate vernacular form of address with the Coventry pageants. Careless also shares with the pageants an important, and by no means intuitive, inclination to situate prayer and reliance on providence in a community of friends of God who nurture each other's faith in times of trial.

Comfort and mutual prayer function in the Coventry pageants and for Careless's community as means of historical memory, intergenerational continuity, and interpretation of events. This is consistent with the role of prophecy in the Bible. "Comfort ye, comfort ye, my people," declares Isaiah as he interprets Israel's sufferings in light of God's promises and plans for the future (Isa. 40:1, Geneva Bible 1599). "I cum," says Isaiah in the Shearmen and Taylors pageant, "to comforde eyuere creature off birthe, / For I . . . hathe fownde / Many swete matters whereof we ma make myrthe" (15–18). "Profeta" characters in both Coventry pageants function as transitional figures, recalling in the present the prophecies of Isaiah and others and anticipating their imminent fulfillment. In addition to the characters so named, Simeon and Anna are prophetic figures whose lives barely stretch to span the Old and New Testaments. And the shepherds, who in other cycles are the grateful recipients of angels' tidings, here discern the meaning of the Star of Bethlehem before the angels can announce Christ's birth.[144] In the Coventry

---

144. Lines 229–36. York's is the only other extant English nativity in which the shepherds have an inkling of the nativity before the angels' announcement.

pageants, prophetic comfort is the practice by which characters recognize their own historicity and endow their community with historical continuity, and mirth is the attendant affect.

The scene transitions between these prophetic figures are marked by song, a communal expression of the mirth that the Coventry Isaiah wants his comfortable prophecies to make. The characters in Coventry's dramatic Bible comfort each other with songs that create community not only among individuals but also across historical periods. The shepherds exchange songs of "myrth and solas" with the angels, to whose Latinate *Gloria* they respond with their vernacular "Ase I Owte Rodde" (254, 263a). Their mingled strains reach an anxious Joseph, waiting outside the birthing room, as it were. "Now, Lorde, this noise þat I do here / With this grett solemnete, / Gretly amendid hath my chere. I trust hy nevis shortly wol be" (264–67). And immediately the comforting news arrives that the "Kyng of blys" has been born (269). Hailing the mother and child, the first shepherd presents as his gift "my pype . . . Thow schallt yt haue to make the myrthe" (297). The shepherds then sing again before they exit, passing two prophets who echo their "novellis, novellis" upon entry (313)—the tune to which Mary, or a cleverly rigged baby Jesus, could continue to play on the pipe the shepherds left behind. The scene transitions accompanied by singing are then broken up by the appearance of Herod and the new plot of the massacre of the innocents. But song returns as the holy family flees to Egypt and the mothers of Jerusalem come in, singing lullabies to the children who will suffer the death meant for Christ. The stage directions call for an overlap, so that the mothers come on singing before Mary and Joseph depart with Jesus. Their lullaby, the famous Coventry carol, "Lully lulla, þow littell tine child," recorded at the end of the manuscript, seems to join with the angels' and shepherds' songs of praise to Jesus, but then the women are left alone with their own babies whom, they sing, "Herod the king, in his raging," has ordered slain (8).[145] In the Weavers' pageant, too, singing marks the transitions between scenes of prophecy and fulfillment. This

---

145. King and Davidson, eds., *The Coventry Corpus Christi Plays*, 110–11.

pageant invites audience participation to maintain continuity between scenes. When Simeon goes up to the temple just before the scene of the annunciation, he tells his clerks to "syng then with me that conyng hasse," a phrase that invites the audience to join in if they know the song (362).[146] Later Simeon and his clerks sing as they process to meet Mary and Joseph (633), and at the end of the scene they all together sing an "anthem" of praise before the altar (799). All of these musical scene transitions, explicitly associated with "myrth" and "comfort," establish communication between generations and across the periodizing division of promise and fulfillment.

This intergenerational and period-crossing communication is an important concern of Careless and his fellows, who intend their own martyrdoms to communicate the Gospel to younger generations and happier times. Careless uses song in his letters to foster unity among isolated prisoners and persecuted brethren and to comfort them by the musical intimation of future glory. He alternates between invoking song in an eschatological sense and bringing it into the daily intercourse of prayer and literary correspondence as a figure of proleptic comfort. Answering John Philpot's "comfortable letter," Careless writes that he "wil now with Gods grace sing Psalmes of prayse and thankesgeuing with you. . . . O that I were with you in body, as presently I am in spirit, that I might sing all care away in Christ: for nowe the time of comforte is

---

146. The invitation reflects what Richard Rastall, in his major study of the intersection of musical and dramatic cultures, has described as "a general context of audience participation and interaction in late medieval drama," in which "an audience . . . could be expected to be able to fulfill a number of functions as a sort of unwritten cast." Richard Rastall, *The Heaven Singing*, vol. 1 of *Music in Early English Religious Drama* (Cambridge: D. S. Brewer, 1996), 376. In the present context, Rastall notes that Simeon and his clerks sing the song assigned to them much later (at 633), so the song here must be sung by others. The general appeal of this internal stage direction suggests that all present would take up the song. Richard Rastall, *Minstrels Playing*, vol. 2 of *Music in Early English Religious Drama* (Cambridge: D. S. Brewer, 2001), 188. For examples of audience participation in the singing of liturgical hymns in other plays, see Rastall, *The Heaven Singing*, 373–78.

come."[147] Careless anticipates the comfort of heaven where he and Philpot will be able to sing together, body and spirit. The Psalms they sing together now in spirit bridge the gap of martyrdom, joining this age to the next. Careless consoles his wife with a similar image of heavenly harmony, enjoining her to rejoice that God is taking him "into his celestiall kingdom," where he "will shortlye bring you and your deare children thither to me, that we maye moste ioyfully together sing prayses vnto his glorious name for euer."[148]

By singing God's praises now in the midst of tribulation, Careless and his persecuted brothers and sisters can also participate in biblical history, and indeed in the invention of scripture. Careless urges "brother T. V." to put himself in the role of David, the inventor of holy song, who

> was even in the same case that you are now in: but he still comforted himselfe with the sweet promises of God. . . . Oh . . . that you might say with Dauid: Awake my glory, awake Lute and Harpe, bring forth the Psalter with the merry song, that I might sing a newe song of prayse and thankesgeuing vnto the Lord.[149]

Careless himself invented "merry songs" to comfort the persecuted. He likely wrote a popular conversion narrative in ballad form that lent its "tune of John Carelesse" to other ballads.[150] For Agnes Glasscock, who

---

147. Foxe, *Actes and Monuments* (1583), 1945.

148. Ibid., 1946.

149. Ibid., 1950.

150. On the tune, see Hyder Edward Rollins, ed., *Old English Ballads, 1553–1625* (Cambridge: Cambridge University Press, 1920), 46. The ballad, which survives in London, British Library, Sloane MS 1896, fols. 6r–6v, probably circulated in broadside. Its first extant printing is Miles Coverdale, ed., *Certain Most Godly, Fruitful, and Comfortable Letters of Such True Saintes and Holy Martyrs of God, as in the Late Bloodye Persecution Here within This Realme, Gaue Their Lyues for the Defence of Christes Holy Gospel Written in the Tyme of Their Affliction and Cruell Imprysonment*, Early English Books Online, 1475–1640 / 217:02 (London: Iohn Day, 1564), 634–38. Coverdale attributes the ballad to Careless and includes it with Careless's letters and two other lyrics of consolation not printed by Foxe.

wavered between her reformed faith and outward conformity to the restored Roman Mass, he composed a lyric that he inscribed in a book of
hers when she visited him in prison: "My sister deare, God geue you
grace / With stedfast faith in Christes name: / His Gospell still for to
embrace, / And liue according to the same."[151] These simple verses en-
capsulate the tropological impulse to live according to the Gospel that
motivates Careless's singing, letter writing, and firm resolve to undergo
martyrdom.

These songs that circulated first privately and then publicly forged
a spiritual communion among individuals and generations. Careless
understands their actual and figurative songs of prayer for each other to
foster mutual participation in each others' trials, which participate in
Christ's own sufferings. "O howe happy are we then," Careless writes to
"sister E. K.,"

if God of hys goodnesse appoint vs to pay natures dette wyth suff-
eryng for hys trueth and Gospels sake, and so making vs his faithfull witnesses wyth Prophetes, Apostles, Martyrs, and Confessours,
yea wyth his dearely beloued sonne Iesus Christe, to whome he
doeth heere begin to fashion vs lyke in suffering, that we myght be
like hym also in glory.[152]

The important function played by song in Careless's sense of mutual
participation can certainly be ascribed in part to what Hannibal Hamlin
has called "Psalm culture."[153] But Careless's careful use of song to give
comfort, excite mirth, and bridge the gaps between people and ages
places it in close relationship to Coventry biblical drama as well.

Careless repeatedly draws on dramatic analogies to identify how
members of his community participate in Christ's suffering. He praises
M. Greene, prisoner in Newgate, "Oh happy Peter, whose part thou hast

---

151. Foxe, *Actes and Monuments* (1583), 1956.
152. Ibid., 1955.
153. Hannibal Hamlin, *Psalm Culture and Early Modern English Literature* (New York: Cambridge University Press, 2004).

wel played: therefore thy reward and portion shall be like unto his."[154] Other prisoners in Newgate he writes into the parable of the wise virgins:

> Praised be God for you mine own sweet sisters, which hath made you to play such wise virgins parts. He hath plentifully poured the oyle of his spirite into the lampes of your faythe, so that the light thereof shall neuer be extinct. You shal enter with your bridegrome into euerlasting ioy, wherunto you were chosen in him from the beginning.[155]

He may have these women in mind when he exhorts his wife, "Take heede, Margaret, and play the wise womans part. You haue warning by other, if you will take an example."[156] Careless commends biblical behavior, but his Bible in these cases is a dramatic Bible played out by a local community. He goes so far as to script this local biblical drama himself, writing lines for Harry Adlington—"a simple man"—to use when he comes before the tribunal. He even gives delivery instructions, with audience effect in mind: "This kinde of aunswere will cut their combes moste, and edifie the people that stand by, so that the same bee done coldly with sobrietie, meekenes, and patience."[157]

As these examples suggest, Careless was a master of dramatic material and techniques, particularly the techniques of traditional participatory biblical drama. But when such techniques give shape to theological expression, they yield a participatory theology as well. While Careless in the conversion ballad, "Some men for sodayne ioye do weep," sketches a dialectic of law and gospel, his letters imagine the persecuted attaining glory through their participation in Christ's sufferings. God "doeth heere begin to fashion vs lyke in suffering [to Christ], that we myght be like hym also in glory."[158] Careless is too skillful a drama-

---

154. Foxe, *Actes and Monuments* (1583), 1949.
155. Ibid.
156. Ibid., 1946.
157. Ibid., 1952–53.
158. Ibid., 1955.

tist to have fallen accidentally into a participatory soteriology. And he is too cautious about Roman claims regarding the participatory sacrifice of the Mass to subscribe naively to an outmoded theology. In fact, Careless's anxiety about the Mass has nothing in common with other Protestant dismissals of it as vain, theatrical "juggling."[159] Quite to the contrary, the Mass is the theater of apocalyptic history. It makes the devil himself present in a dramatic mode, and to participate in it is to commune with the damned. "Drinke not of the whore of Babylons cuppe by no meanes, for it will infecte the body, and poyson the soule. Be not partakers of her sinnes (sayth the Aungell) least you be partakers of the plagues that shortly shall be powred vppon her."[160] Catholic participatory soteriology is all too real, yet inverted. Careless devoutly believes in the dramatic nature of salvation and in sacramental drama. But the medium of participation must be scripture, not Eucharist, and it is possible to participate in scripture because it is essentially dramatic. Careless does not begin with the notion of scripture as a textual object and then draw an analogy to drama that then generates an oddly participatory reformed soteriology. Rather, formed from a young age by Coventry's biblical drama, his Protestant conversion (involving as it must a new reverence for scripture as the privileged locus of Christ's presence) entailed a turn from Mass to Bible, which meant a turn from sacrament to *drama*—not from sacrament to textual object. Despite this theological revolution, he conserved what must have been his most fundamental theological intuition: a tropological understanding of human action participating in the drama of salvation as revealed in the Bible. Having dropped out of the sacramental economy, dramatic tropology sustained his faith unto a soft martyrdom—death in prison, and burial "on a dungehill."[161]

In the previous chapter I posed the question of tropology's fate after the sacramental system had gone into eclipse. This chapter has explored

---

159. Tamara Atkin, *The Drama of Reform: Theology and Theatricality, 1461–1553* (Turnhout: Brepols, 2013), 146–47.

160. Foxe, *Actes and Monuments* (1583), 1955.

161. Coverdale, *Certain Most Godly . . . Letters*, 560.

a number of different fates. Most of the Protestants studied here, with the exceptions of Tyndale, Morison, and Careless, affirmed a fairly robust sacramental economy, even if they rejected Catholic understandings of penance. But because they magnified the roles of scripture and faith in the Christian life, they were not compelled to relate tropological invention directly to the sacramental economy. Whereas Langland felt obliged to apologize for his tropological writing by fashioning it as a work of mercy in a life of open-ended penitential satisfaction, Protestant writers did not bear the same burden of connecting their tropological inventions with the sacraments. Far more important was their participation in the world of scripture, or in the providential history playing out in the present day. Of all the Protestant practices of tropological invention surveyed here, Careless's comes closest to the Langlandian sense of crucicentric invention. Aware that God is making him Christlike through his sufferings, Careless anticipates "that we myght be like hym also in glory."[162] Like Langland, Careless believes in the patristic dictum "God became man that man might become God."[163] Careless bypasses the penitential system with a direct grasp after martyrdom. In so doing, he reminds us that the sacramental economy is not the final dispensation of humanity's participation in God, and suggests that medieval tropological making could be soteriologically participatory outside the sacramental system.

The next and final chapter entertains sacramental and nonsacramental versions of tropological participation at the same time—or rather in two concurrent temporalities. It imagines the final performances of the York Play in a Protestant age, produced and appreciated by people like Careless—or Bucer, Calvin, and Luther.

---

162. Foxe, *Actes and Monuments* (1583), 1955.
163. See chapter 4, section "Alliterative Chiasmus and Langland's Theology of the Cross."

6

Mirror of Scripture

Ethics and Anagogy in the York Doomsday Pageant

So far in this book tropology has been understood to involve actions of the human will. The assumption has been that the human can take the initiative to participate in the divine life (which nevertheless comes first in the order of grace). This final chapter reverses the initiative to consider tropology from the direction of anagogy, from the end of this world's history, and from the perspective of the judicial gaze of Christ the King. Here the action, the initiative, the will, is all God's. This is also the realm of what Protestant reformers would call passive righteousness. Seen from Judgment Day—the end of ethics—tropological participation looks different. Individual agents do not step into the stream of salvation history so much as they are swept up in it: the good souls in Jesus' parable of Judgment Day (Matt. 25) are not aware that they have intimately cared for Christ, who was present to them in the poor and needy whom they helped. Christ took the initiative and came to them; they responded well. This anagogical approach to ethical participation in salvation history exerts a salutary counter-pressure on tropological invention, keeping it from devolving into what Protestants would call works-righteousness. Entertaining a Protestant skepticism about good works and human initiative, this chapter speculatively probes the limits of tropological participation in the Doomsday pageant of the York Play, a participatory biblical drama that occupied multiple positions relative to the sacramental economy and communal ethical practices over the two centuries of its performance. This reversal of perspective opens a critical space to reconsider how the play's mode of participatory theater—commonly understood to consummate the Eucharist in tropological acts of communal justice—rebuffs individuals' and guilds' claims to possess the body of Christ through works of charity.

In the Middle Ages, drama and the liturgy of the Mass shared powerful experiential elements, prompting theologians to draw an analogy between the two kinds of performance. For Honorius of Autun, writing around 1100, the priest reciting the canon of the Mass is like an actor representing "in the theatre of the church the conflict of Christ" and his victory over death.[1] Reversing the analogy, Sarah Beckwith identifies the body of Christ in the community that participated in York's Corpus Christi play, the "sacramental theater" that rendered Christ present in acts of mutual recognition.[2] In this reading, the sensible experience of Corpus Christi theater compensates for the scandal of the doctrine of transubstantiation. Christ's sensible absence in the Eucharist's simple meal of bread, wine, and friendship has tempted the ecclesiastical authorities to overcompensate by enforcing a superstructure of rickety doctrinal conceits. To twist a line from Thomas Aquinas's Eucharistic hymn *Pange lingua*, where the senses fail, the hierarchy supplies rationalist doctrines, on pain of death. Not so the sacramental theater of York, which employs the senses of the audience and bodies of the actors to confect the very body of Christ, the *corpus verum*, in a social body ordered to justice. The York cycle therefore exposes the hierarchy's will

---

1. Honorius of Autun, *Gemma animae*, in Karl Young, *The Drama of the Medieval Church* (Oxford: Clarendon Press, 1933), 1:83; for an extended discussion of Honorius, see O. B. Hardison, *Christian Rite and Christian Drama in the Middle Ages: Essays in the Origin and Early History of Modern Drama* (Baltimore: Johns Hopkins University Press, 1965), 35–79.

2. Most influentially, Sarah Beckwith, *Signifying God: Social Relation and Symbolic Act in the York Corpus Christi Plays* (Chicago: University of Chicago Press, 2003).

to power and essential negativity. It denies the institutional church's pretensions to secular power in its putatively most sacred domain, the Eucharist. Meanwhile, the *saeculum* of the laity and of their labors emerges as the true domain of the incarnate and salvific God. The chief mode of participation in this God's life therefore migrates from Eucharist to tropology, to the invention of justice and charity out of habits of participation in enacted biblical history. Like Max Weber's Protestant theology of labor, the York Play both critiques and sacralizes the labors of the city and its lay investments. Its critique has been appreciated by the less theological line of criticism that sees York's civic theater as triumphantly lay, secular, and trade-centered.[3]

However, Beckwith's argument also demonstrates the limitations of the Weberian hypothesis that Christ is most authentically present in the *saeculum* if we extend it to the final pageant of the cycle, Doomsday, which shatters the image of social ethics on which York's sacramental and civic theater depends. For if other pageants had questioned the mandate of the ecclesiastically licensed Eucharist, the Doomsday pageant interrogates the social body's capacity to make Christ present. Here—removed by some eighteen hours and forty-six episodes from the Fall of the Angels that rolled into the streets of York before dawn—Christ invites his apostles to sit down with him and watch a play. The action: the Last Judgment. The characters: all souls. The scene: York's Pavement, a large plaza that served as both market square and site of public assizes and executions, bordered on one side by the jail and butcheries and on the other by All Saints Pavement church, in whose

---

3. Martin Stevens, *Four Middle English Mystery Cycles: Textual, Contextual, and Critical Interpretations* (Princeton: Princeton University Press, 1987), 17–87; Lawrence M. Clopper, *Drama, Play, and Game: English Festive Culture in the Medieval and Early Modern Period* (Chicago: University of Chicago Press, 2001), 155–59; Ruth Nisse, *Defining Acts: Drama and the Politics of Interpretation in Late Medieval England* (Notre Dame, IN: University of Notre Dame Press, 2005), 23–74; Kate Crassons, *The Claims of Poverty: Literature, Culture, and Ideology in Late Medieval England* (Notre Dame, IN: University of Notre Dame Press, 2010), 221–73.

cemetery rested many venerable mayors and burgesses of old.[4] The *dramatis personae*: the once dead and now resurrected good souls and evil souls who must be sorted and sent to their respective dooms. But the Nicene Creed specifies that Christ will come to judge *the living* and the dead. Where are the living? They are on the Pavement, too. They are sometimes referred to as the audience. This pageant will call that designation into question. For Christ has ascended his judgment seat to watch and take part in the play of Doomsday, and all souls, quick and dead, must play their parts.

And so the York Doomsday reverses the theatrical perspective of the play, as many critics have noted.[5] Less noticed has been the play's own theorization of the optics and performance dynamics involved in this reversal, specifically in its deft deployment of mirror topoi informed by the fourteenth-century discourse of moralized optics. According to this discourse, the drama is a mirror of scripture, while scripture is a mirror of goodness. And Christ, as he proclaims in the Baptism pageant of the York Play, is a mirror for humanity by virtue of his incarnation.[6] When Christ himself becomes the mirror, humans are

---

4. On the sites and customs of public execution and pillory on the Pavement, see Angelo Raine, *Mediaeval York: A Topographical Survey Based on Original Sources* (London: J. Murray, 1955), 178–79.

5. An early inspiration of this chapter was Ralph Hanna's observation about "the redefinition of what the stage is at *The Play*'s end, when the performance goes defiantly metatheatrical." Hanna notes that Christ in the Ascension gets lifted into the clouds beyond any stage area, and the pageant wagon in the Assumption becomes "some heavenly anteroom." "Such transpositions establish the final reversal of The Doom: the audience, who has gazed, becomes the object gazed upon—by divinity. The action, . . . the acts of communal charity, is going to get played in the street, as unconscious acts of daily life. Insofar as audience remains audience, it is in this instruction and in their reciprocal view of the wounds, the fleshly penitent medium." Ralph Hanna III, "York and Yorkshire," in *Europe: A Literary History, 1348–1415*, ed. David Wallace (New York: Oxford University Press, forthcoming). I am grateful to Prof. Hanna for sharing a draft of his article before publication.

6. "And sithen myselffe haue taken mankynde, / For men schall me þer myrroure make / And haue my doyng in ther mynde, / Also I do þe baptyme take." Richard Beadle, ed., *The York Plays: The Text*, vol. 1 of 2 vols., EETS, s.s., 23 (Oxford: Oxford University Press, 2009), 21.92–95.

no longer simply in the role of viewer. If the mirror is a person who also sees, then the act of seeing, and not just the object of sight, can be reversed. This reversal of perspective, enacted when Christ mounts the seat of judgment to watch and enact the ultimate drama of salvation, also animates late medieval Eucharistic devotion, of which the York Play is perhaps the most elaborate expression. On Judgment Day God's vision will damn and save, yet the Doomsday pageant occurs on the Eucharistic feast of Corpus Christi, blending the finality of the Last Day with the Mass's repetitive participation in salvation—a repetition that will come to an end in heaven when Christ's immediate presence supersedes and obviates the Eucharist. The Doomsday pageant deploys the figure of the mirror in the Last Judgment to invite an eschatological counter-vision into Eucharistic life. The Eucharist then becomes an eschatological mirror, both the origin of God's counter-vision, and the means by which the faithful can be found to bear the image of Christ.

Because the York Play is "sacramental theater," the Doomsday pageant's theatrical reversal also enacts the more radical phenomenological reversal that takes place in the Eucharist—at least, according to those orthodox theologies of transubstantiation commonly thought to be inimical to the York Play's more demotic modes of distributed divine presence. When God is both the producer and audience of the play, then the experience of community and sacrament is most authentically what Jean-Luc Marion calls counter-experience. To act is to be acted; to observe is to be observed; to judge is to be judged. I enlist the discourse of phenomenology because of its importance to the history of the emotions and the affective turn in medieval and early modern drama criticism. The medieval dramatic, theological, and optical texts discussed here point to a limitation in drama studies that remain focused on experience, and the recent religious turn in phenomenology helps to explain, within a discourse perhaps more relevant to contemporary performance studies, how medieval and early modern performance can function beyond experience.

The Doomsday Christ's counter-vision points to a dimension of Eucharistic doctrine and devotion that precedes experience, whether affective or intellectual. The pageant's eschatology, manifest in its mirror inversion of theatrical optics, bears out Jean-Yves Lacoste's astute observation that "Man can encounter God, exist in the presence of God [*coram Deo*] without requiring him to grant us the fruition of his presence. The affective experience of God therefore loses all right to verify or falsify the relation between man and God."[7] While the York Doomsday acknowledges and productively enlists affective experience to achieve its effects, it reconfigures the liturgy of Corpus Christi in eschatological perspective and renders experience just one aspect of Christ's sacramental presence. The other aspect is Eucharistic counter-experience, which originates in the mystical presence of the body of Christ uncircumscribed in the Eucharistic host.

While the York Play challenges a narrowly idolatrous dogma of the Eucharist that would limit God's presence to the host, the Doomsday pageant also places God's *other* body, the community of the faithful, under scrutiny, questioning its ability to bear the presence of Christ. The Doomsday pageant thus negates both social and sacramental modes of Eucharistic hegemony. It negates the experience of Christ's body in the host *and* in the community in order to affirm God's presence in both, suspending sacrament and society before the gaze of a God who sees all from its end. In this joining of experience and counter-experience, of communal devotion and the spectating *corpus Christi*, the Doomsday pageant dissolves the dichotomy between Eucharistic host and Eucharistic community—without resolving the salutary tension that Beckwith and others have perceived. Our dominant critical model of "sacramental theater" as a corrective to hegemonic ecclesiastical sacraments has yet to grapple with the Doomsday pageant's scrutiny of theatrical and communal experience.

This mirror reversal does not allow virtue—whether individual or communal—to be the final horizon of ethics. The Doomsday mirror dilates ethics by resituating the practices of charity within the horizon of salvation history. Moreover, it refuses tropological invention the status of exclusive and sufficient means of participation in salvation history. The Doomsday pageant's Eucharistic, eschatological mirror therefore rebuffs Edwardian participatory tropology and its confident identifica-

---

7. Jean-Yves Lacoste, *Experience and the Absolute: Disputed Questions on the Humanity of Man*, trans. Mark Raftery-Skehan (New York: Fordham University Press, 2004), 191.

tion of present historical action with biblical narrative. The Eucharist's anagogical counter-vision conflicts with Nicholas Udall's tropology in an apocalyptic key.[8] Yet this conflict does not play out along inevitable Catholic/Protestant battle lines. In fact, as I argue near the end of this chapter, certain Protestant theologies of justification make this reading of the Doomsday pageant more readily visible, effectively revealing the York Play's most trenchant confrontation with traditional tropology in the years when it fell under the suspicion of the Protestant elite.

In what follows, I challenge the dominant model of "sacramental theater," elaborating how the pageant manipulates ethics and ethical interpretation by way of Eucharistic counter-experience. The phenomenological analysis I pursue responds to the York Play's attention to mirroring. Playing with the practices of seeing and being seen, the Doomsday pageant takes advantage of the convergence in the fourteenth century of four disparate discourses and practices: drama, ethics, exegesis, and optics. These fields converge in the important late medieval figures of mirrors and mirroring, figures the York Play deploys with remarkable cunning.

First, I will examine the relationship between the Eucharist and the Last Judgment in order to describe the kinds of theological and sacramental work that the pageant proposes to accomplish. Next, I will address two important aspects of tropology in the York Play—temporality and biblical exemplarity—and show how the play deploys mirror figures and the optics of seeing and being seen to manipulate tropology. I will contextualize these mirror figures by comparing a fifteenth-century French play, *Mystère de la Passion* by Arnoul Gréban, and the tradition of moralized optics as a tool of biblical exegesis and ethical formation. Those discourses' unique phenomenology of vision prompts an engagement with Marion's theory of counter-experience, which captures the dynamics of these related practices. Finally, I will sketch three conflicting options for performing and interpreting the pageant in light of its mirror optics, with each reading inflected by a different theology of salvation and ethics. The first reading considers how the soteriology of

---

8. See chapter 5, section "Erasmus and Udall: Vernacular Tropology."

the magisterial Reformation might have resonated with the pageant's emphasis on the primacy of God's vision. The second reading develops research on the economics of the York Play and guild charity to argue that the Mercers produced the Doomsday pageant in order to consolidate their control over the social body of Christ by means of their charitable activities. In the third reading, I compare the Mercers' hypothetical hegemony over the body of Christ to the dominant critical view that the play critiques and displaces the ecclesiastical hierarchy's hegemony over the Eucharistic body of Christ. Refracted through Protestant theology, the play challenges works-based soteriology. By holding the tension between tropological and anagogical modes of reading the Last Judgment, the play refuses a "Protestant" collapse of anagogy into apocalyptic (such as Ochino's play for Edward VI) as well as a "Catholic" collapse of tropology into the social gospel.

Eucharist and Last Judgment

In the Doomsday pageant, the Eucharistic occasion of the York Play comes to the fore. Like several other pageants (e.g., the Crucifixion and Resurrection), the Doomsday pageant is markedly paraliturgical, depending on and participating in oblique ways in the liturgy of the Mass and other liturgies of veneration of Christ's body associated with the feast of Corpus Christi and the maintenance of York's civic cult. In this case, the pageant elicits a complex theology linking Eucharist to Last Judgment.

As Beckwith has argued, the York Play's "sacramental theater" relied on a structure of signification akin to the one that underwrote premodern understandings of the sacraments. On analogy to the way that "the sacraments as signs participate in the reality that they signify and are not 'mere signs,'" illusion and actuality cohered in the York Play, such that the play achieved that participatory union of signifier and signified that theology understood to occur in the Eucharist.[9] As Pamela King

---

9. Beckwith, *Signifying God*, 61. The clearest example of this is how the church community that constitutes the mystical body of Christ collaborated to

points out, the play often models itself on forms of lay participation in the Mass and uses familiarity with those forms to assert its relationship to the Feast of Corpus Christi as another faithful representation of Christ's body and as a devotional aid.[10]

The York Play repeatedly calls attention to this relationship when it adopts the form of vernacular levation prayers. These pious ejaculations that laypeople were encouraged to say at the elevation of the host are punctuated by greetings—usually "Hayle"—and epideictic apostrophes, such as Mary's speech upon giving birth to Jesus: "Hayle, my lord god, hayle prince of pees, / Hayle my fadir, and hayle my sone" (14.57–58).[11] The first human responses to God in the Doomsday pageant read like levation prayers, praising God and bidding mercy on their sins, protection from the fiend, and grace to "wonne [dwell] in paradise" (47.97–112; 104).[12] King reads the Doomsday pageant as "an enacted Host miracle: *corpus Christi* does descend among the people. . . . His transportation of the wounded body to earth, familiar from the Mass of St. Gregory and other Host miracles, reciprocates the reuniting of bodies and souls of the saved and damned, but also enacts for all time and from

---

represent Christ's body on the stage. In order for the York Play to successfully present Christ's one body in a full cycle, approximately twenty-four actors had to play the part. Playing Christ's body was a corporate activity. Beckwith contrasts this communal confection of Christ's body with the ecclesiastical hierarchy's exclusive claims to control the body of Christ in the Eucharistic host confected by a hegemonic priesthood. The York Play, then, relates to the Mass by subverting its claims to Christ's presence and providing an alternative mode of real presence.

10. Pamela M. King, *The York Mystery Cycle and the Worship of the City* (Cambridge: D. S. Brewer, 2006), 20.

11. Ibid., 19–29.

12. For a representative selection of levation prayers, see Rossell Hope Robbins, "Levation Prayers in Middle English Verse," *Modern Philology* 40, no. 2 (November 1, 1942): 131–46. King does not recognize the addresses to God in the Doomsday pageant as levation prayers, perhaps because they do not include the characteristic "Hayle" greetings. However, Robbins's specimens of levation prayers do not all include "Hayle" greetings, although they do all perform at least some of the Doomsday pageant's souls' acts of praise and petition. It is therefore reasonable to consider the souls' acclamations as levation prayers.

a heavenly perspective, the moment of consecration of the Host, when Christ comes among his people."[13]

The demonstratively Eucharistic character of Christ's second coming in the pageant entails an important theological teaching about the Eucharist itself. Just as the Doomsday pageant can be said to enact the Eucharistic consecration, the Eucharist enacts judgment. While the Eucharist was understood to confer great benefits on those in a state of grace, the Apostle Paul's admonition to "unworthy" Corinthians testified to its power to curse as well as to bless: "For he that eateth and drinketh unworthily eateth and drinketh judgment to himself, not discerning the body of the Lord" (1 Cor. 11:29). The judgment Paul speaks of was often associated in patristic and medieval theology with the Last Judgment. The *Glossa ordinaria* places Paul's discussion of Eucharist and judgment in an eschatological context. Citing Augustine via Bede, it encourages would-be communicants to set up a court in the privacy of their minds to adjudicate and correct their own behavior now so that later, when they receive the Eucharist, they will not be judged unworthy by God. If a man should determine that he is indeed unworthy, he should refrain from the Eucharist and, "while others approach the altar of God, where he cannot go, let him revolve the image of the future judgment before his eyes, and think how worthy of trembling is that punishment wherein, while some are taking possession of eternal life, the rest are cast down into eternal death."[14] If the York Doomsday is a host miracle, then it is also the kind of waking nightmare that Augustine urged the mortal sinner to imagine during the Mass.

Meditation on the Doomsday in connection with the Eucharist was hardly just a pious accretion. As theologian Geoffrey Wainwright has observed, Paul's Eucharistic theology expresses deep structures of

---

13. P. King, *The York Mystery Cycle and the Worship of the City*, 27–28.

14. *Biblia latina cum Glossa ordinaria*, 6:298–99. The gloss here cites Bede citing Augustine's "Liber de poenitentia"—Augustine's sermons 351 and 352, which often circulated together. See Michael Lapidge, "Booklists from Anglo-Saxon England," in *Learning and Literature in Anglo-Saxon England*, ed. Michael Lapidge and Helmut Gneuss (Cambridge: Cambridge University Press, 1985), 79n19. Cf. Augustine, Sermon 351, PL 39:1542–43.

Christian soteriology and temporality: "The Eucharist is a repeated projection of the last judgment which each time partly fulfills, and therefore strengthens, the promise of judgment and pardon which we received in hope in our baptism. . . . [A]lready the Lord comes in judgment at every Eucharist."[15] Perhaps the most ambitious meditation on Eucharistic eschatology is Michelangelo's *Last Judgment* fresco in the Sistine Chapel (1536–41), which, despite its enormous dimensions, functions liturgically as an altarpiece, "intended as a complement to the mensa-altar, located at the center below and before it, and as a spiritual preparation for the believer about to receive the sacrament."[16] Michelangelo was participating in a long tradition of Doomsday scenes in altarpieces and on chancel arches and walls over the altar, stretching from the twelfth century and reaching a pitch of intensity in the fifteenth.[17]

For purposes of personal devotion, the vital connection between Eucharist and Last Judgment may be seen vividly in illustrations of the Seven Penitential Psalms in English primers, or *horae*, where the Last Judgment frames scenes of Eucharistic reception. As Clare Costley

---

15. Geoffrey Wainwright, *Eucharist and Eschatology* (London: Epworth Press, 1971), 80; on Paul and other biblical and early liturgical contexts, 81–89.

16. Charles Tolnay, *Michelangelo*, vol. 5, *The Final Period* (Princeton: Princeton University Press, 1960), 28; cited in Ann W. Astell, *Eating Beauty: The Eucharist and the Spiritual Arts of the Middle Ages* (Ithaca, NY: Cornell University Press, 2006), 214. For an insightful discussion of the Eucharistic dimensions of the Sistine Chapel's altarpiece, see Astell, 212–18.

17. Inside English churches, "'the Doom, with the Seven Deadly Sins, and the Seven Corporal Works of Mercy, all allied subjects, are more often found after c. 1350 than any others, except perhaps figures of Saints.' At least seventy-eight examples of paintings of the Doom still survive in England. These Dooms are usually located above the arch separating the nave, the space of the laity, from the choir or chancel, the space of the clergy. A congregation facing the altar from the nave must then behold a huge painting of Doomsday on the arch that frames the chancel." Pamela Sheingorn and David Bevington, "'Alle This Was Token Domysday to Drede': Visual Signs of Last Judgment in the *Corpus Christi* Cycles and in Late Gothic Art," in *Homo, Memento Finis: The Iconography of Just Judgment in Medieval Art and Drama*, ed. David Bevington (Kalamazoo, MI: Medieval Institute Publications, 1985), 123.

King'oo has noted, late medieval lay Christians used these psalms in their self-directed penitential preparation for Mass. This practice, informed by Augustine's commentaries, "positions the Penitential Psalms in the context of the inevitable moment when God will bring his perfectly just, yet utterly intimidating, sentence to bear upon mankind."[18] An image of the Doomsday Christ "was universally preferred" for the facing page or initial that marked the beginning of the Penitential Psalms in thirteenth- and fourteenth-century *horae*.[19] This penitential association of Eucharist and Last Judgment extended into the English Reformation in doctrine and personal devotion. It was retained in the Eucharistic prayer of the 1549 Book of Common Prayer, which petitions God the Father, "Graunt . . . that, at the day of the generall resurreccion, we and all they which bee of the misticall body of thy sonne, may altogether be set on his right hand."[20] As Eamon Duffy has shown, the lay faithful of the Church of England continued to use old books of hours for personal devotion and to prepare for the sacraments well into the Reformation.[21] Even after *horae* declined in use, the Penitential Psalms remained the most prominent vehicle for meditation on the Last Judgment and one's eschatological fate well into the seventeenth century.

The Pavement Hours (York Minster, MS XVI.K.19), produced in York in the first quarter of the fifteenth century, attests to the currency of the Eucharist-as-Judgment motif during the flourishing of the mature York cycle (fig. 6.1). The wounded Christ seated on a rainbow is reflected

---

18. King'oo, *Miserere Mei*, 8; on para-penitential use of the psalms, see 16–17.

19. But "images of David gained ground" in the fifteenth century. "The Last Judgment remained prevalent, however, in Dutch and Flemish Books of Hours." Roger S. Wieck, *Painted Prayers: The Book of Hours in Medieval and Renaissance Art* (New York: George Braziller, 1997), 96. For a fuller discussion of the iconography, see Roger S. Wieck, *Time Sanctified: The Book of Hours in Medieval Art and Life* (New York: George Braziller, 2001), 97–99.

20. Cited in Wainwright, *Eucharist and Eschatology*, 88. This passage was dropped from later editions of the Book of Common Prayer.

21. Eamon Duffy, *Marking the Hours: English People and Their Prayers, 1240–1570* (New Haven: Yale University Press, 2006), 147–70.

Fig. 6.1. Christ displays his wounds at the Last Judgment. York Minster, MS
XVI.K.19, fol. 31r. © Chapter of York: Reproduced by kind permission.

in the fuller tableau titled "Last Judgm(en)t at Domesdai" and situated as the final image in another *horae* of York provenance, the Bolton Hours (York Minster, MS Add. 2), also produced in the first quarter of the fifteenth century (fig. 6.2). This final illumination functions as a colophon, and renders all of the book's foregoing contents as penitential preparation for the Last Judgment. When used during the Mass to facilitate vicarious participation in the sacrament of the altar, as the book likely was, this image of final judgment would have framed the reader's Eucharistic experience.[22]

An Italian book of hours contemporary with the York Play brings all of these temporalities and stages of sacramental preparation together in one tableau. On a full folio opposite the beginning of the Penitential Psalms, scenes of worthy and unworthy Eucharistic reception play out in front of a backdrop that conflates the crucified Christ, the unbloody sacrifice of the Mass, and the Doomsday division of good and evil souls (fig. 6.3). Here two similar scenes of confession and Eucharistic reception are marked as worthy and unworthy by visual embellishments. The good penitent, in black on the left, seems to breathe out a vapor, perhaps in the form of a dove, that shares the ghostly white pigment of Christ's body. The spiritual breath of the good confession severs the long leash held by an attendant demon. On the right, a demon's leash transfixes the host like a lance before it descends unbroken to throttle the penitent making a bad confession. A dove hovers over the host on the left, and a black creature—perhaps a fly?—over the host on the right. All of these books of hours gave their penitent readers the opportunity, whether in

---

22. This layered temporality is built into the structure of an earlier *horae* of Yorkshire provenance, the De Lisle Hours produced for Margaret de Beauchamp, c. 1320–25. As Kathryn A. Smith has observed, the De Lisle Hours "features two distinct temporal cycles," the single-day cycle of Christ's passion and the life-cycle of the Ages of Man. The resurrected Doomsday Christ illustrating the Penitential Psalms brings both of these cycles together, fittingly completing the Passion sequence with the resurrected body in triumph, and depicting the final life event in the Ages of Man. Kathryn A. Smith, *Art, Identity, and Devotion in Fourteenth-Century England: Three Women and Their Books of Hours* (London: British Library, 2003), 58–59.

Fig. 6.2. Christ judges the good and the evil souls on Doomsday. York Minster, MS Add. 2, fol. 208r. © Chapter of York: Reproduced by kind permission.

Fig. 6.3. New York, Pierpont Morgan Library, MS Morgan 1089, fol. 118v. Northern Italy, possibly the Veneto, c. 1425–1450. Reprinted by kind permission. Photo: The Pierpont Morgan Library, New York.

Mass or preparing for Mass, to "revolve the image of the future judgment before [their] eyes . . . while others approach the altar of God."[23]

As in the Doomsday pageant's sacramental theater, Christ's sacrificed body, flowing with Eucharistic blood, makes the celebration of the Eucharist the occasion for final judgment. Christ the high judge is a Eucharistic Christ, and his perception of the souls before him, including the audience-participants of the pageant, is a Eucharistic perception. To gaze on this judge is to gaze on the Eucharist in anticipation of the salvation and damnation that it effects. And while such a vision could have salutary effects on would-be penitents, it is equally important for what it teaches about how God's counter-vision, looking back at the faithful, acts on and within them. The Doomsday pageant draws on tableaux such as these, but instead of telescoping the temporality of salvation into the moment of Eucharistic reception, it uses the element of God's embodied presence and his counter-vision to dilate the time of salvation.

The Tropological Temporality of Salvation and the Body in Time

When the last pageant of the York Play rolled onto the final station at the Pavement, usually it had already been performed eleven times along the pageant route, and it could be performed as many as fifteen times. All humanity had been judged at least eleven times, the good souls divided from the evil at least eleven times, and the second-to-last of the day's approximately twenty-four Christs had uttered the ostensibly conclusive lines—"Nowe is fulfilled all my forþoght, / For endid is all erthely thyng"—eleven times.[24] If you had been watching the sequence of pageants along Coney Street or at any of the other stations, once the Doomsday pageant ended all earthly things at your spot, you might have made

---

23. *Biblia latina cum Glossa ordinaria*, 6:298–99.

24. Beadle, ed., *The York Plays: The Text*, 47.373–74; cited hereafter in the text by pageant and line number. The estimates of the number of actors needed to play Christ vary depending on the model of performance assumed. For a good discussion of the issues, see Alan H. Nelson, "Principles of Processional Staging: York Cycle," *Modern Philology* 67, no. 4 (May 1, 1970): 319–20.

your way southeast and then left around the corner on High Ousegate to reach the Pavement from the opposite direction of the pageant. You might have two or three hours to refresh yourself before assembling along with hundreds of other souls to participate in the Last Judgment again. For according to the mysterious temporality of the York Play, it is never too late (for now) to experience that fatal finality again.

The saved souls in the pageant are, like their damned counterparts, unaware that they have been saved. But they recognize the mysterious temporality that grants them the time to throw themselves on God's mercy. It is as if they stand outside a Schrödinger's box of predestination, with their hope staked on the indeterminacy of election and God's infinite mercy. The bad souls know only their final assignment to hell and never the mercy-prone providential indeterminacy on which the good souls presume when they pray,

> Of oure ill dedis, lorde, þou not mene [remember not],
> That we haue wroght vppon sere wise [in various ways],
> But graunte vs for thy grace, bedene,
> Þat we may wonne [dwell] in paradise.
>
> (47.101–4)

The good souls' prayers reveal how the final pageant's stark options incompletely present the cycle's dramatic soteriology. To be sure, the Father calls his angels to divide good from evil, right from left, according to the judgment he has already made: "Þis day þer domys þus haue I dight / To ilke a man as he hath serued me" (47.79–80). But the Father's will does not put an end to things; on the contrary, the tension between God's providential "grace" (47.103) and the record of how each man has served God (47.80) complicates and extends the drama.[25] Because the Father's doom is the beginning and not the end, even if you are among

---

25. In this way it is like Truth's laconic, disputed pardon in *Piers Plowman* that gives rise to much of the poem's plot, such as it is. The pardon's simple, decisive soteriology—"*Et qui bona egerunt ibunt in vitam eternam; / Qui vero mala in ignem eternum*" (C.9.286a–b)—functions as the beginning, rather than the end, of a complex inquiry.

the goats on the Pavement this year, you could always be among the sheep next year.

Just how dilatory York renders its Judgment Day may be appreciated by comparison to another Yorkshire meditation on last things, the *Prick of Conscience*, which dedicates its fifth book to the Doomsday, episodes from which are depicted in a window installed in 1410 in All Saints North Street, York. Unlike the York Play cycle, which jumps from the events of the very early church to the Last Judgment, the *Prick of Conscience* rehearses the events of the end times, elaborating the apocalypses of Daniel, Matthew, and John. The signs of the times and the rule of Antichrist take up a thousand lines, followed by the wrath of Christ anatomized in his wounds:

> He sal shew, to þar confusioun,
> Alle þe signes of his passioun,
> And þe enchesoun [reason] and þe manere
> Of his ded þat he tholed [suffered] here.
> And alle þis sal he do þos openly,
> To reprove þe synful men þarby,
> And þat sal be þair shenschip [disgrace] þan.[26]

Christ displays his wounds in order to reprove the sinful and prove their disgrace. Where the Mercers' Christ invites the gratitude of affective crucifixion lyrics—"Here may ȝe see my woundes wide . . . To bye you blisse þus wolde I bleede" (47.245, 252)—the Christ of the *Prick of Conscience* shows his wounds only to accuse. Some twenty-three hundred lines of apocalypse and judgment must pass before the tropological moment at the end of the book when a homiletical voice adds, as if in afterthought,

> Na [no] man þarfor suld in dispayre be;
> For alle þat has mercy here sal be save,

26. Ralph Hanna and Sarah Joy Wood, eds., *Richard Morris's "Prick of Conscience": A Corrected and Amplified Reading Text*, EETS, o.s., 342 (Oxford: Oxford University Press, 2013), ll. 5309–15; punctuation silently altered. Hereafter cited in the text.

And alle þat here askes mercy sal it have,
Yf þai it sekes whiles þai lyf bodily . . .
Byfor þe tyme ar þe dede [death] þam take.

(6293–99)

Besides these brief lines affirming the efficacy of conversion, the *Prick of Conscience* never takes up the temporality of repentance and therefore never explicitly invites its readers to consider their own lifetime. The book's temporality is built around the apocalypse, with the Doomsday firmly lodged at the end of time. The brief reminder at the end that now is the day of salvation hardly merges with the book's teleology of the damned. This comparison points up just how merciful is the York Doomsday pageant, with its temporizing plot, its tropologically ambiguous "this day."

York's mysterious temporality rewards further attention because it clarifies how the play makes present in human bodies the correspondence between a lifetime and the time of salvation—or, we could say, between history and salvation history. Like the Eucharist-as-Judgment motif, the Doomsday pageant makes the Last Judgment immanent to the time that remains. Of course it is meant to call the audience to consider the end, but it holds the grim finality of Doomsday in tension with the possibilities on offer from a merciful God. This God, who commenced the day's play at dawn with a proclamation of his own eternity, can play with time. This God "vnendande, withoutyn any endyng" (1.8), can temporize. While the day of the Lord will come as a thief in the night, "one day with God is as a thousand years and a thousand years as one day" (2 Pet. 3:8). This God keeps his promises, but he is leisurely about them, "sed patienter agit" (2 Pet. 3:9). Consistent with 2 Peter and the cycle's interest in God's temporal play, the Doomsday pageant holds the urgency of the Day of Judgment in tension with the leisure of God's merciful patience.[27]

So when the Father declares that the verdicts have already been settled for each person "þis day," the audience should be prepared to take

---

27. Noah underscores the urgency in the Flood pageant's paraphrase of 2 Pet. 3:10: "For it [the world] sall ones be waste with fyre, / And never worþe to worlde agayne" (9.301–2).

the frame of time tropologically. As discussed briefly in chapter 1, tropological commentary on scripture frequently employs temporal proximal deixis, inviting the reader to realize that the history he encounters in scripture entails truths about his own history, his own time. "The day" becomes the figure for this telescoping of history, and the adverb "daily" (*cotidie*) functions as a proximal temporal deictic. Each day the plot of salvation history plays out in the life of the church and the individual Christian soul.[28] The York Play, which took up all the daylight hours of a long bright day, and then some, is perhaps the most ambitious and lavish expression in medieval culture of the daily arc of salvation history. By squeezing all of history into one day, unlike the French biblical plays that stretched over several days, the York Play figures the tropological day as both complete and iterable. Salvation history has a clear beginning, middle, and end, but because it is contained within a cyclical unit of time, its linear plot will repeat the next day—or the next year. This dual characteristic of completeness and iterability nuances the doctrine of election: the traditional (Western) Christian teaching, influentially articulated by Augustine, that God providentially elects before all time which souls will be saved without impinging on individuals' temporally conditioned freedom. The play's plotting maintains both the finality of election and souls' freedom for salvation. It maintains the decisive fact of election from a perspective that sees all of salvation history (completeness). From the perspective of new beginnings and second chances (iterability), it maintains the openness and freedom of individual lives to participate tropologically in the history of salvation.

God the Father at the beginning of the pageant declares, "Þis day þer domys þus haue I dight" (47.79), and by doing so, his syntax renders settled judgments present, the subject of the ongoing play that is temporally coterminous with *the day*, today.[29] The mysterious temporality

---

28. De Lubac, *Medieval Exegesis*, 2:138.

29. Cf. Sheingorn and Bevington, "Alle This Was Token," 142. "In order for the subject to be effective, the audience must experience it as an accurate vision of the closure of history, and yet must remember that all individual Christians in the audience have time still to repent—unlike their counterparts who are being judged in the play or painting."

entailed by the tropological expression "þis day" opens the judgments to change, putting them quite literally "in play." In the French tradition, Passion plays were divided into *journées*, or days, instead of acts or pageants, and in this sense the Father could simply be proclaiming the matter of the pageant, namely, judgment. The Last Judgment was known to be appointed for a particular day, "dies illa" (Luke 21:34), of which the great requiem hymn of the Latin church, the *Dies irae*, speaks so movingly: "Quantus tremor est futurus, / Quando iudex est venturus, / Cuncta stricte discussurus!" (What a tremor there will be / When the judge is to appear, / All things harshly to review!).[30] But where the hymn of the Mass for the Dead centers on an inscribed doomsday book "in which all is contained,"[31] the Doomsday pageant's Father presents a living body and the wounds it has acquired this day, over the course of the cycle: "Ther schall þei see þe woundes fyve / Þat my sone suffered for þem all" (47.71–72).

The body and its wounds are "live" in that only a few hours have passed since they were incurred. In the case of the five crucifixion wounds, less real time will have passed between the pageant in which they were inflicted and the Doomsday pageant than the three hours Christ actually spent on the cross. While the cycle has telescoped time to fit the history of redemption into one day, it has thereby dilated the time of each episode and, by extension, the time of the Day of Judgment, which becomes coterminous with the tropological "today."[32] The Father does not present for evidence a doomsday book, but the living record of his Son's flesh.[33]

---

30. P. G. Walsh, ed., *One Hundred Latin Hymns: Ambrose to Aquinas*, trans. P. G. Walsh (Cambridge, MA: Harvard University Press, 2012), 346–47.

31. Ibid.

32. For an incisive consideration of this complex temporality, see Andreas Kablitz, "Representation and Participation: Some Remarks on Medieval French Drama," in *Rethinking the Medieval Senses: Heritage, Fascinations, Frames*, ed. Stephen G. Nichols, Alison Calhoun, and Andreas Kablitz (Baltimore: Johns Hopkins University Press, 2008), 194–205.

33. Recognition of this contrast requires familiarity with the Doomsday narrative of Rev. 7, in which the book of life figures prominently. In York's vari-

In contrast to biblical representations of the Last Judgment, the York Doomsday conspicuously declines to represent the doom as a legal proceeding contingent on written records. Instead, when Christ appears as judge, victim, and witness, he testifies to the wounds he has received and the benefactions he has enjoyed when he interacted with the souls in the person of the naked, the hungry, the thirsty. The judgment depends not on the written testimony inscribed in the book of life but on the interpersonal interactions Christ has had with individual people. The record of those interactions is inscribed on his body, not by the scribal-incarnational transactions of texts such as "The Long Charter of Christ" and related deed-poems,[34] but by the dramatic action of the day, by the buffeting from the Bowers and Flecchers' soldiers (in Christ before Annas and Caiaphas), the ropes and cords of the Tapiteres and Couchers (in Christ before Pilate [I]), the jeers of the Littisteres (in Christ before Herod), the lashes of the Tillemakers at his own judgment (likely performed at one point simultaneous with the Doomsday within earshot of the Pavement at the intersection of Ouse Gate and Coney Street),[35] the jostling and falls along the Shermans' route to Calvary, the Pynneres' nails (in the Crucifixion of Christ), and the Bocheres' spearpoint in the hands of Longeus Lateus (in the Death of Christ). When the Doomsday pageant was first performed at Micklegate, the first station, the judgment depended on wounds that were still being inflicted further

---

ous representations of Doomsday—in windows and books of hours as well as drama—"the narratives drawn from Matthew 25 and from Revelations 7 are not treated as competing versions of the last day, but are cast as two different figural valencies, the one, Doomsday and the division of the sheep from the goats, tropological, the other, culminating in a vision of the permanence of access to heavenly bliss through divine atonement, anagogical." Pamela M. King, "The End of the World in Medieval English Religious Drama," *Literature and Theology* 26, no. 4 (2012): 386.

34. On charter poetry, see Cervone, *Poetics of the Incarnation*, 85–105; and Emily Steiner, *Documentary Culture and the Making of Medieval English Literature* (New York: Cambridge University Press, 2003), 47–92.

35. On the possibilities of overhearing pageants other than the one at your station, see Pamela M. King, "Seeing and Hearing; Looking and Listening," *Early Theater* 3 (2000): 155–66.

down the pageant course, and would continue for several hours. And by the time the Doomsday pageant reached the last station, the Pavement, the judgment would depend on wounds that were the bodily traces of personal interactions with characters whose actors in previous pageants could very well already be standing in the audience next to their fellow butchers or fletchers or tilemakers. The judgment depends on evidence that is in the process of being made, and that will disappear when the human figure who bears it in his body leaves the stage.

When the Father commands the general resurrection and proclaims his intention to "make ende," he describes the last judgment in terms of vision. The God who proclaims that each person will receive his or her "dome" also specifies that the act of seeing is the means by which the judgment will be carried out. Once all souls have been raised up from the graves, "Ther schall þei see þe woundes fyve / Þat my sone suffered for þem all" (47.71–72). The play will later show in detail how that bodily testimony works, but first, God the Father's sight divides the blessed and damned souls relative to his visual perspective. He commands the angels to divide the souls "before my sight" so that "Mi blissed childre . . . / On my right hande I schall thame see" (47.73–76). After the blessed souls have been divided from the damned, God the Son descends to earth to display his wounded body so that "All mankynde þere schall it see" (47.184). As Christ descends to the throne of judgment, he calls his apostles to sit "Beside myselffe to se þat sight, / And for to deme [judge] folke ferre and nere / Aftir [according to] þer werkyng, wronge or right" (47.190–92). Like the lord mayor and other city dignitaries, Christ and his apostles will sit in "seetis sere" (various seats) to watch the proceedings (189). In this pageant of judgment, seeing runs in two directions, from God to humanity, and from humanity to God, but God's vision is determinative.

The Body in the Mirror and the Discovery of Spiritual Evidence

God the Father captures the pageant's mysterious temporality, extended in space and rendered dramatic by the interactions of human bodies, with the figure of the mirror. In what amounts to the final pageant's prologue, the Father poses the question of why, after all he and his Son have done for humanity, "þei als wrecchis, wittirly, / Has ledde þer liffe in lithirnesse" (47.43–44). Why do they persist in sin, when God is "Full of grace and forgifnesse" (47.42)? It is not, God reasons, for lack of basic wisdom. "Men seis þe worlde but vanité, / ȝitt will no manne beware þerby" (47.49–50). How can people agree with Quohelleth that all is vanity, but take no precautions? It must be because they do not consider the fact that they will die. However, their senses should remind them that they are only growing older: "Ilke a day þer mirroure may þei se, / ȝitt thynke þei noȝt þat þei schall dye" (47.51–52). God deploys this mirror figure subtly, setting the literal practice of looking in a mirror in the anagogical context of the Last Judgment, but opening the figure to the tropological "today" that is the time for repentance, all the while allegorically hearkening back to the mirror of Christ manifested in the Baptism and Temptation pageants. Each aspect of this mirror figure—literal, allegorical, tropological, and anagogical—repays further attention, and the remainder of this section elaborates on each in turn.

Literal Mirrors

Unlike most mirrors in fourteenth-century English religious writing, God's mirror topos here derives its literal sense from the practices of everyday life. People looking in their mirrors each day should be able to tell that they are aging, and therefore that death is approaching. This reference to the daily use of a mirror comes early in Herbert Grabes's chronology of "real mirrors" in Middle English literature, which he finds begins with Chaucer and Gower.[36] At the height of the York Play's civic prominence in the mid-fifteenth century, mirrors for inspecting one's appearance would have been familiar objects in York, as attested by the inventory of the chapman (merchant retailer) Thomas Gryssop, who in 1446 had in his possession two "barber myrors" worth two

---

36. Herbert Grabes, *The Mutable Glass: Mirror-Imagery in Titles and Texts of the Middle Ages and English Renaissance,* trans. Gordon Collier (New York: Cambridge University Press, 1982), 71–73.

ducats (the same value as two pairs of gloves), as well as six dozen "myrours, hapeny ware."[37] The affordability of these mirrors suggests that they were common and easily attainable. The pageant's producers and their audience would know that there is no excuse not to recognize that you are not getting any younger.

The evidence that you are growing older is found in the flesh, the same place where the pageant's judicial process discovers evidence. Like the evidence of sins inscribed on Christ's body as wounds, the evidence of age and approaching death comes from bodies, not books. Like the dramatic evidence of the plays, the evidence of your advancing years is in the process of being made. God himself commends looking at the material body as a practice by which you may come to a necessary stage of saving knowledge, the recognition that death approaches.

Allegorical Mirrors

As much as God the Father's mirror topos depends for its meaning on the use of real mirrors, the context in which he deploys it opens up figurative, allegorical significance as well. Christ has already twice manifested himself as a mirror: at his baptism and at the conclusion of the Temptation pageant. In the Barbours' Baptism pageant, Jesus likens himself to a mirror in order to answer two objections posed by John the Baptist. John, who has been preaching a baptism of repentance according to Jewish law, objects that Jesus cannot be baptized because he cannot repent, for "wele I wotte þat synne is none / In hym, withoute ne withinne" (21.79–80). Jesus replies that because he has taken on human nature, he will undergo the baptism that all humans must receive if they are to be saved.

> And sithen myselffe haue taken mankynde,
> For men schall me þer myrroure make
> [And] haue my doyng in ther mynde,

---

37. James Raine, ed., *Testamenta Eboracensia: A Selection of Wills from the Registry at York*, vol. 3, Surtees Society 45 (Durham: Andrews and Co., 1865), 102–3; Benjamin Goldberg, *The Mirror and Man* (Charlottesville: University Press of Virginia, 1985), 112.

Also I do þe baptyme take.
I will forthy
Myselfe be baptiste for ther sake,
Full oppynly.

(21.92–98)

The third line here suggests that the mirror is a person's memory, in which Christ's life on earth is imprinted as a pattern to follow. But the syntax of the second line suggests a different configuration, one in which collective humanity compels Christ to reflect not only its nature but its actions. The logic of the incarnation binds Christ to the imitation of mankind. As "þer myrroure," whatever they do, he must do, or at least reflect. He might have responded to John with the rhetorical question, What would mankind do? Alternatively, he complicates the conventional mirror-as-moral-exemplar topos, putting mankind in the subject position and thereby accentuating the ambivalence of the mirror. Men will make Christ reflect their actions, whether good or ill, for that is the logic of incarnational exchange, which, taken to its limit, turns into the sacrificial exchange of the Passion and the *sacrosanctum commercium*— the holy exchange—of gifts in the Mass. When Christ says, "Men shal me their mirror make," he complicates exemplarity with the exchange that effects atonement. The line suggests a catoptric account of atonement, according to which the mirror of Christ's body reflects the sinful deeds of humanity, just as Christ "bore our sins in his body upon the tree" (1 Peter 2:24).

Tropological Mirrors

John's other objection is that he, an unrighteous man, should not baptize a righteous man. Christ responds by redefining righteousness not as the absence of sin, but as the fulfillment of word by deed. In his own variation on the tropological commonplace of the homiletic tradition, "first he wroghte, and afterward he taughte,"[38] Jesus declares, "Fyrst schall I take, sen schall I preche" (21.134). He challenges John to baptize him so "þat rightwisnesse be noȝt oonlye / Fullfillid in worde, but also in

---

38. Chaucer, *The Canterbury Tales*, General Prologue, 497.

dede, / Thrughe baptyme clere" (21.129–31). By this twofold argument for his baptism, Jesus builds into the mirror topos the tropological imperative to turn words into works. Because his mirror figure goes beyond mere exemplarity, tropology is revealed to have depths beyond moral exemplarity and imitation. The tropological circulation that converts words into works also converts human attributes into divine attributes, and vice versa. This exchange or communication of attributes results finally in humanity's salvation, through Christ's sacrifice that mirrors the death that sin inflicts on fallen humanity.

Anagogical Mirrors

Jesus' double mirror figure responds to the gap between exemplary knowledge and salvation that frustrates other protagonists of medieval religious literature, such as Will in *Piers Plowman*. Even if "men . . . haue my doyng in ther mynde" (21.94)—even if Will knows and remembers the characteristics of Dowel, Dobet, and Dobest—those exemplars still do not suffice for salvation. As long as God and humans stand alienated from each other by virtue of their different natures or substances—one uncreated, the other created; one infinite, the other finite; one immaterial, the other material—humans will never be able to imitate God, no matter how clear the example and upright the will. Only an exchange of substance and form between God and humanity will suffice to save creatures of flesh and blood. That this exchange occurs in the Eucharist, where the substance of bread and wine are transformed into the substance of Christ's body and blood, stands out most clearly in the *secreta* (secret prayer) appointed in the York rite (as well as most other Western rites) for one of the two great solemnities of the incarnation, the first Christmas Mass:

> May the sacrifice of today's feast be acceptable to you, Lord, we pray, so that, through the outpouring of your grace, by these holy exchanges we might be found in the form of Him, in whom with you is our substance, Jesus Christ your Son our Lord.[39]

---

39. "Accepta tibi sit, Domine, quaesumus, hodiernae festivitatis oblatio, ut, tua gratia largiente, per haec sacrosancta commercia in illius inveniamur forma, in quo tecum est nostra substantia, Jesus Christus Filius tuus Dominus

The change desired here exceeds the hopes of a perfectionist program of moral improvement. It goes beyond the removal of original sin and return to the innocence of Adam and Eve before the Fall, the "likeness" to God in which humanity was created. As liturgical theologians have noted, the language of form in the Latin Mass

> is used principally to denote the restoration as an entirely new state: in Christ humanity not only returns to the likeness of God of the original creation, but is transformed to the likeness with the *forma*, the nature of Him in whom our human nature is united with God himself. And precisely this transformation to the image of Christ which has its origin in Christ's incarnation, is more admirable than the original creation . . . : it implies namely that we can become sharers in the divinity of Jesus Christ, the Son of God, who deigned to participate in our human nature.[40]

As an anagogical reading of the mystery of transubstantiation, this prayer envisions the way in which the commerce of the Mass will transform the substance of the participants from human into divine, just as the people's gifts of bread and wine are transformed into God's gifts of Christ's body and blood.

This prayer and related prayers that stress salvific exchange would have been well known in late medieval York, and their Eucharistic context resonates with the goals of York's sacramental theater, especially the eschatological Doomsday pageant. Like the Doomsday pageant, this particular prayer envisions the transformation of humanity into the form of Christ in the context of the Last Judgment, asking not that "we might *be changed* into the form of Him" but that "we might *be found* [*inveniamur*] in the form of Christ." And so Christ's judicial task at

---

noster." William George Henderson, ed., *Missale ad usum insignis ecclesiæ eboracensis*, vol. 1, Publications of the Surtees Society 59 (Durham: Andrews and Co., 1874), 15.

40. Gerard Lukken, *Original Sin in the Roman Liturgy: Research into the Theology of Original Sin in the Roman Sacramentaria and the Early Baptismal Liturgy* (Leiden: Brill, 1973), 387.

Doomsday is the task of *inventio*, or in legal parlance, of "discovery." The evidence of salvation that he must discover is his own form in the souls of the living and the dead. Just as the audience of the play have been challenged throughout to see the form of Christ, now Christ must look for his own form, as if in a mirror, in the souls on the Pavement.

Mirror of Drama, Mirror of Scripture: A Prologue to a French Passion Play

The tropological temporality of the Doomsday pageant renders Christ's body a site of interactivity with the audience. What they do will have an effect on what Christ's body looks like, the evidence to which it testifies, and, finally, the outcome of the play. Although this effect of embodied interactivity is particularly pronounced in the York Doomsday, it is a feature of many biblical dramas. In order to explicate these effects and their relationship to the temporality of other pageants and the mirroring function of Christ's body, I will first consider a prologue to a roughly contemporary French biblical play, Arnoul Gréban's *Mystère de la Passion*.[41] Composed around 1455, the play was first produced about twenty years after the York Play text reached the approximate form in which we know it today, and the two plays' nearly annual performance overlapped for another eighty-odd years.[42] Derived from vernacular verse narra-

---

41. Gréban was a choirmaster at the Cathedral of Notre Dame in Paris. The approximately 35,000 lines are divided into four days that comprise many of the episodes of salvation history treated in the English play cycles such as York's. The Third Day interweaves the trials and passion of Christ with a conspiracy of devils, including scenes set in hell derived from the Gospel of Nicodemus. The play was performed at least seventeen times before 1536, including a finely documented performance at Mons in 1501, attended by an audience as large as 6,300 people. The best English-language introduction is Arnoul Gréban, *The Mystery of the Passion: The Third Day*, trans. Paula Giuliano (Asheville, NC: Pegasus Press, 1996).

42. The extant text of the York Play dates from the late 1470s and reflects a twenty-year period of significant development and revision under the Common Clerkship of Roger Burton, 1415–35. Richard Beadle, ed., *The York Plays:*

tives that also transmitted the central sources for the York Play, the *Mystère de la Passion* opens a window onto the theological and dramaturgical perspectives of the international dramatic tradition in which the York cycle developed.[43] Like the York Doomsday pageant, Gréban's play draws together four disparate discourses and practices that underwent significant innovation in the late fourteenth and early fifteenth centuries: drama, ethics, exegesis, and optics. Its explicit discussion of embodied performance vividly theorizes the mirror topoi and implicit dramaturgy that shape the York Play's style of participatory drama. The prologue articulates how drama, scripture, bodies, and optics work together to invite spectators to participate in the drama of salvation. It also clarifies the relationship of two other discourses that inform the York Doomsday: the tradition of moralized optics, and the experience of seeing and being seen by Christ in the Eucharist.

The prologue to the Third Day of the four-day *Mystère* considers how the biblical story of the passion of Jesus becomes available to the audience of a play. The prologue posits a complex analogy: the spectators relate to the actors in the same way that readers of biblical narrative relate to salvation history. Just as readers of the biblical narrative can participate in the narrative tropologically and thereby activate it as salvation history, so can members of the audience participate in the play by their embodied correspondence to the actors. The actors "incorporate" the story by giving their bodies-in-action over to the performance

---

Introduction, Commentary, Glossary, vol. 2 of 2 vols., EETS, s.s., 24 (Oxford: Oxford University Press, 2013), xxiii–xxvi.

43. On the shared international dramatic culture in which the *Mystère de la Passion* provides a constant point of comparison, see Lynette R. Muir, *The Biblical Drama of Medieval Europe* (New York: Cambridge University Press, 1995). It has long been recognized that the York Play draws heavily from the verse *Northern Passion* (Frances H. Miller, "The Northern Passion and the Mysteries," *Modern Language Notes* 34, no. 2 [1919]: 88–92), but that Middle English text is an amplified translation of the late Old French *Passion*, the narrative and textual backbone of Gréban's play. Other shared sources are the Anglo-Norman (and then Middle English) verse *Gospel of Nicodemus* and, obliquely by way of its inspirations for the *Northern Passion*, Robert of Gretham's Anglo-Norman homily cycle, the *Miroir*.

of the narrative as characters in the narrative. In real life, humans can also give their bodies over to performance of the story of Christ's passion. The prologue explains that "this passion" can lead humans to participate in Christ's perfect love and suffering, if they will ready their understanding to "incorporate" it.

> [S]eigneurs, humblement vous supply
> qu'ung peu de silence prestez
> et l'entendement apprestez
> a incorporer la doulour,
> charité et parfaicte amour
> ou ceste passion admaine
> et joinct nostre nature humaine[.]

> ---

> Lords, I humbly beg you
> to lend a little silence
> and ready your understanding
> to incorporate the suffering,
> charity, and perfect love
> to which this passion leads
> and joins our human nature.[44]

But what is "this passion?" We are given several options. This passion could be the play itself, for such productions were typically called "passion" or "passion par parsonnages."[45] Or it could be the story—"ceste histoire"—the narrative itself, which the prologue calls more morally

---

44. Arnoul Gréban, *Le mystère de la passion d'Arnould Greban*, ed. Gaston Paris and Gaston Raynaud (F. Vieweg, 1878), ll. 19,959–66; repr. Geneva: Slatkine Reprints, 1970; hereafter cited in the text by line number. In making my translations, I have consulted Gréban, *The Mystery of the Passion: The Third Day.*

45. Lynette R. Muir, "Playing God in Medieval Europe," in *The Stage as Mirror: Civic Theatre in Late Medieval Europe*, ed. Alan E. Knight (Cambridge: Boydell & Brewer, 1997), 25.

fertile and fecund than any other story in the world. But the passion is also called a work, "ceste oeuvre":

> pensez que celuy qui s'instruit
> en ceste œuvre porte grant fruit,
> et qu'il n'est histoire en ce monde
> si fertille ne si feconde,
> ne qui doyve mieulx faire entendre
> le cueur au bien ou il doit tendre;

> ─────────────

> think that he who learns
> from this work bears great fruit,
> and there is no story in the world
> so fertile or so fecund,
> or which makes the heart more attentive
> to the good to which it must tend.

(19967–72)

"Oeuvre" here could have a range of referents: the saving actions of Christ in history, the scripture re-presented in the play, Gréban's script of the play, or the collaborative labor involved in one of the productions.

When he invokes the polyvalent terms *histoire* and *oeuvre*, Gréban raises two questions that have long interested medievalists but only recently attained the attention they deserve: what is the relationship between a text and a work, and how is the audience responsible to and for this relationship? In forcing this question, Gréban playfully antici-pates Paul Zumthor's distinction between *texte* and *oeuvre*, according to which the text as subject of editorial attention is but one of many factors involved in the work, including voice and performance. Zumthor ar-gues, "The text is but a surface phenomenon . . . . For the medieval audience . . . the poem was its performance."[46] Pamela Sheingorn and Robert L. A. Clark have extended Zumthor's theory of the work to

─────────────

46. Paul Zumthor, *Toward a Medieval Poetics* (Minneapolis: University of Minnesota Press, 1992), 54.

include the manuscripts of medieval drama and narrative poetry, upsetting generic distinctions that oriented the field for years. By focusing on "the work as embracing all dimensions of perception," Clark and Sheingorn have been able to reveal how illuminated manuscripts of so-called "narrative poetry" generate gesture, voice, and characterization, while eliciting from their audiences practices of "performative reading," thereby "cross[ing] the threshold between the narrative and drama and becom[ing], in a very real sense, play texts."[47] Gréban's prologue and the York Doomsday's optics of seeing and being seen deploy the liminal space not only between the texts and performances of biblical narrative and drama, but also between drama, liturgy, and the practices that make manifest the relationships between humans and God.

Gréban's prologue suggests that we cannot choose just one or two of the factors composing the *oeuvre*, and it deploys the image of a mirror to capture the moral and soteriological functions of a performed Bible. It therefore combines two mirror topoi pervasive in medieval culture—the mirror of scripture and the mirror as moral exemplar—displacing them from their conventional medium, the book, onto drama, thus producing what would become another pervasive mirror topos, the drama-as-mirror. So the prologue raises the following question: What becomes of the Bible, and of biblical translation, when the medium translated is not a book but a mirror, and the content translated is not text (or not only text) but human figures-in-action? What do we do with a "Passion par personnages et sans parler" (a Passion in human figures and without speech), as a contemporaneous account of a silent pageant puts it?[48]

---

47. Robert L. A. Clark, "Liminality and Literary Genres: Texts *Par Personnages* in Late Medieval Manuscript Culture," in *Thresholds of Medieval Visual Culture: Liminal Spaces*, ed. Elina Gertsman and Jill Stevenson (Woodbridge, Suffolk: Boydell Press, 2012), 262.

48. The eye-witness account is from the journal of Jean de Roye, describing the 1461 royal entry of Louis XI: "Et, ung peu au dessoubz dudict ponceau, à l'endroit de la Trinité, y avoit une Passion par personnages et sans parler, Dieu estendu en la croix et les deux larrons à destre et à senestre." Jean de Roye, *Jour-

Working through these questions, Gréban runs the mirror topos through an impressive range of transformations as he rings changes on the root *mirer* (to look). I will cite and discuss each transformation in turn.

> Ainsi va son veil moderant
> en ce miroir considerant
> ou tout cueur pour son dueil mirer
> se doit doucement remirer;

> Thus his will is moderated
> as he considers this mirror
> where every heart, to reflect/heal its suffering
> must examine itself with care.

(19989–92)

The story of the work of the passion is a mirror with respect to example and memory, two of the most prominent uses for the mirror topos. With Christ's example fixed in the memory, one can judge the sufferings and pleasures of the world as the fleeting things they really are. One can be healed of suffering by reflecting the exemplar, Christ.

Next the prolocutor speaks for the play's producers, describing how they are making that salutary mirror available to the audience.

> et affin que vous y mirez
> et humblement la remirez,
> ce devost miroir pour le mieulx
> vous ramenons devant les yeulx
> sensiblement par parsonnages[.]

> And so that you may look at yourselves
> and humbly regard there,

---

nal de Jean de Roye: Connu sous le nom de Chronique scandaleuse, 1460–1483, ed. Bernard de Mandrot, vol. 1 (Paris: Renouard, 1894), 28.

we present before your eyes
this devout mirror for your benefit
through live actors available to the senses.

(19992–96)

The play presents the passion to the audience's eyes by means of actors playing characters whom the audience can see, hear, and even
touch—"sensiblement par parsonnages." Here the metaphor tilts, as it
were, to take on another tenor. The mirror that had contained the story
of the work of the passion now also contains the bodies of the actors,
which correspond to the bodies of the audience as mirror images:

mirez vous, si serez bien sages;
chacun sa forme y entrevoit;
qui bien se mire, bien se voit.

————————

Observe yourselves and you will indeed be wise;
each one glimpses his own form there;
he who observes himself well, sees himself well.

(19996–98)

The prolocutor suggests that because the actors have bodies like the
spectators' bodies, the spectators can see themselves embodied and emplotted, so to speak, in the action taking place on the stage or platea (the
ground-level playing space). When the spectators look at the actors,
they are considering themselves. They consider (*mirez*) themselves in
the actors first, and through this consideration of themselves emplotted
in the biblical drama they are able to reconsider (*remirez*) themselves.
In order to be themselves as God would have them be—healed, wise,
good—they must first experience themselves as others, receiving back
from the drama their own selves renewed.

This new tweak adds something truly distinctive to the mirror of
scripture topos. Up to this point, the prologue has drawn on numerous
conventional aspects of the mirror topos, many of which are covered in
Alan of Lille's catalogue of mirror topoi in his art of preaching. There,
readers are encouraged to observe themselves well in the mirrors of

conscience and experience, and to employ the mirrors of memory and reason to do so, guided by the mirror of scripture.[49] For Alan of Lille and many others, this mirror apprehension was both moral and conceptual.[50] In the mirror of scripture you recognized your condition, in the mirror of creation your wretchedness, and in the mirror of nature your guilt. But here the prologue actualizes the metaphor. It is not *as if* you recognize yourself in the mirror of scripture. You actually *do* encounter your own form there as a human figure in action, and only subsequently do you re-cognize (*re-mirez*) yourself in terms of an identity provided first by the *personnages* on stage. In Gréban's mirror, you recognize your own form with your senses. And, as in a real mirror, the figures face each other. Because of this, you can see your own form more completely and accurately than from the first-person perspective. This mirror-play does not reflect an existing subject-position, but instead creates that position in the image of a *personnage*—like Christ, who reflects back on humans their transformed nature as an image made available only through his incarnation.[51]

The prolocutor has set up this relationship from the beginning of the prologue. This passion, he said, will join "our" human nature to Christ's passion, with the first-person plural pronoun uniting the audience to those producing and acting the *oeuvre*. An audience member not only sees his own human form but sees it *as participating* in the biblical drama. He also might see his own counterpart in society playing a role up there on the stage. For example, an audience member who is a miller and father of four could plausibly see another miller and father of four playing Herod on the stage. Likewise, the collective audience,

---

49. Alan of Lille, *Ars praedicandi*, PL 210:118d–119a; Alan of Lille, *The Art of Preaching*, trans. Gillian R. Evans (Kalamazoo, MI: Cistercian Publications, 1981), 29–30.

50. On classical and medieval mirror topoi, see Ritamary Bradley, "Backgrounds of the Title *Speculum* in Mediaeval Literature," *Speculum* 29, no. 1 (1954): 100–115; Grabes, *The Mutable Glass*; and Goldberg, *The Mirror and Man*.

51. I am grateful to Billy Junker for helping me to refine and extend this paragraph.

representing the demographic diversity of the locality—the whole range of social persons, in Elizabeth Fowler's phrase—sees its diversity reflected in the cast of approximately one hundred named characters from all walks of life.[52]

The prolocutor calls attention to the way in which the mirror function of drama draws the audience into the performance in a manner different from reading or looking at a narrative picture. To be sure, as Mary Carruthers has argued, "Even silent reading, the medium of meditation, is thought of as a performance by the reader . . . , actively and inventively memorizing, responding, recalling, and seeing and hearing inwardly."[53] But although the audience of Gréban's passion would need to engage in such interactive "reading" in order to interpret the play, the prolocutor claims that even before interpretation, the audience's mirror counterparts are performing the passion in speech and actions. While the mirror-as-moral-exemplar always invites readers to complete the act of interpretation by performing an imitation, Gréban's prologue claims that the dramatic mirror can reverse the priority, placing the audience's performance within the *histoire*, and therefore prior to interpretation.

These points have important parallels in the York Doomsday pageant's manipulations of seeing and being seen. As the culminating pageant of a play designed to enact in dramatic form the mystery of the Eucharist, the Doomsday pageant plays out as a Eucharistic mirror in which God's intentions "on stage" mysteriously precede and exceed the audience's acts of interpretation. In the Doomsday pageant, the live audience finds its own end anticipated and given to it before it has even reached it. Each one sees his own form there, in the judicial emergency of the Eucharist—an emergency that is also the source of all love and mercy. As Ann Astell has observed, "The very blankness of the bread

---

52. Elizabeth Fowler, *Literary Character: The Human Figure in Early English Writing* (Ithaca, NY: Cornell University Press, 2003), 1–31.

53. Mary Carruthers, "Rhetorical *Ductus*, or, Moving through a Composition," in *Acting on the Past: Historical Performance across the Disciplines*, ed. Mark Franko and Annette Richards (Hanover, NH: University Press of New England, 2000), 99–100.

makes the Host, as it were, a pure mirror (*speculum*), capable of reflecting different images and forms of Christ's beauty into the world."[54] Gréban articulates how a biblical drama can perform a similar mirroring function. The Doomsday pageant merges the mirror of drama with the mirror of the Eucharist to make a sophisticated argument about the nature of virtue in anagogical perspective, viewed from the end. The play as Eucharistic mirror takes temporal, ontological, and interpretive priority over the mirrored audience, even as more traditional uses of the mirror topos remain in effect. The medieval science of perspectivist optics and the related theory of moralized optics make this argument about drama, vision, and virtue intelligible. What, then, is the full significance of this moralized optics for the study of biblical drama?

Moralized Optics and the Mirror of Scripture

Gréban could not have been the first person to whom the idea of the stage as mirror had occurred, even though I have not found an earlier example of its articulation. For Gréban deftly interweaves the strands of several well-developed traditions, from the optics of mirrors and their practical use to moralizations of their functions and the theology of the beatific vision. At least since Robert Grosseteste (c. 1168–1253) developed a mathematically astute metaphysics of light,[55] mirrors provided a way to think about how the God "dwelling in light inaccessible" (1 Tim. 6:16) could be made accessible and be accommodated by mediation to the limited and fallen vision of humans. The mirror could help explain how the transcendent might be present in the immanent, the infinite in

---

54. Astell, *Eating Beauty*, 31.

55. Robert Grosseteste, "De luce seu de inchoatione formarum," in *Die Philosophischen Werke des Robert Grosseteste, Bischofs von Lincoln*, ed. Ludwig Baur (Münster: Aschendorffsche Verlagsbuchhandlung, 1912), 51–59; Robert Grosseteste, *On Light (De Luce)*, trans. Clare C. Riedl (Milwaukee, WI: Marquette University Press, 1942); J. J. McEvoy, *Robert Grosseteste* (New York: Oxford University Press, 2000), 84–97.

the finite, with the image of God reflected in the human soul, and the whole human person, crucially, reflected in the incarnate Son of God.

At the same time, mirror optics could help account for the failures and successes of this reflection by demonstrating how sin and goodness vitiate or augment a person's capacity for the vision of God. In a wide range of homiletic, penitential, and pedagogical literature, the mirror connected visible action in the world to invisible spiritual and ethical realities. The "mirror without blemish" (*speculum sine macula*) of Wisdom 7:26 could describe Mary immaculate and provide optical grounds on which to understand the incarnation.[56] And it could explain how souls full of charity are able to multiply their gifts to share with others.[57] Conversely, persistent sinners could be likened to ugly people who refuse to look in the mirror. But "since God and the soul are in the same image, when the soul contemplates God's purity, it carefully considers its own vileness." So penitent sinners will dare "to look in that mirror frequently so that we can discern in ourselves the blemishes of our mind and cleanse them."[58] Close to a thousand late medieval and early modern works adopted *speculum* as their title, alluding to this rich tradition of theological-ethical optics.[59]

Gréban's sophisticated deployment of this tradition depends on the great leaps in optical science made in the late thirteenth century. At about the same time as Thomas Aquinas was synthesizing Aristotelian and Augustinian metaphysics with an eye on Arab philosophy, Roger Bacon elaborated the recently discovered optical science of Ibn al-Haytham (latinized Alhacen). Bacon's *Perspectiva* laid the groundwork for the later experimental science of Johannes Kepler and Isaac New-

---

56. Jacobus de Voragine, *Marialis Liber*, s.v. "speculum;" available in Jacques de Voragine, *Mariale de laudibus deiparae virginis* (Lyon: Martin, 1688), 472.

57. See Bromyard, *Summa praedicantium*, s.v. "gratitudinis."

58. Peter of Limoges, *The Moral Treatise on the Eye*, trans. Richard Newhauser (Toronto: Pontifical Institute of Mediaeval Studies, 2012), 186–87.

59. Herbert Grabes lists 385 works before 1500 with "mirror" in the title, and 398 in England alone between 1500 and 1700. See the appendices to Grabes, *The Mutable Glass*. See also Bradley, "Backgrounds of the Title *Speculum* in Mediaeval Literature."

ton,[60] yet he claims to have undertaken his mathematically sophisticated work as an aid to biblical exegesis: "for in divine scripture, nothing is dealt with as frequently as matters pertaining to the eye and vision . . . and therefore nothing is more essential to a grasp of the literal and spiritual sense than the certitude supplied by this science."[61] Bacon assumes that profound analogies are at work between the optics of vision and the perception by faith of spiritual realities. What is true of how we see material phenomena will also be true of how we perceive immaterial phenomena. For Bacon, a correct understanding of optics will help us to understand not only biblical discussions of visual phenomena, but also the allegorical, tropological, and anagogical senses of scripture, which are properly the objects of faith, understood commonly as spiritual vision. The new optics received its heartiest reception from preachers and confessors because it demonstrated in the realm of natural philosophy problems of perception and error akin to those constantly encountered in the field of practical ethics. Bacon's treatment of mirrors is an anatomy of error, and his geometrical reasoning repeatedly corrects the conclusions that unreflective perception would draw. The image we see *in* the mirror is "not according to the truth of its existence there but only according to its appearance."[62]

Two decades or so after Bacon composed the *Perspectiva*, a master of theology named Peter of Limoges took Bacon up on the challenge to integrate the insights of perspectivist optics with scriptural exegesis. In the aftermath of the University of Paris Condemnations of 1277, which tarnished Bacon's reputation, Peter interwove a natural-tropological reading of the *Perspectiva* with agile scriptural exegesis and related *exempla* without ever mentioning Bacon or his work by name. The resulting *Tractatus moralis de oculo* far outcirculated its source text as well as the most widely disseminated perspectivist treatise, John Pecham's

---

60. David C. Lindberg, *Roger Bacon and the Origins of "Perspectiva" in the Middle Ages: A Critical Edition and English Translation of Bacon's "Perspectiva," with Introduction and Notes* (New York: Oxford University Press, 1996), xciv–c.

61. Ibid., 323.

62. Ibid., 267.

Perspectiva communis.[63] At the same time, Peter's hybrid treatise was one of the most popular texts in the vast field of homiletic aids.[64]

The *Tractatus moralis de oculo* gained popularity in England as well. It is estimated that more than fifty manuscript copies originated in England, including an early, abbreviated copy that traveled as far as Estonia.[65] While most of the early copies were anonymous, in England many were ascribed subsequently to Robert Grosseteste, a convenient disguise that diffused late-thirteenth- and early-fourteenth-century suspicions of the new Parisian Aristotelianism condemned in 1277.[66] Its attribution

---

63. Scholars have identified more than 220 extant manuscript copies of *The Moral Treatise on the Eye*, compared to 66 of Pecham's treatise, which became "a standard university text"; was required to gain an M.A. at Prague in 1390; and in the fifteenth century was regularly lectured on at Vienna, Leipzig, and Cracow. R. G. Newhauser, "Peter of Limoges, Optics, and the Science of the Senses," *The Senses and Society* 5, no. 1 (2010): 31; Lindberg, *Roger Bacon and the Origins of "Perspectiva,"* xcvi–xcvii.

64. Comparing the evidence of manuscript transmission and survival, Richard Newhauser remarks, "Even measured against such other near-contemporary popular and moral treatments of natural philosophy as Thomas of Cantimpré's *Bonum universale de apibus* . . . Peter's text must be given a place of pre-eminence." Newhauser, "Nature's Moral Eye: Peter of Limoges' *Tractatus Moralis De Oculo*," in *Man and Nature in the Middle Ages*, ed. Susan J. Ridyard and Robert G. Benson (Sewanee, TN: University of the South Press, 1995), 133–34.

65. Richard Newhauser, Tiina Kala, and Meelis Friedenthal, "The Work of an English Scribe in a Manuscript in Estonia," *Scriptorium* 62, no. 1 (2008): 139–48.

66. The quotations from the *Tractatus moralis* in sermons of which we are aware attribute the text to Grosseteste, illustrating Newhauser's conclusion that the text circulated primarily as a homiletical aid rather than as an optical treatise (Peter of Limoges, *The Moral Treatise on the Eye*, xxx). The ascription also folded Peter's work into the mainstream of what Siegfried Wenzel has identified as "English theology," a kind of homegrown homiletical magisterium of trustworthy texts by or ascribed to Grosseteste, John Bromyard, and Robert Holcot. See Wenzel, *Latin Sermon Collections from Later Medieval England: Orthodox Preaching in the Age of Wyclif* (New York: Cambridge University Press, 2005), 322–32. The English authorities were closely integrated with the homiletical aids of the day, as well as perennial, pan-European authorities. On the

to Grosseteste lent the *Tractatus moralis* a special cachet in England, where, as Peter Brown has shown, "By the late fourteenth century . . . a working knowledge of the rudiments of optical theory was not confined to the cognoscenti: through various kinds of reading and listening, wider sections of society were aware of the processes, effects and significance of visual phenomena."[67]

Although Bacon only infrequently connects scripture and optics, Peter of Limoges in the *Tractatus moralis de oculo* offers a comprehensive meditation on the spiritual sense of optical phenomena in scripture. Comparing the effects of scripture to the perspectival reversal of a plane mirror, Peter concludes, "So, therefore, when we turn our eye to the mirror of Holy Scriptures, the right seems to us the left and vice versa. Likewise, what is thought to be below will appear to be above and vice versa. For Holy Scriptures bless the poor and raise them up."[68] Peter notes that life is full of topsy-turvy values such as this, including even the natural

---

broader European aspects of "English theology," see 316–21. The ascription to Grosseteste would have been particularly apt, given his theology of divine illumination, and Peter's care to moralize each optical phenomenon would have complemented the typical use of Grosseteste as a theological and exegetical sourcebook for preachers (327–28).

67. Peter Brown, *Chaucer and the Making of Optical Space* (Oxford: Peter Lang, 2007), 108–9. Brown's sketch of perspectivist optics in fourteenth-century encyclopedic and homiletic literature as well as vernacular poetry confirms that Peter of Limoges's text was one among many responsible for the wide dissemination of recent scientific advances in optics throughout fourteenth-century English culture. Exempla collections such as Bromyard's *Summa praedicantium* spread the theories and optical phenomena found in Alhacen, Bacon, and John Pecham. Robert Holcot's commentaries on Wisdom moralized perspectivist optics, and were then in turn mined by homilists and Geoffrey Chaucer (ibid., 104–6). Chaucer also drew from Guillaume de Lorris and Jean de Meun, with Nature's learned discourse on captoptrics in the *Roman de la Rose* likely an influence on the magical mirror of the Squire's Tale (Guillaume de Lorris and Jean de Meun, *Roman de la Rose*, 18123–18268). On Jean's debt to Bacon, see Suzanne Conklin Akbari, *Seeing Through the Veil: Optical Theory and Medieval Allegory* (Toronto: University of Toronto Press, 2004), 88–96. On Chaucer's debt to Jean, see Brown, *Chaucer and the Making of Optical Space*, 123–35.

68. Peter of Limoges, *The Moral Treatise on the Eye*, 36.

aversion to calamity and preference for comfort. To illustrate this point, he considers the liturgical space of the church, where the congregation and the rood screen face each other. The crucifix atop the rood screen in church, "raised up . . . like a book for the laity," performs the mirror-like reversal of humans' natural inclinations:

> For he stretches his right hand to the north wind, while he extends his left hand to the south wind. Now, prosperity is signified by the south wind; misfortune by the north wind. In this way one ought to remark that the image of the Blessed Virgin has been placed on the side of the north wind under the right hand of Jesus on the cross, since the Blessed Virgin was exposed to misfortunes in this present life. . . . We know, however, that she was loved above all others by God and has now been raised up to God's right hand. For the Lord exposes those dear to him to misfortunes and afflictions in this world when he has determined to place them on the right hand of his glory at the end of time.[69]

The mirror of scripture can teach the faithful to correct their perceptions according to its own paradoxical logic, but the physical crucifix teaches its lesson with the simple mirror-like effect of reversing right and left, the relative directions. The congregation and the priest facing *ad orientem* favor with their right hands the gifts and comforts of the south wind, while the Christ on the crucifix favors the north wind's adversities. Hand to hand, the people and their God face each other *par parsonnages*.

Just as mirror topoi enabled Gréban to speak simultaneously of the story (*histoire*) of the Bible and the work (*oeuvre*) of the play, and so to move seamlessly between texts and bodies, between narratives and actions, similarly, perspectivist optics enable Peter's ethical ruminations to circulate among scripture, contemplative vision, and embodied sanctity. Alhacen had observed that if a person is in a dark room and stares

---

69. Ibid.

at a bright window for a long time, when he closes his eyes he will "see" an image of the window. Peter argues by analogy,

> The opening which all of us should pay attention to and look at frequently is Christ's side pierced on the cross. For this reason . . . [consider] Zechariah 12: 'they will look at him, whom they have pierced.' He said 'they have pierced' in the plural, for all of us have pierced Christ, or rather we have crucified him, since Christ was crucified for everyone. Let each and every person enter the house of his conscience and consider Christ's wounds with the eyes of his mind, so that in his own small measure he might conform himself to the suffering Christ.[70]

From the body of Christ to the Christ of the scriptures, Peter's analogical thought traffics in optical effects. Traditional allegorical readings, such as that of Zecharaiah 12, prompt him to moralize optical phenomena, which in turn produces new commentary on scripture. "But few look at this opening, and for this reason the Lord laments in Proverbs 1, 'I stretched out my hand'—add here: pierced on the cross—'and there was no one who paid any heed.'"[71] Here Christ is both the origin of the proper perspective on relative directions and the origin of attention. Christ exhibits the proper orientation to suffering and ease, right and left, and his wound opens a space for people to enter into and share his orientation. By stretching out his hand, Christ extends his attention to passersby, but they do not repay him with attention. Just as the mirror of scripture corrects the natural perspective and therefore reveals itself to be prior in the order of knowledge to natural vision, so Christ reveals that his own attention prevenes the attentions of would-be spectators. Like the figures-in-action in Gréban's drama, and especially like the Christ in the York Doomsday, Peter's Christ extends himself and intends the world, paying heed to the passersby on their own behalf before they pay heed to him.

---

70. Ibid., 60.
71. Ibid.

This understanding of Christ's presence and attention as preceding the viewers' attention and, indeed, giving their own attention to them is central to how late medieval theology conceived of Christ's presence in the Eucharistic host in the Mass and in liturgical and paraliturgical celebrations of Corpus Christi in processions and drama. The apparently insensate image or object turns out to be the origin of attention, both the giver and the gift of perception in those who look on it. For this reason devotional objects or, in the case of drama, bodies could become the origin of spiritual seeing and be understood optically not simply as objects of vision but as originators of vision or intention.

Devotional Images and Objects as the Origins of Intention

When Peter of Limoges applies optical theory to the rood-screen crucifix, he does not assume that the crucifix itself can actually see, even though he maintains the language of vision and optics. But he does impute intention to the crucifix, *as if it were looking out at us.* I draw this latter term, intention, from the modern discipline of phenomenology because it embraces all kinds of attention, perception, and directedness of consciousness. The concept of intentionality is helpful in the present context because it can be invoked for both (sentient) people and (nonsentient) things, and discourses of moralized optics frequently use the language of vision for both kinds of phenomena.

Indeed, in contrast to Husserl, whose analysis of intention I adopt here,[72] medieval writers, artists, dramatists, and their audiences did not

---

72. For Edmund Husserl, the founder of the modern discipline of phenomenology, consciousness is always consciousness *of* something; it inclines toward one object or another. This inclination or directedness of consciousness is known as intention. Edmund Husserl, *Ideas Pertaining to a Pure Phenomenology and to a Phenomenological Philosophy: First Book,* trans. F. Kersten (Boston: M. Nijhoff, 1982), 63–78. Human sensory perception is also a kind of intention. When a communicant at Mass sees the elevated host, smells the incense, hears the sacring bells, and understands the words "Hoc est corpus meum," she intends the Mass. Each of these individual sensory intentions combines as a complex intention of the complex liturgical phenomenon, the Mass.

limit intentionality to sentient beings. Images or objects could intend their viewers just as much as their viewers intended them.[73] In the thought of Jean-Luc Marion, the intentionality we encounter "looking back at us" takes on central importance. When we intend certain phenomena such as icons or the Eucharist, Marion argues, we discover that they were already intending us, and have indeed given to us the very structure of intention by which we intended them.[74] If they had not given us this structure, we would not have had the capacity to intend

---

To keep things simple, I am here calling on only a part of Husserl's account of experience. A fuller account must note that experience involves subjective and objective poles. When a subject intends an object, she applies structures of signification. What the subject receives from the object is called intuition. For a phenomenon to appear, then, intention must be "filled" by intuition, and this filling is called constitution. When I see a red apple, I intend it as red and my intuition of its color fills my intention; I have thereby constituted the apple so that it might appear as a red apple (something a color-blind person could not do). In Marion's account, counter-experience occurs when the intuition supplied by the object exceeds the structures of signification available to the intending subject. Counter-experience is a surplus of intuition over intention. In another context, a fuller discussion would include an analysis of intuition as well as intention, but for the purposes of this argument, an analysis of intention will suffice.

73. In most cases this is not because a crucifix literally sees the people who gaze upon it, but because the object is directed toward their gaze, and to this extent it is helpful to speak of its directedness toward viewers as intention. In other cases discussed below, however, the presence of a spiritual gaze is attributed to the object. In those cases we must speak of a phenomenal experience that goes beyond constitution, beyond the cooperation of subjective intention and objective intuition available from the object. When a material thing is understood as a locus of personal divine presence, it functions not only as an objective pole, but also as a subjective pole, like the face. This phenomenon cannot be reduced to an object.

74. Again, here I speak of experience that is not only of a phenomenon whose intuition exceeds intention—what Marion calls a "saturated phenomenon"—but one that also involves, like an encounter with another's face, a counter-intentionality that gives some of the structures of meaning that the subject needs in order to intend it. For Marion's analysis of the face's counter-intentionality, see Jean-Luc Marion, *The Erotic Phenomenon*, trans. Stephen E. Lewis (Chicago: University of Chicago Press, 2007), 97–99.

them. Because we encounter our intentionality as having been given to us from the phenomena in question, it follows that our own intentionality cannot be said to exhaust these phenomena, whose intentionality exists in advance and in excess of that which it produces in us.

Marion's term "counter-experience" helpfully differentiates Eucharistic experience from the subject-centered categories of experience that tend to dominate historical and literary treatments of Eucharistic culture. Instead of focusing on what a devotional subject experiences of a sacramental object, an inquiry into sacramental counter-experience will focus on how the sacraments exceed, escape, and ultimately *give* the subject's perceptions, intentions, and affective capacities. Marion explicates counter-experience not as the absence or impossibility of experience, but as the experience of some thing or state of affairs that manifestly exceeds our conceptual and affective categories of experience.[75] To illustrate this, Marion uses optical analogies to suggest that the phenomenon has an "eye" of its own, a kind of vision that the perceiving subject encounters as always already looking at him.[76] Marion's analysis of counter-experience significantly turns repeatedly to the figural po-

---

75. "Counter-experience offers the experience of what irreducibly contradicts the conditions for the experience of objects." Marion, *Being Given*, 215.

76. The phenomenon that triggers counter-experience (a "saturated phenomenon") is like "the speed of something in motion, unrepresentable in a frozen image[, which] nevertheless appears there in and through the smudge that its very unrepresentability makes on the paper." In this analogy, counter-experience is the smudge made by excess motion. When the intending I or eye—Marion plays these two terms of subjectivity together—witnesses such an excessive phenomenon, he realizes that he no longer has the initiative in intention and can no longer predetermine the forms in which the phenomenon will arrive to his eye. To the extent that he understands himself as a subject, as a perceiving I, he must consider himself subsequent to the phenomenon that precedes and exceeds his act of seeing. As Marion puts it, "the I loses its anteriority as egoic pole . . . and cannot yet identify itself, except by admitting the precedence of such an unconstitutable phenomenon. This reversal leaves him stupefied and taken aback, essentially surprised by the more original event, which takes him away from himself." This reversal implies that the phenomenon has an "eye" of its own. Ibid., 216, 217.

tential of the basic terminology of phenomenology, especially the language of optics and judgment, which in his work begins to chime with late medieval theological developments of the same figures. When the subjective I undergoes the reversal of the gaze, he cannot remain a subject, but becomes instead a "witness" who lets himself "be judged . . . by what he himself cannot say or think adequately."[77]

According to a story made famous in the life of St. John Vianney, when a peasant contemplating the Eucharist in the tabernacle was asked what he was doing, he replied, "I look at him, and he looks at me." Using the language of vision, the peasant imputes intentionality to the Eucharist.[78] In these terms, medieval liturgical and paraliturgical practices of devotion to the Eucharist, which are often explained pastorally or devotionally in terms of vision, imply a theory of intentionality when they ascribe vision to the Eucharistic host. Peter speaks of the "eyes of the mind," but the desire to "pay heed" to the wounds of Christ generated a set of material practices contemporary with the growing popularity of his moralized optics. The moralization of optics was a two-way street. While Peter tends to draw lessons about spiritual seeing and related devotions from the visual examples, optical spirituality also encouraged devotees to engage the visual and material presence of devotional objects with the expectation that they were origins of intention. As many art historians exploring performativity have come to see, medieval images and objects are often designed or "framed" to interact with a viewer in a way that assumes the objects' intentionality.[79] Caroline Walker Bynum discusses this phenomenology of devotion in relation to an image of the wound in Christ's side that manifestly elicited the kind of interactive meditation that Peter of Limoges commended. Kisses or caresses have worn away the color and parchment from a large mandorla representing Christ's side wound in a full-page depiction of the *arma Christi* in a

---

77. Ibid., 217.

78. Alfred Monnin, *Le curé d'Ars, vie de M. Jean-Baptiste-Marie Vianney* (Paris: C. Douniol, 1868), 80.

79. See, for example, Elina Gertsman, ed., *Visualizing Medieval Performance: Perspectives, Histories, Contexts* (Burlington, VT: Ashgate, 2008), especially the articles by Richard K. Emmerson, Pamela Sheingorn, and Gertsman.

French luxury manuscript made around 1320 for the future chancellor of France, Guillaume Flote. Bynum argues not only that "the flagrant tactility of the handling of materials" could "draw viewers toward the unseen," but also that "the medieval devout frequently treated such images as a locus of the divine. Indeed, the images themselves sometimes instructed the devout to venerate them with mouths and fingers."[80] The manuscripts themselves imputed intentionality to the images, and the devout responded in kind.

Jill Stevenson's research at the intersection of cognitive theory and performance studies resonates with the catoptric intentionality of moralized optics. Stevenson relates the physical manipulation by York citizens of their books of hours to the embodied interpersonal encounters these citizens produced in the York Play. In studying the Pavement Hours, a book in which eight images were sewn in as flaps that covered (or uncovered) text, Stevenson observes that the book's users converted abstract meditational or ethical goals into concrete actions by engaging the physical book as a locus of intentionality:

> By placing these images over texts, the owner of the Pavement Hours does not reduce the text's value or erase it from the devotional encounter; instead, this act embellishes the textual content with associations and possibilities. . . . The manuscript invites users to lift and lower images literally and thereby lift and lower ways of devotional seeing. . . . More fundamentally, these images may also materially insert the book's owner(s) into the blends of specific devotional moments and therefore into a subsequent user's experience of those blends. If purchased by or for a female user, the image of the female saint holding a book mirrors the reader herself and thereby sews her physical presence into the book's pages.[81]

---

80. Caroline Walker Bynum, *Christian Materiality: An Essay on Religion in Late Medieval Europe* (New York: Zone, 2011), 65. The image is placed at the end of a copy of Gossouin de Metz's *Image du monde*: fol. 140v, Paris, BNF MS Fr. 574, available online through Gallica, http://gallica.bnf.fr.

81. Stevenson, *Performance, Cognitive Theory, and Devotional Culture: Sensual Piety in Late Medieval York* (New York: Palgrave Macmillan, 2010), 109–10.

The practices that Stevenson describes take Peter of Limoges's moralized optics to another level. Whereas Peter uses optical examples to explain optical phenomena in scripture, Stevenson's "hackers" of the Pavement Hours deploy the optical principles Peter discusses in order to capitalize on the material presence of bodies and the cognitive networks that interpersonal embodied interactions activate.

The York Play also brings Peter of Limoges's moral exegesis of scripture into live action and real life, as all good tropological invention must do. The final pageant of the cycle elaborates a phenomenology of ethical exegesis and invention that resists the inclination to think about the good merely by the light of the present world. By presenting Christ and the apostles as spectators of the spectators, the Doomsday pageant reverses the operative intentionality of most of the pageants. It stages counter-experience, a reversal of perspective and experiential priority that exceeds human perceptions and calls ethical action into question. It does so by blending the counter-experience of the Eucharist with the counter-experience of the Last Judgment.

I have now introduced several discourses and practices of devotion that operate in and on the York Doomsday pageant: the dilated temporality of the tropological "now"; the exemplarity of the drama-as-mirror topos by which spectators and actors, Christ and humanity exchange positions; the tradition of moralized optics that relates the optics of visible phenomena to invisible ethical and spiritual phenomena; the counter-intention of devotional objects; and the counter-experience par excellence in the Eucharistic anticipation of the Last Judgment. These discourses and practices open up a wide range of potential performances and responses. In the rest of this chapter, I draw on these discourses to develop three potential, interrelated readings refracted through Reformation-era theology. It will be evident that I consider the final reading to develop the York Play's potential most fully, but the other readings are powerful options that map onto competing theologies of the fifteenth and sixteenth centuries, as well as recent critical perspectives on the play. In pursuing all three, I wish not only to demonstrate the complex religious periodization of a play that was performed over some two hundred years, but also to appreciate the play's potential for thinking about ethical and theological approaches to scripture that could have resonated with the Protestant tropologies discussed in the previous chapter.

God's Vision and the (Reformed) Optics of Imputed Righteousness

God's vision determines the end because human vision is incapable of seeing properly. Peter of Limoges's *Tractatus moralis de oculo* bears a structure similar to that of the York cycle, moving from an examination of human perception, with its challenges and failures, to divine perception, with the emphasis on God's vision of humans. Like the Doomsday pageant, the last section of the *Tractatus moralis* considers how the divine gaze manifests the truth of individual human lives, not only as judge but also as instrument of repair. Peter's text is a meditation on optical as well as moral error, and its program for reform requires that the person in error convert his gaze, not only by changing his perspective, but by changing his habits, often through ascetic disciplines.[82]

The Doomsday pageant likewise attends to the frailty of human vision and the need for virtuous action, encapsulated in the works of mercy, but it takes human frailty a step further in its emphasis on the souls' inability to see even when they encounter Christ. When Christ

---

82. For example, the student who would lead an exemplary life of study must keep the eyes of his soul healthy by avoiding "the swelling of pride, the dust of avarice, and the congealed fluid of lust." Peter of Limoges, *The Moral Treatise on the Eye*, 114. Therefore the student should lead a life of patient humility, poverty, chastity, and temperance. Attendant considerations include a lengthy disquisition on why good food and drink are not eligible business expenses: "Since sobriety at the table and the study of wisdom are connected and have been joined together in such a strong alliance, it is not fitting for academics to make time for sumptuous dishes and to be eager to drain off goblets" (125). But university administrators should not be too quick to recruit Peter for the Board of Visitors if they wish to downsize programs that do not have an immediate economic payoff: "For even when Fortune bestows every one of her rewards, she easily takes them away. But the learning that has been joined to the soul remains with one permanently until the end of life. Hence, the foolishness of some moderns is clear who judge all knowledge a useless effort unless some money results from it, although it is evident according to the judgment of the wise man that knowledge should be sought more than health and all beauty, Wisdom 7: 'More than health and splendor,' and so on" (121–22).

displays his body to the assembled souls, he presents it as evidence of the suffering he incurred on behalf of all souls. But it is unclear what his repeated commands to "loke" and "behalde" are supposed to achieve. Although Christ's reproaches participate in a lyric and liturgical tradition of passion meditation, the risen souls cannot respond to alter their fate. Nor does it seem that recognition of Christ's body as *Christ's* body can change their final destination. Even the blessed souls testify that they did not recognize Christ when they clothed and fed him. Christ describes even their charitable motivation in the negative: "ȝe wolde no sorowe vppon me see" (47.288). These souls did well, but like the evil souls they did not discern Christ's body as such. Even the vision of Christ's resurrected body, bearing the marks of his passion, does not enable the souls to make the connection between their works of mercy and his passion. Gazing on Christ's wounds, the good souls can only say, "Whanne was'te þat we þe clothes brought, / Or visite þe in any nede[?]" (47.305–6). Even the good souls, examining their own consciences, cannot recognize Christ in the history of their own works of mercy. Only Christ's judgment, his own vision of the souls' deeds, can render their lives intelligible within the story of salvation. Christ's vision overcomes their lack of perception. Only by being seen can they truly see Christ and themselves.

The end of the York Play, with its conversion of the gaze, corresponds to the final section of the *Tractatus moralis*, where God's vision comes as a relief from the foregoing rigorous counsel on the need for reform. Now God does all the work, and although his gaze or aversion thereof will decide whether you go to heaven or hell, it can also elicit true contrition and "heal the infirmity of the soul," restoring spiritual health, strength, and goods.[83] According to Peter, it is good to undergo the all-seeing scrutiny of God, especially if it is not really Doomsday. It is good because looking in the mirror does not usually work for you. As much as you look, you do not let yourself *be looked at*. God has a number of solutions to this problem. First, he gives his Son's body for you to look at. Second, God (the Son) looks at you with the gaze that "dissolves

---

83. Ibid., 191–92.

a sinner into tears. . . . For this reason it is said in Luke 22[:61]: The Lord looked at Peter 'and he went outside and wept bitterly.'"[84] The divine gaze of the Doomsday pageant reverses the intentionality of the dramatic experience, implicating the audience more intensely than before in the action of the play, to the point that they can hardly be called spectators. "Spectated" would be more to the point, though they are also already the players according to Gréban's mirror-theory of drama. At the end of the *Tractatus moralis*, however, the divine gaze not only undoes the soul's claims to autonomy and prompt contrition, but also fosters conversion and healing and prompts a return to the world where tropological action can recommence. The souls in the pageant cannot return to the world, but their mirror figures and collaborators in the play can. Once they have been taken up into the pageant's Eucharistic-judicial counter-experience and have received their own selves and works of mercy back again, the audience can go forth with renewed hope.

These reflections gain significant systematic expression in Reformation theology, and it may be instructive to imagine how a York reader of Calvin, Luther, or any of the English reformers influenced by them might have experienced the Doomsday pageant before its last performance in 1569.[85] Viewed from the perspective of reformed theology, Christ's recognition of the good souls' good works—beyond the agents' own ability to recognize them—could be a comfort to those who doubt their own salvation and the reality of the promises of the Gospel.

---

84. Ibid., 191.

85. Calvin and Luther, my sources here, were hardly the most prominent influences in early Yorkshire reformist thought. But their expansive, systematic range of theological thought serves the purpose here better than that of homegrown reformists, such as Thomas Bigod of Yorkshire, who wrote primarily in protest against Roman abuses. My hypothetical viewers of the York Play who have read the magisterial reformers become more plausible after the return of Marian exiles from the Low Countries, so I will imagine this performance as happening in the 1560s. For evidence of Protestant influence in York to the end of Mary's reign, see A. G. Dickens, *Lollards and Protestants in the Diocese of York, 1509-1558* (New York: A&C Black, 1959).

John Calvin's commentary on the Last Judgment episode in Matthew 25 eloquently explicates the Doomsday pageant's portrayal of counter-vision. Our senses do not yet grasp how much Christ values the works of charity, and Calvin suggests as a remedy that "so oft as we do waxe slow to help the pore, let vs loke vpon the sonne of God."[86] But like the pageant's God the Father, who laments humanity's inattention to his Son, Calvin also recognizes humans' tendency not to "loke vpon the sonne of God." In fact, although Christ loves to reward good works, works are never the cause of salvation. The cause of salvation happened earlier in the pageant, when God divided the saved souls from the damned to reflect his election before all time. Calvin comments on this episode in Matthew:

> But before that he will speake of the rewarde of good woorkes, he sheweth by the way that the spring of saluation ariseth from an higher fountaine. For by calling them the blessed of the father, he declareth that their saluation proceedeth of the free fauour of God . . . Wherefore it is not to be doubted, but that Christ describing the saluation of the godly beginneth at the free loue of GOD, whereby they which by the direction of Gods spirite do aspire to righteousnesse in this life, are predestinated to life.[87]

The true cause of the souls' salvation is God's unconditional election of certain souls to blessedness. God is happy to reward these souls for their good works, but those works have not caused their salvation, nor could they know in this life, based on their works, that they would attain salvation. Assurance of salvation comes not through reflection on works

---

86. John Calvin, *A Harmonie vpon the Three Euangelists, Matthew, Mark and Luke with the Commentarie of M. Iohn Caluine*, trans. Eusebius Pagit (London: Thomas Dawson, 1584), 674. Pagit's translation elides Calvin's reference to the senses in the Latin version: "sensum nostrum nondum capere quanti ipse aestimet charitatis officia." Calvin, *Harmonia ex evangelistis tribvs composita, Matthaeo, Marco, & Luca, commentariis Iohannis Calvini exposita* (Geneva: Vignon, 1582), 326.

87. Calvin, *A Harmonie*, 671–72.

but through reflection on Christ: "But when consciences are carefull how they may haue God mercifull, what they shall answer, & vpon what affiance they shall stand if they be called to his iudgement, there is not to be reckoned what the law requireth, but onely Christ must be set forth for righteousnesse, whiche passeth all perfection of the lawe."[88]

We have seen already how, when Christ surveys the assembled souls, living and dead, he seeks his own form in them. He must do this because works alone will not determine the souls' appointed ends. As Martin Luther argued, only because God imputes Christ's righteousness to sinners can they be saved on the day of judgment. In Luther's theology of justification, humans remain depraved by sin on the last day, and they are accounted righteous only because the Father imputes the Son's righteousness to them. Commenting on Galatians 2:16, Luther argued, "Yea sinne is in deede alwaies in vs, and the godly doe feele it: but it is couered and is not imputed vnto us of God for Christes sake: whom because we doe apprehend by Faith, all our sinnes are now no sinnes."[89] Viewing the souls in judgment, the Father chooses to see only his Son in them.

---

88. John Calvin, *The Institution of Christian Religion*, trans. Thomas Norton (London: Wolfe and Harison, 1561), 3.19.2; fol. 209r.

89. Martin Luther, *A Commentarie of M. Doctor Martin Luther vpon the Epistle of S. Paul to the Galathians* (London: Thomas Vautroullier, 1575), fol. 62r. Although the doctrine of imputation became a prominent feature of seventeenth-century Lutheran and Reformed doctrines of justification, scholars dispute whether Luther himself accorded imputation the prominence it later achieved. The 1535 *Commentary on Galatians* represents Luther's mature doctrine of justification, in which imputation plays an important role. On the development of this doctrine, see R. Scott Clark, "*Iustitia imputata Christi*: Alien or Proper to Luther's Doctrine of Justification?," *Concordia Theological Quarterly* 70, no. 3 (2006): 269–310. For a conflicting reading that downplays imputation and promotes union with Christ and deification, see Mark Seifrid, "Luther, Melanchthon and Paul on the Question of Imputation: Recommendations on a Current Debate," in *Justification: What's at Stake in the Current Debates*, ed. Mark A. Husbands and Daniel J. Treier (Downers Grove, IL: InterVarsity Press, 2004), 137–76. It will be apparent that the York Doomsday could be appreciated from both positions.

The York Doomsday employs the technology of the mirror to imagine how the Father will identify the Son in the righteous souls on Judgment Day. The Son displays his wounds, which can then be made present in those who pay heed: "For men schall me þer myrroure make / And haue my doyng in ther mynde" (21.93–94). Christ does not cover up the souls, as certain reformed analogies suggest,[90] but instead imputes his sacrificial body to them by means of a triangulating mirror. Roger Bacon called mirrors the technology by which "anything hidden in an out-of-the-way place in cities, armies, and the like can be brought to light" and made to appear in a place where it was not.[91] We can imagine a performance of the pageant in which the good souls would hold mirrors that presented God the Father with the image of Christ, thereby depicting how their minds and hearts, with the vision of faith fixed on Christ, "have his doing" within them.

In fact, the mirror technology of the Doomsday could explain how Luther could rely on two apparently conflicting ways of describing justification: imputation and union with Christ. In this imagined performance of the York Doomsday—in which bodies, souls, and the play itself are figurative mirrors, and the good souls hold actual mirrors—humans' visions of Christ matter as much as Christ's vision of them because by looking at Christ, their souls mirror Christ to the Father. If the soul is essentially a mirror, then the righteousness of Christ in that mirror is not simply extrinsic; it is intrinsic to the soul, and Christ is united to the soul as an image is united to a mirror.[92] Christ's righteousness is

---

90. One of many possible examples is a line from a Wesleyan hymn, "When this unspotted robe we wear / Our sins are cover'd all by Thee." John Wesley, *Hymns and Spiritual Songs, Intended for the Use of Real Christians of All Denominations* (London: William Strahan, 1753), 105.

91. Lindberg, *Roger Bacon and the Origins of "Perspectiva"*, 331.

92. Of course this unity is not particularly strong and has everything to do with perspective and angle, as Roger Bacon and Peter of Limoges were quick to point out. The image in the mirror is not really *in* the mirror. For this analogy to work, one would need to think about the human soul as *imago Dei*, which is restored by mirroring the image of Christ, so that in this case the image in the mirror really does "stick."

then both imputed and intrinsic, in a manner that is both passive, because the mirror only reflects the image, and active, because the souls
must orient their mirrors to Christ so that Christ then "has his doing"
in them.[93] Since the soul is also made in the image of God, when it reflects the face of God in Christ, the image "sticks." As in a single-lens
reflex camera, the mirror is used to orient the soul toward the image,
and then the mirror momentarily lifts to allow the image to impress the
same image onto the film, which receives the image as a gift and becomes it.

However we might want to parse the logistics of justification here,
the key point is that people cannot recognize their own salvation based
on their works. Only God's vision justifies, for salvation is first and last
an act of God. The primacy of God's vision overwhelms conventional
virtue ethics. Not only can people do nothing that will merit their own
salvation; they also cannot know when they are ministering to Christ's
body in a manner that will receive a reward. On the other hand, like the
little apocalypse of Matthew 25 on which the pageant is based, the
Doomsday promotes indiscriminate works of charity. The saved souls
did not know they were ministering to Christ, so the moral here would
seem to be that one should perform the works of mercy and all the other
duties of a Christian no matter what, in anticipation of the rewards—
not the salvation—that Christ has promised. As Calvin commented on
the Matthean apocalypse, "Wherfore those fantasticall men do very
preposterously vnder pretence of this place withdrawe themselues, both
from the hearing of the word, and also from receiuing the holy supper:
for vnder the same coloure they might also cast away faith and bearing
of the crosse, and prayers, and chastitie."[94]

Calvin's admonitions helpfully frame the incipient fanaticism of
certain English proponents of the Reformation, particularly those gal-
vanized in the course of their exile in Germany and the Low Countries
during the reign of Queen Mary. The circle of reformers that coalesced
around the publications of John Foxe and John Bale during the years

---

93. On the double operation of justification, passive and active, see Luther's full comments on Gal. 2.

94. Calvin, *A Harmonie*, 673.

1553–58 had good reason to "withdraw from" religious practices as defined by the Catholic Church. In their histories and polemics (often the same thing), the act of withdrawal or refusal of sacramental participation often becomes the very manner of "bearing the cross," with heavy consequences including exile and martyrdom. As long as English Protestants had to insist, with Calvin, that faith, cross-bearing, prayer, chastity, "and the other spiritual exercises" remained indispensable aspects of the Christian life, the sacrament of the Eucharist became the central point of contestation.[95] But Calvin's admonitions remind us how even in a highly charged context such as the early Reformation, the doctrine of the Last Judgment necessarily activates the doctrine of the Last Supper, notions of bodily sacrifice, and communal practices of participation in the drama of salvation.

All of these elements work together to profound and surprising effect on the title page of Foxe's *Actes and Monuments*, commonly known as Foxe's *Book of Martyrs* (fig. 6.4). Like the illumination in the Italian book of hours discussed above (fig. 6.3), the title page presents images of worthy and unworthy sacrifice in a Last Judgment tableau. If recognized as a Last Judgment tableau, the column of images on Christ's right hand must represent the blessed and the column on the left the damned. In the bottom diptych, both groups attend to God's revelation, though the blessed listen to the word of God and see his name, the tetragrammaton, mystically inscribed as in the Book of Daniel, while the damned count their beads and take part in Corpus Christi devotions. In the central diptych, the two communities are engaged in worthy and unworthy forms of sacrifice: martyrdom and the Mass.

Although this tableau may seem to divide Protestants from Catholics, just as the sheep are divided from the goats, even a cursory reading of it points to greater nuance and theological depth.[96] The small

---

95. Ibid.

96. Jennifer Rust has noted that later editions seem to have responded to viewers' tendency to read nuance and ambiguity in the image because they label the respective groups as "the persecuted church" and "the persecuting church." Jennifer R. Rust, "Reforming the Mystical Body: From Mass to Martyr in John Foxe's *Acts and Monuments*," *ELH* 80, no. 3 (2013): 638.

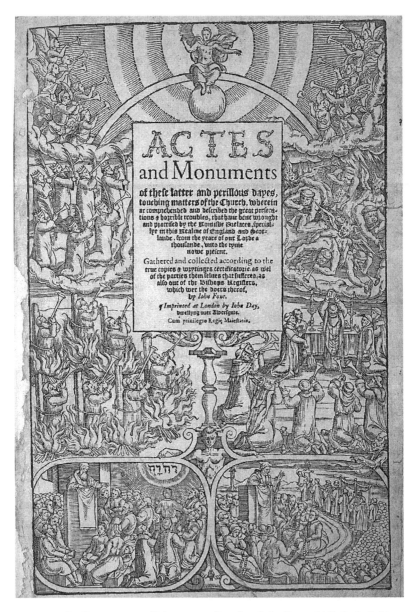

Fig. 6.4. John Foxe, *Actes and Monuments* (London: John Day, 1563). Oxford, Magdalen College, Old Library, Arch.B.I.4.13. Title page of the first edition. Reprinted by kind permission of the President and Fellows of Magdalen College Oxford.

image of the crucified Christ on the Eucharistic host in the right frame counts as a "dead idol," in contrast to the "lively images" of the martyrs on the left. This contrast between dead and lively images pervaded Protestant discourse of images, bodies, and sacraments. But as Jennifer Waldron has argued, the same contrast becomes the basis for an account of Christ's real presence and a robust ecclesiology. The title page tableau encapsulates how *Actes and Monuments* "emphasizes the suffering body as the common attribute of Christians across time and space: contemporary martyrs appear to suffer side by side in the pages of the book with those of earlier times. Their experiences and actions reveal to Foxe's readers a mobile but continuous and visible church, borne in the bodily 'temples' of the faithful."[97] Moreover, all but the more radical Protestants would have to acknowledge that a valid Eucharist, "duly received," authentically made Christ present.[98] Calvin, Luther, and

---

97. Waldron, *Reformations of the Body*, 43.

98. Just how and under what circumstances Christ was present were matters of continual dispute, productive of a wide range of theological accounts. Many important English theologians of the early Reformation—e.g., Thomas Becon, John Hooper, Roger Hutchinson—were influenced by radical Eucharistic theology from the continent (Carlstadt, Zwingli) and explicitly denied any kind of real presence. Brian Douglas, *A Companion to Anglican Eucharistic Theology*, vol. 1, *The Reformation to the 19th Century* (Leiden: Brill, 2011), 65–289. But official Church of England doctrine and liturgy maintained at a minimum that those who "duely receiued these holy misteries" would be fed "with the spirituall foode of the most precious body and bloud of thy sonne our sauiour Jesus Chryst," as the 1552 Book of Common Prayer—the short-lived and most radical version of the communion liturgy—put it. *The Boke of Common Prayer, and Administracion of the Sacramentes, and Other Rites and Ceremonies in the Churche of Englande*, Early English Books Online, 1475–1640 / 1855:19 (London: Edward Whitchurch, 1552), fol. P.2r. According to George Huntston Willliams, an anti-sacramental doctrine of the Lord's Supper was not the most prominent feature of the more radical sorts of English Protestantism in the sixteenth century, compared to those of continental Protestant radicals. Williams, *The Radical Reformation*, 3rd ed. (Kirksville, MO: Truman State University Press, 1995), 1191–1211. But see the discussion of Yorkshire heresy trials during the reign of Mary in Dickens, *Lollards and Protestants*, 222–31. On radical Eucharistic doctrines on the continent that influenced some English

Cranmer all maintained that the Eucharist was the sacrament of unity ordained by Christ.[99] The most widely used Elizabethan catechism taught that "when we rightly receiue the Lordes supper, with the very diuine nourishment of hys body and bloud . . . we are continually fedde and susteyned to eternall life, growing together in them both into one body with Christ."[100] In the second half of the sixteenth century there was a broad, though by no means unanimous, Protestant understanding that the unity of Christ's body was constituted specifically by participation in the Lord's supper. Foxe's title page, with its images of unified communities of bodies, depends on this understanding.

---

reformers and lay radicals, see Williams, *The Radical Reformation*, 109–20, 175–211; Dickens, *Lollards and Protestants*, 33–34; Bryan D. Spinks, *Do This in Remembrance of Me: The Eucharist from the Early Church to the Present Day* (London: SCM Press, 2013), 347–56.

99. Spinks observes that the communion liturgy of the 1552 Book of Common Prayer "could be construed as some Protestant ecumenical rite. It affirmed what all agreed, and . . . avoided those things that were controversial." *Do This in Remembrance of Me*, 346. But already during the late 1540s and early 1550s the mainstream of English doctrine was moving further toward a Reformed position that emphasized Christ's personal presence. "What the Articles, Nowell's catechism, Fenner, Perkins and Hooker all illustrate is a wide Reformed understanding of sacraments and the Eucharist." Ibid., 327. Mystical participation was also a prominent feature of Eucharistic doctrine. Preaching in the mid-1550s, Edwin Sandys, later archbishop of York (1576–88), affirmed that "in the eucharist, or supper of the Lord, our corporal tasting of the visible elements, bread and wine, sheweth the heavenly nourishing of our souls unto life by the mystical participation of the glorious body and blood of Christ." Edwin Sandys, *The Sermons of Edwin Sandys*, ed. John Ayre (Cambridge: Parker Society, 1842), 302.

100. Alexander Nowell, *A Catechisme, or First Instruction and Learning of Christian Religion*, Early English Books Online, 1475–1640 / 1525:12 (London: John Day, 1570), fol. 75r. Even one of the most radical sixteenth-century nonconformists, Robert Browne, affirmed that the Eucharist was the sacrament of unity: "Likewise also must he take the cuppe and blesse and geue thankes, and so pronounce it to be the bloud of Christ in the newe Testament, which was shed for the remission of sinnes, that by faith we might drinke it spirituallie, and so be nourished in one spirituall bodie of Christ." Cited in Spinks, *Do This in Remembrance of Me*, 355.

Although this is not the place to linger over the variety of tropologies in *Actes and Monuments*, one passage should suffice to indicate how Foxe might want the image of martyrs on the title page to be interpreted. It suggests the tropological means by which, as Jennifer Rust has argued, "Foxe's title page trains a community of readers accustomed to this form of sacramental celebration to transfer the values associated with the Mass to a newer martyrological scheme of community."[101] In Book II, Foxe translates an address by Jan Hus that involves, as tropological arguments so often do, Gregory the Great's *Moralia in Iob*. "And Gregory in hys thre and twenty boke of moralles, sayeth thus, God in the holy scripture hathe comprehended what soeuer thyng may hapen vnto any man, and in the same hathe, by the exampels of those whyche are gone afore, taught them whyche are to come, how to reforme theyr lyues."[102] This understanding of generational exemplarity and reformation of life informs the title page illustration. The faithful community in the bottom diptych hears the Gospel of Christ, who sacrificed his body for the sake of the elect. In the middle frame, the elect follow Christ's example, reforming their lives even unto death. They make the ultimate sacrifice for the sake of the community. The sacrificial suffering of the few participates in Christ's own martyrdom on behalf of the entire community, who are shown by this witness the truth of the Gospel. According to John Borthwick, on trial for heresy in Scotland in 1540, the martyrs fulfill Paul's claim that his own sufferings fill up what was lacking in the sufferings of Christ, on behalf "of his body, which is the church" (Col. 1:24). "For Christ hath vouchsaued to honour vs with this honour, that he doth impute and call our afflictions to be his."[103] The martyrs are fully converted to Christ's death so that others who are not called to martyrdom might nevertheless be inspired to do good and bear their sufferings

---

101. Rust, "Reforming the Mystical Body," 636. My treatment of Foxe's title page is inspired by Rust's analogous treatment in this incisive article.

102. John Foxe, *Actes and Monuments* (1563), 161. For all editions I cite from *The Unabridged Acts and Monuments Online*, giving the year and page number of the edition cited.

103. Foxe, *Actes and Monuments* (1583), 1285.

patiently for the sake of the church. "[T]he profit and fruit [of the martyrs] is aboundant to glorify God by their death, to subscribe and beare witness vnto the truth by their bloud, and by the contempt of this present lyfe, to witnesse, that he doth seeke after a better lyfe, by his constancie and stedfastnesse to confirme and establish the fayth of the church, and subdue and vanquish the enemy."[104]

This theology of martyrdom guards the act of witness from becoming a work of righteousness in the same way that the Protestant theory of justification handles any good work: by imputation. Christ "doth impute and call our afflictions his." The mere fact of persecution is not a mark of salvation, just as in the Doomsday pageant, works of mercy are not automatically marks of salvation. Only the vision of God determines whether any work, including martyrdom, is to be accounted as Christ's. Foxe and his readers were keenly aware that there had been Catholic "martyrs" whose persecution did not render *them* among the elect. Likewise, the Church of England daily prayed in its Mass that its Eucharistic "sacrifice of praise and thanksgiving" might be deemed worthy of acceptance by God the Father. A worthy Eucharist effectively offered the Father "our selves, our soules and bodies, to be a reasonable, holy, and lively sacrifice," in the words of the Elizabethan Book of Common Prayer.[105] So even though the left-hand figures in Foxe's title page are labeled "blessed" in some editions and contrasted to the "cursed," without these labels the martyrs could be interpreted as a type of lively sacrifice that is in fact fulfilled in the right-hand frame's image of the Eucharistic offering. According to this interpretation, then, there are worthy and unworthy martyrdoms, as well as worthy and unworthy Eucharists—even within Protestant communities.

Interpreted carefully as a tropological rendering of Matthew 25, Foxe's title page functions like the depiction of worthy and unworthy receptions of the Eucharist in the illumination prefacing the Penitential

---

104. Ibid.

105. *The Book of Common Prayer: Commonly Called the First Book of Queen Elizabeth. Printed by Grafton 1559* (Chiswick: W. Pickering, 1844), fol. 86v.

Psalms of the late medieval book of hours discussed above (fig. 6.3). It forces all those who would be martyrs, or who would offer their lesser afflictions up to God, to examine their hearts lest they "presume to come to this thy table . . . trustinge in oure owne rightuousnesse," as the Book of Common Prayer's prayer before reception put it.[106] This interpretation of Foxe's title page as a penitential primer does not subvert or deconstruct its message or the reformed theology on which it is based. Rather, it reveals a depth of soteriology where the surface antagonisms of Protestant and Catholic thought diminish. This depth is approached first through tropological reflection on Matthew 25, and then finally reached in the eschatological perspective demanded by the Eucharist, from which point God's counter-vision comes to the fore.

As this "Protestant" reading of the pageant suggests, its deep investment in the priority of counter-experience places it well within the conceptual world of Protestant soteriology, with its emphases on election and imputation. Viewers of and participants in a Reformation-era production of the Doomsday pageant might have found it, therefore, a poignant form of the counter-experience that their own Protestant theology and liturgy offered them, as in a mirror, on a daily basis.

Sacramental Hegemony and the Complacency of the Rich

Because we know a great deal about the charitable activities of the Mercers' guild that produced the Doomsday pageant, we can inquire with a certain amount of empirical evidence into the conditions of the pageant's practical reception and its producers' tropological inventions. This inquiry enables judgments about the play's Eucharistic theology and its implications for ethical participation in the history of salvation. Of all the York Play's pageants, the Doomsday pageant most explicitly addresses social inequities and the Gospel's preferential option for the poor. While the Crucifixion pageant identifies Christ as naked, poor, and thirsty, encouraging concern for the vulnerable by empathetic

---

106. Ibid., fol. 86r.

transference, the Doomsday pageant, like the Gospel on which it is based, explicitly exhorts Christians to do the works of mercy. That the city's wealthiest guild, the Mercers, should take responsibility for this pageant invites scrutiny of their motives. The pageant's exhortations to charity have opened the Mercers' guild up to charges of hypocrisy. The mercers, however, were indeed quite charitable, following the counsel of their own pageant. The chief risk to their souls is not hypocrisy but presumption. York's wealthy providers of charity and sponsors of lay sacramental theater risk claiming hegemony over the social body of Christ. But the Doomsday pageant, as I will argue in the final section of this chapter, will not allow providers of charity to possess the body of Christ in the bodies of the poor and ill.

The Doomsday was the most elaborate of all the York pageants. Its effects included "a brandreth of Iren þat god sall sitte vppon when he sall fly vppe to heuen," eleven "gilted" angels "holding the passion," and four smaller angels "to renne aboute in þe heuen."[107] The Mercers' guild expended on average thirty shillings on each production, roughly sixty days' wages for a skilled carpenter.[108] Expenses included breakfast, lunch, and dinner for many of the performers and workers, as well as "drynk vpon corpus cristi day be þe way."[109] Of all the York guilds, the Mercers could most comfortably afford the outlay. "The mercers were the wealthiest citizens of York and played an important role in civic politics. Of the eighty-eight mayors between 1399 and 1509, sixty-eight were mercers. In some years they dominated the city council; for example, in 1420 twenty of the twenty-nine members of the council were mercers."[110]

In accordance with their wealth, the mercers were also charitable. Yet their rhetoric and practices of charity, expressed in their own guild ordinances and the city's labor structure that they established and main-

---

107. Cited from documents in the archives of the Merchant Adventurers of York in Alexandra F. Johnston and Margaret Dorrell, "The York Mercers and Their Pageant of Doomsday," *Leeds Studies in English*, n.s., 6 (1972): 15.

108. Ibid., 21–22.

109. Ibid., 14.

110. Ibid., 11.

tained in their prominent positions on the city council, contorted the simple council of alms portrayed in other pageants. According to one analysis, which I dispute below, the guild system redefined "charity" and reduced it to a system of fines exchanged among guilds when they impinged on each other's proprietary trade rights.[111] By institutionalizing charity in this way, according to this line of argument, the Mercers neglected the corporal works of mercy commended in their own pageant. But however much the Mercers may have been responsible for labor's economic woes—an issue much debated among historians—the craft guild's membership overlapped with that of the religious guilds, which did provide corporal charity. Christ's second coming and judgment therefore ratify the works that individual mercers have made possible through their membership in and gifts to the religious guilds. In Pamela King's reading, "*corpus Christi* does descend among the people and those who are saved are those who, like the members of the Corpus Christi guild, have endeavored to perform significant corporal acts of mercy."[112] While the Corpus Christi guild, a religious confraternity,

---

111. As Kate Crassons argues, "the city's insistence on charity ironically emerges from the conflicts created by its own requirement that artisans be divided into artificially rigid labor classifications. Rather than encouraging artisans to recognize their common interests and work collectively, the guild system split the body of craftsmen into competing parts. The resultant disputes, as we have seen, demand a version of charity in which the mercantile oligarchy steps in to 'resolve' the very conflicts it creates. It restores the broken bonds among craftsmen by administering a form of charity that requires one guild to pay money toward another's pageant as a 'meene of soccour and supportacion.' In this particular context, the language of charity once again differs from that of the Last Judgment pageant, where food, drink, and clothing constitute the primary means of relief voluntarily given by one individual to another. Here, charity becomes a part of business negotiations, and it functions as the oligarchic body's attempt to mediate the conflicts it creates and depends on within the body of artisan workers." *The Claims of Poverty*, 265. For another suspicious view of guild charity that focuses on the inequitable structures of economic institutions, see Christina Marie Fitzgerald, *The Drama of Masculinity and Medieval English Guild Culture* (New York: Palgrave Macmillan, 2007), 28–33.

112. P. King, *The York Mystery Cycle and the Worship of the City*, 27.

focused its resources on liturgical devotion rather than corporal works of mercy, the merchants associated with the Mercers' trade guild and its religious counterpart, the confraternity of Holy Trinity in Fossgate, certainly did perform charitable deeds, readily visible to the citizens of York in the hospital that the confraternity sponsored.[113] This particular history reflects the complexity of the relationships between religious, craft, and mercantile guilds.

These charitable activities have aroused the suspicions of some literary scholars who have relied on the work of the historian Heather Swanson.[114] Swanson studied the shifting application of funds derived from craft-ordinance fines during the period in which the York Play was devised and came to take on a central and resource-intensive role in the city's civic life. Before the rise of the play, half of craft-ordinance fines had been devoted to "spiritual and fraternal purposes," while the other half went into the guild coffers.[115] As the play demanded more guild resources, the guilds devoted the fine money to the "spiritual and fraternal purpose" of producing their pageants. Swanson suggests that the play therefore diverted charitable funds from the poor to the maintenance of the civic cult. What Swanson does not make explicit in this frequently cited passage is that the "spiritual and fraternal purposes" of fine money rarely entailed care for the poor. Nor does Swanson mention that religious and craft guilds that provided aid to the poor and disabled continued to do so throughout the fifteenth century, either because they were not responsible for the pageants (in the case of the religious confraternities) or because their charitable funds came from sources other than "pageant silver."[116]

---

113. David J. F. Crouch, *Piety, Fraternity, and Power: Religious Gilds in Late Medieval Yorkshire, 1389–1547* (Cambridge: Boydell and Brewer, 2000), 139–40.

114. Heather Swanson, *Medieval Artisans: An Urban Class in Late Medieval England* (Oxford: Basil Blackwell, 1989). In addition to Crassons and Fitzgerald, cited above, see the trenchant Marxian-theological assessment of the historiography of guild economics in Beckwith, *Signifying God*, 42–55.

115. Swanson, *Medieval Artisans*, 119.

116. On the charitable activities of guilds, see, besides Crouch cited above, P. H. Cullum and P. J. P. Goldberg, "Charitable Provision in Late-

Crassons argues that the Mercers' trade guild did not provide any aid to the poor (of the kind commended by Christ in their own pageant).[117] Yet in 1420 more than two thirds of the members of the Holy Trinity confraternity responsible for the hospital were mercers.[118] After its incorporation in 1430, the Mercers' guild shared account rolls with the Holy Trinity Fossgate hospital; they were overseen by the same people. When the Mercers' guild was incorporated, the mercers, who had run the hospital probably since its founding in 1371, had the chance to divest themselves of the responsibility of Holy Trinity hospital and its salaries for chaplain, master, and room and board for more than a dozen full-time residents. Yet they chose to put the charity on the account rolls of their guild, which amounted to undertaking full financial responsibility.[119] A hospital such as Holy Trinity Fossgate was not a profit center. There was no chance for the Mercers' trade guild to line their pockets with rents. Rather, their official sponsorship of the hospital and shared accounts likely streamlined the finances for a group of individuals who had supported the hospital, along with other citizens, including a mason, a draper, a clerk, and two bakers.[120] These records demonstrate that the membership of the Mercers' guild and eventually the guild itself were involved in a long-term, well-organized, costly provision of charity to York's poor, sick, and disabled.

Whatever suspicions historians might harbor concerning the motives of the wealthy in their care for the poor and ill, the mercers and their elite counterparts gave generously. Many charitable bequests of York's wealthy endowed in-home hospitals or orphanages that they had established and maintained in their own lifetimes. Cecily Giry, for example, "provided three featherbeds to be kept in her guestchamber for

---

Medieval York: 'To the Praise of God and the Use of the Poor,'" *Northern History* 29 (1993): 24–39.

117. Crassons, *The Claims of Poverty*, 254–59.

118. Crouch, *Piety, Fraternity, and Power*, 139.

119. Maud Sellers, *The York Mercers and Merchant Adventurers, 1356–1917*, Publications of the Surtees Society 129 (Durham: Andrews and Co., 1918), xvi–xvii.

120. Crouch, *Piety, Fraternity, and Power*, 140.

the hospitality of the poor."[121] These "maisons dieu" were not bureau-cratic institutions that applied capitalist managerial efficiency to the problem of indigence, nor did they emerge from a counter-cultural religious fringe such as the modern Catholic Worker houses. Rather, they responded directly and intimately to mainstream cultural adaptations of Christ's exhortations in Matthew 25, conceived as "works of mercy." Such works were depicted in a fourteenth-century glass window in All Saints, North Street (next to the *Prick of Conscience* window depicting the apocalypse). And just beyond that window, they were depicted once a year in the Doomsday pageant. As Cullum and Goldberg have argued, the wealthy performed charity consciously as works of mercy. "A significant proportion of the charitable provision in later medieval York wills was likewise conceived in terms of these Seven Works, and they may have continued as a model for testamentary charitable provision even into the Reformation era. As late as 1542, for example, Jane Huntingdon of Hull provided that, in the event of her legatee dying, her house be sold and the proceeds used to support the Seven Works of Mercy."[122] As this brief discussion suggests, and failing the clear light of the Last Judgment, readings of the Doomsday pageant's ethics against the supposedly craven and insouciant practices of the Mercers' guild and York's other rich and powerful citizens overstep the proper bounds of human and historical judgment.

Rather, the more subtle critique to which the Mercers and their pageant are vulnerable concerns the certainty that works of mercy constitute saving care for the hidden Christ. The Mercers and other wealthy institutions and individuals risked establishing a hegemony over the works of mercy. The case for the Mercers' sanctity and their hegemony over Christ's body might go something like the following, admittedly tongue-in-cheek, line of argument:

Although the play of Corpus Christi might have made the body of Christ present through "sacramental theater," the wealthy citizens'

---

121. Cullum and Goldberg, "Charitable Provision," 33.
122. Ibid., 28.

works of mercy had a Gospel promise attached to them that theater did not: "As long as you did it to one of these my least brethren, you did it to me" (Matt. 25:40). The Doomsday pageant advertised the Mercers' guild's continual rendering of Christ's body throughout the year in their charitable activities. As the city's poor and ill came through the doors of its hospitals and *maisons dieu*, they were transfigured into Christ by the charitable gaze of the wealthy who provided for them.

How fitting, then, that the Eucharistic procession should have shifted from the feast of Corpus Christi to the following day in 1476, replaced by the sacramental theater and its representations of York's charitable confections of the body of Christ. This migration answered to a crisis of community in late medieval church practice. The true body of Christ had become displaced from the bonds of charity enacted in a communal meal to be circumscribed in a wafer magically consecrated by the precise rubrics of a priest and thereafter available to the community only by remote vision.[123]

In terms of John Bossy's influential narrative, the social function of the Mass had migrated to the rituals of Corpus Christi, and now further to the play of Corpus Christi. Freed from misplaced devotion to the Eucharistic host in procession, which had after all

---

123. As Dom Gregory Dix concluded his magisterial study of medieval liturgy, "The old corporate worship of the eucharist is declining into a mere focus for the subjective devotion of each separate worshipper in the isolation of his own mind and it is the latter which is beginning to seem to him more important than the corporate act. The part of the individual layman in that corporate action had long ago been reduced from 'doing' to 'seeing' and 'hearing.' Now he is even beginning to think that over much 'seeing' (ceremonial) and 'hearing' (music) are detrimental to proper 'thinking' and 'feeling'. While the catholic doctrines of the priesthood and the conversion of the elements were retained, the remnants of the corporate action still provided an objective centre which was identical for all present. But it needed only a continuation of the shift of emphasis for the eucharistic action to come to be regarded as a mere occasion for or accompaniment to the individual's subjective thought and emotion." Cited in Sarah Beckwith, *Christ's Body: Identity, Culture, and Society in Late Medieval Writings* (New York: Routledge, 1993), 136n58.

been excised from its properly embedded place in the rich liturgical and social fabric of the Mass, the citizens could now attend fully to the tropological imperative of Matthew 25 and tend to Christ's body by the bonds of affection he himself had instituted for his church. Just as the idea of the consecrated host as Christ's real presence emerged to consolidate the function of the priesthood,[124] so the merchant class consolidated its soteriological function by confecting Christ under its charitable gaze, on behalf of the larger community, the consolidation of which Mervyn James has argued was a chief function of the feast.[125] These migrations of symbolic capital and religious significance were not only natural,[126] but they also tended progressively to more authentic responses to the Gospel revelation that God is charity. By consolidating their role as stewards of active charity, the Mercers placed themselves on the side of progress and communal solidarity, and against the creeping tide of individualism. They anticipated in less troubled times the migration of Eucharistic function depicted on the title page of Foxe's *Actes and Monuments*, where the perfect sacrifice is made not in bread and wine but in the bodily suffering of some members of Christ's body on behalf of others. Let the priests have their Mass; the laity had the *koinonia* of the true church.

If the above thought experiment grates against some common sensibilities, it may be because it is difficult to think of the wealthy, even the generous wealthy, as holy. As Peter Brown has observed, we tend to "treat the renouncers of wealth as the heroes and heroines of a 'true' Christianity and to view all other forms of religious giving as somehow

---

124. Ibid., 30.

125. Mervyn James, "Ritual, Drama and Social Body in the Late Medieval English Town," *Past and Present* 98 (1983): 3–29.

126. As Miri Rubin asserts in her programmatic observation that "Corpus Christi is . . . part of a system of meaning, of a chain of associations, in which the eucharist possessed a central signifying power." *Corpus Christi: The Eucharist in Late Medieval Culture* (New York: Cambridge University Press, 1991), 5.

a betrayal of the essential radicalism of the Christian movement."[127] But this line of argument should set off other alarms as well, the same alarms triggered by late medieval ecclesiastical claims to hegemony over Christ's body in a confected wafer—those attempts to circumscribe the uncircumscribable symptomatic of "an exclusive concentration and focus on one moment of the canon of the mass" by which "Eucharistic discourse and practice became assimilated to Eucharistic dogma."[128] Our suspicion of sacramental hegemony should extend also to what I am imagining as the Mercers' claim to confect the body of Christ in the objects of their charity.

The Mercers' pretensions to possess Christ's body by works of mercy would reflect an exclusively literal reading of Christ's exhortations to charity. The problem is not that the Mercers do not get the moral, but that they get only the moral. To grasp the moral of a literally didactic passage of scripture is not to read tropologically. Tropology is the circulatory system of scripture, pushing the blood of the literal sense into action and circulating it through the lungs of the allegorical sense in order to animate and inhabit the body with an anagogical completeness. Any literal moral injunction must be carefully applied in the context of today as a way of participating in the history of redemption in anticipation of the perfect justice of the kingdom of heaven. Carried out simply as moral acts, divorced from salvation-historical participation and without respect to a comprehensive vision of justice, good deeds do not merit salvation. To put it in terms that are both reformed and Tridentine, good works are meritorious when they are the result of grace. John Bale puts the point in characteristically stark but traditionally mainstream terms when he comments on John's Apocalypse, wherein the two "books of reckonings" opened by the final judge are the book of conscience and

---

127. Peter Brown, *Through the Eye of a Needle: Wealth, the Fall of Rome, and the Making of Christianity in the West, 350–550 AD* (Princeton: Princeton University Press, 2012), xxv.

128. David Aers and Sarah Beckwith, "The Eucharist," in *Cultural Reformations: Medieval and Renaissance in Literary History*, ed. Brian Cummings and James Simpson (New York: Oxford University Press, 2010), 159.

the book of life. Those who "had led their lives here without faith and the Spirit of Christ" are judged strictly by the book of conscience and do not receive any reward for their good deeds. Rather, they are judged "according to the filthy works whereof their desperate consciences accused them."[129] Good works, in order to be saving works, must be ratified by the vision of God.

The Mercers' hypothetical pretensions to possess the body of Christ by an instrumentalizing gaze of charity ignore the fact that Christ's presence can damn as well as save, as in the examples of worthy and unworthy reception of the Eucharist. Craven motives will not disappear Christ's body from the naked, thirsty, and hungry recipients of charity, but they could inflict judgment on those who would unworthily receive the body of Christ by a false hospitality. To ignore the knock of the needy is not the only way to sin against hospitality. The historical evidence suggests that the Mercers were indeed quite charitable according to the literal instructions of Matthew 25. The danger was that by providing and advertising their charity, they might claim to possess and control the body of Christ in the "least of these."

The Primacy of Eucharistic Counter-Experience

The foregoing thought experiment points to a potential red herring in recent literary critical historiographies of medieval and early modern Eucharistic culture. In 1944, Henri de Lubac produced *Corpus mysticum: L'eucharistie et l'Église au Moyen Age*, a searching, widely appreciated genealogy of how a late medieval concern to secure the realism of the Eucharist as Christ's "true body" had led some theologians to contrast the "true body" of the Eucharist to the "mystical"—read "irreal"—body of Christ in the church.[130] Inspired by de Lubac's narrative, Ernst

---

129. John Bale, *Select Works of John Bale, D. D., Bishop of Ossory: Containing the Examinations of Lord Cobham, William Thorpe and Anne Askewe and "The Image of Both Churches,"* ed. Henry Christmas (Cambridge: Cambridge University Press, 1849), 577–78.

130. Henri de Lubac, *Corpus mysticum: L'eucharistie et l'Église au Moyen âge. Étude historique* (Paris: Aubier, 1949); Henri de Lubac, *Corpus Mysticum:*

Kantorowicz in 1957 extended the argument to show how the social community, no longer Christ's "true" body, turned into the king's mystical body, an immanent, secular body politic, which was the communal dimension of "the king's two bodies."[131] However, as Jennifer Rust has compellingly argued, Kantorowicz flattened out de Lubac's much more subtle argument and transformed the meaning of the key term, "mystical," from an index of material and social realism as in de Lubac to an index of ethereal abstraction: "the primordial stuff of secularism . . . malleable for new ideological purposes once the church has unleashed it from the liturgical sphere."[132] Yet Kantorowicz's narrative, or de Lubac's

---

The Eucharist and the Church in the Middle Ages: Historical Survey, trans. Gemma Simmonds (Notre Dame, IN: University of Notre Dame Press, 2007).

131. Ernst Hartwig Kantorowicz, *The King's Two Bodies: A Study in Mediaeval Political Theology* (Princeton: Princeton University Press, 1957).

132. Jennifer R. Rust, "Political Theologies of the *Corpus Mysticum*: Kantorowicz, Schmitt, de Lubac," in *Political Theology and Early Modernity*, ed. Graham L. Hammill, Julia Reinhard Lupton, and Etienne Balibar (Chicago: University of Chicago Press, 2012), 117. Rust's central contention is such an important and timely corrective that it is worth quoting at length: "On one level, Kantorowicz is faithful to the outline of de Lubac's claims about the significant change in the idea of the 'mystical body' that occurred around the twelfth century—the *curieux chassé-croisé* that transferred 'mystical' from a sacramental to a primarily ecclesiastical sense. However, if we recall de Lubac's original text, it is also clear that Kantorowicz flattens out what de Lubac presents as an originally dynamic situation which involves a fluid relation between *ecclesia* and Eucharist, to further his own idea of a genealogy of secular polity, one in which theological structures are progressively taken over by political secular forces as metaphors or fictions. For de Lubac, it is simply not the case that in the early Middle Ages *corpus mysticum* 'referred not at all to the body of the Church nor to the oneness and unity of human society' as Kantorowicz insists. Instead, it would be more accurate to say that *Corpus Mysticum* seeks to demonstrate that the 'liturgical or sacramental' was always already 'sociological' in the milieu of the early church. Kantorowicz seeks to play down the claim about the earlier 'sociological' aspect of the 'sacramental' because it could interfere with the progressively immanentizing thrust of his larger argument. As theological tropes become sociological in *The King's Two Bodies*, they tend also to be tamed into pliable fictional material for representing specific political, very human, interests, evacuated of all but the barest hint of transcendent content" (114).

read through Kantorowicz, has dominated literary critical accounts of the Eucharist and the social body in the late Middle Ages.

In fact, although de Lubac focuses on the hegemonic dangers of Eucharistic realism, he also registers the equally hegemonic danger of a myopic ecclesial realism—the equivalent of the Mercers' hypothetical claim to hegemony over Christ's body in the poor. In de Lubac's view, any claim to possess Christ by possessing either the Eucharist or the social mission of the church transmutes into idolatry. De Lubac appreciates the goods of the Eucharistic doctrines that developed in the thirteenth to seventeenth centuries concerning transubstantiation and the worship of the Eucharist outside of the Mass.[133] Throughout *Corpus Mysticum* de Lubac assumes that Christ's Eucharistic and social bodies equally and mutually constitute the "true" and the "mystical" bodies. He insists that the church needs both the "communitarian" and the sacramental understandings of Christ's body.[134] Although he understands

---

133. Often invoked in literary studies as a static dogma, transubstantiation was anything but. Thomas Aquinas's formulation did not address important metaphysical issues concerning substance and dimension that were later revealed by John Duns Scotus and William of Ockham, among others, to whom various strands of Thomistic thinkers gave various answers over another hundred years. A similar refining of the doctrine was occurring also in the seventeenth century as John of St. Thomas responded to Descartes's new metaphysics. For a conspectus of this history, as well as the intricacies of transubstantiation, in the context of the devotional practice of Eucharistic adoration, see Reinhard Hütter, "Eucharistic Adoration in the Personal Presence of Christ: Making Explicit the Mystery of Faith by Way of Metaphysical Contemplation," *Nova et Vetera*, English Edition 7, no. 1 (2009): 199–204.

134. "Eucharistic realism and ecclesial realism: these two realisms support one another, each is the guarantee of the other. Ecclesial realism safeguards Eucharistic realism and the latter confirms the former. The same unity of the Word is reflected in both. Today, it is above all our faith in the 'real presence,' made explicit thanks to centuries of controversy and analysis, that introduces us to faith in the ecclesial body: effectively signified by the mystery of the Altar, the mystery of the Church has to share the same nature and the same depth. Among the ancients, the perspective was often inverted. The accent was habitually placed on the effect rather than on the cause. But the ecclesial realism to which they universally offer us the most explicit testimony is at the same time, and when necessary, the guarantee of their Eucharistic realism. This is

himself to be narrating an inexorable evolution,[135] he allows that Eucharistic doctrine had to develop in order to bring about certain goods.[136] De Lubac maintains that during all periods of the history he narrates, Eucharist and church *were* actually interpenetrating and mutually informative in precisely the way that "bad" Eucharistic doctrine missed: "I am certainly not so naïve as to think that this living synthesis [in which the church and Eucharist are 'formed by one another day by day'] was never realized in its perfect state in the thinking of the Doctors or the practice of the people of any century."[137]

Returning to York, if we place the righteous mercers into de Lubac's account, we can see how they err on the side of the social dimension of the Mass. Eucharistic hegemony can cut both ways. For this reason Sarah Beckwith's profound reading of the Doomsday pageant as resisting Eucharistic hegemony remains within a problematic approach to the Eucharist that is best characterized as experiential. For Beckwith, the play's finale on the Pavement consolidates its implicit critique of late medieval Eucharistic theology and practice by presenting a more authentic alternative, the church as theater.[138] Sacramental theater improves on ecclesiastical liturgy because it works from "acknowledgment

---

because the cause has to be proportionate to the effect." De Lubac, *Corpus Mysticum*, 251–52.

135. Ibid., 256.

136. "We should not conclude, from all this, that evolution was a negative thing in itself. It was normal and therefore good. Furthermore, it was needed in order to remedy error and to offer a response to the questions inevitably raised by progress in understanding. Preserving the *status quo* in theories and viewpoints has never been and can never be an adequate means of safeguarding the truth. In the present case, many misunderstandings that the ensuing changes brought about were the sorts of inconveniences that all good brings in its wake." Ibid., 258–59.

137. Ibid., 260.

138. "The Corpus Christi pageants enact the church as a series of dramatic performances through which the visibility of the body of Christ is rendered in relation to the possibility of recovery of reception in liturgical action. For in these pageants, the life of the church is told with utter concreteness in relation to our response to and recognition of the passion and resurrection of Christ." Beckwith, *Signifying God*, 114.

rather than knowledge, trust and imagination rather than doctrine."[139] It can therefore make Christ's body present more authentically than that other sacramental theater, the Mass.[140] In Beckwith's reading, the York Play responds to the late medieval tendency to understand the Eucharistic host as the "true body" of Christ, in contradistinction to the social community as a kind of virtual body. The Doomsday pageant stages Christ's presence as a relationship of mutual acknowledgment through the cultivation of the bonds of charity in works of mercy. "The possibilities of scapegoating are ruled out about as scrupulously as they could be."[141] The pageant turns on "a genuine indeterminacy" that refuses to tell "us in advance of performance whether the souls are good and bad."[142] And because it happens in an eschatological future, "the city of God never becomes one that is transparently identified on earth as being the possession of any particular jurisdiction."[143] But why not? Why shouldn't the city of God be identified with the providers of charity, especially the institutions sponsored by the sponsors of the pageant? Only Eucharistic counter-experience could radically undercut both social-charitable *and* Eucharistic hegemony of the body of Christ.

The Doomsday pageant exposes the social hegemony of sacramental theater by inciting a sense of eschatological emergency, the sense that this is my last chance to love before the end. In representing the time at which it is too late to love, it holds out the present moment as the time

---

139. Ibid., 89.

140. "The Corpus Christi plays of the late Middle Ages understand the sacramental relation between form and grace as *best* realized in theater. Theater is . . . the perfectly consonant form for the religion of incarnation. Precisely because sacraments are best understood as actions and not things, it is in the theater of dramatic action that they are best understood. In theater's phenomenality, in its central resource of the body of an actor, . . . sacrament is no longer the little wafer held aloft between priestly hands but strives to fulfill and point toward the host's most ardent and outrageous claims—its most generously utopian aspirations to cause what it signifies, to perform a bond of love in the community of the faithful" (ibid., 59–60).

141. Ibid.

142. Ibid., 112.

143. Ibid., 113.

in which to love.[144] The counter-experience of the Eucharist "sets itself up as a judge of the worldly ambiguities of immediacy."[145] Just as in the liturgy of the Mass, temporal succession "rests against the eternal life of God."[146] Eucharistic counter-experience relativizes both urgency and tardiness by rebuffing the certitude of both. The pageant occurs between too late and too soon. It refuses to set the day or the hour. Like the liturgy itself, it "refuses sensible certitude."[147]

Taken together with the rest of the York Play, then, the Doomsday pageant is arguing that if you want social justice, if you want a reconciled community that confects Christ's body in works of mercy, you also need the adorable transubstantiated body of Christ confected by a priest and given by the institutional church. The cult of Corpus Christi must continually direct the gaze to the uncircumscribable host and insist on the transubstantial real presence there in order to counter the affective, epistemological, and ethical certitude given in the perceptible phenomenon of a reconciled or reconciling community. The transubstantiated body of Christ in the Eucharist itself resists possession and places under judgment all those who would possess it. If the Doomsday pageant is a host miracle, it is one designed to counter the certitudes of another kind of host miracle, one that would claim the audience, the gathered community, as the true body of Christ. The social doctrine of the Eucharist can objectify and circumscribe Christ's body just as much as dematerializing claims for the *corpus verum*. The Doomsday pageant refuses the either/or of social/sacramental realism, and also the reduction of the Christian life to ethics. It insists that works of mercy be transformed into works of love (*caritas*), which can be discerned only insofar as they participate in Christ. But as the mirror optics of Christ's

---

144. "The point is to transform one instant among others—a simple insignificant *item* of repetition—into a final instance. . . . love now as if your next act of love were to accomplish your final possibility of loving." Marion, *The Erotic Phenomenon*, 208.

145. Lacoste, *Experience and the Absolute*, 143.

146. Robert Sokolowski, *Eucharistic Presence: A Study in the Theology of Disclosure* (Washington, DC: Catholic University of America Press, 1994), 106.

147. Lacoste, *Experience and the Absolute*, 143–44.

search for the marks of his own wounds among the gathered body of the faithful suggests, the works of love, though hidden, are also external.

Even as it rebuffs human claims to certitude about salvation and works, the Doomsday pageant enacts the return from counter-experience back to experience, and from anagogy back to tropology, when Christ identifies the good souls' works of mercy as saving works performed for him. These souls become "good" when Christ gives back to them their own works, now constituted as saving works of love. As for the audience, their mirror figures in the play prevened their selves and gave them back to themselves as participants in the drama of salvation. When Christ transforms the souls' good works into saving works, he also validates the audience's works of mercy, but with the proviso that any work must pass through Eucharistic counter-experience, by which it participates by grace in Christ's saving work.

On this account, a properly theological ethics is sustained only in the circulation between tropological and anagogical readings of scripture within the church's sacramental life. The tropological emphasis on works is immediately countered by an eschatological recoil that sends tremors through a concept of works founded merely on virtue ethics. Works can no longer refer only to agents' own deeds but must now dilate to include the divine life that enables and infinitely exceeds them. In this anagogical mode, scripture does not so much apply to our experience, as in tropology, but rather overwhelms the concepts and categories provided by experience as such, producing a counter-experience instead. By means of the sacraments, anagogical interpretation then returns "works" to tropological performance, though under a description that tropology alone cannot provide. The Doomsday pageant functions as an anagogical interlude, interceding between tropology's injunction to works and the works whose performance follows. This circulation of tropology and anagogy prevents theological ethics from reducing to a theology of works, a dead doing of the dead law. The arguments pursued in this vein demonstrate the resources of late medieval Catholic culture to think beyond merit when considering the relationship between scripture, works, and salvation.

Conclusion

Tropology Today

"Not everyone who says to me, 'Lord, Lord,' will enter the kingdom of heaven, but the one who does the will of my Father who is in heaven. On that day many will say to me, 'Lord, Lord, did we not prophesy in your name, and cast out demons in your name, and do many mighty works in your name?' And then will I declare to them, 'I never knew you; depart from me, you workers of lawlessness.'"
                    —Matthew 7:21–23 (English Standard Version)

On November 21, 2012, one B. Littlefield highlighted this passage in his Kindle edition of the English Standard Version Bible, the "most high-lighted book of all time."[1] Evidently moved, he made a note: "Sobering.

---

1. "Amazon Kindle: Most Highlighted Books of All Time 1–25," accessed November 21, 2012, https://kindle.amazon.com/most_popular/books_by_popular_highlights_all_time. Six other Kindle editions of the Bible make the list of the top twenty-five. The ESV Kindle edition, which is free, outranks Walter Isaacson's biography of Steve Jobs and the first volume of the *Hunger Games*

Where do I say I stand with Jesus and where do I actually stand. What does Jesus say?"[2] This Doomsday scenario inspired a qualm in its reader, who entertains the bracing consideration that even the "mighty works" he performs might not accord with the will of his Father who is in heaven. His open question invites, or perhaps stands for, an examination of conscience, the spiritual inventory to which Christ exhorts the audience in the York pageant of Doomsday: "All this I suffered for thi sake / Say, man, what suffered thou for me?" (274–75). The question resonates down the social media feeds of the present day. "What Have You Done!" demands Twitter user @7ENJ7, glossing Matthew 25:35–36, "For I Was Hungry And You Gave Me Food; I Was Thirsty And You Gave Me Drink; For I Was . . . Stranger . . . Naked." Others urge concrete action. @PainterRandy glosses the Matthew 25 Last Judgment interrogation with a link to the donation page for the Supernatural Life Transition Ranch for the Homeless in Red Bluff, California. Glossing the same verse, @thegospelhand exhorts, "Give the gift of clean water," and links to a six-minute inspirational video on the work of the faith-based non-profit Imagine Water. On Thanksgiving Day, @melsoriano tweets, "Thank you all who teach me that to be alive means to bring life to others—'For I was hungry and you gave Me food. . . .'"[3] On YouVersion, a mobile app and Web site with more than 150 million registered users, Zen Wijeyesinghe applies the Doomsday lessons of Matthew 25 to an earlier episode in which Jesus predicts his passion:

---

trilogy. Another edition of the Bible, designed to facilitate reading the entire Bible in one year, occupies fourth place, just above *The 7 Habits of Highly Effective People*. Amazon stopped publishing this list sometime in 2013, but an analysis of highlighting data released privately to *The Atlantic* near the end of 2014 confirms the 2012 patterns. Robinson Meyer, "The Most Popular Passages in Books, According to Kindle Data," *The Atlantic*, November 2, 2014, http://www.theatlantic.com/technology/archive/2014/11/the-passages-that-readers-love/381373/.

2. *The Holy Bible, English Standard Version (with Cross-References)*, Kindle Edition (Crossway, 2011), http://www.amazon.com.

3. These comments were accessed 23 November 2012, and appeared on the noted Web sites on 17, 18, and 22 November 2012 (in order of citation).

I wish that I was a man who could have encouraged Him as it seems evident that He was starting to show signs of the struggle that would culminate in Gethsemane. I recognise that I am not naturally like that however. But with The Holy Spirit in my life I can be. But how can I minister to Jesus?

Skip over a few chapters. Jesus talks about doing things for others as if it was done to Him personally. This is great news as it gives us the opportunity to minister to others as if we were being here for Christ.

What an amazing opportunity to serve. Wonder if we will take it![4]

These acts of vernacular digital exegesis attest to an array of tropological responses to scripture, from eschatologically motivated introspection and affective aspiration to collective action and individual participation in salvation history. They also defy Whiggish grand narratives of the history of exegesis, according to which historical criticism has triumphed over premodern practices of spiritual exegesis.

A recent document of the Pontifical Institute of Biblical Studies exemplifies this distortion of the history of exegesis:

But [premodern spiritual exegesis] was not based on the commentated text. It was superimposed on it. It was inevitable, therefore, that at the moment of its greatest success, it went into irreversible decline. . . . Starting from the Middle Ages, the literal sense has been restored to a place of honour and has not ceased to prove its value. The critical study of the Old Testament has progressed steadily in that direction culminating in the supremacy of the historical-critical method.[5]

---

4. Public note on Matt. 20:17–28 and Matt. 25:40. 5 March 2015. www.bible.com. Accessed 6 March 2015.

5. The Pontifical Biblical Commission, *The Jewish People and Their Sacred Scriptures in the Christian Bible* (Vatican City: Libreria Editrice Vaticana, 2002), sec. 20, http://www.vatican.va.

On the face of it, this brief genealogy cannot be disputed: despite a renewed interest in spiritual exegesis among theologians and some biblical studies scholars in the past two decades, the historical-critical method dominates the field, and academic commentators on scripture hardly ever advance allegorical readings. Granted, the authors of the document approve of Paul's allegorical reading of Sarah and Hagar as types of the Old and New Covenants (Gal. 4:21–31) because he speaks of "persons . . . in the ancient text . . . without the slightest doubt being cast on their historicity." Nevertheless, while such Auerbachian figuralism passes muster, the authors caution against tropological exegesis: "The Fathers of the Church and the medieval authors, in contrast, make systematic use of [spiritual exegesis] for the entire Bible, even to the least detail . . . to give a contemporary interpretation capable of application to the Christian life."[6] Historical criticism has rescued the Bible from the immoderate presentism of tropology. However, in its turn to tropology, the document's genealogy breaks down, for if there is one kind of scriptural discourse over which the historical-critical method has not triumphed—not through the magisterial or radical Reformations, not through the Enlightenment, not through "the eclipse of biblical narrative"—it is tropology. After the "literal sense had been restored to a place of honor," tropological spiritual exegesis may have seemed relegated in academic discourse to a few lines titled "moraliter" at the bottom of the page in early modern printings of Nicholas of Lyra's biblical commentary, but it persisted in a vast range of scriptural discourses in Latin and, increasingly, in the European vernaculars. And it persists to this day in everything from Sunday sermons and the VeggieTales to Kindle readers' private notes and YouVersion users' public commentary. Tropological interpretation and invention has always been a mass phenomenon, and will continue to be as long as readers respond to the biblical imperative, resounding from Moses to John the Evangelist, to turn words into works for the love of God and neighbor and, ultimately,

---

6. Ibid. In context, this passage is talking about "allegory," which can refer to all the spiritual senses. The objection to "contemporary . . . application to the Christian life" clearly refers to tropology.

for the sake of salvation. Tropology can therefore be considered a vernacular phenomenon in the sense used by scholars of modern media to entail mass access to a prominent cultural discourse and translation across time, space, and linguistic registers.[7]

Yet I have argued in this book for more than just the persistence of tropological practices, which is fairly easily demonstrated in sixteenth-century reformed practices of "religious reading," as well as in the lived theology of the world's two billion Christians today. As Matthew Levering notes, "[participatory] exegesis is ongoing whenever people presume that a biblical text about Jesus is about the Jesus whom they worship in the Church . . . . It is ongoing whenever people pray, receive the sacraments, or ask forgiveness in the context of the reading and teaching of Scripture. . . . Yet it is one whose justification has largely been lost and needs reclaiming."[8] Levering may be right about the present situation, but I have argued that in the late Middle Ages and early Reformation tropological theory supplied a robust intellectual and not just practical rationale for participatory exegesis, even if the theoretical apparatus of the sacramental framework became detached from scriptural study.[9] For this reason, the ongoing theory and practice of tropology, precisely as a form of participatory exegesis, defies the narratives of eclipse and disintegration in which both triumphalist and critical histories of exegesis have framed the passage to modernity.

Tropology has eluded histories of modern exegesis in part because the field for a long time ignored vernacular theology, understood loosely as the body of religious literature that falls outside the boundaries of the institutionally legitimized theology and major mystical writing that comprise the monumental compendia of historical theology,

---

7. Miriam Hansen, "The Mass Production of the Senses: Classical Cinema as Vernacular Modernism," *Modernism/Modernity* 6, no. 2 (1999): 59–77.

8. Levering, *Participatory Biblical Exegesis*, 5–6.

9. I suspect that further research into practices of lay vernacular exegesis will complicate this settled judgment. As I have attempted to demonstrate, non-academic, lay, and vernacular practices of exegesis typically generate their own justifications. The common academic remark that a practice is "untheorized" belies the continuum between theory and practice.

as represented by the Patrologia Latina and the Corpus Christiano-rum series, as well as their early modern and modern counterparts. More importantly, though, tropology has eluded histories of spiritual exegesis because it is by definition not designed for official use; it is not ordered to the accretive development of biblical knowledge, as is literal-historical exegesis, or to the systematic elucidation of doctrine, as is allegorical exegesis. Because tropology necessarily circulates biblical meaning out into the lives of readers, it belongs more comfortably in coterie manuscript culture or on social media than it does in the official publications of ecclesial bodies such as the Pontifical Biblical Commission, in the "covertly magisterial" glossing of major Bible publishing companies, or in the published academic commentary that systematically cultivates the objective detachment of its practitioners from their objects of study.[10]

In these terms, the study of tropology suggests a new perspective on what vernacular theology is and why it matters. Although tropological exegesis is widespread in Latinate biblical commentary, tropological habits foster various forms of translation: from words into works, ideas into actions, affects into effects, past into present, and of course source language into target language. Considered as a tropological phenomenon, vernacularity is characterized by the intimate application of scripture in the contingent circumstances of individual and communal lives, as well as by the consequent recirculation of lived, applied meaning back into scriptural and theological discourse. In these terms, in order to understand tropology and the history of exegesis, we need to study vernacular theology.

These remarks are intended not to align tropology with a more legitimate, because more demotic, form of theological authority but rather to point out that in order to give a good account of tropology, and therefore of spiritual exegesis generally and the fate of participatory exegesis, we have to attend to readers' tropological inventions, which in

---

10. David Dault, "The Covert Magisterium: Theology, Textuality and the Question of Scripture," Ph.D. diss., Vanderbilt University, 2009, http://grad works.umi.com/34/79/3479819.html.

many cases are their very lives. This suggests a rationale for the study of vernacular theology that is based neither on an impulse to democratize theology and its history nor on the academic responsibility to study the understudied but on the fact that a crucial dimension of exegesis and theology happens outside the formal discourses of exegesis and theology, in the lives of the readers of scripture. Here, exegesis is intimately involved in the practices of everyday life, and we detect it by listening for a tropological voice accented in ways we more conventionally associate with the vernacular: in the intimacy of the mother tongue, in occasional rather than sustained exegesis, in poetry rather than academic commentary, in tweets rather than in the pulpit. Literary studies grant access to several forms of vernacular tropological invention; other forms will require conventional historical theology, still others ethnography. In this sense, then, vernacular theology is defined not by its resistance to or independence from the conventional authorizing institutions and forms but by its participatory mode, the tropological phase of the hermeneutical circle that is ordered to the lives of readers of scripture before it circulates back to matters of history and doctrine. Detectable as a contingent historical phenomenon, vernacular theology in this tropological mode sustains the intimate voice of lived theology for, and indeed within, academic, ecclesial, and pastoral theology.

Tropological Periodization

Arguments about periodization, especially in the age of religious reform in England, the period this book covers, tend to circle around dynamics of continuity and rupture. Was translation of the Bible a conservative act of reformist tendencies, as the Middle English *Mirror* frames it, or a revolutionary, liberating act that ushered in the modern age, as John Bale and more recent commentators such as David Daniell would have it?[11] Did the turn to the literal sense of scripture pave the way for

---

11. David Daniell, *The Bible in English: Its History and Influence* (New Haven: Yale University Press, 2003).

instrumental rationality, or did it make God even more intimately present in the language of the text?[12] These are important debates. Big questions require big answers. But they can also cause us to lose sight of the genealogies of modernity that frame them in the first place, the teleological narratives that condition our historical imagination and what we are able to see and not to see. One phenomenon we have not yet seen well enough is tropology. By studying tropology, we are able in turn to see more of this complex period.

The trouble with genealogies of modernity is that they can know too much about the present. A case in point is the radical reformer John Bale's apocalyptic history, *The Image of Both Churches* (1547), where the past already reflects the division of good and evil that will become manifest at the Last Judgment. But even Bale must scour the English age of Antichrist (after the year 1000) for figures of hope. One of those figures is "Robertus Langelande," who wrote "in sermone Anglicane" the "pium opus . . . *Visionem petri aratoris.*" Bale's Langland spoke out against the blasphemies of the papacy with a spirit of fervor and prophesied "many things which we have seen fulfilled in our own day," namely, the dissolution of the monasteries, one of the most violent percussions of the English Reformation.[13] Bale's reading of the deeply Catholic *Piers Plowman* evinces a brutal charity that reimagines Langland in order to recuperate him in a history whose conclusion is known. We can admire Bale's charitable imagination, but we should resist the apocalyptic hermeneutic, shared with some current genealogies of modernity, according to which "we have seen these things fulfilled in our own day."

At the same time, Bale's sense of providential history, minus the apocalyptic certainty, is well attuned to all of the works studied in this book. Although tropological writers handle history in diverse, some-

---

12. For the former argument, see Peter Harrison, *The Bible, Protestantism, and the Rise of Natural Science* (New York: Cambridge University Press, 2001); for the latter, see Ocker, *Biblical Poetics Before Humanism and Reformation.* These two arguments often overlap more than they contradict each other.

13. John Bale, *Scriptorum illustrium maioris Brytanniae catalogus* (Basle, 1557, 1559): With the Dedication to Queen Elizabeth from the Grenville Library Copy in the British Museum, repr., 2 vols. (Westmead: Gregg International, 1971), 1:474.

times conflicting, ways, they share the understanding that the march of human events is embedded in the larger history of creation, the drama of God's self-donation and subsequent relationship with God's creatures. Because providential history takes God seriously as a first and final cause, it renders history far more contingent than the "complexity" that modern historicism, which admits only efficient causes, cites as the source of contingency. So while the writers I study here resist "treating historical periods as self-enclosed, self-explanatory, and petrified in their oppositions one to the other," they also have an expansive understanding of what it means for a phenomenon to be "historically determined."[14] For them, human and natural events unfold in the broad horizon of providential history, an expanse in which periodization, contingency, and complexity look quite different.

Inspired by these tropological inventions, I have sought to reimagine historical processes as underdetermined and open to contingencies and alternatives at every point of development, even in their consequences, even in the present. Tropological invention circulates the promises of the past through the present in anticipation of future fulfillment. Inventing a tropological literary and theological history, I have tried to allow these texts' hopes and promises to exceed or reconfigure their protagonists' historical horizons—and also our own. Like many literary historians, I admire from afar the communities who engaged in forms of reading and writing that are not available to me today. But these texts need not inspire a sense of belatedness, because they so often perform ethical and scriptural work that defies fatalist genealogies of decline.

This book is not, however, an embattled protest against periodization. That argument was settled theoretically long ago, and it is by now a truism that literary and historical periods are intellectual and ideological constructs. I have layered each chapter with a variety of temporalities and discourses not to reveal complexity or generate nuance—though of course that is one result—but in order to appreciate the richness and meaning of what we too often *explain away* as historical complexity. If the alternative to an artificial and tacitly ideological periodization

---

14. Simpson, *Reform and Cultural Revolution*, 32.

is simply the constant refining of our sensitivity to complexity and continuity, then we would be better off periodizing wildly. In fact, the latter is closer to what I have attempted here than proposing to offer a more nuanced, and thereby somehow more faithful, account of literary and religious change across the Reformation. The study of tropology adds complexity to the field, but it also generates meaning. It does so primarily through the periodizing imaginations of the writers studied here, who conceive of historical meaning as emerging in the interplay of likeness and difference between historically distant persons and events. Their method, and mine, could therefore be viewed as a kind of tropological periodization, that is, a constantly periodizing, constantly reforming habit of historical imagination that is occasional and provisional but also responsible and ordered to the good, necessarily circulating the past through the present in order to invent the future.

Comparative Literary Ethics

Tropology is not the only way to do literary ethics; indeed, it is not even the only way to approach biblical ethics. Chaucer is a case in point, and it is instructive to follow his brief engagements with tropology in order to understand why he generally chose not to invest in tropological invention. Few readers have recognized *Piers Plowman*'s tropological genius as clearly as Chaucer, whose Parson exemplifies and gently satirizes the habits of tropological interpretation and invention. Besides his brother the Plowman, who never tells a tale, the Parson is Chaucer's most Langlandian character. His primary invention is his own life, modeled on and incarnating the life of Christ the shepherd. "To drawen folk to hevene by fairnesse, / By good ensample, this was his bisynesse."[15] That business perhaps explains why the Parson does not exactly tell a tale when his turn comes up at the end of *The Canterbury Tales*. All *sentence* and no *solas*, the Parson's "meditacioun" (X.55) on the seven deadly sins has no chance of winning the Host's prize for the best tale on the pilgrimage. However, even as the Parson refuses to tell "fables

---

15. Chaucer, *Canterbury Tales*, I.520.

and swich wrecchednesse" (X.34), Chaucer keeps his meta-fiction running. As the Parson's oral, homiletic air congeals into the textual discourse of the pastoral manuals, the pilgrimage motif evaporates, leaving only Chaucer's authorial voice—at once earnest and satirical—to retract in penitential and testamentary terms his "translacions and enditynges of worldly vanitees," including whichever "tales of Caunterbury . . . sownen into synne" (X.1085).

Whatever Chaucer's intentions might have been for a complete work, this actual ending in twenty-eight of the surviving manuscripts plays a characteristically Chaucerian joke on its readers, its author, and its unspoken "Langlandian shadowpresence."[16] For when the Host exhorts the Parson to tell a "fructuous" tale "in litel space," he echoes *Piers Plowman*'s most insistent spur to poetic invention: "to *do wel* God sende yow his grace!" (X.72). The Parson does not in fact do well according to the Host's criteria—he tells no fable, nor does he confine himself to "litel space." By this irony, Chaucer pokes fun at Langland's endless quest for Dowel and his eager ventriloquizing of clerical and scriptural discourses. But Chaucer also loves to "make earnest of game," as he puts it, and this joke refers back to the Parson's style of scriptural exegesis as described in the General Prologue. There we learn that the Parson interprets the Bible first by doing well, and only subsequently by teaching. The portrait puts the Parson's didactic "tale" in perspective, for "first he wroghte, and afterward he taughte: / Out of the gospel he tho wordes caughte" (I.497–98). Calling on an "incarnational poetic" associated with meditative lyrics and mystical texts, Chaucer has the Parson "catch" the words of the Gospel, just as Langland's Marian figure "clennesse" catches the Son of God at the moment of incarnation:[17]

And loue shal lepe out aftur into þis lowe erthe
And clennesse shal cach hit and clerkes shollen hit fynde:
Pastores loquebantur ad invicem &c. [The shepherds (on Christmas
morning) said to one another . . .]
(*Piers Plowman*, C.14.85–86a)

---

16. John M. Bowers, *Chaucer and Langland: The Antagonistic Tradition* (Notre Dame, IN: University of Notre Dame Press, 2007), 160.

17. Cervone, *Poetics of the Incarnation*, 114–18.

Chaucer then shows how a cleric, a good shepherd (*pastor*), who has incarnated the Word in his own actions, might then invent further words. In indirect speech, the Parson adds a "figure" of speech to elaborate the figural or typological relationship he embodies between Christ the shepherd and the priest who acts as *alter Christus*, another Christ:

> And this figure he added eek therto,
> That if gold ruste, what shal iren do?
> For if a preest be foul, on whom we truste,
> No wonder is a lewed man to ruste;
> And shame it is, if a prest take keep,
> A shiten shepherde and a clene sheep.
>
> (I.499–504)

As the final line absorbs *Piers Plowman*'s alliterative idiom, we hear the Langlandian voice that Chaucer deflects and ironizes in the prose Parson's Tale. Taken together, the Parson's portrait and Tale suggest that while Chaucer admires tropological invention in the parish, he also identifies its potential to overwhelm poetic invention with pastoral literature. He fears that the model will displace the copy. In his agile deployment and critique of the Langlandian imagination, Chaucer recognizes the versatile habit of literary invention that I have explored in this book, while also identifying reasons not to invest in tropology as his chief mode of invention.[18] We have much more to learn about the comparative affordances of tropological and non-tropological literary ethics and their shifting relationships in medieval and early modern culture.

---

18. As many readers have appreciated, Chaucer is deeply interested in both ethics and the Bible. For a lucid account of how Chaucer pursues these interests without engaging in tropological invention, see Chad Schrock, "The Ends of Reading in the *Merchant's Tale*," *Philological Quarterly* 91 (2012): 591–609.

Bibliography

Aers, David. *Faith, Ethics, Church: Writing in England, 1360–1409.* Cambridge: D. S. Brewer, 2000.

———. "Langland on the Church and the End of the Cardinal Virtues." *Journal of Medieval and Early Modern Studies* 42, no. 1 (2012): 59–81.

———. *Piers Plowman and Christian Allegory.* London: Edward Arnold, 1975.

———. *Salvation and Sin: Augustine, Langland, and Fourteenth-Century Theology.* Notre Dame, IN: University of Notre Dame Press, 2009.

———. *Sanctifying Signs: Making Christian Tradition in Late Medieval England.* Notre Dame, IN: University of Notre Dame Press, 2004.

Aers, David, and Sarah Beckwith. "The Eucharist." In *Cultural Reformations: Medieval and Renaissance in Literary History,* edited by Brian Cummings and James Simpson, 153–65. New York: Oxford University Press, 2010.

Akbari, Suzanne Conklin. *Seeing Through the Veil: Optical Theory and Medieval Allegory.* Toronto: University of Toronto Press, 2004.

Alan of Lille. *Ars praedicandi.* PL 210, n.d.

———. *The Art of Preaching.* Translated by Gillian R. Evans. Kalamazoo, MI: Cistercian Publications, 1981.

———. *Distinctiones dictionum theologicalium.* PL 210, n.d.

———. *Liber parabolarum (Una raccolta di aforismi).* Edited by Oronzo Limone. Lecce: Congedo Editore, 1993.

Alford, John A. "Some Unidentified Quotations in *Piers Plowman*." *Modern Philology* 72, no. 4 (1975): 390–99.

Alford, Stephen. *Kingship and Politics in the Reign of Edward VI.* New York: Cambridge University Press, 2002.

Allen, Elizabeth. *False Fables and Exemplary Truth in Later Middle English Literature.* New York: Palgrave Macmillan, 2005.

Allen, Judson Boyce. *The Ethical Poetic of the Later Middle Ages: A Decorum of Convenient Distinction.* Toronto: University of Toronto Press, 1982.

Andrée, Alexander, ed. *Anselmi Laudunensis Glosae super Iohannem.* CCSL 267. Turnhout: Brepols, 2014.

———. "Anselm of Laon Unveiled: The *Glosae super Iohanem* and the Origins of the *Glossa ordinaria* on the Bible." *Mediaeval Studies* 73 (2011): 217–40.

———, ed. *Gilbertus Universalis: "Glossa ordinaria in Lamentationes Ieremie prophete," Prothemata et Liber I: A Critical Edition with an Introduction and a Translation.* Stockholm: Almqvist and Wiksell, 2005.

———. "The Rhetorical Hermeneutics of Gilbert the Universal in His Gloss on Lamentations." *Journal of Medieval Latin* 17 (2007): 143–58.

Andrew, Malcolm. "Jonah and Christ in 'Patience.'" *Modern Philology* 70, no. 3 (1973): 230–33.

———. "The Realizing Imagination in Late Medieval English Literature." *English Studies* 76, no. 2 (1995): 113–28.

Andrew, Malcolm, and Ronald Waldron, eds. *The Poems of the "Pearl" Manuscript: "Pearl," "Cleanness," "Patience," "Sir Gawain and the Green Knight."* Exeter: Exeter University Press, 2002.

Anglo, Sydney. "An Early Tudor Programme for Plays and Other Demonstrations against the Pope." *Journal of the Warburg and Courtauld Institutes* 20, no. 1/2 (January 1, 1957): 176–79.

Arnold, Thomas, ed. *Select English Works of John Wyclif.* 3 vols. Oxford: Clarendon Press, 1871.

Astell, Ann W. *Eating Beauty: The Eucharist and the Spiritual Arts of the Middle Ages.* Ithaca, NY: Cornell University Press, 2006.

Athanasius. *De incarnatione Dei Verbum.* In *Select Writings and Letters of Athanasius, Bishop of Alexandria.* Edited by Archibald Robertson. Nicene and Post-Nicene Fathers, 2nd series, vol. 4. Edited by Philip Schaff and Henry Wace. Grand Rapids, MI: William B. Eerdmans, 1953.

Atkin, Tamara. *The Drama of Reform: Theology and Theatricality, 1461–1553.* Turnhout: Brepols, 2013.

Attridge, Derek. *The Singularity of Literature*. New York: Routledge, 2004.

Auerbach, Erich. "Figura." In *Gesammelte Aufsätze zur Romanischen Philologie*, 55–92. Bern: Francke, 1967.

———. "Figura." In *Scenes from the Drama of European Literature*, translated by Ralph Manheim, 11–76. Minneapolis: University of Minnesota Press, 1984.

Augustine [of Hippo]. *Enarrationes in Psalmos*. PL 37.

———. *On Christian Doctrine*. Translated by D. W. Robertson. Upper Saddle River, NJ: Prentice-Hall, 1958.

———. *The Trinity*. Translated by Edmund Hill. Brooklyn, NY: New City Press, 1991.

Augustine of Denmark. "Augustini de Dacia, O. P., 'Rotulus pugillaris.'" Edited by A. Walz. *Angelicum* 6 (1929): 253–78.

Ayres, Lewis. *Nicaea and Its Legacy: An Approach to Fourth-Century Trinitarian Theology*. New York: Oxford University Press, 2006.

———. "The Soul and the Reading of Scripture: A Note on Henri de Lubac." *Scottish Journal of Theology* 61, no. 2 (2008): 173–90.

Baasten, Matthew. *Pride according to Gregory the Great: A Study of the "Moralia."* Lewiston, NY: E. Mellen Press, 1986.

Bale, John. *Scriptorum illustrium maioris Brytanniae catalogus (Basle, 1557, 1559): With the Dedication to Queen Elizabeth from the Grenville Library Copy in the British Museum*. Repr. 2 vols. Westmead: Gregg International, 1971.

———. *Select Works of John Bale, D. D., Bishop of Ossory: Containing the Examinations of Lord Cobham, William Thorpe and Anne Askewe and "The Image of Both Churches."* Edited by Henry Christmas. Cambridge: Cambridge University Press, 1849.

Barnett, Mary Jane. "Erasmus and the Hermeneutics of Linguistic Praxis." *Renaissance Quarterly* 49, no. 3 (1996): 542–72.

Barney, Stephen A. *The Penn Commentary on "Piers Plowman."* Vol. 5, *C Passūs 20–22; B Passūs 18–20*. Philadelphia: University of Pennsylvania Press, 2006.

———. "The Plowshare of the Tongue: The Progress of a Symbol from the Bible to *Piers Plowman*." *Mediaeval Studies* 35 (1973): 261–93.

Barr, Helen, ed. *The "Piers Plowman" Tradition: A Critical Edition of "Pierce the Ploughman's Crede," "Richard the Redeless," "Mum and the Sothsegger," and "The Crowned King."* London: J. M. Dent, 1993.

Barton, Benjamin Herbert, Thomas Castle, and John Reader Jackson, eds. *The British Flora Medica: A History of the Medicinal Plants of Great Britain.* London: Chatto and Windus, 1877.

Beadle, Richard, ed. *The York Plays: Introduction, Commentary, Glossary.* Vol. 2 of 2 vols. EETS, s.s., 24. Oxford: Oxford University Press, 2013.

———, ed. *The York Plays: The Text.* Vol. 1 of 2 vols. EETS, s.s., 23. Oxford: Oxford University Press, 2009.

Beckwith, Sarah. *Christ's Body: Identity, Culture, and Society in Late Medieval Writings.* New York: Routledge, 1993.

———. *Shakespeare and the Grammar of Forgiveness.* Ithaca, NY: Cornell University Press, 2011.

———. *Signifying God: Social Relation and Symbolic Act in the York Corpus Christi Plays.* Chicago: University of Chicago Press, 2003.

Bede. *Opera didascalica.* Edited by C. B. Kendall. CCSL 123A. Turnhout: Brepols, 1975.

———. *The Venerable Bede: Commentary on the Acts of the Apostles.* Translated by Lawrence T. Martin. Kalamazoo, MI: Cistercian Publications, 1989.

Benrath, Gustav Adolf. *Wyclifs Bibelkommentar.* Berlin: Walter de Gruyter, 1966.

Bernard of Clairvaux. *Bernard of Clairvaux: Selected Works.* Translated by Gillian R. Evans. New York: Paulist Press, 1987.

———. *Epistolae.* Edited by Jean Leclercq and Henri Rochais. Vol. 8. Sancti Bernardi opera. Rome: Editiones Cistercienses, 1977.

Betz, John R. "Beyond the Sublime: The Aesthetics of the Analogy of Being (Part One)." *Modern Theology* 21, no. 3 (2005): 367–411.

Biblia latina cum Glossa ordinaria. 6 vols. Venice, 1603.

Blacketer, Raymond Andrew. *The School of God: Pedagogy and Rhetoric in Calvin's Interpretation of Deuteronomy.* Dordrecht: Springer, 2006.

Bloomfield, Morton W. *"Piers Plowman" as a Fourteenth-Century Apocalypse.* New Brunswick, NJ: Rutgers University Press, 1961.

Boccaccio, Giovanni. "Short Treatise in Praise of Dante." In *Medieval Literary Theory and Criticism, c. 1100–c. 1375: The Commentary Tradition,* edited by A. J. Minnis and A. B. Scott, translated by David Wallace, rev. ed., 492–503. Oxford: Clarendon Press, 1988.

The Boke of Common Prayer, and Administracion of the Sacramentes, and Other Rites and Ceremonies in the Churche of Englande. Early English Books Online, 1475–1640 / 1855:19. London: Edward Whitchurch, 1552.

Bonaventure. *Collations on the Six Days*. In *The Works of St. Bonaventure*. Vol. 5. Translated by José de Vinck. Paterson, NJ: St. Anthony Guild Press, 1970.

———. *Saint Bonaventure's "De reductione artium ad theologiam."* Translated by Emma Thérèse Healy. 2nd ed. Saint Bonaventure, NY: The Franciscan Institute, 1955.

The Book of Common Prayer: Commonly Called the First Book of Queen Elizabeth. Printed by Grafton 1559. Chiswick: W. Pickering, 1844.

Bori, Pier Cesare. *L'interpretazione infinita: L'ermeneutica cristiana antica e le sue trasformazioni*. Bologna: Il Mulino, 1987.

Bossy, John. "Practices of Satisfaction, 1215–1700." In *Retribution, Repentance, and Reconciliation: Papers Read at the 2002 Summer and 2003 Winter Meeting of the Ecclesiastical History Society*, edited by Kate Cooper and Jeremy Gregory, 106–18. Woodbridge, Suffolk: Boydell Press, 2004.

———. "The Social History of Confession in the Age of the Reformation." *Transactions of the Royal Historical Society (Fifth Series)* 25, no. 1 (1975): 21–38.

Bowers, John M. *Chaucer and Langland: The Antagonistic Tradition*. Notre Dame, IN: University of Notre Dame Press, 2007.

———. *The Crisis of Will in "Piers Plowman."* Washington, DC: Catholic University of America Press, 1986.

Bradley, Ritamary. "Backgrounds of the Title *Speculum* in Mediaeval Literature." *Speculum* 29, no. 1 (1954): 100–115.

Brague, Rémi. *The Law of God: The Philosophical History of an Idea*. Translated by Lydia G. Cochrane. Chicago: University of Chicago Press, 2007.

———. *The Wisdom of the World: The Human Experience of the Universe in Western Thought*. Translated by Teresa Lavender Fagan. Chicago: University of Chicago Press, 2003.

Bray, Gerald Lewis. *Documents of the English Reformation, 1526–1701*. Cambridge: James Clarke, 2004.

Breck, John. *The Shape of Biblical Language: Chiasmus in the Scriptures and Beyond*. Crestwood, NY: St. Vladimir's Seminary Press, 1994.

Brenz, Johannes. *Newes from Niniue to Englande, Brought by the Prophete Ionas*. Translated by Thomas Tymme. Early English Books Online, 1475–1640 / 523:07. London: Henrie Denham, 1570.

Brinkmann, Hennig. *Mittelalterliche Hermeneutik*. Darmstadt: Wissenschaftliche Buchgesellschaft, 1980.

Bromyard, John. *Summa praedicantium*. 2 vols. Venice, 1586. Available online at www.archive.org.

Brown, Peter. *Chaucer and the Making of Optical Space*. Oxford: Peter Lang, 2007.

Brown, Peter. *Through the Eye of a Needle: Wealth, the Fall of Rome, and the Making of Christianity in the West, 350–550 AD*. Princeton: Princeton University Press, 2012.

Bucer, Martin. *De regno Christi*. In *Melanchthon and Bucer*, edited by Wilhelm Pauck, 174–394. Philadelphia: Westminster Press, 1969.

———. *Enarratio in Evangelion Iohannis (1528, 1530, 1536)*. Edited by Irena Backus. Martini Buceri Opera Omnia 2. Gütersloh: Mohn, 1988.

Buell, Lawrence. "In Pursuit of Ethics." *PMLA* 114, no. 1 (1999): 7–19.

Burrow, John. *Langland's Fictions*. Oxford: Clarendon Press, 1993.

Bynum, Caroline Walker. *Christian Materiality: An Essay on Religion in Late Medieval Europe*. New York: Zone, 2011.

———. *Jesus as Mother: Studies in the Spirituality of the High Middle Ages*. Berkeley and Los Angeles: University of California Press, 1982.

Cairns, Francis. "Latin Sources and Analogues of the Middle English *Patience*." *Studia Neophilologica* 59 (1987): 7–18.

Calvin, John. *Harmonia ex evangelistis tribvs composita, Matthaeo, Marco, & Luca, commentariis Iohannis Calvini exposita*. Geneva: Vignon, 1582.

———. *A Harmonie vpon the Three Euangelists, Matthew, Mark and Luke with the Commentarie of M. Iohn Caluine*. Translated by Eusebius Pagit. Early English Books Online, 1475–1640 / 1370:15. London: Thomas Dawson, 1584.

———. *The Institution of Christian Religion*. Translated by Thomas Norton. Early English Books Online, 1475–1640 / 415:01. London: Wolfe and Harison, 1561.

———. *The Sermons of M. Iohn Caluin vpon the Fifth Booke of Moses Called Deuteronomie Faithfully Gathered Word for Word as He Preached Them in Open Pulpet*. Translated by Arthur Golding. Early English Books Online, 1475–1640 / 199:02. London: Henry Middleton for George Bishop, 1583.

Caplan, Harry, trans. *Ad C. Herennium: De ratione dicendi (Rhetorica ad Herennium)*. Cambridge, MA: Harvard University Press, 1964.

Carruthers, Mary. *The Book of Memory: A Study of Memory in Medieval Culture*. Rev. ed. New York: Cambridge University Press, 2008.

———. *The Craft of Thought: Meditation, Rhetoric, and the Making of Images, 400–1200.* New York: Cambridge University Press, 2000.

———. "Rhetorical *Ductus*, or, Moving through a Composition." In *Acting on the Past: Historical Performance across the Disciplines*, edited by Mark Franko and Annette Richards, 99–117. Hanover, NH: University Press of New England, 2000.

———. *The Search for St. Truth: A Study of Meaning in "Piers Plowman."* Evanston, IL: Northwestern University Press, 1973.

Cayley, David. "The Corruption of Christianity: Ivan Illich on Gospel, Church and Society." *Ideas.* Toronto: Canadian Broadcasting Corporation, 2000.

Certeau, Michel de. *The Practice of Everyday Life.* Translated by Steven Rendall. Berkeley and Los Angeles: University of California Press, 1988.

Cervone, Cristina Maria. *Poetics of the Incarnation: Middle English Writing and the Leap of Love.* Philadelphia: University of Pennsylvania Press, 2013.

Châtillon, François. "Vocabulaire et prosodie du distique attribué à Augustin de Dacie sur les quatre sens de l'écriture." In *L'Homme devant Dieu: Mélanges offerts au Père Henri de Lubac*, 3 vols., 2:17–28. Lyons: Aubier, 1964.

Chaucer, Geoffrey. *Book of the Duchess.* In *The Riverside Chaucer.* Edited by Larry D. Benson. 3rd ed. Boston: Houghton Mifflin Company, 1987.

———. *The Canterbury Tales.* In *The Riverside Chaucer.* Edited by Larry D. Benson. 3rd ed. Boston: Houghton Mifflin Company, 1987.

Chrétien, Jean-Louis. *The Call and the Response.* Translated by Anne A. Davenport. New York: Fordham University Press, 2004.

Church of England. *The Boke of the Common Praier and Administratio[n] of the Sacramentes and Other Rytes and Ceremonies of the Churche, after the Vse of the Churche of Englande.* Early English Books Online, 1475–1640 / 482:04. Worcester, England: John Oswen, 1549.

Clark, R. Scott. "*Iustitia imputata Christi*: Alien or Proper to Luther's Doctrine of Justification?" *Concordia Theological Quarterly* 70, no. 3 (2006): 269–310.

Clark, Robert L. A. "Liminality and Literary Genres: Texts *Par Parsonnages* in Late Medieval Manuscript Culture." In *Thresholds of Medieval Visual Culture: Liminal Spaces*, edited by Elina Gertsman and Jill Stevenson, 260–80. Woodbridge, Suffolk: Boydell Press, 2012.

Clopper, Lawrence M. *Drama, Play, and Game: English Festive Culture in the Medieval and Early Modern Period.* Chicago: University of Chicago Press, 2001.

———. *Songs of Rechelesnesse: Langland and the Franciscans*. Ann Arbor: University of Michigan Press, 1997.

Comet, Georges. "Technology and Agricultural Expansion in the Middle Ages: The Example of France North of the Loire." In *Medieval Farming and Technology: The Impact of Agricultural Change in Northwest Europe*, edited by Grenville Astill and John Langdon, 11–39. New York: Brill, 1997.

Condren, Edward I. *The Numerical Universe of the "Gawain"-"Pearl" Poet: Beyond Phi*. Gainesville: University Press of Florida, 2002.

Constable, Giles. *Three Studies in Medieval Religious and Social Thought: The Interpretation of Mary and Martha, the Ideal of the Imitation of Christ, the Orders of Society*. New York: Cambridge University Press, 1995.

Contreni, John. "Review of *Medieval Exegesis, Vol. 1: The Four Senses of Scripture* by Henri de Lubac." *The Medieval Review*, August 13, 1999. http://hdl.handle.net/2022/4700.

Cook, Eleanor. "The Figure of Enigma: Rhetoric, History, Poetry." *Rhetorica* 19, no. 4 (2001): 349–78.

Cooper, Helen. *Shakespeare and the Medieval World*. London: Methuen Drama, 2010.

———. "Shakespeare and the Mystery Plays." In *Shakespeare and Elizabethan Popular Culture: Arden Critical Companion*, edited by Stuart Gillespie and Neil Rhodes, 18–41. London: Arden Shakespeare, 2006.

Copeland, Rita. "The Fortunes of 'Non Verbum pro Verbo': Or, Why Jerome Is Not a Ciceronian." In *The Medieval Translator*, edited by Roger Ellis, 15–35. Wolfeboro, NH: D. S. Brewer, 1989.

———. "Medieval Theory and Criticism." In *The Johns Hopkins Guide to Literary Theory and Criticism*. 2nd ed. Baltimore: Johns Hopkins University Press, 2005. http://litguide.press.jhu.edu/.

———. "*Pathos* and Pastoralism: Aristotle's *Rhetoric* in Medieval England." *Speculum* 89, no. 1 (2014): 96–127.

———. *Rhetoric, Hermeneutics, and Translation in the Middle Ages: Academic Traditions and Vernacular Texts*. New York: Cambridge University Press, 1991.

Cottier, Jean-François. "Erasmus's *Paraphrases*: A 'New Kind of Commentary'?" In *The Unfolding of Words: Commentary in the Age of Erasmus*, edited by Judith Rice Henderson, 27–45. Toronto: University of Toronto Press, 2012.

Coverdale, Miles, ed. *Certain Most Godly, Fruitful, and Comfortable Letters of Such True Saintes and Holy Martyrs of God, as in the Late Bloodye Persecution Here within This Realme, Gaue Their Lyues for the Defence of Christes Holy Gospel Written in the Tyme of Their Affliction and Cruell Imprysonment.* Early English Books Online, 1475–1640 / 217:02. London: Iohn Day, 1564.

Craig, John. "Forming a Protestant Consciousness? Erasmus' *Paraphrases* in English Parishes, 1547–1666." In *Holy Scripture Speaks: The Production and Reception of Erasmus' "Paraphrases on the New Testament,"* edited by Hilmar M. Pabel and Mark Vessey, 313–59. Toronto: University of Toronto Press, 2002.

Cranmer, Thomas. *The Byble in Englyshe . . . Apoynted to the Vse of the Churches.* Early English Books Online, 1475–1640 / 129:02. London: Rychard Grafton, 1540.

———. *Certayne Sermons, or Homelies Appoynted by the Kynges Maiestie, to Be Declared and Redde, by All Persones, Vicars, or Curates, Euery Sondaye in Their Churches, Where They Haue Cure.* Early English Books Online, 1475–1640 / 48:03. London: Rychard Grafton, 1547.

———. *Remains.* Edited by Henry Jenkyns. 4 vols. Oxford: Oxford University Press, 1833. Available online at www.archive.org.

Crassons, Kate. *The Claims of Poverty: Literature, Culture, and Ideology in Late Medieval England.* Notre Dame, IN: University of Notre Dame Press, 2010.

Crouch, David J. F. *Piety, Fraternity, and Power: Religious Gilds in Late Medieval Yorkshire, 1389–1547.* Cambridge: Boydell and Brewer, 2000.

Cullum, P. H., and P. J. P. Goldberg. "Charitable Provision in Late-Medieval York: 'To the Praise of God and the Use of the Poor.'" *Northern History* 29 (1993): 24–39.

Cummings, Brian. *The Literary Culture of the Reformation: Grammar and Grace.* New York: Oxford University Press, 2002.

———. "Protestant Allegory." In *The Cambridge Companion to Allegory*, edited by Rita Copeland and Peter T. Struck, 177–90. New York: Cambridge University Press, 2010.

Dagenais, John. *The Ethics of Reading in Manuscript Culture: Glossing the Libro de Buen Amor.* Princeton: Princeton University Press, 1994.

Dahan, Gilbert. *L'exégèse chrétienne de la Bible en Occident médiéval, XIIe–XIVe siècle.* Paris: Cerf, 1999.

Daniell, David. *The Bible in English: Its History and Influence.* New Haven: Yale University Press, 2003.

Dault, David. "The Covert Magisterium: Theology, Textuality and the Question of Scripture." Ph.D. diss., Vanderbilt University, 2009. http://gradworks .umi.com/34/79/3479819.html.

Dawson, Christopher. "The Vision of *Piers Plowman*." In *Medieval Essays*, 206–34. Washington, DC: Catholic University of America Press, 2002.

Deagman, Rachael. "The Formation of Forgiveness in *Piers Plowman*." *Journal of Medieval and Early Modern Studies* 40, no. 2 (2010): 273–97.

Defensor Locogiacensis. *Liber scintillarum.* Edited by H. M. Rochais. CCSL 117. Turnhout: Brepols, 1957.

Denziger, Heinrich, and Adolf Schönmetzer, eds. *Enchiridion symbolorum, definitionum et declarationum de rebus fidei et morum.* Barcinone: Herder, 1973.

Derrida, Jacques. "Psyche: Invention of the Other." Translated by Catherine Porter. In *Psyche: Inventions of the Other*, edited by Peggy Kamuf and Elizabeth Rottenberg, 1:1–47. Stanford, CA: Stanford University Press, 2007.

Devereux, E. J. "The Publication of the English Paraphrases of Erasmus." *Bulletin of the John Rylands Library* 51 (1969): 348–67.

Dickens, A. G. *Lollards and Protestants in the Diocese of York, 1509–1558.* New York: A&C Black, 1959.

Diekstra, F. N. M., ed. *Book for a Simple and Devout Woman: A Late Middle English Adaptation of Peraldus's "Summa de Vitiis et Virtutibus" and Friar Laurent's "Somme Le Roi": Edited from British Library Mss Harley 6571 and Additional 30944.* Groningen: Egbert Forsten, 1998.

Dodds, Gregory D. *Exploiting Erasmus: The Erasmian Legacy and Religious Change in Early Modern England.* Toronto: University of Toronto Press, 2009.

Donagan, Alan. "Thomas Aquinas on Human Action." In *The Cambridge History of Later Medieval Philosophy: From the Rediscovery of Aristotle to the Disintegration of Scholasticism, 1100–1600*, edited by Norman Kretzmann, Anthony Kenny, and Jan Pinborg, 642–54. New York: Cambridge University Press, 1982.

Douglas, Brian. *A Companion to Anglican Eucharistic Theology.* Vol. 1, *The Reformation to the 19th Century.* Leiden: Brill, 2011.

Dreves, Guido Maria, ed. *Hymnographi Latini: Lateinische Hymnendichter des Mittelalters*. Vol. 2. Analecta hymnica Medii Aevi 50. Leipzig, 1907. Repr. New York: Johnson Reprint Company, 1961.

Duffy, Eamon. *Marking the Hours: English People and Their Prayers, 1240–1570*. New Haven: Yale University Press, 2006.

Dugdale, William, Sir. *The Antiquities of Warwickshire Illustrated from Records, Leiger-Books, Manuscripts, Charters, Evidences, Tombes, and Armes: Beautified with Maps, Prospects and Portraictures*. Early English Books Online, 1641–1700 / 182:03. London: Thomas Warren, 1656.

Duggan, Hoyt N. "Notes toward a Theory of Langland's Meter." *Yearbook of Langland Studies* 1 (1987): 41–70.

Ebeling, Gerhard. "Die Anfänge von Luthers Hermeneutik." *Die Zeitschrift für Theologie und Kirche* 48 (1951): 172–230.

Eco, Umberto. *A Theory of Semiotics*. Bloomington: Indiana University Press, 1976.

Eliade, Mircea. *Myth and Reality*. Translated by Willard R. Trask. New York: Harper and Row, 1963.

Emerson, Ralph Waldo. *Essays and Lectures*. Edited by Joel Porte. New York: Viking Press, 1983.

Emmerson, Richard K. "The Prophetic, the Apocalyptic, and the Study of Medieval Literature." In *Poetic Prophecy in Western Literature*, edited by Jan Wojcik and Raymond-Jean Frontain, 40–54. Cranbury, NJ: Fairleigh Dickinson University Press, 1984.

Engel, William E. *Chiastic Designs in English Literature from Sidney to Shakespeare*. Burlington, VT: Ashgate, 2009.

"The Epitome of the Formula of Concord." *The Book of Concord: The Confessions of the Lutheran Church*, 2008. http://bookofconcord.org.

Erasmus, Desiderius. *An Exhortation to the Diligent Studye of Scripture, Made by Erasmus Roterodamus. And Tra[n]slated in to Inglissh. An Exposition in to the Seventh Chaptre of the First Pistle to the Corinthians*. Early English Books Online, 1475–1640 / 39:05. Antwerp: Hans Luft, 1529.

———. *The First Tome or Volume of the Paraphrase of Erasmus upon the Newe Testamente*. Edited by Nicholas Udall. Early English Books Online, 1475–1640 / 1772:01. London: Edwarde Whitchurche, 1548.

———. *The First Tome or Volume of the Paraphrases of Erasmus vpon the Newe Testament Conteinyng the Fower Euangelistes, with the Actes of the Apostles:*

Eftsones Conferred with the Latine and Throughly Corrected as It Is by the Kinges Highnes Iniunccions Commaunded to Be Had in Euerie Churche of This Royalme. Edited by Nicholas Udall. 2nd ed. Early English Books Online, 1475–1640 / 2057:01. London: Edward Whitchurch, 1551.

———. *Opera omnia Desiderii Erasmi Roterodami: Ordinis noni Tomus Quartus*. Edited by Erika Rummel and Edwin Rabbie. Amsterdam: Huygens Instituut/Brill, 2003.

———. *Paraphrase on Matthew*. Edited by Dean Simpson. Collected Works of Erasmus: New Testament Scholarship 45. Toronto: University of Toronto Press, 2008.

Evans, G. R. *The Language and Logic of the Bible: The Road to Reformation*. New York: Cambridge University Press, 1985.

Fassler, Margot. *Gothic Song: Victorine Sequences and Augustinian Reform in Twelfth-Century Paris*. Cambridge: Cambridge University Press, 1993.

Feasey, Henry John. *Ancient English Holy Week Ceremonial*. London: Thomas Baker, 1897.

Fein, Susanna Greer, ed. "The Four Leaves of the Truelove." In *Moral Love Songs and Laments*. Kalamazoo, MI: Medieval Institute Publications, 1998.

Feuillerat, Albert, ed. *Documents Relating to the Revels at Court in the Time of King Edward VI and Queen Mary (the Loseley Manuscripts) Edited with Notes and Indexes*. Louvain: A. Uystpruyst, 1914.

Fitzgerald, Christina Marie. *The Drama of Masculinity and Medieval English Guild Culture*. New York: Palgrave Macmillan, 2007.

Fletcher, Alan J. "The Essential (Ephemeral) William Langland: Textual Revision as Ethical Process in Piers Plowman." *Yearbook of Langland Studies* 15 (2001): 61–98.

Forshall, J., and F. Madden, eds. *The Holy Bible . . . by John Wycliffe and His Followers*. 4 vols. Oxford: Oxford University Press, 1950.

Foucault, Michel. *The Hermeneutics of the Subject*. Edited and translated by Frederic Gros. New York: Palgrave Macmillan, 2005.

Fowler, Elizabeth. *Literary Character: The Human Figure in Early English Writing*. Ithaca, NY: Cornell University Press, 2003.

Foxe, John. *The Unabridged Acts and Monuments Online*. Sheffield: HRI Online Publications, 2011. http://www.johnfoxe.org.

Franklin, R. William. "A Model for a New Joint Declaration: An Episcopalian Reaction to the Joint Declaration on Justification." In *Justification and the*

Future of the Ecumenical Movement, edited by William G. Rusch, 35–46. Collegeville, MN: Liturgical Press, 2003.

Frei, Hans W. *The Eclipse of Biblical Narrative: A Study in Eighteenth and Nineteenth Century Hermeneutics.* New Haven: Yale University Press, 1974.

Frere, Walter Howard, and William Paul McClure Kennedy, eds. *Visitation Articles and Injunctions of the Period of the Reformation.* 3 vols. London, New York: Longmans, Green & Co., 1910.

Friedman, John B. "Figural Typology in the Middle English *Patience.*" In *The Alliterative Tradition in the Fourteenth Century*, edited by Bernard S. Levy and Paul E. Szarmach, 99–129. Kent, OH: Kent State University Press, 1981.

Froehlich, Karlfried. "'Always to Keep the Literal Sense in Holy Scripture Means to Kill One's Soul': The State of Biblical Hermeneutics at the Beginning of the Fifteenth Century." In *Literary Uses of Typology from the Late Middle Ages to the Present*, edited by Earl Miner, 20–48. Princeton: Princeton University Press, 1977.

Froehlich, Karlfried, and Margaret T. Gibson, eds. *Biblia latina cum Glossa ordinaria: Facsimile Reprint of the Editio Princeps Adolph Rusch of Strassburg 1480/81.* 4 vols. Turnhout: Brepols, 1992.

Gelber, Hester Goodenough. *It Could Have Been Otherwise: Contingency and Necessity in Dominican Theology at Oxford, 1300–1350.* Leiden: Brill, 2004.

Gertsman, Elina, ed. *Visualizing Medieval Performance: Perspectives, Histories, Contexts.* Burlington, VT: Ashgate, 2008.

Ghosh, Kantik. *The Wycliffite Heresy: Authority and the Interpretation of Texts.* Cambridge: Cambridge University Press, 2002.

Gillespie, Vincent. "The Study of Classical Authors from the Twelfth Century to *c.* 1450." In *The Cambridge History of Literary Criticism*, vol. 2, *The Middle Ages*, edited by Alastair Minnis and Ian Johnson, 160–78. New York: Cambridge University Press, 2005.

Goering, Joseph. "The Scholastic Turn (1100–1500): Penitential Theology and Law in the Schools." In *A New History of Penance*, edited by Abigail Firey, 219–37. Leiden: Brill, 2008.

Goldberg, Benjamin. *The Mirror and Man.* Charlottesville: University Press of Virginia, 1985.

Goldsmith, Margaret E. *The Image of "Piers Plowman": The Image on the Coin.* Cambridge: D. S. Brewer, 1981.

Grabes, Herbert. *The Mutable Glass: Mirror-Imagery in Titles and Texts of the Middle Ages and English Renaissance*. Translated by Gordon Collier. New York: Cambridge University Press, 1982.

Gréban, Arnoul. *Le mystère de la passion d'Arnould Greban*. Edited by Gaston Paris and Gaston Raynaud. F. Vieweg, 1878. Repr. Geneva: Slatkine Reprints, 1970.

——. *The Mystery of the Passion: The Third Day*. Translated by Paula Giuliano. Asheville, NC: Pegasus Press, 1996.

Gregory, Brad S. *The Unintended Reformation: How a Religious Revolution Secularized Society*. Cambridge, MA: Belknap Press, 2012.

Gregory of Nyssa. *The Life of Moses*. Translated by Abraham J. Malherbe and Everett Ferguson. New York: Paulist Press, 1978.

Gregory the Great. *S. Gregorii Magni Moralia in Job*. Edited by M. Adriaen. 3 vols. CCSL 143. Turnhout: Brepols, 1979.

Greschat, Catharina. *Die "Moralia in Job" Gregors des Grossen*. Tübingen: Mohr Siebeck, 2005.

Gretham, Robert de. *The Middle English "Mirror": An Edition Based on Bodleian Library, MS Holkham Misc. 40*. Edited by Kathleen Marie Blumreich. Tempe: Arizona Center for Medieval and Renaissance Studies, 2002.

Griffiths, Paul J. *Decreation: The Last Things of All Creatures*. Waco, TX: Baylor University Press, 2014.

——. *Religious Reading: The Place of Reading in the Practice of Religion*. New York: Oxford University Press, 1999.

Grosseteste, Robert. "De luce seu de inchoatione formarum." In *Die Philosophischen Werke des Robert Grosseteste, Bischofs von Lincoln*, edited by Ludwig Baur, 51–59. Münster: Aschendorffsche Verlagsbuchhandlung, 1912.

——. *On Light (De luce)*. Translated by Clare C. Riedl. Milwaukee, WI: Marquette University Press, 1942.

Groves, Beatrice. *Texts and Traditions: Religion in Shakespeare, 1592–1604*. Oxford: Clarendon Press, 2007.

Hailey, R. Carter. "'Geuyng Light to the Reader': Robert Crowley's Editions of *Piers Plowman* (1550)." *Papers of the Bibliographical Society of America* 94 (2001): 483–502.

——. "Robert Crowley and the Editing of *Piers Plowman* (1550)." *Yearbook of Langland Studies* 21 (2007): 143–70.

Hale, Dorothy J. "Aesthetics and the New Ethics: Theorizing the Novel in the Twenty-First Century." *PMLA* 124, no. 3 (2009): 896–905.

Hamlin, Hannibal. "Piety and Poetry: English Psalms from Miles Coverdale to Mary Sidney." In *The Oxford Handbook of Tudor Literature, 1485–1603*, edited by Mike Pincombe and Cathy Shrank, 203–21. New York: Oxford University Press, 2009.

———. *Psalm Culture and Early Modern English Literature*. New York: Cambridge University Press, 2004.

Hanna, Ralph. *London Literature, 1300–1380*. New York: Cambridge University Press, 2005.

———. "York and Yorkshire." In *Europe: A Literary History, 1348–1415*, edited by David Wallace. New York: Oxford University Press, forthcoming.

Hanna, Ralph, and Sarah Joy Wood, eds. *Richard Morris's "Prick of Conscience": A Corrected and Amplified Reading Text*. EETS, o.s., 342. Oxford: Oxford University Press, 2013.

Hansen, Miriam. "The Mass Production of the Senses: Classical Cinema as Vernacular Modernism." *Modernism/Modernity* 6, no. 2 (1999): 59–77.

Hardison, O. B. *Christian Rite and Christian Drama in the Middle Ages: Essays in the Origin and Early History of Modern Drama*. Baltimore: Johns Hopkins University Press, 1965.

Harrison, Peter. *The Bible, Protestantism, and the Rise of Natural Science*. New York: Cambridge University Press, 2001.

Hart, Kevin. "Introduction." In *Counter-Experiences: Reading Jean-Luc Marion*, edited by Kevin Hart, 1–54. Notre Dame, IN: University of Notre Dame Press, 2007.

Hartshorne, Henry, ed. *Household Cyclopedia*. New York: Thomas Kelly, 1881.

Henderson, William George, ed. *Missale ad usum insignis ecclesiæ eboracensis*. Vol. 1 of 2 vols. Publications of the Surtees Society 59. Durham: Andrews and Co., 1874.

Henry, Avril, ed. *The Pilgrimage of the Lyfe of the Manhode*. 2 vols. New York: Oxford University Press, 1988.

Henry of Ghent. *Summae quaestionum ordinarium theologii*. In A. J. Minnis and A. B. Scott, eds., *Medieval Literary Theory and Criticism, c. 1100–c. 1375: The Commentary Tradition*, rev. ed., 250–66. Oxford: Clarendon Press, 1988.

Herdt, Jennifer A. *Putting on Virtue: The Legacy of the Splendid Vices*. Chicago: University of Chicago Press, 2008.

Hill, Ordelle G. "The Audience of 'Patience.'" *Modern Philology* 66, no. 2 (1968): 103–9.

Hirsch, Emil G., Karl Budde, and Solomon Schechter, eds. "Jonah." *Jewish Encyclopedia*. New York: Funk and Wagnalls, 1906.

Hoffmann, Manfred. *Erkenntnis und Verwirklichung der wahren Theologie nach Erasmus von Rotterdam*. Tübingen: Mohr, 1972.

Horace. *The Art of Poetry*. Translated by Burton Raffel and James Hynd. Albany: State University of New York Press, 1974.

Horobin, Simon. "Stephen Batman and His Manuscripts of *Piers Plowman*." *Review of English Studies*, n.s., 62, no. 255 (2010): 358–72.

Howlett, David R. *British Books in Biblical Style*. Dublin: Four Courts Press, 1997.

Hudson, Anne, ed. "Prologue to the Wycliffite Bible, Chapter 15." In *Selections from English Wycliffite Writings*. Toronto: University of Toronto Press, 1997.

Hudson, Anne, and Pamela Gradon, eds. *English Wycliffite Sermons*. 5 vols. Oxford: Clarendon Press, 1983.

Hugh of St. Victor. *De sacramentis christiane fidei*. PL 176.

———. *The Didascalicon of Hugh of Saint Victor: A Medieval Guide to the Arts*. Translated by Jerome Taylor. New York: Columbia University Press, 1991.

Hughes, Kevin L. "'The Fourfold Sense': De Lubac, Blondel and Contemporary Theology." *Heythrop Journal* 42 (2001): 451–62.

Husserl, Edmund. *Ideas Pertaining to a Pure Phenomenology and to a Phenomenological Philosophy: First Book*. Translated by F. Kersten. Boston: M. Nijhoff, 1982.

Hütter, Reinhard. "Eucharistic Adoration in the Personal Presence of Christ: Making Explicit the Mystery of Faith by Way of Metaphysical Contemplation." *Nova et Vetera*, English Edition 7, no. 1 (2009): 175–216.

Iguchi, Atsushi. "Translating Grace: The *Scala Claustralium* and *A Ladder of Foure Ronges*." *Review of English Studies* 59, no. 242 (2007): 659–76.

———. "The Visibility of the Translator: The *Speculum Ecclesie* and *The Mirror of Holy Church*." *Neophilologus* 93, no. 3 (2009): 537–52.

Illich, Ivan. *The Rivers North of the Future: The Last Testament of Ivan Illich*. Edited by David Cayley. Toronto: House of Anansi Press, 2005.

Ingram, R. W. "Fifteen Seventy-Nine and the Decline of Civic Religious Drama in Coventry." *Elizabethan Theatre* 8 (1982): 114–28.

———, ed. *Records of Early English Drama: Coventry*. Toronto: University of Toronto Press, 1981.

Irvin, Matthew W. *Poetic Voices of John Gower: Politics and Personae in the "Confessio Amantis."* Suffolk: D. S. Brewer, 2014.

Iser, Wolfgang. *The Act of Reading: A Theory of Aesthetic Response*. Baltimore: Johns Hopkins University Press, 1978.

James, Mervyn. "Ritual, Drama and Social Body in the Late Medieval English Town." *Past and Present* 98 (1983): 3–29.

Jeauneau, Éduard. "Thomas of Ireland and His *De tribus sensibus sacrae scripturae*." In *With Reverence for the Word: Medieval Scriptural Exegesis in Judaism, Christianity, and Islam*, edited by Jane Dammen McAuliffe, Barry Walfish, and Joseph Ward Goering, 284–91. New York: Oxford University Press, 2003.

Jeffrey, David Lyle. *People of the Book: Christian Identity and Literary Culture*. Grand Rapids, MI: William B. Eerdmans, 1996.

Jerome. *Commentarium in Ionam*. In *Commentarii in prophetas minores*, edited by M. Adriaen. CCSL 76. Turnhout: Brepols, 1969.

Jewel, John. *An Apologie or Answere in Defence of the Churche of Englande with a Briefe and Plaine Declaration of the True Religion Professed and Vsed in the Same*. Translated by Anne Cooke Bacon. London: Reginald Wolfe, 1564.

John of Burgh. *Pupilla oculi*. Strasburg: Schott, Knobloch, and Götz, 1516. Available online through Gateway Bayern, http://gateway-bayern.de.

Johnston, Alexandra F., and Margaret Dorrell. "The York Mercers and Their Pageant of Doomsday." *Leeds Studies in English*, n.s., 6 (1972): 11–35.

Johnston, Alexandra F., and Margaret Rogerson, eds. *Records of Early English Drama: York*. 2 vols. Toronto: University of Toronto Press, 1979.

Jusserand, J. J. *"Piers Plowman": A Contribution to the History of English Mysticism*. Translated by M. E. R. London: T. Fisher Unwin, 1894.

Justice, Steven. "Did the Middle Ages Believe in Their Miracles?" *Representations* 103 (2008): 1–29.

Kablitz, Andreas. "Representation and Participation: Some Remarks on Medieval French Drama." In *Rethinking the Medieval Senses: Heritage, Fascinations, Frames*, edited by Stephen G. Nichols, Alison Calhoun, and Andreas Kablitz, 194–205. Baltimore: Johns Hopkins University Press, 2008.

Kane, George. "The Text." In *A Companion to Piers Plowman*, edited by John A. Alford, 175–200. Berkeley and Los Angeles: University of California Press, 1988.

Kantorowicz, Ernst Hartwig. *The King's Two Bodies: A Study in Mediaeval Political Theology*. Princeton: Princeton University Press, 1957.

Karnes, Michelle. *Imagination, Meditation, and Cognition in the Middle Ages.* Chicago: University of Chicago Press, 2011.

———. "Will's Imagination in *Piers Plowman.*" *Journal of English and Germanic Philology* 108, no. 1 (2009): 27–58.

Kelen, Sarah A. *Langland's Early Modern Identities.* New York: Palgrave Macmillan, 2007.

Kelly, Douglas. "The *Fidus interpres*: Aid or Impediment to Medieval Translation and *Translatio.*" In *Translation Theory and Practice in the Middle Ages*, edited by Jeanette Beer, 47–58. Kalamazoo, MI: Medieval Institute Publications, 1997.

Kelly, Henry Ansgar. "Penitential Theology and Law at the Turn of the Fifteenth Century." In *A New History of Penance*, edited by Abigail Firey, 239–98. Leiden: Brill, 2008.

Kendall, Ritchie D. *The Drama of Dissent: The Radical Poetics of Nonconformity, 1380–1590.* Chapel Hill: University of North Carolina Press, 1986.

Kerby-Fulton, Kathryn. *Reformist Apocalypticism and "Piers Plowman."* New York: Cambridge University Press, 1990.

Kerby-Fulton, Kathryn, and Denise L. Despres. *Iconography and the Professional Reader: The Politics of Book Production in the Douce "Piers Plowman."* Minneapolis: University of Minnesota Press, 1999.

King, John N. *English Reformation Literature: The Tudor Origins of the Protestant Tradition.* Princeton: Princeton University Press, 1982.

King, Pamela M. "The End of the World in Medieval English Religious Drama." *Literature and Theology* 26, no. 4 (2012): 384–99.

———. "Seeing and Hearing; Looking and Listening." *Early Theater* 3 (2000): 155–66.

———. *The York Mystery Cycle and the Worship of the City.* Cambridge: D. S. Brewer, 2006.

King, Pamela M., and Clifford Davidson, eds. *The Coventry Corpus Christi Plays.* Kalamazoo, MI: Medieval Institute Publications, 2000.

King'oo, Clare Costley. *Miserere Mei: The Penitential Psalms in Late Medieval and Early Modern England.* Notre Dame, IN: University of Notre Dame Press, 2012.

Kleist, James A., trans. *The Epistles of Saint Clement of Rome and Saint Ignatius of Antioch.* Westminster, MD: The Newman Bookshop, 1946.

Kolb, Robert, and Timothy J. Wengert, eds. *The Book of Concord: The Confessions of the Evangelical Lutheran Church.* Translated by Charles Arand et al. Minneapolis: Fortress Press, 2000.

Krey, Philip D., and Lesley Janette Smith, eds. *Nicholas of Lyra: The Senses of Scripture*. Leiden: Brill, 2000.

Krüger, Friedhelm. *Humanistische Evangelienauslegung: Desiderius Erasmus von Rotterdam als Ausleger der Evangelien in seinen Paraphrasen*. Tübingen: J. C. B. Mohr, 1986.

Kruger, Steven F. *Dreaming in the Middle Ages*. Cambridge: Cambridge University Press, 1992.

Kuczynski, Michael P. *Prophetic Song: The Psalms as Moral Discourse in Late Medieval England*. Philadelphia: University of Pennsylvania Press, 1995.

Lacoste, Jean-Yves. *Experience and the Absolute: Disputed Questions on the Humanity of Man*. Translated by Mark Raftery-Skehan. New York: Fordham University Press, 2004.

Lake, Peter. *Moderate Puritans and the Elizabethan Church*. New York: Cambridge University Press, 1982.

Lancashire, Ian, ed. *Dramatic Texts and Records of Britain: A Chronological Topography to 1558*. Toronto: University of Toronto Press, 1984.

Langland, William. *Piers Plowman: A Parallel-Text Edition of the A, B, C and Z Versions*. Edited by A. V. C. Schmidt. 2 vols. Kalamazoo, MI: Medieval Institute Publications, 2011.

———. *Piers Plowman: The A Version*. Edited by George Kane. London: Athlone Press, 1960.

———. *Piers Plowman: The B Version*. Edited by George Kane and E. Talbot Donaldson. London: Athlone Press, 1988.

———. *Piers Plowman: The C Version*. Edited by George Russell and George Kane. London: Athlone Press, 1997.

———. *Piers Plowman: The C-Text*. Edited by Derek Pearsall. Exeter: University of Exeter Press, 1994.

———. *The Vision of Pierce Plowman*. Edited by Robert Crowley. Early English Books Online, 1475–1640 / 122:19. London: Robert Crowley, 1550.

———. *Visio Willi de Petro Plouhman*. Edited by Thomas Dunham Whitaker. London: J. Murray, 1813.

Lapidge, Michael. "Booklists from Anglo-Saxon England." In *Learning and Literature in Anglo-Saxon England*, edited by Michael Lapidge and Helmut Gneuss, 33–89. Cambridge: Cambridge University Press, 1985.

Largier, Niklaus. "Allegorie und Figuration: Figuraler Realismus bei Heinrich Seuse und Erich Auerbach." *Paragrana* 21, no. 2 (2012): 36–46.

Latham, R. E., ed. *Revised Medieval Latin Word-List from British and Irish Sources*. London: Oxford University Press, 1980.

Lausberg, Heinrich. *Handbook of Literary Rhetoric: A Foundation for Literary Study*. Edited by David E. Orton and R. Dean Anderson. Leiden: Brill, 1998.

Lavere, Suzanne. "From Contemplation to Action: The Role of the Active Life in the *Glossa ordinaria* on the Song of Songs." *Speculum* 82 (2007): 54–69.

Lawler, Traugott. "The Pardon Formula in *Piers Plowman*: Its Ubiquity, Its Binary Shape, Its Silent Middle Term." *Yearbook of Langland Studies* 14 (2000): 117–52.

Legg, J. Wickham, ed. *The Sarum Missal: Edited from Three Early Manuscripts*. Oxford: Clarendon Press, 1916.

Leithart, Peter J. *Deep Exegesis: The Mystery of Reading Scripture*. Waco, TX: Baylor University Press, 2009.

Leo the Great, Pope. "Letter 28." In *Leo the Great, Gregory the Great*, edited by Charles Lett Feltoe, 38–43. Nicene and Post-Nicene Fathers, 2nd series, vol. 12. Edited by Philip Schaff and Henry Wace. Buffalo, NY: Christian Literature Publishing Co., 1895.

Lerer, Seth. *Chaucer and His Readers: Imagining the Author in Late Medieval England*. Princeton: Princeton University Press, 1993.

Levering, Matthew. *Participatory Biblical Exegesis: A Theology of Biblical Interpretation*. Notre Dame, IN: University of Notre Dame Press, 2008.

Lévinas, Emmanuel. *Ethics and Infinity*. Translated by Philippe Nemo. Pittsburgh: Duquesne University Press, 1985.

———. "A Religion for Adults." In *Difficult Freedom: Essays on Judaism*, translated by Seán Hand, 11–24. Baltimore: Johns Hopkins University Press, 1990.

———. "Revelation in the Jewish Tradition." In *The Levinas Reader*, edited by Seán Hand, 190–210. Malden, MA: Blackwell, 1999.

Levy, Ian Christopher. *John Wyclif: Scriptural Logic, Real Presence, and the Parameters of Orthodoxy*. Milwaukee: Marquette University Press, 2003.

———. *Reading the Scriptures: Holy Scripture and the Quest for Authority at the End of the Middle Ages*. Notre Dame, IN: University of Notre Dame Press, 2012.

Lindberg, David C., ed. *Roger Bacon and the Origins of "Perspectiva" in the Middle Ages: A Critical Edition and English Translation of Bacon's "Perspectiva," with Introduction and Notes*. New York: Oxford University Press, 1996.

Little, Katherine C. *Confession and Resistance: Defining the Self in Late Medieval England*. Notre Dame, IN: University of Notre Dame Press, 2006.

———. "Transforming Work: Protestantism and the *Piers Plowman* Tradition." *Journal of Medieval and Early Modern Studies* 40, no. 3 (2010): 497–526.

Livingston, Michael, ed. *The Middle English Metrical Paraphrase of the Old Testament*. Kalamazoo, MI: Medieval Institute Publications, 2011.

Lloyd, Charles, ed. *Formularies of Faith Put forth by Authority during the Reign of Henry VIII*. Oxford: Oxford University Press, 1856.

Lodge, Thomas, and Robert Greene. *A Looking Glasse for London and England*. Edited by George Alan Clugston. New York: Garland, 1980.

de Lubac, Henri. *Augustinisme et théologie moderne*. Paris: Aubier, 1965.

———. *Corpus mysticum: L'eucharistie et l'Église au Moyen âge. Étude historique*. Paris: Aubier, 1949.

———. *Corpus Mysticum: The Eucharist and the Church in the Middle Ages: Historical Survey*. Translated by Gemma Simmonds. Notre Dame, IN: University of Notre Dame Press, 2007.

———. *Exégèse médiévale: Les quatre sens de l'écriture*. 4 vols. Paris: Aubier, 1959–64.

———. *Medieval Exegesis: The Four Senses of Scripture*. Translated by Mark Sebanc and E. M. Macierowski. 3 vols. Grand Rapids, MI: William B. Eerdmans, 1998–2009.

———. *Scripture in the Tradition*. Translated by Luke O'Neill. New York: Herder and Herder, 2000.

Lukken, Gerard. *Original Sin in the Roman Liturgy: Research into the Theology of Original Sin in the Roman Sacramentaria and the Early Baptismal Liturgy*. Leiden: Brill, 1973.

Lumiansky, Robert M., and David Mills. *The Chester Mystery Cycle: Essays and Documents*. Chapel Hill: University of North Carolina Press, 1983.

Luther, Martin. *A Commentarie of M. Doctor Martin Luther vpon the Epistle of S. Paul to the Galathians*. Early English Books Online, 1475–1640 / 408:06. London: Thomas Vautroullier, 1575.

———. *Disputatio pro declaratione virtutis indulgentiarum*. Project Wittenberg, n.d. http://www.projectwittenberg.org/.

———. *D. Martin Luthers Werke*. Edited by J. F. K. Knaake et al. 72 vols. Kritische Gesamtausgabe. Weimar: Böhlau, 1883–.

———. *Luther's Works*. Edited by Jaroslav Pelikan, Hilton C. Oswald, Helmut T. Lehmann, and Christopher Boyd Brown. 69 vols. Saint Louis and Philadelphia: Concordia and Fortress, 1955–.

———. *Der Prophet Jona ausgelegt*. Augsburg, 1526.

Lutheran World Federation, and the Catholic Church. *Joint Declaration on the Doctrine of Justification*, 1999. http://www.vatican.va/.

Lyons, J. D. *Exemplum: The Rhetoric of Example in Early Modern France and Italy*. Princeton: Princeton University Press, 1989.

MacCulloch, Diarmaid. *The Boy King: Edward VI and the Protestant Reformation*. Berkeley and Los Angeles: University of California Press, 2002.

Mane, Perrine. *Le travail à la campagne au Moyen Age: Étude iconographique*. Paris: Picard, 2006.

Mann, Jill. "'He Knew Nat Catoun': Medieval School-Texts and Middle English Literature." In *The Text in the Community: Essays on Medieval Works, Manuscripts, Authors, and Readers*, edited by Jill Mann and Maura Nolan, 41–74. Notre Dame, IN: University of Notre Dame Press, 2006.

Marion, Jean-Luc. *Being Given: Toward a Phenomenology of Givenness*. Translated by Jeffrey L. Kosky. Stanford, CA: Stanford University Press, 2002.

———. "'Christian Philosophy': Hermeneutic or Heuristic?" In *The Visible and the Revealed*, translated by Christina M. Gschwandtner, 66–79. New York: Fordham University Press, 2008.

———. *The Erotic Phenomenon*. Translated by Stephen E. Lewis. Chicago: University of Chicago Press, 2007.

———. *God without Being: Hors Texte*. Translated by Thomas A. Carlson. Chicago: University of Chicago Press, 1991.

Marlowe, Christopher. *Doctor Faustus and Other Plays: A Text*. Edited by David Bevington and Eric Rasmussen. New York: Oxford University Press, 2008.

Marsh, George P. *The Origin and History of the English Language and of the Early Literature It Embodies*. Rev. ed. New York: Charles Scribner's Sons, 1892.

Martin, Priscilla. "Allegory and Symbolism." In *A Companion to the "Gawain"-Poet*, edited by Derek Brewer and Jonathan Gibson, 315–28. Woodbridge, Suffolk: D. S. Brewer, 1997.

Maskell, William, ed. *Monumenta ritualia ecclesiae Anglicanae: or, Occasional Offices of the Church of England According to the Ancient Use of Salisbury, the Prymer in English, and Other Prayers and Forms*. Vol. 1. London: W. Pickering, 1846.

Matsushita, Tomonori, ed. *A Glossarial Concordance to William Langland's "The Vision of Piers Plowman," the B-Text*. 3 vols. Tokyo: Yushodo Press, 1998.

Matthews, David. *The Making of Middle English, 1765–1910*. Minneapolis: University of Minnesota Press, 1999.

McDermott, Ryan. "Henri de Lubac's Genealogy of Modern Exegesis and Nicholas of Lyra's Literal Sense of Scripture." *Modern Theology* 29, no. 1 (2013): 124–56.

——, trans. "The Ordinary Gloss on Jonah." *PMLA* 128, no. 2 (2013): 424–38.

McEvoy, J. J. *Robert Grosseteste*. New York: Oxford University Press, 2000.

McEwan, Ian. *Atonement*. New York: Doubleday, 2001.

McGrath, Alister E. *The Intellectual Origins of the European Reformation*. 2nd ed. Malden, MA: Blackwell, 2004.

McMahon, Robert. *Understanding the Medieval Meditative Ascent: Augustine, Anselm, Boethius, and Dante*. Washington, DC: Catholic University of America Press, 2006.

Meyer, Robinson. "The Most Popular Passages in Books, According to Kindle Data." *The Atlantic*. November 2, 2014. http://www.theatlantic.com/technology/archive/2014/11/the-passages-that-readers-love/381373/.

Middleton, Anne. "Acts of Vagrancy: The C Version 'Autobiography' and the Statute of 1388." In *Written Work: Langland, Labor, and Authorship*, edited by Steven Justice and Kathryn Kerby-Fulton, 208–317. Philadelphia: University of Pennsylvania Press, 1997.

——. "Introduction: The Critical Heritage." In *A Companion to Piers Plowman*, edited by John A. Alford, 1–25. Berkeley and Los Angeles: University of California Press, 1988.

——. "Making a Good End: John But as a Reader of *Piers Plowman*." In *Medieval English Studies Presented to George Kane*, edited by Edward Donald Kennedy, Ronald Waldron, and Joseph S. Wittig, 243–63. Wolfeboro, NH: D. S. Brewer, 1988.

——. "Narration and the Invention of Experience: Episodic Form in *Piers Plowman*." In *The Wisdom of Poetry: Essays in Early English Literature in Honor of Morton W. Bloomfield*, edited by Larry Dean Benson and Siegfried Wenzel, 91–122. Kalamazoo, MI: Medieval Institute Publications, 1982.

——. "William Langland's 'Kynde Name': Authorial Signature and Social Identity in Late Fourteenth-Century England." In *Literary Practice and Social Change in Britain, 1380–1530*, edited by Lee Patterson, 15–82. Berkeley and Los Angeles: University of California Press, 1990.

Miller, Frances H. "The Northern Passion and the Mysteries." *Modern Language Notes* 34, no. 2 (1919): 88–92.

Miller, Patrick Lee. *Becoming God: Pure Reason in Early Greek Philosophy.* New York: Continuum, 2011.

Minnis, Alastair. "Ethical Poetry, Poetic Theology: A Crisis of Medieval Authority?" In *Medieval and Early Modern Authorship*, edited by Guillemette Bolens and Lukas Erne, 293–308. SPELL: Swiss Papers in English Language and Literature 25. Tübingen: Narr, 2011.

———. *Fallible Authors: Chaucer's Pardoner and Wife of Bath.* Philadelphia: University of Pennsylvania Press, 2008.

———. "Langland's Ymaginatif and Late-Medieval Theories of Imagination." *Comparative Criticism* 3 (1981): 71–103.

———. *Medieval Theory of Authorship: Scholastic Literary Attitudes in the Later Middle Ages.* 2nd ed. Philadelphia: University of Pennsylvania Press, 2011.

———. "The Trouble with Theology: Ethical Poetics and the Ends of Scripture." In *Author, Reader, Book: Medieval Authorship in Theory and Practice*, edited by Stephen Bradford Partridge and Erik Kwakkel, 20–37. Toronto: University of Toronto Press, 2012.

Minnis, Alastair, Ralph Hanna, Tony Hunt, R. G. Keightley, and Nigel F. Palmer. "Latin Commentary Tradition and Vernacular Literature." In *The Cambridge History of Literary Criticism*, vol. 2, *The Middle Ages*, edited by Alastair Minnis and Ian Johnson, 363–421. New York: Cambridge University Press, 2005.

Minnis, Alastair, and Ian Johnson, eds. *The Cambridge History of Literary Criticism*, vol. 2, *The Middle Ages.* New York: Cambridge University Press, 2005.

Minnis, A. [Alastair] J., and A. B. Scott, eds. *Medieval Literary Theory and Criticism, c. 1100–c. 1375: The Commentary Tradition.* Rev. ed. Oxford: Clarendon Press, 1988.

Mirk, John. *Instructions for Parish Priests.* Edited by Gillis Kristensson. Lund: Gleerup, 1974.

Mitchell, J. Allan. *Ethics and Eventfulness in Middle English Literature.* New York: Palgrave Macmillan, 2009.

———. *Ethics and Exemplary Narrative in Chaucer and Gower.* Rochester, NY: D. S. Brewer, 2004.

Monnin, Alfred. *Le curé d'Ars, vie de M. Jean-Baptiste-Marie Vianney.* Paris: C. Douniol, 1868.

Moorman, Charles. "The Role of the Narrator in *Patience*." *Modern Philology* 61 (1963): 90–95.

More, Thomas. *The Confutation of Tyndale's Answer*. In vol. 8 (with 3 pts.) of *The Complete Works of St. Thomas More*, edited by Louis A. Schuster, Richard C. Marius, James P. Lusardi, and Richard J. Schoeck. 15 vols. New Haven: Yale University Press, 1973.

Morey, James H. *Book and Verse: A Guide to Middle English Biblical Literature*. Urbana-Champaign: University of Illinois Press, 2000.

Muir, Lynette R. *The Biblical Drama of Medieval Europe*. New York: Cambridge University Press, 1995.

———. "Playing God in Medieval Europe." In *The Stage as Mirror: Civic Theatre in Late Medieval Europe*, edited by Alan E. Knight, 25–47. Cambridge: Boydell & Brewer, 1997.

Müller, Johannes. *Martin Bucers Hermeneutik*. Gütersloh: Gütersloher Verlagshaus G. Mohn, 1965.

Muller, Richard A. "Biblical Interpretation in the Era of the Reformation: The View from the Middle Ages." In *Biblical Interpretation in the Era of the Reformation: Essays Presented to David C. Steinmetz in Honor of His Sixtieth Birthday*, edited by Richard A. Muller and John Lee Thompson, 3–22. Grand Rapids, MI: William B. Eerdmans, 1996.

Muscatine, Charles. *Chaucer and the French Tradition: A Study in Style and Meaning*. Berkeley and Los Angeles: University of California Press, 1957.

Myers, A. R., ed. *English Historical Documents*, vol. 4, *1327–1485*. London: Eyre and Spottiswoode, 1969.

Nelson, Alan H. "Principles of Processional Staging: York Cycle." *Modern Philology* 67, no. 4 (May 1, 1970): 303–20.

———, ed. *Records of Early English Drama: Cambridge*. 2 vols. Toronto: University of Toronto Press, 1989.

Newhauser, Richard. "Nature's Moral Eye: Peter of Limoges' *Tractatus Moralis de Oculo*." In *Man and Nature in the Middle Ages*, edited by Susan J. Ridyard and Robert G. Benson, 125–36. Sewanee, TN: University of the South Press, 1995.

———. "Peter of Limoges, Optics, and the Science of the Senses." *The Senses and Society* 5, no. 1 (2010): 28–44.

———. "Sources II: Scriptural and Devotional Sources." In *A Companion to the "Gawain"-Poet*, edited by Derek Brewer and Jonathan Gibson, 257–76. Woodbridge, Suffolk: D. S. Brewer, 1997.

Newhauser, Richard, Tiina Kala, and Meelis Friedenthal. "The Work of an English Scribe in a Manuscript in Estonia." *Scriptorium* 62, no. 1 (2008): 139–48.

Newman, Martha G. *The Boundaries of Charity: Cistercian Culture and Ecclesiastical Reform, 1098–1180.* Stanford, CA: Stanford University Press, 1996.

Nicholas of Lyra. *Nicholas of Lyra's Apocalypse Commentary.* Edited by Philip D. W. Krey. Kalamazoo, MI: Medieval Institute Publications, 1997.

———. *Postilla.* In *Biblia latina cum Glossa ordinaria.* 6 vols. Venice, 1603.

———. *Postilla super totam bibliam.* Vol. 4. Strasburg, 1492.

———. "Second Prologue." *Postilla super totam bibliam.* In A. J. Minnis and A. B. Scott, eds., *Medieval Literary Theory and Criticism, c. 1100–c. 1375: The Commentary Tradition,* rev. ed., 268–70. Oxford: Clarendon Press, 1988.

Nisse, Ruth. *Defining Acts: Drama and the Politics of Interpretation in Late Medieval England.* Notre Dame, IN: University of Notre Dame Press, 2005.

Nowell, Alexander. *A Catechisme, or First Instruction and Learning of Christian Religion.* Early English Books Online, 1475–1640 / 1525:12. London: John Day, 1570.

O'Brian, Patrick. *H.M.S. Surprise.* New York: W. W. Norton, 1994.

Ochino, Bernardino. *A Tragoedie or Dialoge of the Vniuste Vsurped Primacie of the Bishop of Rome, and of All the Iust Abolishyng of the Same.* Translated by John Ponet. Early English Books Online, 1475–1640 / 327:10. London: N. Hill for Gwalter Lynne, 1549.

Ocker, Christopher. *Biblical Poetics before Humanism and Reformation.* New York: Cambridge University Press, 2002.

O'Mara, Veronica, and Suzanne Paul, eds. *A Repertorium of Middle English Prose Sermons.* 4 vols. Turnhout: Brepols, 2007.

Origen. *Homilies on Genesis and Exodus.* Translated by Ronald E. Heine. Washington, DC: Catholic University of America Press, 1982.

Orme, Nicholas. *Medieval Schools from Roman Britain to Renaissance England.* New Haven: Yale University Press, 2006.

Overell, Anne M. *Italian Reform and English Reformations, c. 1535–c. 1585.* Abingdon, UK: Ashgate, 2008.

Overmyer, Sheryl. "The Wayfarer's Way and Two Texts for the Journey: The 'Summa Theologiae' and 'Piers Plowman.'" Ph.D. diss., Duke University, 2010. ProQuest Dissertations & Theses Full Text (741140836).

Pabel, Hilmar M. "Exegesis and Marriage in Erasmus' *Paraphrases on the New Testament*." In *Holy Scripture Speaks: The Production and Reception of Erasmus' "Paraphrases on the New Testament*," edited by Hilmar M. Pabel and Mark Vessey, 175–209. Toronto: University of Toronto Press, 2002.

Parkes, M. B. "Stephen Batman's Manuscripts." In *Medieval Heritage: Essays in Honour of Tadahiro Ikegami*, ed. Masahiko Kanno et al., 125–56. Tokyo: Yushodo Press, 1997.

Parshall, Peter W. "Albrecht Dürer's St. Jerome in His Study: A Philological Reference." *The Art Bulletin* 53, no. 3 (1971): 303–5.

Pasternack, Carol Braun. "Stylistic Disjunctions in 'The Dream of the Rood.'" *Anglo-Saxon England* 13 (1984): 167–86.

Patrick, Saint. *Liber epistolarum Sancti Patricii episcopi*. Edited by David R. Howlett. Dublin: Four Courts Press, 1994.

Pearson, A. Harford, ed. *The Sarum Missal Done into English*. 2nd ed. London: The Church Printing Company, 1884.

Peter of Limoges. *The Moral Treatise on the Eye*. Translated by Richard Newhauser. Toronto: Pontifical Institute of Mediaeval Studies, 2012.

Phillips, Jane E. "On the Road to Emmaus: Erasmus' Paraphrase of Luke 24:27." *Erasmus of Rotterdam Society Yearbook* 22 (2002): 68–80.

Poleg, Eyal. *Approaching the Bible in Medieval England*. Manchester: Manchester University Press, 2013.

Pontifical Biblical Commission. *The Jewish People and Their Sacred Scriptures in the Christian Bible*. Vatican City: Libreria Editrice Vaticana, 2002. http://www.vatican.va/.

Prior, Sandra Pierson. *The Fayre Formez of the Pearl Poet*. East Lansing: Michigan State University Press, 1996.

Przywara, Erich. *"Analogia entis": Metaphysics: Original Structure and Universal Rhythm*. Translated by John R. Betz and David Bentley Hart. Grand Rapids, MI: William B. Eerdmans, 2014.

Putter, Ad. *An Introduction to the "Gawain"-Poet*. New York: Longman, 1996.

Quain, Edwin A. "The Medieval Accessus ad Auctores." *Traditio* 3 (January 1, 1945): 215–64.

Quantin, Jean-Louis. *The Church of England and Christian Antiquity: The Construction of a Confessional Identity in the 17th Century*. New York: Oxford University Press, 2009.

Quinto, Riccardo. "Peter the Chanter and the 'Miscellanea del Codice del Tesoro' (Etymology as a Way for Constructing a Sermon)." In *Constructing the Medieval Sermon*, edited by Roger Anderson, 33–81. Turnhout: Brepols, 2007.

Raabe, Pamela. *Imitating God: The Allegory of Faith in "Piers Plowman" B.* Athens: University of Georgia Press, 1990.

Raepsaet, Georges. "The Development of Farming Implements between the Seine and the Rhine from the Second to the Twelfth Centuries." In *Medieval Farming and Technology: The Impact of Agricultural Change in Northwest Europe*, edited by Grenville Astill and John Langdon, 41–68. New York: Brill, 1997.

Raine, Angelo. *Mediaeval York: A Topographical Survey Based on Original Sources.* London: J. Murray, 1955.

Raine, James, ed. *Testamenta Eboracensia: A Selection of Wills from the Registry at York.* Vol. 3. Surtees Society 45. Durham: Andrews and Co., 1865.

Rastall, Richard. *The Heaven Singing.* Vol. 1 of *Music in Early English Religious Drama.* Cambridge: D. S. Brewer, 1996.

———. *Minstrels Playing.* Vol. 2 of *Music in Early English Religious Drama.* Cambridge: D. S. Brewer, 2001.

Raw, Barbara. "Piers and the Image of God in Man." In *"Piers Plowman": Critical Approaches*, edited by S. S. Hussey, 143–79. London: Methuen, 1969.

Reilly, Robert. "A Middle English Summary of the Bible: An Edition of Trinity College (Oxon) Ms. 93." Ph.D. diss., University of Washington, 1966.

Reventlow, Hennig Graf. *Epochen der Bibelauslegung: Von der Spätantike bis zum Ausgang des Mittelalters.* 2 vols. Munich: C. H. Beck, 1994.

Rhodes, E. W. *Defensor's "Liber Scintillarum," with an Interlinear Anglo-Saxon Version Made Early in the Eleventh Century.* EETS, o.s., 93. London: N. Trübner, 1889.

Rhodes, Jim. *Poetry Does Theology: Chaucer, Grosseteste, and the Pearl-Poet.* Notre Dame, IN: University of Notre Dame Press, 2001.

Riches, Aaron. "Being Good: Thomas Aquinas and Dionysian Causal Predication." *Nova et Vetera: The English Edition of the International Theological Journal* 7, no. 2 (2009): 439–76.

Rituale romanum Pauli Quinti. Rome, 1636.

Robbins, Rossell Hope. "Levation Prayers in Middle English Verse." *Modern Philology* 40, no. 2 (November 1, 1942): 131–46.

Robert of Basevorn. *Forma praedicandi*. Translated by Leopold Krul. In *Three Medieval Rhetorical Arts*. edited by James J. Murphy, 114–215. Tempe: Arizona Center for Medieval and Renaissance Studies, 2001.

Robertson, D. W., and Bernard F. Huppé. *"Piers Plowman" and Scriptural Tradition*. Princeton: Princeton University Press, 1951.

Rogers, E. F. "How the Virtues of an Interpreter Presuppose and Perfect Hermeneutics: The Case of Thomas Aquinas." *Journal of Religion* 76, no. 1 (1996): 64–81.

Rolle, Richard. *The Form of Living*. In *Richard Rolle, Prose and Verse*. Edited by S. J. Ogilvie-Thomson. EETS, o.s., 293. Oxford: Oxford University Press, 1988.

Rollins, Hyder Edward, ed. *Old English Ballads, 1553–1625*. Cambridge: Cambridge University Press, 1920.

Rosemann, Philipp W. *The Story of a Great Medieval Book: Peter Lombard's "Sentences."* Toronto: University of Toronto Press, 2007.

Rosenfeld, Jessica. *Ethics and Enjoyment in Late Medieval Poetry: Love after Aristotle*. New York: Cambridge University Press, 2010.

Roye, Jean de. *Journal de Jean de Roye: Connu sous le nom de Chronique scandaleuse, 1460–1483*. Edited by Bernard de Mandrot. Vol. 1. 2 vols. Paris: Renouard, 1894.

Rubin, Miri. *Corpus Christi: The Eucharist in Late Medieval Culture*. New York: Cambridge University Press, 1991.

Rust, Jennifer R. "Political Theologies of the *Corpus Mysticum*: Kantorowicz, Schmitt, de Lubac." In *Political Theology and Early Modernity*, edited by Graham L. Hammill, Julia Reinhard Lupton, and Etienne Balibar, 102–23. Chicago: University of Chicago Press, 2012.

———. "Reforming the Mystical Body: From Mass to Martyr in John Foxe's *Acts and Monuments*." *ELH* 80, no. 3 (2013): 627–59.

Salter, Elizabeth. "Introduction." In *Piers Plowman*, by William Langland, edited by Elizabeth Salter and Derek Pearsall, 9–28. Evanston, IL: Northwestern University Press, 1967.

———. *"Piers Plowman": An Introduction*. 2nd ed. Cambridge, MA: Harvard University Press, 1969.

Sandys, Edwin. *The Sermons of Edwin Sandys*. Edited by John Ayre. Cambridge: Parker Society, 1842.

Sayers, William. "Sailing Scenes in Works of the *Pearl* Poet (*Cleanness* and *Patience*)." *Amsterdamer Beiträge zur älteren Germanistik* 63 (2007): 129–55.

Scanlon, Larry. "Langland, Apocalypse, and the Early Modern Editor." In *Reading the Medieval in Early Modern England*, edited by Gordon McMullan and David Matthews, 51–73. New York: Cambridge University Press, 2007.

———. *Narrative, Authority, and Power: The Medieval Exemplum and the Chaucerian Tradition*. New York: Cambridge University Press, 1994.

———. "Personification and Penance." *Yearbook of Langland Studies* 21 (2007): 1–29.

Scase, Wendy. "Writing and the Plowman: Langland and Literacy." *Yearbook of Langland Studies* 9 (1995): 121–31.

Schleusener, Jay. "History and Action in *Patience*." *PMLA* 85, no. 5 (1971): 959–65.

Schmidt, A. V. C. *The Clerkly Maker: Langland's Poetic Art*. Cambridge: D. S. Brewer, 1987.

Schott, Christine. "The Intimate Reader at Work: Medieval Annotators of *Piers Plowman* B." *Yearbook of Langland Studies* 26 (2012): 163–85.

Schrock, Chad. "The Ends of Reading in the *Merchant's Tale*." *Philological Quarterly* 91 (2012): 591–609.

Seifrid, Mark. "Luther, Melanchthon and Paul on the Question of Imputation: Recommendations on a Current Debate." In *Justification: What's at Stake in the Current Debates*, edited by Mark A. Husbands and Daniel J. Treier, 137–76. Downers Grove, IL: InterVarsity Press, 2004.

Sellers, Maud. *The York Mercers and Merchant Adventurers, 1356–1917*. Publications of the Surtees Society 129. Durham: Andrews and Co., 1918.

Selwyn, David Gordon. *The Library of Thomas Cranmer*. Oxford: Oxford Bibliographical Society, 1996.

Sheingorn, Pamela, and David Bevington. "'Alle This Was Token Domysday to Drede': Visual Signs of Last Judgment in the *Corpus Christi* Cycles and in Late Gothic Art." In *Homo, Memento Finis: The Iconography of Just Judgment in Medieval Art and Drama*, edited by David Bevington, 121–45. Kalamazoo, MI: Medieval Institute Publications, 1985.

Shuger, Debora. "The Reformation of Penance." *Huntington Library Quarterly* 71, no. 4 (December 2008): 557–71.

Simpson, James. *Burning to Read: English Fundamentalism and Its Reformation Opponents*. Cambridge, MA: Harvard University Press, 2009.

———. "Desire and the Scriptural Text: Will as Reader in *Piers Plowman*." In *Criticism and Dissent in the Middle Ages*, edited by Rita Copeland, 215–43. New York: Cambridge University Press, 1996.

———. *Reform and Cultural Revolution: 1350–1547*. The Oxford English Literary History 2. New York: Oxford University Press, 2004.

Skeat, Walter, W., ed. *The Vision of William Concerning Piers the Plowman*. Vol. 2, *Preface, Notes, and Glossary*. Oxford: Oxford University Press, 1885. Repr. 1961.

Smalley, Beryl. "The Bible and Eternity: John Wyclif's Dilemma." *Journal of the Warburg and Courtauld Institutes* 27 (1964): 73–89.

———. *The Study of the Bible in the Middle Ages*. Oxford: Blackwell, 1952.

Smith, D. Vance. *The Book of the Incipit: Beginnings in the Fourteenth Century*. Minneapolis: University of Minnesota Press, 2001.

———. "Negative Langland." *Yearbook of Langland Studies* 23 (2009): 33–59.

Smith, Kathryn A. *Art, Identity, and Devotion in Fourteenth-Century England: Three Women and Their Books of Hours*. London: British Library, 2003.

Smith, Lesley. *The "Glossa ordinaria": The Making of a Medieval Bible Commentary*. Leiden: Brill, 2009.

Smith, Macklin. "Balancing Tactics in *Piers Plowman*." Paper presented at the Fifth International *Piers Plowman* Conference, Oxford, England, 2011.

———. "Chiastic Form in *Piers Plowman*." Paper presented at the Forty-Fourth Annual International Congress on Medieval Studies, Kalamazoo, MI, 2009.

———. "Langland's Alliterative Line(s)." *Yearbook of Langland Studies* 23 (2009): 163–216.

Sokolowski, Robert. *Eucharistic Presence: A Study in the Theology of Disclosure*. Washington, DC: Catholic University of America Press, 1994.

Somerset, Fiona. "'Al þe comonys with o voys atonys': Multilingual Latin and Vernacular Voice in *Piers Plowman*." *Yearbook of Langland Studies* 19 (2005): 107–36.

———. *Feeling Like Saints: Lollard Writings after Wyclif*. Ithaca, NY: Cornell University Press, 2014.

Soskice, Janet Martin. *Metaphor and Religious Language*. Oxford: Clarendon Press, 1985.

Spearing, A. C. *Criticism and Medieval Poetry*. New York: Barnes and Noble, 1964.

———. *The "Gawain"-Poet: A Critical Study*. Cambridge: Cambridge University Press, 1970.

———. *Medieval Dream-Poetry.* Cambridge: Cambridge University Press, 1976.

———. "Verbal Repetition in *Piers Plowman* B and C." *Journal of English and Germanic Philology* 62 (1963): 722–37.

Spinks, Bryan D. *Do This in Remembrance of Me: The Eucharist from the Early Church to the Present Day.* London: SCM Press, 2013.

Staley, Lynn. *Languages of Power in the Age of Richard II.* University Park: Pennsylvania State University Press, 2005.

———. *The Voice of the "Gawain"-Poet.* Madison: University of Wisconsin Press, 1984.

Stanbury, Sarah. *Seeing the "Gawain"-Poet: Description and the Act of Perception.* Philadelphia: University of Pennsylvania Press, 1991.

Steiner, Emily. *Documentary Culture and the Making of Medieval English Literature.* New York: Cambridge University Press, 2003.

Steinmetz, David C. "John Calvin as an Interpreter of the Bible." In *Calvin and the Bible*, edited by Donald K. McKim, 282–92. New York: Cambridge University Press, 2006.

Stevens, Martin. *Four Middle English Mystery Cycles: Textual, Contextual, and Critical Interpretations.* Princeton: Princeton University Press, 1987.

Stevenson, Jill. *Performance, Cognitive Theory, and Devotional Culture: Sensual Piety in Late Medieval York.* New York: Palgrave Macmillan, 2010.

Stierle, Karl-Heinz. "Story as *Exemplum—Exemplum* as Story: On the Pragmatics and Poetics of Narrative Texts." In *New Perspectives in German Literary Criticism: A Collection of Essays*, edited by Richard E. Lange and Victor Amacher, translated by David Henry Wilson, 389–417. Princeton: Princeton University Press, 1979.

St.-Jacques, Raymond. "Conscience's Final Pilgrimage in *Piers Plowman* and the Cyclical Structure of the Liturgy." *Revue de l'Université d'Ottawa* 40, no. 2 (1970): 210–23.

———. "Langland's Bells of the Resurrection and the Easter Liturgy." *English Studies in Canada* 3, no. 2 (1977): 129–35.

Stock, Brian. *The Implications of Literacy: Written Language and Models of Interpretation in the Eleventh and Twelfth Centuries.* Princeton: Princeton University Press, 1987.

Streete, Adrian. "Introduction." In *Early Modern Drama and the Bible: Contexts and Readings, 1570–1625*, edited by Adrian Streete, 1–23. New York: Palgrave Macmillan, 2012.

Streitberger, W. R. *Court Revels, 1485–1559*. Toronto: University of Toronto Press, 1994.

Strohm, Paul. *England's Empty Throne: Usurpation and the Language of Legitimation, 1399–1422*. New Haven: Yale University Press, 1998.

Summit, Jennifer. *Memory's Library: Medieval Books in Early Modern England*. Chicago: University of Chicago Press, 2008.

Swanson, Heather. *Medieval Artisans: An Urban Class in Late Medieval England*. Oxford: Basil Blackwell, 1989.

Swanton, Michael, ed. *The Dream of the Rood*. Manchester: Manchester University Press, 1970.

Synan, Edward. "The Four 'Senses' and Four Exegetes." In *With Reverence for the Word: Medieval Scriptural Exegesis in Judaism, Christianity, and Islam*, edited by Jane Damman McAuliffe, Barry D. Walfish, and Joseph W. Goering, 226–36. New York: Oxford University Press, 2003.

Taylor, Charles. *A Secular Age*. Cambridge, MA: Belknap Press, 2007.

Tentler, Thomas N. "Postscript." In *Penitence in the Age of Reformations*, edited by Katharine Jackson Lualdi and Anne T. Thayer, 240–59. Burlington, VT: Ashgate, 2000.

———. *Sin and Confession on the Eve of the Reformation*. Princeton: Princeton University Press, 1977.

Thomas Aquinas. *Ethicorum Aristotelis expositio*. Corpus Thomisticum, n.d. www.corpusthomisticum.org.

———. *In psalmos Davidis expositio*. Corpus Thomisticum, n.d. www.corpus thomisticum.org.

———. *Quaestiones de quodlibet*. Corpus Thomisticum, n.d. www.corpustho misticum.org.

———. *Summa theologica*. 5 vols. Translated by Fathers of the English Dominican Province. New York: Benziger Bros., 1948. Repr. Notre Dame, IN: Ave Maria Press, 1991.

Thomson, Ian, and Louis Perraud, eds. *Ten Latin Schooltexts of the Later Middle Ages*. Lewiston, NY: E. Mellen Press, 1990.

Tolnay, Charles. *Michelangelo*. Vol. 5, *The Final Period*. Princeton: Princeton University Press, 1960.

Tydeman, William, ed. *The Medieval European Stage, 500–1550*. Theatre in Europe: A Documentary History. Cambridge: Cambridge University Press, 2001.

Tyndale, William. *The Obedyence of a Christian Man and How Christen Rulers Ought to Gouerne*. Early English Books Online, 1475–1640 / 156:08. London: William Hill, 1548.

———. *The Prophete Ionas with an Introduccio[n] before Teachinge to Vndersto[n]de Him and the Right vse Also of All the Scripture, and Why It Was Written, and What Is Therin to Be Sought, and Shewenge Wherewith the Scripture Is Locked Vpp That He Which Readeth It, Can Not Vndersto[n]de It, Though He Studie Therin Never so Moch: And Agayne with What Keyes It Is so Opened, That the Reader Can Be Stopped out with No Sotilte or False Doctrine of Man, from the True Sense and Vderstondynge Therof*. Early English Books Online, 1475–1640 / 950:10. Antwerp: M. de Keyser, 1531.

Vantuono, William. "The Structure and Sources of *Patience*." *Medieval Studies* 34 (1972): 401–21.

Vaughan, Míċeál F. "The Liturgical Perspectives of *Piers Plowman* B, XVI–XIX." *Studies in Medieval and Renaissance History* 3 (1980): 87–155.

———. "'Til I gan awake': The Conversion of Dreamer into Narrator in *Piers Plowman* B." *Yearbook of Langland Studies* 5 (1991): 175–92.

Vessey, Mark. "The Actor in the Story: Horizons of Interpretation in Erasmus's *Annotations on Luke*." In *The Unfolding of Words: Commentary in the Age of Erasmus*, edited by Judith Rice Henderson, 55–69. Toronto: University of Toronto Press, 2012.

———. "The Tongue and the Book: Erasmus' *Paraphrases on the New Testament* and the Arts of Scripture." In *Holy Scripture Speaks: The Production and Reception of Erasmus' "Paraphrases on the New Testament,"* edited by Hilmar M. Pabel and Mark Vessey, 29–58. Toronto: University of Toronto Press, 2002.

Voragine, Jacobus de. *Legenda aurea: Vulgo historia lombardica dicta*. Edited by Johann Georg Theodor Grässe. Dresden and Leipzig: Impensis Librariae Arnoldianae, 1846.

———. *Marialis Liber*. In Jacques de Voragine, *Mariale de laudibus deiparae virginis*. Lyon: Martin, 1688.

Wainwright, Geoffrey. *Eucharist and Eschatology*. London: Epworth Press, 1971.

Waldron, Jennifer. *Reformations of the Body: Idolatry, Sacrifice, and Early Modern Theater*. New York: Palgrave Macmillan, 2013.

Walker, Greg, ed. "Chester, The Post-Reformation Banns." In *Medieval Drama: An Anthology*, 201–5. Malden, MA: Wiley-Blackwell, 2000.

Walsh, P. G., ed. *One Hundred Latin Hymns: Ambrose to Aquinas*. Translated by P. G. Walsh. Cambridge, MA: Harvard University Press, 2012.

Warner, Lawrence. *The Lost History of Piers Plowman: The Earliest Transmission of Langland's Work*. Philadelphia: University of Pennsylvania Press, 2011.

Warren, Nancy Bradley. "Incarnational (Auto)biography." In *Oxford Twenty-First Century Approaches to Literature: Middle English*, edited by Paul Strohm, 369–85. New York: Oxford University Press, 2007.

Watson, Nicholas. "*Piers Plowman*, Pastoral Theology, and Spiritual Perfectionism: Hawkyn's Cloak and Patience's Pater Noster." *Yearbook of Langland Studies* 21 (2007): 83–118.

———. *Richard Rolle and the Invention of Authority*. New York: Cambridge University Press, 1991.

Wenzel, Siegfried. "The Continuing Life of William Peraldus's *Summa vitiorum*." In *Ad litteram: Authoritative Texts and Their Medieval Readers*, edited by Mark D. Jordan and Kent Emery, 135–64. Notre Dame, IN: University of Notre Dame Press, 1992.

———, ed. *Fasciculus morum: A Fourteenth-Century Preacher's Handbook*. Translated by Siegfried Wenzel. University Park: Pennsylvania State University Press, 1989.

———. *Latin Sermon Collections from Later Medieval England: Orthodox Preaching in the Age of Wyclif*. New York: Cambridge University Press, 2005.

Wesley, John. *Hymns and Spiritual Songs, Intended for the Use of Real Christians of All Denominations*. London: William Strahan, 1753.

Westberg, Daniel. *Right Practical Reason: Aristotle, Action, and Prudence in Aquinas*. Oxford: Clarendon Press, 1994.

White, Paul Whitfield. *Drama and Religion in English Provincial Society, 1485–1660*. New York: Cambridge University Press, 2008.

———. "Reforming Mysteries' End: A New Look at Protestant Intervention in English Provincial Drama." *Journal of Medieval and Early Modern Studies* 29, no. 1 (1999): 121–47.

———. *Theatre and Reformation: Protestantism, Patronage, and Playing in Tudor England*. New York: Cambridge University Press, 1993.

White, Robert Meadows, ed. *The Ormulum*. 2 vols. Oxford: Oxford University Press, 1852.

Wieck, Roger S. *Painted Prayers: The Book of Hours in Medieval and Renaissance Art.* New York: George Braziller, 1997.

———. *Time Sanctified: The Book of Hours in Medieval Art and Life.* New York: George Braziller, 2001.

Wieland, George. "Happiness: The Perfection of Man." In *The Cambridge History of Later Medieval Philosophy: From the Rediscovery of Aristotle to the Disintegration of Scholasticism, 1100–1600,* edited by Norman Kretzmann, Anthony Kenny, and Jan Pinborg, 673–86. New York: Cambridge University Press, 1982.

Williams, George Huntston. *The Radical Reformation.* 3rd ed. Kirksville, MO: Truman State University Press, 1995.

Wood, Diana. *Medieval Economic Thought.* New York: Cambridge University Press, 2002.

Woolf, D. R. *Reading History in Early Modern England.* New York: Cambridge University Press, 2001.

Wright, D. F. "Martin Bucer." *Dictionary of Major Biblical Interpreters.* Downers Grove, IL: InterVarsity Press, 2007.

Wyatt, Michael. *The Italian Encounter with Tudor England: A Cultural Politics of Translation.* Cambridge: Cambridge University Press, 2005.

Wyatt, Sir Thomas. *The Complete Poems.* Edited by R. A. Rebholz. Harmondsworth: Penguin, 1978.

Wyclif, John. *On the Truth of Holy Scripture.* Translated by Ian Christopher Levy. Kalamazoo, MI: Medieval Institute Publications, 2001.

——— "Principium." Edited by Gustav Adolf Benrath. In Gustav Adolf Benrath, *Wyclifs Bibelkommentar,* 338–45. Berlin: Walter de Gruyter, 1966.

Yeago, David. "The Office of the Keys: On the Disappearance of Discipline in Protestant Modernity." In *Marks of the Body of Christ,* edited by Carl E. Braaten and Robert W. Jenson, 95–122. Grand Rapids, MI: William B. Eerdmans, 1999.

Young, Frances. *Biblical Exegesis and the Formation of Christian Culture.* New York: Cambridge University Press, 1997.

Young, Karl. *The Drama of the Medieval Church.* 2 vols. Oxford: Clarendon Press, 1933.

Zahora, Tomas. *Nature, Virtue, and the Boundaries of Encyclopaedic Knowledge: The Tropological Universe of Alexander Neckam (1157–1217).* Turnhout: Brepols, 2014.

Zeeman, Nicolette. *"Piers Plowman" and the Medieval Discourse of Desire*. New York: Cambridge University Press, 2006.

Zieman, Katherine. *Singing the New Song: Literacy and Liturgy in Late Medieval England*. Philadelphia: University of Pennsylvania Press, 2008.

Zim, Rivkah. "Stephan Batman." Edited by H. C. G. Matthew and B. Harrison. *The Oxford Dictionary of National Biography*. Oxford: Oxford University Press, 2004. http://www.oxforddnb.com.

Zinn, Grover A. "Exegesis and Spirituality in the Writings of Gregory the Great." In *Gregory the Great: A Symposium*, edited by John Cavadini, 168–80. Notre Dame, IN: University of Notre Dame Press, 1995.

Zumthor, Paul. *Toward a Medieval Poetics*. Minneapolis: University of Minnesota Press, 1992.

Index

accessus ad auctores, 13–18

action. *See* ethics, action, action theory

active life, 2, 34–35, 41–42, 45–46, 70–72, 334

Adam of St. Victor, 97

Aers, David, 46n81, 235

affections, 17, 19–20, 33, 68, 101–3, 140–42, 252–55

Alan of Lille, 40, 169, 184, 326–27

Alexander of Hales, 37

Alhacen, 330, 333n67, 334–35

allegory
  literary, 50–57, 72–75, 103
  theological, 2–3, 35, 37–39, 88–94, 112–35, 261–64, 373–74. *See also* exegesis, fourfold theory of; Jesus Christ, allegorical correspondence to

Allen, Elizabeth, 154n22, 155n24

Allen, Judson Boyce, 14, 116, 147n6

alliterative verse, 108, 199–200, 202–7

amplification, 94–99, 107

anagogy, 77, 180–82, 186–88, 256, 270, 291–92, 318–20, 369–70. *See also* eschatology; exegesis, fourfold theory of; *Piers Plowman*, anagogy and eschatology of

analogy, doctrine of, 164–65, 187–88, 268

Anselm of Laon, 100

Antichrist, 65–66, 272, 277, 309, 378

apocalyptic, 9, 196, 225n77, 240, 270–76, 289, 297–98, 309–10, 378–79

Arator, 138

Aristotle, 14–15, 19–20, 269–70, 272

Articles about Religion (Ten Articles), 225–27

Astell, Ann, 328–29

Athanasius, 198, 204

Attridge, Derek, 150n14

Auerbach, Erich, 2, 93–94, 136, 374

Augustine of Denmark, 16, 180

Augustine of Hippo, 6, 24, 31, 35, 38, 46n81, 48, 63, 246, 300, 302, 311

Bacon, Roger, 330–31, 333, 347

Bale, John, 136n94, 274–75, 278, 348, 363–64, 377–78

Batman, Stephen, 6, 78–85, 224

Beckwith, Sarah, 228, 292–93, 296, 298, 358n114, 363, 367–68

Becon, Thomas, 351n98

Bede, 24, 35

Bernard of Clairvaux, 6, 148, 180

Bible, 11–12

  concept of, 21

  episodes and books

  —Deuteronomy, 240–42

  —Emmaus, road to, 167–70, 263–64

  —harrowing of hell, 121–22, 130, 198, 205–7

  —Jonah, 87–142

  —Last Judgment. *See* Last Judgment

  —massacre of the innocents, 284

  —Moses and the burning bush, 117–18

  —nativity and childhood of Christ, 282–85

  —parable of the sower, 55, 80–84

  —Pauline epistles, 2, 22, 35, 193, 234, 236, 246–49, 253, 256–57, 270, 300–301, 346, 353, 374

  —Pentecost, 7, 152–56, 173–78

  —Psalms, 243–48. *See also* Penitential Psalms

  —Sermon on the Mount, 59–60

  —Song of Songs, 34–35

  —Ten Commandments, 3

  Kindle edition, 371–72

  practices of scripture, 62, 66

  vernacular biblical literature, 16, 18, 19n15, 70, 94, 257–71, 320–21

  YouVersion, 372–73

Biblia pauperum, 99–100

Bloomfield, Morton W., 207–8

Boccaccio, Giovanni, 14

Bolton Hours, 304–5

Bonaventure, 6, 99

  arts correspond to four senses of scripture, 16–17, 166–67

  Gregory the Great as master of tropology, 39

  integrates spirit and letter, 114, 116

  spiritual senses as theological virtues, 29–30, 165

  tropology and wisdom are circulatory, 41–42

Boniface III, pope, 272

Book of Common Prayer, 227, 302, 351n98, 352n99, 354–55

Borthwick, John, 353–54

Bossy, John, 191

Brague, Rémi, 172

Brenz, Johannes, 138

Bromyard, John, 154n21, 330, 332n66

Brown, Peter, 333

Browne, Robert, 352n100

Bucer, Martin, 9, 264–72, 274, 290

But, John, 224

Bynum, Caroline Walker, 162, 339–40

Calvin, John, 9, 266, 290, 344
   commentary on the Last Judg-
     ment, 345–46
   Eucharistic doctrine, 351–52
   on refusing the sacraments,
     348–49
   tropological theory, 239–43
Careless, John, 9, 240, 278–90
Carruthers, Mary, 18–19, 38, 148,
   170, 328
Cawarden, Thomas, 273
Certeau, Michel de, 125, 132
Cervone, Cristina Maria, 197–98
Chalcedon, Council of, 203
charity. *See* works of mercy
Chaucer, Geoffrey, 7
   on ambiguity of *doctrina*, 244
   "first he wroghte . . . ," 317
   "glosing," 41
   inventive habits compared to
     Langland, 146–47
   and *Liber Catonis*, 184
   as reader of *Piers Plowman*,
     380–82
   scripture, definition of, 21
   as translator, 158–59
   waking to write in *Book of the*
     Duchess, 211–12
chiasmus, 195, 197–210
Chrétien, Jean-Louis, 177
Cicero, 150–51
Clark, Robert L. A., 323–24
Cleanness, 131
confession, 214–18
contemplative life, 2, 16, 28–29,
   34–35, 41–42, 45–46, 70–72,
   334
contrition, 214, 216n57, 217–18,
   251–53

conversion, 2, 8, 67, 90n10, 121, 128,
   142, 168, 169n49, 178, 216, 233,
   254–56, 264, 270, 275, 286,
   288–89, 310, 344
Copeland, Rita, 7, 148, 150, 156–59,
   162–63
Corpus Christi, Feast of, 279, 281,
   295–96, 298–99, 336, 349, 357,
   361
Corpus Christi Guild, 357
counter-experience, 295–97, 337n72,
   338–39, 341, 344, 355, 364–70
Coventry Play, 274, 278–90
Cranmer, Thomas, 191, 226, 252,
   255–58, 265, 271–72, 352
Crassons, Kate, 357n111, 359
Cromwell, Thomas, 276
Crowley, Robert, 9, 229–30
Cummings, Brian, 246, 254n38

Dagenais, John, 75, 84
Dahan, Gilbert, 3, 28–29, 165
Daniell, David, 377
Dante Alighieri, 222
de Deguileville, Guillaume, 213–14
De Lisle Hours, 304n22
de Lubac, Henri, 22n23, 23–24, 28,
   32–34, 42–43, 46n81, 112, 311,
   364–67
Derrida, Jacques, 150–51, 170–80
Descartes, René, 366n133
Dies irae, 312
Dix, Gregory, 361n123
Doomsday. *See* Last Judgment; York
   Play, Doomsday
drama
   biblical, 265, 269–70, 274–75. *See*
    also Coventry Play; York Play
   comedy, 269–70

court, 273–74
Mass, relationship to, 292
Protestant, 264, 268–90
"sacramental theater," 10, 292–93,
   295–98, 307, 319, 355–58,
   360–70
school drama, 273–74, 278
song in, 284–87
tragedy, 269–70
The Dream of the Rood, 200
ductus, 103–13
Duffy, Eamon, 302
Dugdale, William, 279

Ebeling, Gerhard, 244
ecclesiology, 65–66
Eco, Umberto, 44
Edward VI, king, 4, 9, 240, 259–64,
   271–76, 278, 296, 298
election, doctrine of, 231, 251–56,
   275, 308, 311, 345–46, 353–55
Elizabeth I, queen, 259, 274, 279
Emerson, Ralph Waldo, 33
Erasmus, Desiderius, 6–7, 9, 137n96,
   138–40, 228n87, 239, 257–64,
   266, 271
eschatology, 9, 27. *See also* anagogy;
   Last Judgment; *Piers Plowman*,
   anagogy and eschatology of
ethics. *See also* exemplarity;
   tropology; works of mercy
action, action theory, 2, 6, 17,
   19–20, 42, 165–67, 170, 245–52
literary, 3–5, 14, 16–20, 150–151,
   170–80, 380–82
moralized optics, 294, 321,
   329–36
moral philosophy, 5, 13–14, 18–21,
   42, 60–62, 66, 70, 248–49

virtue ethics, 10, 20, 46n82, 57–66,
   228, 296, 329, 348, 370. *See also*
   virtue
writing as ethical action, 166–67,
   208–24
Eucharist, 10, 55n97, 189, 289,
   292–98, 300, 304–7, 321,
   351–52, 357, 360–70
exegesis. *See also* allegory; anagogy;
   literal sense of scripture;
   tropology
fourfold theory of, 2–3, 11–12,
   22–32, 103, 181
history of, 4–5, 11–28, 47–48,
   110–19, 238–71, 375–77
relationship of literal sense to allegorical sense, 110–19, 135–37,
   254–56, 331
vernacular, 10, 18, 70, 89–90,
   257–64, 371–77
exemplarity, 141, 150, 152–56,
   162–64, 182–88, 268–69,
   316–18, 353

Fasciculus morum, 218–19
Fletcher, Alan, 216n57
Foucault, Michel, 192
"The Four Leaves of the Truelove,"
   201
Fourth Lateran Council, 17, 164–65,
   235
Foxe, John, 9, 252n33, 275, 281,
   348–55, 362
Franciscanism, 181
Frei, Hans, 92–93, 112, 135–36

Ghosh, Kantik, 61
Giles of Rome, 34
Glasscock, Agnes, 286–87

Glossa ordinaria, 6, 23n25, 92,
    99–110, 120, 155, 300, 307
Gower, John, 158–59, 222n71
Gratian, 191
Gréban, Arnoul, 270n103, 297,
    320–30, 334
Greene, Robert, 141–42
Gregory, Brad, 196
Gregory of Nyssa, 165
Gregory the Great
    exegetical analogy of head and
        body, 33–34
    Gospel homilies as source for
        Middle English *Mirror*, 80
    master of tropology, 17
    Moralia in Job, purpose of, 1
    order of the senses of scripture, 39
    participatory exegesis, 28–29
    significance in *Piers Plowman*,
        70–72
    significance in Reformation, 252,
        353
    "transform what we read" into our
        lives, 57
    whether God's will changes, 133
Griffiths, Paul, 26–27
Grosseteste, Robert, 272n112, 329,
    332–33

Hanna, Ralph, 5, 80, 221, 294n5
Heidegger, Martin, 175n67
Henry VIII, king, 228n88, 260–61,
    264, 272–73, 276–77
Henry of Ghent, 24–25
hermeneutical theory (modern), 12,
    43, 49, 59–60, 92, 223, 377
Holcot, Robert, 115–16, 332n66
homiletics, 15, 58, 97–98, 141,
    161–62, 329–32

Honorius of Autun, 34, 292
Hooper, John, 351n98
Horace, 157, 159, 162–63
Howlett, David, 198–99
Hugh of St. Victor, 16, 24, 36–37,
    40n68
Hus, Jan, 353
Husserl, Edmund, 175n67,
    336
Hutchinson, Roger, 351n98
Hutton, Matthew, 278–79

Iguchi, Atsushi, 158n32
Illich, Ivan, 192
imitation, 159–64. *See also* Jesus
    Christ, imitation and example of
incarnation. *See* Jesus Christ, incar-
    nation of
incarnational poetics, 197–99, 279,
    313, 368, 381–82
Instructions for Parish Priests. See
    Mirk, John
intentionality, 336–41
invention
    of Antichrist, 272
    competitive and noncompetitive,
        156–64
    as discovery, 320
    ethical, 3, 7, 25
    of institutions, 44–45
    literary, 3, 7, 76–79, 210–15,
        223–24
    participatory, 107–10
    rhetorical, 156–64
    of scripture, 286–87
    translation as, 155–64
    tropological. *See* tropology, and
        invention
Irvin, Matthew, 222n71

Jerome, 88, 101–2, 137–39, 149n10
Jesus Christ
  allegorical correspondence to, 88,
    91, 95, 98, 99, 102, 105, 110,
    113, 120–22, 128–35
  baptism of, 294, 315–19
  body of
  —ecclesial, 246, 292–98, 353–54,
    355–70
  —Eucharistic, 55n97, 357, 360–70
  —physical, 307n24, 309, 312–13,
    315–16, 321–27, 335, 342–43
  chiasmus, relation to, 200–206
  Eucharistic presence of, 10,
    292–98, 300, 304–7, 321,
    351–52, 360–70
  hidden in the poor, 355–64
  imitation and example of, 48,
    58–59, 81, 131–35, 160–63,
    167–69, 228n87, 262–64,
    282–90, 294–95, 315–17, 335,
    347–48, 380–82
  incarnation of, 197–99, 201,
    204–10, 272, 294, 317–19,
    330, 381
  institutor of penance, 226, 229–31,
    250
  interpreter of scripture, 121, 130,
    137, 169, 263–64, 315–19
  judge, 9, 46, 293–95, 302–7,
    309–10, 314, 342–51, 372–73
  meditation on, 221–22
  and the metaphysics of history,
    33–34, 37, 115–18
  participation in life of, 231,
    233–35, 256, 268–69, 282–90,
    321–29
  resurrection of, 88, 109, 135, 182,
    198, 205–7

  salvific work of Passion, satisfac-
    tion, resurrection, 182, 191, 195,
    197–98, 202–10, 216, 231n95,
    321–29
  and the spiritual senses of scrip-
    ture, 2, 4, 22, 24–25, 29–30,
    115–18, 179, 240, 242n8,
    245–49, 255–56
  union with, 42, 236
Joachim of Fiore, 181
John of St. Thomas, 366n133
Joint Declaration on the Doctrine of
    Justification, 232–34
Jusserand, J. J., 145–46
justification, doctrine of, 74, 230–34,
    243–49, 345–48
Juvencus, 138

Kantorowicz, Ernst, 364–66
Karnes, Michelle, 94
Kepler, Johannes, 330
Kerby-Fulton, Kathryn, 208
King, Pamela, 298–300, 312n33, 357
King'oo, Clare Costley, 250, 301–2
Kirchmeyer, Thomas, 274
Krüger, Friedhelm, 262–63

Lacoste, Jean-Yves, 295–96, 369
Lake, Peter, 231n95
Langland, William, 78–79, 195–96,
    207–10, 221n67, 222–24,
    235n106. See also Piers Plowman
Largier, Niklaus, 93–94
Last Judgment, 55n98, 291–92,
    296–314, 319–20, 341–55,
    360
Lavere, Suzanne, 35
Lawler, Traugott, 216–17
Leo the Great, pope, 204n35

levation prayers, 299–300
Lever, Thomas, 274, 278, 280
Levering, Matthew, 30–31, 112, 375
Lévinas, Emmanuel, 109, 151, 171
Levy, Ian Christopher, 61n113
Liber Catonis, 184–85
Liber parabolarum, 183–85
literal sense of scripture, 6–7, 29, 63,
    88–99, 104–6, 110–19, 239,
    241–42, 373–74. *See also*
    exegesis, fourfold theory of
Lodge, Thomas, 141–42
Lombard, Peter, 191
"The Long Charter of Christ," 313
*A Looking Glasse for London and
    England*, 141–42
"Love Rune," 201
Luther, Martin, 9, 100, 270, 290
    Bucer, Martin, influence on, 266
    English Reformation, influence on,
    344
    on imputation and justification,
    346–48
    on Nicholas of Lyra and allegory,
    112
    on penance and satisfaction, 192,
    230–31
    on spiritual exegesis, validity of,
    238–39
    translation of Jonah, 137
    tropological theory of, 243–49
Lutheranism, 232–34, 267

Mann, Jill, 184–85
manuscripts discussed
    Cambridge, Magdalene College,
        MS Pepys 2498, 80, 85
    Cambridge, Peterhouse College,
        MS 57, 19n15
    Duke of Westminster's MS (*olim*
        Eaton Hall), 76–79
    London, British Library, Kings MS
        5, 99–100
    London, British Library, MS Addi-
        tional 35287, 76
    New York, Pierpont Morgan
        Library, MS Morgan 1089, 304,
        306–7
    Oxford, Bodleian Library, MS
        Digby 171, 78–83
    Paris, Bibliothèque nationale de
        France, MS Fr. 574, 339–40
    York Minster, MS Add. 2 (The
        Bolton Hours), 304–5
    York Minster, MS XVI.K.19 (The
        Pavement Hours), 302–4
Marion, Jean-Luc, 175–80, 295, 297,
    337–38, 369
Marlowe, Christopher, 192–93, 237
martyrdom, 9, 240, 280–81, 285–90,
    349–51, 353–55
Mary, mother of God, 97n29, 162,
    169, 284–85, 299, 330
Mary I, queen of England, 9, 259–60,
    281, 348, 351n98
McEwan, Ian, 190–94, 196, 224,
    237
mediocriter boni, 215–17, 224n77
Mercers Guild of York, 298, 355–64,
    366–67
metaphor, 51–55
metaphysics. *See* participation, meta-
    physics of
Michelangelo, 301
Middle English Biblical Summary,
    139–40
*Middle English Metrical Paraphrase
    of the Old Testament*, 139

Middleton, Anne, 146–47, 186, 207–9, 222
Minnis, Alastair, 5, 13–15
Mirk, John, 221n66, 223
mirror(s), 314–15, 329–30, 347–48
    anagogical, 318–20
    drama as, 294, 296–97, 320–29
    exemplary, 294, 316–17, 324–25, 328
    literal, 315–16, 333–34
    scripture as, 294, 324–27
    tropological, 317–18
Mirror, Middle English, 80–81, 85, 221. *See also* Robert of Gretham
mixed life, 70–72. *See also* active life; contemplative life
Moralia in Job. See Gregory the Great
More, Thomas, 9, 239, 249–53, 256–57
Morison, Richard, 276–78, 290
Mum and the Sothsegger, 212–13
Muscatine, Charles, 145
myth, 96–97

Neckam, Alexander, 32
Newhauser, Richard, 89, 332
Newman, Martha G., 45
Newton, Isaac, 330–31
Nicholas of Gorran, 116–18
Nicholas of Lyra, 110–13, 155, 239, 374
Northern Passion, 321n43
Nowell, Alexander, 352
N-Town Play, 272n112

Ochino, Bernardino, 9, 264, 271–76, 298
Ocker, Christopher, 14n3, 36n57, 114–19

optics, optical theory, 10, 314, 330–33. *See also* ethics, moralized optics

Pabel, Hilmar, 138–39
paraphrase, 138–39, 142, 257–64, 266
Parker, Matthew, 79
Parr, Catherine, 260
participation
    affective, 139–41
    in community of body of Christ, 256, 283–88
    contemplative, in divine wisdom, 16
    contrasted to imitation, 88
    in drama, 269–70, 288–90, 320–29
    ethical, 49, 106–10
    imaginative, 47, 106–10, 139
    in invention, 107–10, 286–87
    liturgical, 47, 194–95, 201–2, 205–7, 214–15
    metaphysics of, 12, 27, 30–33, 37, 109–10, 164–65, 186–88, 298
    sacramental, 8–9, 47, 141, 208–10
    in salvation history, 3–4, 45, 107–10, 140–41, 189–90, 249, 261, 266–70, 277, 310–11, 327–29, 349
Patience
    amplification of Jonah story, 94–99
    Glossa ordinaria as source of, 99–110
    "realizing imagination," 88–94, 121, 127, 135–43
    reconciliation of literal and allegorical modes, 119–35
    relationship to Protestant paraphrases of Jonah, 135–43
Patrick, Saint, 199

Paul, the Apostle. *See* Bible, episodes and books, Pauline epistles
Pavement Hours, 302–4
Pecham, John, 331–32, 333n67
penance. *See* confession; contrition; repentance; satisfaction
Penitential Psalms, 225–30, 250–54, 301–7, 355–56
Peraldus, Guilelmus, 17, 58, 70
periodization, 78–79, 83–85, 193, 196–97, 229, 232–37, 285, 341, 377–80
Peter of Limoges, 330–36, 339, 341–44, 347n92
Philpot, John, 285–86
Pierke de-Rabbi Eliezer, 96
Piers Plowman
  anagogy and eschatology of, 186–88, 196, 209, 225n77, 236–37
  annotation of manuscripts, 75–86
  barn of Unity and Antichrist (C.21.333–22.57), 65–66
  chiasmus in, 195, 197–210, 236
  compared to Protestant tropology, 290
  contrasted to Chaucer, 380–82
  crucicentric (dynamic) middle (C.20.468–21.14), 201–15, 235–37
  Emmaus episode (C.12.124–31), 167–70
  exemplarity in, 152–56, 164–70, 182–88, 318
  failure in, 186–88, 194
  Four Daughters of God (B.18/C.20), 182–88
  Gregory the Great (C.5.146–51), 70–72

image on the coin (C.17.73–85), 159–64
  imagination, function of, 94
  inventiveness of, 145–52
  love's leap (C.14.85–86a), 381–82
  making, defense of, 164–70, 195–96
  model and copy, 145, 155–64, 182–88
  natural tropology (C.13.132–55, 14.72–83a), 69–70
  pardon or papal bull episode (C.9), 68, 72–75, 216n56, 308n25
Patience, comparison to method of invention, 122
Pentecost (C.21.200–210), 152–56, 173–78, 181–82
  plowing of scripture (C.21.258–73a, 309–16), 50–59, 63–64, 148, 219
  reception in Reformation, 75–86, 224, 229–30, 235–37, 378
  significance in this book, 5, 19n16
  as source of tropological theory, 47–59, 61–75
  vices, pageant of (C.6–7), 68
  waking and writing, 208–15
Plato, 14
Plautus, 185
Pontifical Institute of Biblical Studies, 373–74
preaching. *See* homiletics
Prick of Conscience, 309–10, 360
Prior, Sandra Pierson, 90
pseudo-Dionysius, 24, 186–87
Pupilla oculi, 220n66

Raabe, Pamela, 170n50
Rashi, 113
Rastall, Richard, 285n146
realism, 88–94, 97, 135–42. *See also*
    Patience, "realizing imagination"
repentance, 230–31, 250–54, 269.
    See also confession; contrition;
    conversion; satisfaction
Reventlow, Hennig Graf, 28–29,
    39n66
Rhetorica ad Herennium, 199
rhetorical tradition, 5, 7, 18–19, 24,
    35, 156–64, 199, 262
Rhodes, Jim, 128, 135n92
Robert of Basevorn, 98
Robert of Gretham, 80, 221,
    321n43
Robert of Melun, 168–69
Robertson, D. W., 4–5
Rolle, Richard, 221–23
Rust, Jennifer, 349n96, 353, 365–66

Salter, Elizabeth, 67
salvation history, 3–4, 20n18, 42–43,
    89n5. *See also* participation, in
    salvation history
Sandys, Edwin, 352n99
satisfaction, 8–9, 190–96, 215–37.
    See also works of mercy
Scanlon, Larry, 154n22, 229n91
Schleusener, Jay, 90–92
Schmidt, A. V. C., 203, 206
Schott, Christine, 76
Scotus, John Duns, 366n133
secularism, secularization, 190–96,
    292–93, 365
Shakespeare, William, 279–80
Sheingorn, Pamela, 323–24
Shuger, Deborah, 231–32

Simpson, James, 114, 149n11,
    226–27, 267n91, 379
Skelton, John, 273
Smalley, Beryl, 23
Smith, D. Vance, 48–49, 147n6,
    163–64, 179, 186–87, 208
Smith, Kathryn A., 304n22
Smith, Macklin, 202–5
Somerset, Fiona, 140, 174n64
Spearing, A. C., 53n96, 121, 147n6,
    213
Staley, Lynn, 90
Stanbury, Sarah, 91
Stevenson, Jill, 340–41
Summit, Jennifer, 84–85
Suso, Henry, 93–94
Swanson, Heather, 358

Taylor, Charles, 193n13
teleology, 92, 170–72
Tentler, Thomas, 230
theater. *See* drama
Thomas Aquinas, 99, 330
    analogy, doctrine of, 187–88, 268
    Christ's Passion unlocks the spiri-
        tual sense of the Old Testament,
        22, 29n37
    infinite spiral of signification,
        43–44
    interpretation requires wisdom, 48
    Pange lingua, 292
    praises absolution rubric, 219–20
    on transubstantiation, 366n133
    treatise on the vices, 17
    verbal signs of scripture are revela-
        tory, 36n57
    whether God's will changes,
        114–15
Thomas of Hales, 201

Thomas of Ireland, 44–46

translation, 145, 150, 153, 155–64, 166–67, 376–77

tropology. *See also* exegesis, fourfold theory of

allegory, relationship to, 39, 128–29, 261–64

apocalyptic, 271–76

circulatory, 2–3, 12, 22, 61–66, 136, 247–49, 318, 363, 379

definitions of, 2, 12, 21, 179

distinguished from other ethical discourses, 13–21, 67–68

dramatic, 264–71

etymology of, 1–2, 168–69

and invention, 3–4, 7, 11–12, 44–45, 47, 77–86, 99, 106–9, 128–29, 148–52, 164–88, 202–24, 266–68

literal sense, relationship to, 99, 107–9, 128–29, 136

mirror figure of, 317–18

natural, 32–34, 37, 45–46, 69–70

Nicholas of Lyra's practice of, 113

penitential, 194, 209–10, 221–24

and periodization, 377–80

and propaganda, 276–78

quotidian, 42–43, 310–12

reductive or vicious, 46, 59, 65–67, 255–57, 267, 363–64

Reformation-era theory and practice of

—by Brenz, Johannes, 138

—by Bucer, Martin, 240, 264–72

—by Calvin, John, 239–42

—by Careless, John, 240, 278–90

—by Erasmus, 138–40, 239, 258–64

—in *A Looking Glasse for London and England*, 141–42

—by Luther, Martin, 239, 243–49

—by More, Thomas, 239, 249–53, 256–57

—by Tyndale, William, 138–42, 239, 249–57

—by Udall, Nicholas, 240, 261–64

sacramental system, relationship to, 189–90, 194–96, 202, 209–10, 223–24, 239–40, 289–90

and temporality, 307–15

threatens to efface individuality, 88

varieties of, 67–86

and vernacular theology, 375–77

Tyndale, William, 9, 137–42, 239, 249–57, 290

typology. *See* allegory, theological

Udall, Nicholas, 9, 240, 261–65, 271, 273, 275, 297

Vantuono, William, 101

vernacularity, 10, 156–59, 174, 178, 196, 257–58, 371–77. *See also* Bible, vernacular biblical literature; exegesis, vernacular

Vessey, Mark, 138–39

Vianney, Saint John, 339

Virgil, 185

virtue, 210, 219, 245, 250, 254, 263, 268

natural and theological, 29–30, 42

and the order of grace, 57–66

virtue ethics. *See* ethics, virtue ethics

Voragine, Jacobus de, 330

Wainwright, Geoffrey, 300–301

Waldron, Jennifer, 280, 351

Warner, Lawrence, 235n106
Watson, Nicholas, 222, 224n77
Weber, Max, 293
Whitaker, Thomas Dunham, 144,
    146n3
White, Paul Whitfield, 275, 277–78,
    280–82
will
    in action theory and moral
        philosophy, 19
    function in tropology, 11
    God's will in history, 242
    in Luther's account of salvation,
        248–49
    priority of God's will, 291
    priority of grace (*Piers Plowman*),
        49
    priority of will or intellect, 60–62
    united to intellect in natural
        tropology, 33
    whether God's will can change,
        133–34
William of Ockham, 366n133
wisdom, 42, 48, 60
works of mercy, 10, 47, 195, 218–19,
    221, 224, 227, 232, 275–76, 290,
    294n5, 301n17, 342–44, 348,
    354–64, 368–70
Wyatt, Sir Thomas, 8, 225–28
Wyclif, John, 99
    "hermeneutical catch-22," 48–49,
        59–61

on the metaphysics of scripture,
    30–32, 48–49, 56
scripture the revelation of truth,
    55
Wycliffite texts, 98n30
    Bible translation, 131, 180
    Middle English Biblical Summary,
        139–40
    on Pentecost, 156, 173
    virtue required to understand
        scripture, 61–62

York Play, 9–10, 46–47, 66n117, 279
    Ascension, 294n5
    Baptism and Temptation of Christ,
        294, 315–18
    Creation, 310
    Crucifixion, 298, 355
    Doomsday, 9–10, 291–300,
        307–15, 319–20, 324, 328–29,
        335, 341–48, 354–57, 360,
        367–70
    Nativity, 283n144
    Noah's Flood, 310n27
    Resurrection, 298
Young, Frances, 25–26

Zeeman, Nicolette, 178, 182–83,
    185–86, 188
Zieman, Katherine, 156, 186
Zumthor, Paul, 323

Ryan McDermott

is assistant professor of English at the University of Pittsburgh.

CPSIA information can be obtained
at www.ICGtesting.com
Printed in the USA
FFOW02n0945070716
25583FF